Sydelle, I miss you.

I went out for a walk and finally concluded to stay out till sundown,
for going out, I found, was really going in.
—JOHN MUIR

Over every mountain is a path,
although it may not be seen from the valley.
—THEODORE ROETHKE

This book is dedicated to William Kent,
whose grand vision and incomparable generosity
preserved Mount Tamalpais
for all future generations.

MOUNT TAMALPAIS TRAILS

By Barry Spitz

Golden Gate National Parks Conservancy
San Francisco, California

Also by Barry Spitz

To Save a Mountain: The 100-Year Battle for Mt. Tamalpais (2010)
Frank Howard Allen (2010)
Marin: A History (2006)
San Anselmo (2003)
Open Spaces: Lands of the Marin County Open Space District (2000)
Mill Valley: The Early Years (1997)
Dipsea: The Greatest Race (1993)
Tamalpais Trails (1989)
Best Running Trails of the San Francisco Bay Area (1978)

Golden Gate National Parks Conservancy
Bldg. 201, Fort Mason, San Francisco, California 94123
www.parksconservancy.org

Safety is an important concern in all outdoor activities, and users of this guide are fully responsible for their own well being. Although the author and publisher have made every effort to ensure that the information included herein was correct at press time, they do not assume and hereby disclaim any liability for any loss, damage, or disruption caused by errors, omissions, or miscalculations on the part of the user.

ISBN 978-1-932519-37-2
Library of Congress Control Number: 2015944301

Photos, p. 27 (clockwise from top left): Eric Poelzl (Pacific Madrone, California Poppy), Kirke Wrench (Lupine), Will Elder (Manzanita), Brandon Levinger (Blue-eyed Grass), Stephen Joseph (Bracken Fern)
Photos, p. 34: Kirke Wrench
Photos, p. 42: GGNRA/PARC, Annals of the Bohemian Club (Bohemian Grove)

The publisher thanks all TLC agency partners for their assistance and cooperation during the development of this book.

Project Managers: Matt Leffert, Sharon Farrell, and Robert Lieber
Design: Vivian Young
Editor: Susan Tasaki
Editorial Assistance: Michael Hsu
Cartography: Map created by Ben Pease/Pease Press, *www.peasepress.com*;
  adapted and updated by Michael Norelli and Warren Cheng
Production: Sarah Lau Levitt

GOLDEN GATE
NATIONAL
PARKS
CONSERVANCY

PARKS FOR ALL FOREVER™

PRINTED IN HONG KONG

CONTENTS

FOREWORD

We are delighted that one of Mt. Tam's dearest friends, Barry Spitz, has agreed to expand, update, and refresh his *Tamalpais Trails*—the authoritative guide to the wonders of the mountain, and the depths of its heart. Whether you're a first-time visitor or a long-time devotee, we think you'll find within this book many new adventures on Mt. Tam, as well as a renewed understanding of the need to protect and preserve this remarkable place.

Barry's book—which also includes rich material from his *To Save a Mountain: The 100-Year Battle for Mt. Tamalpais*—comes at a significant juncture in Tam's history. Invasive species, plant diseases, climate change, wildfire, and drought pose constant threats to the mountain's irreplaceable natural and cultural resources and abundant recreational amenities. Those dangers are exacerbated by deferred maintenance, aging infrastructure, and budget cuts.

To more effectively meet these challenges, the Tamalpais Lands Collaborative (TLC) was formed in 2014 by four land management agencies—the National Park Service (NPS); California State Parks; Marin County Parks (MCP), which includes Marin County Open Space District (MCOSP); and Marin Municipal Water District (MMWD)—and one nonprofit, the Golden Gate National Parks Conservancy.

Just as the company of friends can elevate experiences on a trail by revealing fresh insights and imparting new strengths, the TLC was established to share the collective expertise and resources of the member organizations for greater care and benefit.

This unique collaboration inherits a proud legacy of conservation in Marin. In 1905, William Kent purchased and later donated the parcel that would become Muir Woods National Monument—thus preserving one of the first pieces of the majestic mountain (following the parklands donated by the Tamalpais Land and Water Company). Kent's vision and generosity inspired countless philanthropists and activists over the years, who continued to add more patches to the remarkable quilt that constitutes the protected lands of Mt. Tam.

Time and time again, the community has found innovative ways to secure the long-term health of public lands. In 2011, for example, four of the six state parks in Marin County were slated for closure due to California's budget crisis. In response, the NPS contributed additional resources to keep the state parks open, while the Parks Conservancy was given the task of translating that opportunity into immediate results across the Redwood Creek Watershed—the vital swath of land and water stretching from the slopes of Mt. Tam to Muir Beach.

Within just a couple of years, this new Redwood Creek Watershed Collaborative had reopened and enhanced popular trails, improved native habitat by controlling invasive vegetation, supported endangered species monitoring, and implemented a consistent and comprehensive system of signage.

Meanwhile, the Marin Municipal Water District had been looking to form a nonprofit "friends" organization that would give volunteer and philanthropic lift to underfunded projects and programs. The successful Redwood Creek Watershed Collaborative provided a model that could be expanded upon to include the heart of the mountain and to leverage the proven track record of the nonprofit Parks Conservancy. With support from the community, MMWD—and then Marin County Parks—joined in the visioning process to determine what a five-way partnership for Tam might look like.

After a series of workshops and meetings, the partners formally established the TLC—a collaborative that builds on decades of formal and informal relationships among the land agencies and grassroots organizations, coordinates their work in a more focused and holistic manner, and aims to energize the entire community for the stewardship of the mountain.

Toward that end, in 2014, the TLC launched One Tam (*onetam.org*)—a campaign to engage the public in the care of this cherished mountain and its watersheds. One Tam offers a way for residents and visitors to support the completion of priority conservation and restoration projects, the rehabilitation and maintenance of trails and visitor facilities, and the expansion of education and volunteer programs. In other words, One Tam is the TLC's innovative approach to expanding and nurturing Tam's circle of friends.

However, the best way to cultivate your own relationship with the mountain and to contribute to its care is to get out and experience its magic. By following the wayfinding tips and heeding the wise words in *Mount Tamalpais Trails*, your understanding of—and commitment to—Mt. Tam will deepen. By rambling across Tam's creeks, forests, slopes, and ridges, your love for this special place will flourish. And by wandering its trails, your connection with the mountain will grow stronger, and will open the surest path to Mt. Tam's brightest future.

Greg Moore
President & CEO
Golden Gate National Parks Conservancy

INTRODUCTION

There are good reasons why Mount Tamalpais has been revered for millennia, why so many have fought passionately for it over the generations, why millions visit each year, and why dozens of books have been written about it.

For some 8,000 years, the mountain sustained the Coast Miwoks who lived on and around it. In turn, they honored Tamalpais; descendants tell of ancestors who avoided its summit out of fear and respect. Reverence for the mountain continues. The Dalai Lama held a service atop West Peak in 1989, and circumambulating Mt. Tamalpais has become a quasi-religious ritual.

After the Spanish arrived in treeless San Francisco in 1776, they came to Tamalpais for wood for their *presidio* (fort), mission, and small settlement. The core of the place name *Corte Madera del Presidio*, which translates to "cut wood for the presidio," survives today (Corte Madera). Cattle grazing on Tamalpais helped feed the mission in San Rafael, established in 1817. During California's Mexican era (1821–1846), the earliest European settlers relied almost entirely on the cattle that roamed vast ranches on Mt. Tamalpais. Water flowing off the mountain has consistently provided Marin's needs; the Marin Municipal Water District, created in 1912, was the first such district in California.

When gold discovered in the Sierra foothills in 1848 lured millions westward, cattle from Tamalpais nourished the miners and the new boomtown of San Francisco. The mountain's forests supplied the lumber to build San Francisco, and to rebuild it after frequent fires. From the 1860s, dairy ranches supplied the city with milk, butter, cheese, and eggs.

By the late nineteenth century, hikers, campers, and tourists had begun to arrive on Mt. Tam. Their numbers rose markedly after a rail line was laid into Mill Valley in 1889, and then again in 1896, when the Mill Valley & Mt. Tamalpais Scenic Railway, which terminated near the summit, opened. Crowds jammed the mountain's entry paths on summer weekends, and refreshment stands sprang up to serve them. The Sierra Club held some of its first hikes on Tamalpais, and it is still the local branch's most popular destination.

In 1905, runners raced over the mountain from Mill Valley to Stinson Beach in the first Dipsea Race. Today, the Dipsea is the nation's oldest major cross-country race. The sport of mountain biking was born on the slopes of Tamalpais in the 1960s (the "mountain" of "mountain biking" is Tamalpais).

In 1908, Muir Woods became the country's sixth national monument, two days before Grand Canyon. It was also the first to be donated by an individual. The establishment of Mt. Tamalpais State Park led directly to creation of the California Department of Parks (AKA California State Parks); both came into being from the same 1927 legislative bills. Tamalpais represented, by far, the greatest portion of land within the Golden Gate National Recreation Area when it was created in 1972.

Tamalpais is the tallest mountain directly on the Pacific coast for a stretch of 250 miles between Mendocino County and Big Sur. Its profile is an icon of the San Francisco Bay Area.

In 1987, I began work on *Tamalpais Trails*, the first comprehensive guide to the mountain's trails and fire roads. The book remained in print (through five editions and six printings) for more than twenty years. In 2012, I wrote *To Save a Mountain: The 100-Year Battle for Mt. Tamalpais*, the story of how this treasure, in the midst of a huge metropolitan area, had been protected. I thought my Mt. Tamalpais writing days were then over.

But when the new Tamalpais Lands Collaborative (TLC) was launched in 2014—a partnership consisting of the mountain's four principal land managers and the Golden Gate National Parks Conservancy, uniting to work together for the mountain's benefit—it was clear that another book was needed. This is the result. It incorporates the heart of *Tamalpais Trails*—descriptions of all the trails, each revisited and revised—with history from *To Save a Mountain* and information on the visionary projects ahead. The geographic coverage has been expanded north and south to match TLC's range: some 72 square miles, or 46,000 acres. The maps are new.

In all, more than 160 trails and fire roads covering some 250 miles are described in this book. With minimal effort, hikers, runners, bicyclists, equestrians, and other visitors can design thousands of routes for themselves and know the exact length of each, as well as the elevation changes, and learn more about the natural, cultural, and historical landmarks they'll pass along the way.

Come share what I have seen. Go slowly and discover more.

hadyside Trail near Bon Tempe Lake

THE NATURE OF MT. TAM

Tam's geology, weather, and water influence its mosaic of habitats—open grasslands, chaparral and oak-covered knolls, Douglas-fir and California bay forests, and redwood-filled canyons—which, in turn, shelter approximately nine hundred plant and four hundred animal species, fifty of which are rare and endangered. Following is a brief introduction.

Geology

The Earth's lithosphere, its crust and outermost layer of mantle, is composed of enormous plates. Mt. Tamalpais lies at the western edge of the North American Plate. Adjacent is the Pacific Plate, on which the Pt. Reyes peninsula sits. The much smaller Farallon Plate once lay between the two. Millions of years ago, the Pacific Plate drifted head-on into the North American Plate, pushing the Farallon under the North American. Blocked, the Pacific Plate then began a lateral creep northwest, creating an unstable divide, the infamous San Andreas Fault that runs more than 700 miles through and just off offshore of California. (Bolinas Lagoon, Olema Valley, and Tomales Bay sit stop the San Andreas Fault in Marin.) The plate's movement averages some 2 inches a year, but is occasionally more dramatic, such as 20 feet in seconds during the 1906 earthquake along the fault's northernmost section.

The rocks that make up Mt. Tamalpais are roughly 80 to 150 million years old, and were largely formed from sediments eroded from the predecessor of today's Sierra Nevada to the ocean basin that covered western California. These sediments were deposited atop volcanic rock that lay beneath the sea and then compressed. Some of the volcanic rock intruded upward. When the North American Plate overrode the Farallon Plate, these rocks were scraped off, jumbled, and thrust upward as California's Coast Range, of which Tamalpais is a part. This mixture of rocks, difficult to unravel, is called the Franciscan Complex (or Assemblage or Formation). Thus, while Mt. Tamalpais contains rock of volcanic origin, it was never a volcano.

Erosion then began its relentless work. Less-resistant rock was washed away during earthquakes and rain-triggered landslides. The late Salem Rice, who studied the geology of the mountain closely, speculated that Tamalpais's three-peaked profile became recognizable around 100,000 to 150,000 years ago, and that further erosion and slides will someday turn the highly resistant rock core of East Peak into more of a spire.

All three basic rock classes—igneous, metamorphic, and sedimentary—are represented on Mt. Tamalpais, with sedimentary rocks by far the most prevalent. Following are some of the more abundant rock types, which account for more than 95 percent of the mountain.

Sandstone, Mudstone, Shale

These sedimentary rocks form the bulk of Mt. Tamalpais. Sandstone, mudstone, and shale comprise, in decreasing order of particle size, compressed and bound sand, mud, and clay. Graywacke, a dark-gray, compact type of sandstone dominant on the mountain, is made up of medium-sized, angular sand grains between which are mud and clay-sized particles. Because these rocks readily weather to soil, which is in turn covered by vegetation, they are not generally seen exposed. Much of the sandstone, mudstone, and shale have been well fractured and sheared, forming, with other rocks, what is called a "melange."

Greenstone

Greenstone is an igneous basaltic rock of volcanic origin; occasionally, pieces displaying the holes (vesicles) from which gases escaped as the lava cooled can be found. Its green color, which comes from the presence of the mineral chlorite, only appears when fresh. Though highly resistant to fracture, greenstone weathers to a thick, iron-rich soil that oxidizes to a reddish brown. This soil holds moisture well and supports both forests and grasslands. Bolinas Ridge, on the western side of Tamalpais (the most coherent rock mass on the mountain), is greenstone basalt. Pilot Knob and most of Bald Hill are also blocks of greenstone.

Serpentine

Serpentine (or, technically, serpentinite) is the best-known and most distinctive rock on Tamalpais; a broad vein crosses the entire mountain. Its varying gray-green-bluish boulders cover sections of trails such as Rock Spring and Northside, as well as the San Geronimo Ridge Fire Road. The seats of Mountain Theater are blocks of serpentine, hauled across Tam to the site. In 1965, it was officially designated as California's state rock.

Serpentine is a metamorphic rock formed deep in the Earth, below the floor of the Pacific, from peridotite, Earth's most abundant mantle rock. Because serpentine lacks aluminum, a main ingredient of clay soils, it does not weather to soil and thus remains largely exposed. It is also deficient in the important plant nutrients calcium, potassium, and sodium, and has very high levels of magnesium and chrysotile asbestos, which are toxic to many plants. It thus supports a distinct and limited type of plant life; some plants grow only on serpentine, others take different forms or exist there out of their normal ranges.

Chert

Chert is a very hard (harder than steel) sedimentary rock. It is almost 100 percent quartz, which is crystallized silica (silicon dioxide). Chert is formed by the precipitation of silica, originally from microscopic marine protozoans called radiolaria, in the ocean. (Use a good hand lens to see the embedded skeletal radiolaria.) Chert often appears in uniform 1- to 3-inch layered beds. Because chert resists erosion and appears in several colors (white is common on Tam), its few outcroppings stand out.

Quartz Tourmaline

This rather rare metamorphic rock is found in only a few places on Tam. It is highly resistant to erosion. East Peak is a block of quartz tourmaline, and there was once a tourmaline mine there. Quartz tourmaline boulders have fallen from the peak and come to rest on trails below.

Weather

California's coast enjoys one of the world's five Mediterranean climates, which are characterized by year-round moderate temperatures, wet winters, and nearly completely dry summers. (The other four Mediterranean zones are the coast of Chile, the west coasts of Australia and South Africa, and the Mediterranean coastline itself.) But as visitors learn, weather conditions vary across the mountain, and can change rapidly. Indeed, coastal fog gives the west slope of Tamalpais some of the coolest average summer temperatures in the nation.

Fog is a major component of Mt. Tamalpais's weather. The summer fog cycle begins with the current flowing south along the California coast. Surface water is pushed away from the Marin shore and replaced by upwelling water that is 10 to 15 degrees cooler, from deeper in the ocean (this cold water is well known to Marin beachgoers). Inshore winds, moisture-laden after a long journey across the Pacific, come into contact with these cold, coastal waters. Cooler air holds less moisture, so the excess condenses, much of it on salt spray particles, into coastal fog.

When hot inland air rises, as it does on summer afternoons, it forms a low-pressure area that sucks this fog bank in through the Golden Gate. The summit ridge of Tamalpais is usually an effective barrier, keeping the northern slope fog-free in summer, but fog penetrates to the east and south through low-lying gaps such as Frank and Tennessee Valleys. Some summer days, it is 45 degrees warmer on Tam's sunbaked northeast flank than on the fogbound coastal southwest.

By September, diminishing fog gives Tamalpais many of its hottest, driest days of the year. High fire danger warnings are regularly posted and, in extreme conditions, its roads and even trails are closed.

As fall progresses, the Pacific High, a vast high-pressure air mass, retreats south along with the jet stream. This opens Marin to storms tracking across the

Pacific, and the rainy season begins. Annual rainfall averaged 53 inches at Lake Lagunitas (Marin Municipal Water District's standard measuring location) and 41 inches in Muir Woods during the twentieth century, both more than double that of San Francisco. January is usually the wettest month, followed by, in roughly equal pairings, December/February, November/March, and a usually light October/April.

But exceptions are common, and weather patterns may be changing. Shockingly, there was no rain at all in December 1989; even more astonishing, no rain (under .1 inch) in both January 2014 and 2015. The lowest annual rainfall figure at Lake Lagunitas was 20 inches in 1923–1924. A major drought occurred in 1975–1977, consecutive years with less than 25 inches of rain. Exceptionally high rainfall is often associated with an irregular global weather phenomenon known as "El Niño." In 1889–1890, an all-time record of 109 inches fell at Lake Lagunitas. The winter of 1981–1982 brought almost 90 inches of rain, and major flooding. In 1997–1998, rainfall was 97.7 inches, but there was less flooding, as storms were more spread out.

Beyond heavy rainfall, winter can bring other forms of extreme weather. Winds reached 107 miles per hour on December 1, 1951. A long-time historic low temperature of 19 degrees (January 19, 1922) was shattered on both December 23 and 24, 1990, when the Sky Oaks Ranger Station recorded 4 degrees. On May 4, 1921, the aurora borealis, or northern lights, was plainly visible on Tam. Snow does occasionally fall; the largest storm was in January 1922. It melts rapidly, but may linger for a day or two high on the mountain's north slope.

Also in winter, a different type of fog, known as radiation (or tule) fog, prevails, particularly in the northern valleys. Tule fog arises when air near the ground absorbs moisture from the damp earth. In early morning, low temperatures condense the moisture as ground fog. Hilltops may remain sunny. This fog usually burns off by mid-day.

Warm, spring-like days often arrive early. Indeed, more than one hundred plant species may be flowering by early February. The mountain's grasslands usually appear greenest in March, then die back and turn brown as the year goes on. (Note that before cattle were brought to California and the state's perennial native bunchgrasses were outcompeted and replaced by Eurasian annual grasses, this browning was far less pronounced.) The Pacific High returns and rainfall is rare, and light, from May into October.

Creeks

Just as trails lace their way across Mt. Tamalpais, so do creeks. Thus, most trails cross or skirt creeks, and knowing these creeks will enhance your visit. The mountain's three main creeks are presented first, then others in alphabetical order. (Note: A creek's designated left and right bank is based on a downstream view.)

Lagunitas Creek

This is by far the longest, strongest-flowing, and most important creek on Mt. Tamalpais and in all Marin. The three main headwater feeders of Lagunitas Creek—East, Middle, and West Forks—begin flowing from over 2,300 feet on Tamalpais and meet in what is now Lake Lagunitas. (The fire road around the lake crosses all three forks.) Lagunitas Creek then runs 20 miles to Tomales Bay near Point Reyes Station. Along the way, it absorbs every other creek descending Tamalpais's north side.

Four dams across Lagunitas Creek create the reservoir lakes of (in descending order) Lagunitas, Bon Tempe, Alpine, and Kent, which supply most of Marin's drinking water. Below Kent, Lagunitas Creek meanders unimpeded. Lagunitas Creek is also essential to the mountain's wildlife. For example, the largest silver salmon (22 pounds) and steelhead (30 pounds) ever taken in California were caught in Lagunitas Creek, in 1959 and 1906, respectively. Lagunitas Creek also supports the largest population of California freshwater shrimp.

Redwood Creek

A short but significant stream, it flows across the floor of Muir Woods National Monument, so is enjoyed, traversed, and photographed by millions of visitors. Major feeder creeks—Bootjack, Rattlesnake, Spike Buck, and Laguna—unite above the canyon to form the creek. A major project, completed in 2014, improved its flow through its mouth, an area once known as Big Lagoon, into the Pacific Ocean at Muir Beach. It is hoped that this work, plus other measures, will revive its much-reduced annual salmon run.

Corte Madera Creek

The creek flows through the center of the populous Ross Valley communities of Fairfax, San Anselmo, Ross, Kentfield, Greenbrae, and Larkspur on its way to San Francisco Bay. Thus, when it overflows its banks, as it did in 2005, there is extensive property damage. Major upstream feeders include Fairfax, Deer Park, San Anselmo, and Sleepy Hollow Creeks. Overflow from Phoenix Lake enters in Ross. Between the Ross post office and College of Marin athletic fields, Corte Madera Creek has been channeled within concrete walls. At the end of these walls was the nineteenth-century port of Ross Landing, where shallow draft boats carried logs and produce from Ross Valley to San Francisco.

Other Major Creeks

Following, in alphabetical order, are some of Mt. Tamalpais's other major creeks, strong-flowing enough to require bridges where trails cross them. Note that a few large creeks, such as Lone Tree, Cold Stream, and Kent Canyon, are not crossed by any trails.

Arroyo Corte Madera del Presidio Creek is called various names as it flows through Mill Valley, and rarely by this "official" one. Cascade and Old Mill Creeks meet above Three Wells in Cascade Canyon. The united stream meets Arroyo Corte Madera in downtown Mill Valley. Two more major feeder creeks, (Widow) Reed and Warner, join before they all empty into Richardson Bay at the southern edge of Bayfront Park.

Big and Little Carson Creeks both flow from San Geronimo Ridge into Kent Lake (and into Lagunitas Creek prior to creation of the lake). Little Carson is the more southern. It has a much-visited, four-tiered waterfall, Carson Falls, and a trail runs through its lovely lower canyon. Big Carson is more remote, reachable only by the Pine Mountain Fire Road, which crosses over it (or under it after heavy rains). It too has an impressive waterfall.

Cataract Creek produces the most spectacular natural waterfalls on Tamalpais. Hike the Cataract Trail during or immediately after a heavy winter rain to enjoy one of the Bay Area's special treats. Cataract Creek begins just north of the Rock Spring parking area. The mightiest falls are near the Helen Markt trail junction. Before Alpine Dam was built, Cataract Creek met Lagunitas Creek. Now it empties into Alpine Lake.

Easkoot Creek is crossed, in most cases unknowingly, by hundreds of thousands of visitors each year; the road into the Stinson Beach parking lot goes right over it. It descends from Bolinas Ridge to the Pacific Ocean, absorbs its southern neighbor, Table Rock Creek, then meets Matt Davis Trail. Alfred Easkoot was Marin's first county surveyor and is credited with determining the route of what is now Highway 1. In 1871, he opened his section of beach to summer campers, the beginning of Stinson Beach's enduring popularity.

Fern Creek has two upper forks, the higher of which starts at more than 2,200 feet, near the top of Old Railroad Grade. The creek then drops 2,000 feet—accompanied by the two Fern Creek trails—before meeting Redwood Creek on the floor of Muir Woods National Monument. Fern Creek, along with other Redwood Creek feeders, were all tapped for drinking water in the 1890s. Remnants of the intakes and the pipeline are still evident along Troop 80 Trail.

Larkspur Creek is well visited because it is so near the Magnolia Avenue corridor. The creek's two main headwaters are carried under the Southern Marin Line Road and unite at lovely Dawn Falls. Larkspur Creek then flows through redwood-lined Baltimore (also known as Madrone or Larkspur) Canyon. Dawn Falls Trail runs beside it, and crosses it twice. (There is another bridge at the access from Water Way.) Remnants of a dam built of blue basalt around 1900 by the Larkspur Water Company are still visible. Homes line the lower creek before it empties into San Francisco Bay.

Swede George Creek rivals Cataract as the strongest flowing on Tamalpais's rainy north slope. Indeed, it served as a water source until the 1950s, and the intake and pipe are still evident along Kent Trail. High Marsh Trail crosses Swede George's three major forks where they are still slender enough to be forded (but not always easily). Much lower, a substantial bridge, built by Jim Vitek after he floated the logs across Alpine Lake, carries Helen Markt Trail over this creek. Swede George logged the area in the 1860s before becoming paralyzed and living as a ward of the county; he died at "about forty years of age."

Van Wyck Creek drains the canyon northeast of Swede George Creek. It, too, is quite strong flowing and it, too, empties into Alpine Lake (Lagunitas Creek before the lake was formed in 1919). There is a bridge over it on Stocking Trail and another near its mouth along Kent Trail. Sidney Van Wyck, Jr. (1869–1932) was one of the heroes in the creation of Tamalpais State Park. He earned a law degree from the University of California, Berkeley, in 1890, and served in World War I. In 1920, he was elected president of the Tamalpais Conservation Club and headed the club's Tamalpais Park Committee when it was formed the following year. Van Wyck remained the leading public spokesman for a state park during the tumultuous years that followed. Van Wyck Meadow, at the junction of Bootjack and Troop 80 Trails, is also named for him

Webb Creek starts above Matt Davis Trail west of Pantoll. Below Panoramic Highway, it cuts through magnificent Steep Ravine, where it's crossed by nine bridges. Channeled under Highway 1, it empties into the Pacific near the Steep Ravine cabins. Jonathan Webb (1870–1944) was secretary to William Kent, who owned the creek's entire drainage, and was president of the Tamalpais Conservation Club in 1915–1916.

Other named Mt. Tam creeks include Barth's Creek (flows from the Barth's Retreat area into Cataract Creek), Bill Williams Creek (dammed in 1886 but now a feeder of Phoenix Lake), Cold Stream Creek (flows from Coast View Trail to the Pacific north of Slide Ranch), Lone Tree Creek (flows from Lone Tree Spring beside the Dipsea Trail to the Pacific), Phoenix Creek (runs beside lower Shaver Grade into Phoenix Lake), Tamalpais Creek (flows through Kent Woodlands to San Francisco Bay), and Ziesche Creek (flows from the Simmons/Benstein Trails into Cataract Creek).

Lakes

There are no natural lakes on Mt. Tamalpais. Two tiny wet areas, Hidden Lake and Lily Lake, carry the name but are smaller than an acre and just inches in depth. There are, however, now five large, man-made reservoir lakes (Alpine, Bon Tempe, Kent, Lagunitas, and Phoenix) on the mountain, all within the Marin Municipal Water District (MMWD). Before World War II, boating was allowed on Alpine Lake, but today all the lakes are closed to swimming and boating (fishing is permitted, with a state license). The five major lakes are as follows, in order of their year of creation (in parentheses):

Lake Lagunitas (1873)
Elevation: 784 feet
Capacity: 127 million gallons (350 acre feet)
Surface area: 23 acres

Lagunitas is the oldest, highest, and smallest of Tamalpais's reservoirs. The dam impounds water where the three main headwater forks of Lagunitas Creek meet. William Tell Coleman, who established the Marin County Water Company in 1871, hired Herman Schussler, the engineer who helped supply San Francisco's early drinking water, to build the dam. It was completed November 9, 1873, at a cost of $35,000. The state prison at San Quentin was one of the reservoir's original customers. Coleman also built a road to the lake and lined it with eucalyptus trees, and visitors in horse-drawn carriages were soon enjoying outings there. The first long distance telephone line in Marin County ran from San Rafael to the lake keeper's cottage.

The 1.6-mile circuit of Lake Lagunitas, which crosses bridges over the three forks of Lagunitas Creek, remains one of the most popular excursions on Mt. Tamalpais.

Phoenix Lake (1905)
Elevation: 183 feet
Capacity: 172 million gallons (411 acre feet)
Surface area: 25 acres

After Coleman went bankrupt in 1888, his company was reorganized as the Marin Water & Power Co. and headed by San Rafael's Arthur W. Foster. The new company created Phoenix Lake by building a dam at the confluence of Phoenix and Bill Williams Creeks. The name "Phoenix" came from the family (Phenix) who ran a dairy there.

Because water from Phoenix Lake needs to be pumped 400 feet uphill to Marin Municipal Water District's Bon Tempe Filter Plant before distribution, Phoenix is kept full largely as a recreational destination. A mid-lake pump was installed after the mid-1970s drought and has been occasionally activated since.

The full circuit of Phoenix Lake, half on trail, half on fire road, is 2.33 miles, and is also immensely popular.

Alpine Lake (1919)

Elevation: 646 feet

Capacity: 2.9 billion gallons (8,891 acre feet)

Surface area: 219 acres

The first major project of the new Marin Municipal Water District was to build the concrete Alpine Dam at the confluence of Lagunitas and Cascade Creeks, a site known as Alpine. The original 1870s San Rafael–Bolinas Road was rerouted to run over the dam. Water from Alpine Lake flowed into the Pine Mountain Tunnel, then on to Fairfax. To increase storage capacity, the dam was raised 8 feet in 1924, then an additional 30 feet in 1941.

Kent and Helen Markt Trails run along the south shore of Alpine Lake, but no trails border the opposite bank, so a loop is not possible.

Bon Tempe Lake (1948)

Elevation: 718 feet

Capacity: 1.3 billion gallons (4,017 acre feet)

Surface area: 144 acres

To meet increased demand after World War II, MMWD undertook massive capital projects. The former Bautunpi Brothers dairy ranch (a Swiss name, corrupted to Bon Tempe) was flooded by Bon Tempe Dam. A modern filter plant was built less than a mile away. The new Southern Marin Line (the pipe runs under the 3-mile Kentfield–Larkspur Fire Road of that name) carries filtered water to customers. Because water to the plant is entirely drawn from Bon Tempe, the lake is kept full while other MMWD reservoirs drop in summer and fall. A trail, 4 miles if hugging the shore throughout, circles Bon Tempe.

Kent Lake (1953)

Elevation: 400 feet

Capacity: 10.7 billion gallons (32,895 acre feet)

Surface area: 845 acres

Kent Lake is by far the largest of the Mt. Tamalpais reservoirs. Indeed, its capacity is more than double the other four Tam lakes combined. Named for Thomas Kent, son of William Kent and long-time head of the MMWD Board of Directors, it was formed behind Peters Dam, named for MMWD general manager William Peters. The 400-foot-long earthen dam was raised in 1981–1982 to its current height of 115 feet.

Kent Lake is invariably the last MMWD reservoir to fill, which it does only after major storms in wet winters. When it's full, the watershed's storage is at 100 percent capacity, and it has the most impressive waterfall in Marin. (MMWD also has two reservoirs—Nicasio and Soulajoule—outside of the Mt. Tamalpais watershed.) Overflow water leaves the MMWD system, ultimately draining into Tomales Bay. MMWD also regularly releases water from Kent Lake to maintain salmon habitat downstream.

The Kent Pump Fire Road skirts the southeast tip of the lake, and Peters Dam Fire Road borders the northeast end, but no loop is possible. Indeed, the steep, deeply wooded slope west from the lake up to Bolinas Ridge has no trails whatsoever between Fairfax–Bolinas Road and Shafter Grade.

There are also a few smaller reservoir lakes on Tamalpais. Cascade Reservoir, behind a dam on Mill Creek, began supplying water to the new community of Mill Valley in 1895. When it was no longer needed for drinking water, the reservoir became a popular swimming hole. After a drowning death there, the dam was breached, the reservoir drained, and the site posted as closed. Belvedere Reservoir (1903), above Edgewood Avenue in Mill Valley, drew water from intakes along creeks on the south side of Tamalpais and stored it for transmission to Belvedere. In 1967, the open-air reservoir was enclosed within a metal tank. The old intakes and what is left of 12,000 feet of pipe are still visible along Troop 80 Trail and the remaining section of Pipeline Trail. Ross Reservoir, by Worn Spring Fire Road, is enclosed under a wooden frame, but visitors can peek inside. (Ross Reservoir is scheduled to be replaced.) A dam, now breached but still evident where the Dipsea and Steep Ravine Trails meet, created a small reservoir for Stinson Beach.

Flora

The late John Thomas Howell, in his landmark 1949 book, *Marin Flora*, described some 1,400 species of vascular plants—the most evolutionarily advanced, from ferns through those producing flowers—of which more than 900 are found on Mt. Tamalpais. A handful, such as the Tamalpais jewelflower (*Streptanthus batrachopus*) and Tamalpais manzanita (*Arctostaphylos hookeri*, ssp. *montana*), grow only on the mountain. Tamalpais's trees, shrubs, ferns, and wildflowers enhance every visit, never-ending and never-failing sources of beauty and joy. Here is a brief introduction to that flora.

Plant Communities

To greatly simplify, four plant communities—coniferous forest, broad-leaved (hardwood) forest, chaparral, and grassland—cover almost all of Mt. Tamalpais. These plant communities, or associations, are often just yards apart; boundaries change over time, and many species are found in more than one habitat. For greater detail, refer to Howell or to the California Native Plant Society's *Plant Communities of Marin County* by W. David Shuford and Irene Timossi.

Redwood/Douglas-Fir (Coniferous) Forest

Redwoods and Douglas-firs, in pure stands and intermingled with one another and with other trees, make up the mountain's tallest and deepest forests. Both are conifers, their seeds borne in cones.

Logging of redwoods in Marin began when the Spanish visited the Corte Madera shore to cut trees for their presidio in San Francisco. (As mentioned earlier, this is the origin of Corte Madera del Presidio, or "cut wood for the presidio," the name of Marin's first land grant. There is a splendid first-person account of an early expedition in Antonio María Osio's *The History of Alta California*.)

Marin's first sawmill was built by John Reed in the mid-1830s. Reconstructed, it is now the oldest standing mill in Northern California. Most of Tam's virgin stands of redwoods and Douglas-firs were cut to supply San Francisco's building frenzy during the Gold Rush years. Muir Woods, the only old-growth coastal redwood forest in the Bay Area and one of the few left on the planet, reminds us of what was lost.

Second-growth redwoods, now more than 150 years old and reaching the 200-foot-plus heights of the original monarchs, are again abundant on Tamalpais. Competing directly for sunlight with the redwoods, and therefore often just as tall, are Douglas-firs. They are vigorous colonizers, and have successfully invaded Tam's hardwood forests and grasslands over the last several decades.

Broad-leaved (Hardwood) Forest
The other type of woodland on Mt. Tamalpais consists of non-conifers (also called hardwoods) that have broad leaves, as opposed to needles. Five types of trees—laurel (bay), madrone, tanbark oak, coast live oak, and buckeye—make up most of this forest. Of the five, only the buckeye is deciduous (sheds its leaves in winter). This forest tends to occur between the wetter redwood forests and the drier chaparral and grasslands. There is, however, much intermingling. Excellent examples of this type of woodland occur around Lake Lagunitas and Phoenix Lake.

Chaparral
Howell says, "It is the chaparral that gives to Mt. Tamalpais its distinctive texture. . . . From a distance, there is a velvety quality that characterizes it and gives depth to the blues and purples that pervade the slopes; from near at hand there is still that seeming smoothness and a lawnlike quality that belie the tough and rugged character of the plant cover. Up steep slopes, over rolling summits, and across broad flats spreads the unbroken array of shrubs, dense, erect, stiff—the pile in the fabric of the mountain's mantle."

Chaparral is distinctive of coastal California and of the world's four other Mediterranean climates. Largely treeless, the chaparral community is dominated by shrubs, mostly chamise and manzanita, plus chaparral pea and scrub oak. ("Chaparral" is derived from the Spanish word for scrub oak.)

Chaparral covers the mountain's drier exposed slopes and ridges, where shallow soils lack humus or rocks don't hold soil. Late nineteenth-century photos show the upper 1,500 feet of the south side of Mt. Tamalpais as unbroken chaparral. Subsequent tree plantings and range expansion of native trees in the absence of fire have altered that, but chaparral remains dominant. The impenetrable nature of Mt. Tam's chaparral becomes known to anyone who tries to enter it.

Near the ocean, a different type of chaparral cover, called northern coastal scrub, prevails. It, too, is dominated by shrubs, with Baccharis most prevalent, along with blackberry, lupine, sage, and poison oak.

Grassland
The mountain's grasslands now comprise almost entirely non-native grasses. The native perennial bunchgrasses invariably lost out in competition with more vigorous introduced annual grasses. These Old World grasses arrived both deliberately (planted to nourish livestock) and accidentally (carried by cattle and horses) beginning with Spanish settlement of California in 1776. Native bunchgrasses remain, particularly in light woodland, as along Lower Berry Trail.

The mountain's grasslands are presently shrinking as control of fire and elimination of grazing have permitted invasion by bracken fern, Baccharis, and Douglas-fir. Large expanses persist, among other places, along Bolinas Ridge, on Bald Hill, and in the Potrero meadows.

Trees

There are millions of trees on Mt. Tamalpais, but fewer than fifteen species (grouping the oaks together) account for well over 95 percent of them. Thus, it is not difficult for visitors to learn to identify basically all the trees. Trees are often landmarks, and are cited frequently in trail descriptions.

I'll arbitrarily split Tamalpais's trees into two groups, "most abundant" and "abundant," and then describe them in alphabetical order. The groupings are based solely on my own observations, not any census. A few other trees are noted at the end.

Most Abundant
• California Laurel/Bay (*Umbellularia californica*)
Laurel (interchangeably called "bay" in this book) has evergreen leaves, elliptical, 2 to 5 inches in length, and shiny, dark green on top. When crushed or torn, they produce an unmistakable pungent fragrance. The leaf's oils are so much more potent than the bay leaf sold in markets that recipes commonly call for using it in a strength of just 1 part to 10; the definitive *Jepson Manual* of California flora notes that it "may produce toxic effects in some people."

The laurel's shape, which varies according to environmental conditions, ranges from thick-trunked, 80-foot-tall, fully crowned specimens in protected valleys to thin, bent, 6-foot survivors on the windiest exposed ridges. There are a few almost pure laurel forests, such as the one on Old Vee Fire Road. These trees often grow in circles, multiple trunks root-sprouting from a dead "mother" tree. It is also common to see branches growing straight up from a fallen or bent tree.

Laurel nuts were roasted and eaten by local native people. The tree is also commonly called "pepperwood" and "Oregon myrtle" to the north. It is in the same family as the true laurel of the Mediterranean (of the laurel wreath), but is a different genus.

• Douglas-Fir (*Pseudotsuga menziesii*)
It would be difficult to visit Mt. Tamalpais even occasionally and not come away with respect for Douglas-firs. They grow to huge height and girth, rivaling the redwoods with which they often compete for sunlight. For years, the ancient Kent Tree, a now-fallen Douglas-fir in Muir Woods, was the tallest tree in Marin.

Douglas-firs are found along almost all the trails, and are often dominant. They are actively colonizing the mountain's grasslands, converting them to forests. A dramatic example is Lone Tree Hill above the Dipsea Trail. Where just a single tree, a redwood, stood on its southern slope before World War II (hence the name), the hill is today completely covered with Douglas-firs. Indeed, Douglas-firs have been so successful in advancing on Mt. Tamalpais that MMWD thinned them as part of a native plant/oak restoration project at Lake Lagunitas in 2014.

Pseudotsuga means "false hemlock," and the trees display some characteristics of hemlocks and some of true firs. The cones, 2 to 3 ½ inches, are distinctive for their three-clawed bracts. The flexible evergreen needles—singly in rows, not in sheathed bundles like pines—are ¾ to 1 ½ inches long. Douglas-firs have thick, deeply furrowed bark that feels harder to the touch than redwood. The trunks can be branchless for great heights or, if the tree originally grew without having to compete for sunlight, may be circled with low branches. Douglas-fir is the most important lumber tree of the Pacific Northwest.

- Oak (*Quercus* spp.)
There are some ten species of oak growing on Mt. Tamalpais. The species are not always easy to differentiate, as they hybridize with one another and often have different leaves on the same tree. All have alternate leaves, separate male and female flowers on the same twig, and hard-shelled acorns. Acorns were a staple of the Miwok diet.

Coast live oak (*Q. agrifolia*) may be the mountain's most common. Its leaves are convex above, and the midribs on the lower side have small hairs. Canyon live, or goldcup, oaks (*Q. chrysolepis*) have a golden, turning-to-gray pubescence (hairy surface) on the underside of their young leaves. They are found on the upper slopes, such as the Mountain Theater area. The large, usually seven-lobed deciduous leaves of the black oak (*Q. kelloggii*) are distinctive. One shrubby oak, *Q. parvula* var. *tamalpaisensis*, was only recently identified.

Oak seedlings are a favorite food of deer, whose unchecked population on the mountain may have adversely affected oak's ability to compete. Tam's coast live and black oaks have also been victimized by Sudden Oak Death (SOD). Newly infected oaks display cankers bleeding with a brownish to blackish ooze near their base. Later, there is a rapid browning of leaves and infestations by other fungi and bark and ambrosia beetles. The pathogen—*Phytophthora ramorum*, in the same fungal genus linked to the devastating Irish potato blight of the 1840s—was only identified in 2000. It has since been found on other common Tam species such as bay, huckleberry, and madrone. Restrictions on transporting oaks and oak products were put in place beginning in 2001.

- Pacific Madrone (*Arbutus menziesii*)
  The madrone is well known to mountain visitors for its highly distinctive bark, which peels back in summer to reveal smooth, reddish wood that remains cool to the touch on the hottest of summer days. The trunk and branches are often twisted. The 2- to 6-inch-long evergreen leaves are thick and leathery, elliptic in shape, dark green, and shiny on top.

  Madrones lend a distinctive feel to areas they dominate, such as ridges north of Lakes Lagunitas and Bon Tempe. Marin's largest madrones can be found alongside Pilot Knob and Madrone Trails.

  W. L. Jepson, author of the landmark *Manual of the Flowering Plants of California*, wrote of the madrone, "No other of our trees . . . makes so strong an appeal to man's imagination—to his love of color, of joyful bearing, of sense of magic, of surprise and change." Howell adds "[The madrone's] flowers and fruits [are] beyond compare—the former like sculptured ivory urns, the latter like etched carnelian globes."

  The madrone is in the same family (Heather) as the shrub manzanita. Both display peeling bark, and a small madrone can be the same size as a large manzanita. Madrones are distinguished by their much larger leaves. Local native people ate its fruits both cooked and raw.

- Redwood (*Sequoia sempervirens*)
  Redwoods, the state tree, are the tallest trees in the world, with specimens more than 370 feet high in Humboldt County and in excess of 250 feet on Mt. Tamalpais. They are also among the longest lived, some more than 2,000 years old. And, of course, redwoods are among the world's best loved trees, attracting more than one million visitors annually to Muir Woods National Monument, which has the mountain's finest stands. Once wide ranging along the Pacific Rim, redwoods now grow only in coastal Northern California (and a few miles into Oregon).

  Redwoods have very thick, reddish-brown bark. This thick bark lacks flammable resins, which enables the trees to survive fires. The bark is also resistant to insect and fungus infestation. The trees' roots interlock with those of other redwoods, helping them remain standing in high winds.

  The tree's short evergreen needles vary in appearance between the lower and the topmost branches. The cones are surprisingly small, $\frac{1}{2}$ to $1\frac{1}{8}$ inch. Small too are the seeds within the cone, each only $\frac{1}{8,000}$th of an ounce. Most reproduction is vegetative, with new trees sprouting from, and often around, a "mother" tree's roots.

  Redwoods, which require year-round moisture, follow streambeds up Tamalpais. The highest grove is at Redwood Spring, at around 2,100 feet in elevation. Fog also provides a high percentage of the redwood's considerable water needs. Dense groves of thin, relatively short redwoods, as along Sierra Trail, provide examples of mature redwoods struggling at the limits of their range.

The coast, or California, redwood is related to, but a different genus from, the more massive-in-girth giant sequoia (*Sequoiadendron giganteum*) native to the Sierra. (There is a planted grove in Morse's Gulch, north of Stinson Beach.)

- Tanbark Oak (*Notholithocarpus densiflorus*)
Though in the same beech family as the oaks, the tanbark oak, or tanoak, is not a true oak (genus *Quercus*). One difference is that male flowers are erect catkins, as opposed to the drooping catkins of oaks.

Rarely dominant in any one area of Mt. Tamalpais, tanbark oaks are nonetheless widespread and abundant, as on the south shore of Lake Lagunitas and on Old Mine Trail above Pantoll. Tanbark oaks are generally associated with madrones along the redwood forests' drier borders. They range in size from more than 100 feet, as by the junction of Simmons and Kent Trails, to shrubby dwarfs on rocky, exposed ridges.

Tanbark leaves are oblong, thick, leathery, light green above and lighter below, with wavy, toothed borders. They vary significantly in length, from 2 to 8 inches, depending on habitat.

The acorns of tanbark oaks were a principal source of flour for Marin's native people. Later, the bark was the main California source of tannin, used for tanning leather, dyeing, and making ink. Indeed, tanoaks were once commercially harvested on Mt. Tamalpais.

Sudden Oak Death was first identified on dying tanbarks on Tam in 1995 above Mill Valley, and the species has been particularly hard hit. It is now all but impossible to walk amid Tam's woodlands and not see dead tanbarks.

Abundant
- Alder (*Alnus* spp.)
There are two species of alder on the mountain, white alder (*A. rhombifolia*) and red alder (*A. rubra*). The latter, the leaves of which roll inward around the edge, is found only near the coast. Alders grow along stream banks, where they can be fairly abundant, as on lower Steep Ravine Trail. Howell writes of the white alder, "To see the green-gold of their blossoming crowns in January is one of the floral treats of the year."

- Big-leaf Maple (*Acer macrophyllum*)
This tree is aptly named: its leaves are among the largest of any of the world's roughly 125 species of maples. Most people recognize the deeply incised, five-lobed maple leaf. Maple leaves add fall color to the mountain as they turn

red and yellow before dropping. Single seeds are found in each of the paired "wings" of the fruit, called a samara. Look for maples along streams, such as Arroyo Corte Madera Creek on lower Old Railroad Grade.

- California Buckeye (*Aesculus californica*)
  More than other of the mountain's trees, buckeyes markedly change in appearance with the seasons. In winter, the smooth, light-gray branches are bare. In late winter, fresh, distinctive, five-lobed palmate leaves emerge. In spring, pinkish, fragrant, candle-like flower clusters develop and bloom. In summer, pear-like fruit capsules (buckeyes) form and leaves begin to yellow and drop. In fall, the capsules darken and linger on otherwise bare limbs into winter. Many can be seen beside trails, sometimes sprouting in the soil.

  Buckeye seeds are poisonous. The region's native people leached out the toxin, then turned the residue to flour. The toxin was also put to use, added to small, dammed ponds to stupefy fish for easy catching. Buckeye nectar and pollen are said to be poisonous to bees. Buckeyes, in the horse chestnut family, are found throughout Tamalpais; there is a Buckeye Trail on the northwest slope of Bald Hill. (Tam's buckeye is a different species from the state tree of Ohio.)

- California Nutmeg (*Torreya californica*)
  The California nutmeg is fairly common high on the mountain's north slope, often seen along and above Northside Trail. The flat, sharp-pointed needles are 1 to 3 inches long. Accidentally squeeze a row and you'll remember the difference between nutmeg and similar-looking Douglas-fir needles. The tree and seeds are aromatic. Male and female reproductive parts are found on separate trees.

  Though nutmegs are often little more than shrub height, Howell reported that an 86-footer fell in Cataract Creek. Marin's nutmegs are botanically unrelated to the true nutmegs from which the spice is made. The name arose because the elliptical fruits—with their fleshy outer green layer (aril) around a hard-shelled seed—look somewhat similar.

- Chinquapin (*Chrysolepis chrysophylla*)
  Though often shrub-like, chinquapins can reach more than 50 feet tall, as on Benstein Trail. Most distinctive are the spiny, bur-like fruit capsules, often abundant on the ground beneath the trees. The folded, lance-shaped leaves, shiny green on top and yellow underneath, are also indicative. Chinquapins, which are in the same beech family as oaks (but a different genus), generate erect catkins.

- Sargent Cypress (*Hesperocyparis sargentii*)
  Howell notes two aspects of Marin's Sargent cypress. One grows in striking

stands high on the mountain, almost always on exposed serpentine rock. The other grows in a dense pygmy forest—mature specimens just a few feet tall—atop San Geronimo Ridge. Its small, round cones, sectioned into six or eight parts, are distinctive, as are its short, scale-like leaves, which differ from those of other conifers on Tam. Sargent cypresses, which grow only in Calfornia, are often stunted, with twisted trunks. However, the two largest Sargent cypresses in the world were found on Mickey O'Brien Trail, one standing 96 feet, the other, 85 feet. Both fell in 2002–2003.

Howell may have been contemplating the Sargent cypresses of Simmons Trail when he wrote, "These gray-green trees blend with the gray-green rock of the serpentine barrens to form a picturesque and memorable part of the Mt. Tamalpais scene."

- Toyon (*Heteromeles arbutifolia*)
This member of the rose family may be either a shrub or small tree (to 15 feet) on Tamalpais, depending on growing conditions. Its shiny, evergreen leaves are sharply saw-toothed. Also distinctive are its clusters of small red berries—similar to the Christmas berries of the eastern holly—that mature in fall and persist through winter.

- Willow (*Salix* spp.)
Several species of willow grow naturally on Mt. Tamalpais, with the arroyo willow (*S. lasiolepis*) perhaps the most abundant. Willows may be found high on the mountain in wet soils, as at Willow Meadow, but are more abundant along coastal streams.

Introduced
Pines are not native on Mt. Tamalpais but at least four *Pinus* species—Monterey (*P. radiata*), bishop (*P. muricata*), knobcone (*P. attenuata*), and Coulter (*P. coulteri*)—were introduced and have reproduced. Monterey pines have needles in clusters of three and closed cones whorled around the limbs and trunk. Many were planted along the old Mountain Railway line, such as at Mesa Station, West Point, and today's East Peak parking lot.

Bishop pines also have closed cones in whorls, but their needles are arranged in bunches of two. Aside from outlier stands on Pine Mountain and Green Hill Fire Roads, they are found naturally in Marin only on the west side of the San Andreas Fault. There is a large, planted row along Old Plane (Vic Haun) Trail.

Knobcones have slender cones and three needles per bunch. They are found along Laurel Dell Fire Road, between Laurel Dell and Potrero Meadow. Coulters, which have the heaviest cones in the world—up to 5 pounds—were planted in the Bon Tempe and Lake Lagunitas area around 1930. MMWD has removed almost all of them, as along Lakeview Fire Road.

Two Australian natives, eucalyptus and acacia, were introduced on Tamalpais. Many have been removed—for example, the distinctive, 100-year-old row of eucalyptus on Sky Oaks Road near the Lake Lagunitas parking lot was cut down in 1992—to help restore native vegetation and to lessen fire danger, as both trees are high in flammable resins. They are currently being removed from Citron Fire Road.

Shrubs

Shrubs are short (generally less than 10 feet) plants with branched woody stems rather than a single main axis, or trunk. There is, however, some overlap; several species appear on Mt. Tamalpais as both trees and shrubs, depending on growing conditions. The Sargent cypress, for example, is a tree that grows to 75 feet on Mickey O'Brien Trail but a stunted, shrublike, 2 to 3 feet in the serpentine on Northside Trail.

Shrubs are found everywhere on Mt. Tamalpais and define the huge areas of chaparral and coastal scrub. Following are the most common of the mountain's shrubs, grouped into those favoring chaparral and coastal scrub and those more abundant in woodland, and presented alphabetically by common name. Two of the most abundant (but definitely not most beloved) shrubs, poison oak and broom, are found in all habitats.

Chaparral
- Baccharis (*Baccharis pilularis*)
  Baccharis, also called coyote brush, is abundant alongside most of Tamalpais's grassland trails and dominates the coastal scrub. It is quick to colonize grassland after livestock grazing ceases, as is evident on Tam's southwestern slopes. Each shrub contains either male or female flowers. In winter, the seeds are dispersed by the white tufts on their tops, which gives the female shrubs another common name: fuzzy-wuzzy.

- California Sagebrush (*Artemisia californica*)
  The shrub's gray foliage has a distinctive fragrance, and its leaves are divided into thread-like segments. It is abundant in coastal scrub.

- Ceanothus, California Lilac (*Ceanothus* spp.)
  There are some fifty species of ceanothus in California, and at least six can be found on Mt. Tamalpais. Blue-blossom (*C. thyrsiflorus*) is the most common locally. Its branchlets are ridged and its glossy leaves are prominently three-veined. But most distinctive is the sweet, pervasive fragrance exuded from its clusters of blue flowers in early spring. Indigo-brush (*C. foliosus*), buckbrush (*C. cuneatus*), and muskbrush (*C. jepsonii*) of the high serpentine are other common Tamalpais ceanothus species.

- Chamise (*Adenostoma fasciculatum*)
  This member of the rose family makes up, with manzanita, much of Tam's chaparral, and particularly dominates on the south slope. Its short evergreen needles are arranged in bunches (fascicles), and the stems are stiff. Chamise's cream-colored, stalkless flowers bloom in crowded, pyramidal clusters in late spring. They linger and turn purplish, giving Tamalpais's south face its characteristic tint in fall. The plant is also known as greasewood.

- Chaparral Pea (*Pickeringia montana*)
  This shrub has lovely pink-purple, pea-like flowers that linger into September. It also has sharp, spiny stem tips that can be painful to the unwary.

- Lupine (*Lupinus* spp.)
  There are ten lupine species on Mt. Tamalpais, several of them not easy to tell apart. Lupines, in the pea family, have seedpods. Flowers are usually blue. The palmate leaves are also distinctive. Howell calls the low-growing, grayish-leaved Tamalpais lupine (*L. albifrons* var. *douglasii*) "one of the most beautiful flowering shrubs."

- Manzanita (*Arctostaphylos* spp.)
  Manzanita ("little apple") is very abundant on Tam and throughout California's chaparral plant communities. There are dozens of species in the state, at least six of which can be found on Tamalpais. The pinkish-tinged, delicate, urn-shaped flowers are a common sight in winter and early spring, and fallen blossoms sometimes cover sections of trails. Also distinctive is the bark, which peels, like that of the related madrone, to reveal a reddish trunk. Two of the manzanita species have fire-resistant burls at their bases. Another, Tamalpais manzanita (*A. montana*), is found only on Mt. Tamalpais, usually on serpentine. Named by the legendary botanist Alice Eastwood, it is the last blooming of Tam's manzanitas.

- Shrub Oaks (*Quercus* spp.)
  Shrub oaks are abundant on Tam's drier slopes. Most common is a variety of the interior live oak (*Q. wislizeni* var. *frutescens*), with its plane (uncurved) leaves. Leather oak (*Q. durata*) has tough leaves that are convex above, with inward-rolling margins. Leather oak is restricted to serpentine outcrops.

- Sticky (Bush) Monkeyflower (*Mimulus aurantiacus*)
  Most Tam visitors recognize the funnel-shaped, orange/buff flowers of this widespread shrub, which blooms from February through August, and often later. Opposing leaves have a sticky-to-the-touch underside coating, hence the common name.

- Yerba Santa (*Eriodictyon californicum*)
  The leathery, willow-shaped leaves of yerba santa are sticky above, woolly

below and are sometimes spotted with a black mold. Yerba santa has purplish-white, trumpet-shaped flowers. The leaves were used, either smoked or as a tea, by the local native people and early settlers to ease respiratory ailments.

Woodland
- California Hazel (*Corylus cornuta*)
  Hazel is a large shrub, or occasionally, a small tree, commonly found along the mountain's streamside trails. Its round leaves are very soft to the touch. The drooping male catkins begin appearing in January; the tiny, female catkins, with bright red stigmas, are separate and erect. Its nuts, which squirrels and chipmunks usually harvest before hikers find them, resemble the related filberts of the East Coast.

- California Honeysuckle *(Lonicera hispidula)*
  Honeysuckle entwines itself around other plants, and is often seen overhanging woodland trails. The uppermost of the opposing leaves are fused around the stem. It produces pinkish flowers in spring and red berries in late summer. Other berry-producing members of the honeysuckle family on Tamalpais include the red and blue elderberry, two species of snowberry, and twinberry.

- Coffeeberry *(Frangula californica)*
  In fall, the black berries of this shrub resemble coffee beans, hence the name. Coffeeberry, commonly 3 to 5 feet tall, is found in both light woodland and grassland margins.

- Elk Clover *(Aralia californica)*
  Elk clover (also called spikenard and despite its name, not a member of the clover genus) is found in wet places, its roots always near flowing water. It can be identified by its huge leaves, which are as large as any to be found on the mountain. Elk clover dies back each year, growing anew in spring. One of the last shrubs to blossom, it sends up clusters of tiny white flowers in mid-summer and produces inedible purple-black berries in fall. Elk clover is the only North American native of the Ginseng family.

- Huckleberry *(Vaccinium ovatum)*
  Huckleberries line long sections of many forest trails, such as Sierra, Kent, and, of course, Huckleberry. The berries are small, but sweet and tasty when black and ripe at the end of summer. The alternating leaves are shiny on top, with saw-toothed margins. The pinkish-white flowers are urn-shaped like those of manzanita and madrone; all are members of the Heather family.

- Western Azalea *(Rhododendron occidentale)*
  Azaleas are found in wet areas: stream banks, springs, and marshes. Their

showy, fragrant, creamy-white flowers make them one of the mountain's fa-vorites. Azaleas' smooth green leaves sprout in spring and they are usually in peak bloom in June. Azaleas are perhaps most abundant on Tam along the East Fork of Swede George Creek, which includes Azalea Meadow.

Multi-habitat

- French (*Genista monspessulana*) and Scotch (*Cytisus scoparius*) Broom
Broom, an invasive, non-native plant, grows in thick borders on many trail and road cuts, in grassland, and in light woodland, particularly on the east side of the mountain. Indeed, broom has completely overrun and obscured several old routes. Because brooms are so invasive and hardy, with abundant, long-lived seeds, they crowd out native flowers, to the detriment of native understory animals as well.

  Highly flammable, broom is also feared as a fire menace, and all jurisdic-tions have taken steps to control and eradicate it. Some authorities support using herbicides, a step that has triggered opposition. Many individuals pull broom on their walks, particularly after wet weather, or participate in orga-nized broom pulls. (No jurisdiction seems to object to pulling this, and only this, plant. Note that it is unlawful to pick wildflowers or otherwise disturb the mountain's flora.)

  Brooms bear striking yellow blossoms through much of the year. On hot summer days, seeds literally explode outward, expanding the plant's range.

  French broom is more common on Tam. Native to southern France, its specific name, *monspessulana*, means "of Montpelier." Widely planted as a garden ornamental, it eventually migrated onto Tam. Back in 1949 in his *Marin Flora*, Howell said "[French broom is] . . . a pernicious shrub weed exhibiting an aggressive vigor that the native vegetation cannot withstand." Scotch broom has larger flowers and smaller, almost needle-like leaves.

- Poison Oak (*Toxicodendron diversilobum*)
What may be the mountain's most common shrub, poison oak, is, in the words of the Jepson Manual, "one of the most hazardous plants in California." Anyone who has suffered from the itchy rash it causes learns to identify the plant's distinctive lobed, triple-leaf clusters. However, the plant assumes rad-ically different appearances, hence the species name, which translates to "di-verse-leaved." (The genus name is Latin for "poisonous tree.") Poison oak can appear as an isolated plant a few inches high, grow as mats on coastal hills, form thickets several feet tall, climb high as a vine, or even appear to be a small tree. In summer, the leaves turn from green to red; this red colors many a hillside. It is related to poison ivy and poison sumac but not to true oaks.

Ferns

Ferns differ from more evolutionarily advanced flowering plants in that they reproduce by spores, not seeds, and have two distinct, alternate generations. The sporophyte generation, the one commonly seen, bears and drops the spores. Spores germinate into the smaller gametophyte generation, which produces sperm and egg cells. Sperm, dependent on moisture for mobility, fertilize the eggs, which then develop into sporophytes. There are some twenty species of ferns on Mt. Tamalpais; a list of the most abundant follows.

- Bracken (*Pteridium aquilinum*)
  Bracken, one of the more widely distributed plants in the world, may be the most abundant fern on Tamalpais. Though it is found in many habitats, it is most prominent colonizing grasslands, as along the Hogback section of the Dipsea. Bracken's young, rounded shoots (sometimes called "fiddlenecks") are considered a delicacy in parts of the world, but mature fronds have been known to poison cattle.

- Giant Chain (*Woodwardia fimbriata*)
  Giant chain, or Woodwardias, the largest ferns on the mountain, sometimes rise to 6 feet or more in height. They are found only in wet places, such as seeps and along streambeds. Howell cites the stand on Stocking Trail at Van Wyck Creek as containing "the largest and most luxurious specimens."

- Goldback (*Pentagramma triangularis*)
  Goldbacks are found in shaded areas somewhat drier than those favored by the Western sword and giant chain ferns. The leaflets curl up and dry in summer. This fern is well known for leaving a tracing of golden-green "powder" when its underside is pressed against dark clothing.

- Maidenhair (*Adiantum jordanii*)
  The much-admired maidenhair, with its delicate, rounded segments, is common in shaded, rocky canyons. A close relative, *A. pedatum*, with divided stalks, is known as five-finger fern.

- Western Sword (*Polystichum munitum*)
  This large fern is so named because its leaflets have a serrated edge and a hilt-like base. It is very common in redwood forests, such as in Steep Ravine.

Wildflowers

There are, happily, far too many species of wildflowers on Tamalpais to cover even cursorily here (the 2007 revised edition of *Marin Flora* runs to 512 pages!). But scores of wildflowers are noted in the trail descriptions, often with botanical name and months they are likely to be in bloom.

There is floral color on Tam all year. In *California Out of Doors* (1915), Alice

Eastwood, grand lady of the mountain's flora, noted, "There have been years when a hundred native plants could be found in bloom on and around Mt. Tamalpais in early January." Star lilies (*Toxicoscordion fremontii*) sometimes appear in December, just as the last California fuchsias (*Epilobium canum*) and tarweeds (*Hemozonia and Madia*) are departing. The white of milk maids (*Cardamine californica*)—often the annual leader, seen in profusion in January—the blue of hound's tongue (*Cynoglossum grande*); and the brown-spotted, drooping fetid adder's tongue (*Scoliopus bigelovii*) follow. The floral pageant only gets better with the blossoming of showy trilliums, columbines, orchids, violets, calochortuses, clintonias, silenes, larkspurs, and so many others.

And, of course, there is the California poppy (*Eschscholzia californica*), the state flower, which furls its flowers in the evening. Despite the name, it is not a true poppy; the one true poppy species on the mountain, the fire poppy (*Papaver californicum*) is almost never seen except after major fires.

John Thomas Howell's paean to the California poppy is lyrical: "No poet has yet sung the full beauty of our poppy, no painter has successfully portrayed the satiny sheen of its lustrous petals, no scientist has satisfactorily diagnosed the vagaries of its variations and adaptability. In its abundance, this colorful plant should not be slighted: Cherish it and be ever thankful that so rare a flower is common!"

Pacific Madrone   California Poppy   Lupine

Bracken Fern   Blue-eyed Grass   Manzanita

Fauna

As with plants, there are far too many animal species on Mt. Tamalpais for anything but a cursory treatment here. For example, more than 300 species of birds may spend their entire year on Tamalpais, stay for the breeding season or for the winter, or just pass through on longer migrations. And, of course, unlike trees and shrubs, animals can't be pinned onto any single trail description.

Here is a small sampling of animals with special Mt. Tamalpais connections. Some other famous (or infamous) denizens—ticks, bees and wasps, rattlesnakes, mountain lions, coyotes—are discussed in the "Cautions" section. Other large mammals have been extirpated from Tamalpais in historic times: grizzly bears around 1850, black bears around 1890 (although there were reliable sightings of single individuals in 2003 and 2011), elk during the 1870s, and possibly wolves. Feral pigs came, and were removed.

- Banana Slug (*Ariolomax*)
  On any group walk through Tam's wetter woodlands, you'll likely hear, "Watch out, don't step on the slug." Banana slugs are mollusks in the class Gastropoda, or "stomach foot," for their method of slow locomotion atop their own mucus. This mucus deters most (but not all) predators. Slugs, which help decompose detritus on the forest floor, are hermaphroditic; individuals have both male and female organs (and a bizarre sex life not suitable for inclusion in this general-audience book!).

- Newt (*Taricha*)
  Also underfoot and not much faster than slugs, and so vulnerable to being squished, are Tam's two newt species. Rough-skinned (*T. granulosa*) and California (*T. torosa*) newts are similar in appearance. In winter, they waddle across the mountain's wetter trails on their way to the stream of their birth to reproduce. (On a December walk on Kaasi Road after heavy rain, I saw literally hundreds.) There are "newt crossing" caution signs at some of the places with heavier newt "traffic," including Lake Lagunitas and Rocky Point Road. *Note: Do not pick up newts.* They secrete tarichatoxin, a potent neurotoxin and the most poisonous non-protein substance in the animal kingdom.

- Western Fence Lizard (*Sceloporus occidentalis*)
  Lizards dart by or bask in the sun atop rocks, logs, or fences. Males have blue throat patches and blue on the underside of the belly, inspiring one of their common names: "blue-belly." Western fence lizards play an important and beneficial role in reducing the incidence of Lyme disease on Tamalpais and throughout the West. A favorite host for the nymph ticks carrying Lyme disease, they have an enzyme that kills the causal bacteria and thus helps break the cycle.

- Foothill Yellow-legged (*Rana boylii*) and Red-legged (*R. aurora*) Frog
  Worldwide, populations of frog species are radically declining as a consequence of many factors, including a recently identified fungus. MMWD is closely monitoring the two remaining Mt. Tamalpais breeding sites of the foothill yellow-legged frog, which has been designated as a California Species of Special Concern (a sign by Little Carson Falls explains the project, or visit MMWD's website and enter "frog" in the search box to find out more). A GGNRA sign on Kaasi Road describes the comeback of red-legged frogs in lower Redwood Creek.

  Among the other mountain amphibians are the western toad (*Bufo boreas*) and Pacific treefrog (*Pseudacris regilla*). Bullfrogs (*Rana catesbeiana*) were introduced to California and Mt. Tamalpais roughly a century ago.

- Northwestern Pond Turtle (*Actinemys marmorata*)
  Western pond turtles, once common in the Mt. Tam watershed, are now threatened. A 2004 census of MMWD lakes revealed that the species had essentially been replaced by the larger red-eared slider (*Trachemys scripta* ssp. *elegans*), an aggressive nonnative perhaps introduced from pet tanks. The district has been trapping sliders and training volunteers to count turtles. Western pond turtles, which have a life expectancy of forty to seventy years, can often be seen sunning themselves on the log boom near the Lake Lagunitas dam.

- Great Blue Heron (*Ardea herodias*), Great Egret (*A. alba*), Snowy Egret (*Egretta thula*)
  Until 2012, when they were preyed upon by a golden eagle, these three birds all nested in redwood trees inside the Martin Griffin Preserve on the northwest slope of Mt. Tamalpais. (After predation, the three colonies moved to Bolinas, but perhaps will return.) The need to protect this rare nesting site and the birds' feeding grounds in Bolinas Lagoon played a large role in the birth of Audubon Canyon Ranch in 1962. The nesting season, enjoyed by many thousands of visitors each year, begins in late January.

  Great blue herons, 4 to 5 feet tall, stand motionless in shallow water, patiently waiting to spear fish and crustaceans. The all-white great egret is the symbol of the National Audubon Society, which came into being in part to stop their slaughter for plumes (aigrettes) used in women's hats. The smaller snowy egret is also all white, and has a black bill and yellow legs.

- Turkey Vulture (*Cathartes aura*)
  Turkey vultures are ubiquitous around Mt. Tam, and you're more likely to see one of these large birds on your Tam excursion than any other animal. (I'm excluding insects, including butterflies.) With their nearly 6-foot wingspan, they spend most of the day soaring on thermals across huge areas, using their phenomenal sense of smell as well as visual clues to find carrion. If you come

across a turkey vulture rising from the ground, there's likely a dead animal nearby. Turkey vultures, the region's only vulture, can be distinguished from hawks by the black-and-white pattern under their uptilted—V-shape, or dihedral—wings and their small, featherless red head.

- Red-tailed Hawk (*Buteo jamaicensis*)
  The piercing, descending cry of the red-tailed hawk, described as "keeeer-r-r," is one of the most vivid of Tam's wild sounds. (The call is sometimes well imitated, though always a trifle feebly, by Steller's jays.) Red-tails are commonly seen soaring, circling, and sometimes "stilling"—floating motionless against the wind—in search of rodents and other small mammals. They are the area's largest resident hawk, with a wing span of more than 4 feet. The dark brown head is seen in all ages, but coloring is highly variable, and only adults have the distinctive red tail.

- Osprey (*Pandion haliaetus*)
  Osprey circle the mountain's reservoir lakes hunting for fish; when they spot one, they dive into the water to snatch it. Osprey can be distinguished from red-tails by their whiter underparts and heads, as well as by the bend in their outstretched wings. They build huge nests atop Douglas-fir snags at Kent Lake. After years of decline due to the now-banned insecticide DDT, the osprey breeding colony beside Kent Lake is today the largest in California.

- Pileated Woodpecker (*Dryocopus pileatus*)
  The pileated is the largest extant North American woodpecker, with a wingspan of nearly 30 inches; its drumming on trees is loud and unmistakable. Other, more common Tamalpais woodpeckers include the acorn (*Melanerpes formicivorus*), which is abundant at Lake Lagunitas, and the downy (*Picoides pubescens*), hairy (*P. villosus*) and Nuttall's (*Dryobates nuttallii*). The northern flicker (*Colaptes auratus*) is more likely to be seen feeding on the ground (if it hasn't been startled first).

- Wild Turkey (*Meleagris gallopavo*)
  In 1999, wild turkeys, escapees from a population introduced onto private lands for hunting, began to establish themselves around Bon Tempe and Lagunitas Lakes. Within just a few years, they multiplied and expanded enough to be considered a serious nuisance by MMWD and others. Male turkeys reach nearly 4 feet in height and their call can be heard up to a mile away, most often in spring. Females are smaller, and usually lack the breast tuft.

- Common Raven (*Corvus corax*), American Crow (*C. brachyrhynchos*)
  Ravens are considered to be perhaps the most intelligent of all birds, and are

one of the widest ranging. They figure prominently in the cultural narratives of the native Miwok people, and hold a special appeal when they appear in the wilder spaces. Ravens are larger than Tamalpais's other large all-black bird, the more abundant American crow. Ravens have a wedge-shaped tail, as opposed to the fan shape of the crow; a thicker bill; and a more nasal call.

- Coho (*Oncorhynchus kisutch*), Steelhead (*O. mykiss*) Salmon
Lagunitas Creek, which originates on Mt. Tamalpais, has traditionally supported approximately 10 percent of California's coho (also called silver salmon) population. Coho also still spawn in Redwood Creek, which flows through Muir Woods National Monument. But these runs, like others across central California, have been radically reduced in recent decades, and the species is considered threatened.

The 18- to 30-inch-long, silver-to-brick-red adult coho swim in from the Pacific after the onset of winter rains, following the creeks upstream to the places of their own birth to mate. Males develop the hooked nose that gives the genus its name ("oncho" for hooked, "rhyncos" for nose.) Females deposit 2,000 to 3,500 eggs each in shallow depressions (redds) along the creeks' edges. Males, although exhausted, fight for the privilege of fertilizing these eggs, after which the female covers them when she creates another redd nearby. All adults die soon after.

In forty to sixty days, the young emerge and spend the summer in the creek. The first significant fall rains are signals for the young fingerlings, about 2 ½ inches long, to swim downstream. They reach the ocean and adapt to the salt water. After usually twelve to eighteen months in open water, they gather once again offshore. Generally speaking, only six salmon out of every 10,000 eggs complete the full life cycle.

Redwood Creek's coho salmon population hit a low in 1994; only ten adults were counted, along with a few juveniles. Then, in the winter of 2007–2008, almost no adults returned. In 2014, all young coho in Redwood Creek were moved to a hatchery in Sonoma County for rearing. The recently completed project to improve the flow of Redwood Creek at its mouth (Muir Beach) should aid in the run's recovery.

Steelhead salmon have a similar life cycle. Adults swim up Redwood and Lagunitas Creeks late each winter, after the coho run, to spawn. The young head to the ocean in the fall. However, unlike coho, some steelhead adults survive the spawning season, swim back to the Pacific, and return to spawn again. The 26-inch-long adults develop a red lateral band in fresh water. In 1997, steelheads throughout the central California coast were classified as "threatened" under the Endangered Species Act.

Two other salmonids are found in the Tamalpais watershed; in 2014–2015,

94 Chinook salmon (*O. tshawytscha*) were spotted in Lagunitas Creek (a recent high), and three chum salmon (*O. keta*) were also seen.

- Western Gray (*Scirus grisius*) and California Ground (*Citellus beecheyi*) Squirrel

  Squirrels are a familiar sight on the mountain, scurrying up trees and leaping from branch to branch. Gray squirrels make barking sounds, deeper than birds' calls. They feed mainly on acorns (many are stored but not all are found). These squirrels nest in trees, and bear a litter of three to five in spring. The species was almost wiped off the mountain in the 1930s by a rabies epidemic.

  California ground squirrels—which build burrows in grassland—are less common on Tam. They lack the gray squirrel's light underbelly, and have a less bushy tail. They can have two litters a year.

- Sonoma Chipmunk (*Eutamias sonomae*)

  Chipmunks dart among rocks and shrubs high on the mountain, jerking their tails each time they chirp. They pack their fur-lined cheek pouches with seeds, which they often bury for later use. The light striping on their backs provides camouflage. These chipmunks nest around logs, and give birth to four to six pups. Tam's chipmunk was once regarded as a separate species.

- Black-tailed Hare (*Lepus californicus*) and Brush Rabbit (*Sylvilagus bachmani*)

  Their long ears make black-tailed hares, or jackrabbits, immediately recognizable. Startling potential predators by using their long hind limbs to make a sudden, initial leap, they then bound and zig-zag at up to 35 miles per hour. Females scrape the barest of nests, or none at all, and give birth to one to three litters each year; the young hares are fully furred and capable of hopping.

  Brush rabbits, or cottontails, are smaller and less swift than jackrabbits. They stick to dense vegetative cover to avoid predators. Their young, like all true rabbits, are born blind, without fur, and helpless. Protecting rabbits is one reason for leash laws on the mountain.

- River Otter (*Lontra canadensis*)

  River otters, once killed for their pelts, were rare or absent from Mt. Tamalpais for decades. Now they are resident in all five reservoir lakes and in larger creeks as well. (California banned otter trapping in 1962.) "Otter Crossing" warning signs can be seen in various places, such as on Muir Woods Road.

  Otters, in the weasel family, eat primarily fish, but include crustaceans and other aquatic (and sometimes land) animals in their diets. Pups are born blind and helpless in late winter but by the time they're two months old, they're swimming. River otters are distinct from sea otters (*Enhydra lutris*); the latter, famous for feeding on their backs (river otters don't do this), were also hunted to near extinction along the entire Pacific Coast during the first two decades of the nineteenth century.

- Mule (Black-tailed) Deer (*Odocoileus hemionus*)
  The black-tailed is the only deer species on Mt. Tamalpais. With the disappearance of almost all their predators (although some are now returning), and hunting long banned, deer are likely more abundant on Tam now than they were historically. They are most active in early morning and at dusk, their favorite times for browsing on shrubs, berries, sprouting trees, and other plants.

  In fall, males (bucks) use their hardened, bony antlers to spar with one another for mating rights. After breeding season, the bucks shed their antlers and a new set, likely larger than the previous year's, begins to form in winter. In spring, the antlers are covered with "velvet" (skin and soft hairs that carry blood vessels and nerves), which is then scraped off when the antlers reach the end of their growing process.

  Females seek hidden shelters to bear their offspring—usually two fawns—in spring. The spotted fawns, a joyous mountain sight in May and June, are able to walk within minutes of birth.

- Striped (*Mephistis mephistis*) and Spotted (*Spilogale putorius*) Skunk
  Striped skunks, which have two white stripes lining their black backs, reside in deeper woods. The smaller spotted skunks have four broken stripes and a white-tipped tail.

  Skunks are omnivorous, feeding on insects, berries, rodents, eggs, or carrion. Their powerful anal scent gland spray keeps them relatively safe from natural enemies and is a potential menace to unlucky Tamalpais travelers. In spring, two to six young are born and remain in the mother's care, often trailing after her single file, through the summer. Skunks are usually nocturnal; if you see one roaming during the day, it may well be rabid and should be given even wider berth than usual.

- Gray Fox (*Urocyon cinereoargenteus*)
  You have to be alert, and lucky, to see a fox on Mt. Tamalpais, as they are nocturnal, wary, and blend in with chaparral. (One growled at me, bared its teeth, and chased me off Easy Grade Trail in midday. It may have been rabid, or possibly protecting nearby pups.) Gray foxes have a light reddish-brown underside and a black-tipped tail. They are omnivorous, eating rodents, insects, grasses, berries, and other plants, and climbing trees in search of birds' eggs. Gray foxes mate in winter, and both parents share in raising the two to five young born in spring. The supremely adaptable nonnative red fox (*Vulpes vulpes*) has recently established a local breeding population as well.

- Bobcat (*Lynx rufus*)

  Bobcats are seen only infrequently, both because their fur provides excellent camouflage and because they are largely nocturnal. They superficially resemble a domestic cat, but are bigger (usually 15 to 30 pounds, sometimes twice that), have tufted ears, and, most indicative, a short, bobbed tail. The young—usually two—are born in spring and are cared for by their mother until fall. Like all cats except the cheetah, their tracks do not display claw marks. Bobcats capture rodents, rabbits, and birds, and sometimes eat carrion. Experts believe that almost all mountain lions sighted on Tamalpais are actually bobcats. There is a Bobcat Trail in the Marin Headlands.

Bobcat · Black-tailed Deer · Red-tailed Hawk

Anna's Hummingbird · River Otter · Red-legged Frog

THE PEOPLE OF MT. TAM

People had lived on and around Mt. Tamalpais for thousands of years before European explorers first encountered them in the sixteenth century. The new-comers later named the region's native people "Coast Miwok," a designation based on their spoken language.

Although the Miwok moved according to seasonal harvests, they also established villages, several hundred of which have been identified, most along the shoreline. The Miwoks were hunter-gatherers, and there was plentiful game, waterfowl, fish, shellfish, acorns, and edible vegetation for them on and near Mt. Tam. There is some evidence of burning to improve oak habitat and acorn yield, but otherwise, Miwoks little altered the Tamalpais ecosystem. (The Coast Miwoks had no written language, so much of their history has been lost; Betty Goerke's meticulously researched *Chief Marin* [Heyday Books, 2007] is an excellent resource. In 2000, descendants of the Coast Miwok and the neighboring Southern Pomo of Sonoma County were accorded federal tribal status as the Federated Indians of Graton Rancheria, and then opened a gambling casino.)

At the time of the first European settlement in Marin, Mission San Rafael in 1817, there were an estimated 3,000 or more native people in residence. Miwoks had no natural immunity to introduced Eurasian diseases such as smallpox, measles, and mumps. These diseases, along with the disruption of their traditional ways, migration, and intermarriage, devastated the Coast Miwoks within less than two generations.

When California attained statehood in 1850, "Marin," the Spanish baptismal name of a Miwok chief ("Marino"), was chosen for the county. The name "Tamalpais," for "coastal mountain," is of Miwok origin, but the myth of the summit profile of Tamalpais as "the Sleeping Maiden" is not. There is a reference to "Sleeping Lady" in an 1886 Tamalpais summit log, and Dan Totheroh enshrined it in his play *Tamalpa*, first presented at the Mountain Theater in 1921.

Spanish and Mexican Period

Juan Rodriguez Cabrillo was the first European to see Marin, and perhaps Tamalpais, when he sailed past in 1542, the year he formally claimed California for Spain. But Spain did not explore or settle the region. Indeed, the first European to set foot in Marin was an Englishman, Sir Francis Drake, in 1579. He and his men aboard the *Golden Hind* had been raiding Spanish ships when they put in for repairs at Drakes Bay (some claim he landed elsewhere). Drake's crew stayed thirty-six days and, according to a diary kept by the ship's chaplain, had contact with the native people before departing to complete history's second known circumnavigation of the Earth. Sebastian Cermenho, piloting

Spain's annual Manila–Acapulco trade galleon, shipwrecked at Drakes Bay in 1593. He and his crew then made it Mexico in an open boat. Incredibly, no other European set foot in Marin for 222(!) years, until 1775, when Spain's Juan Manuel de Ayala became the first European to sail through the Golden Gate.

In response to encroachments from Russia, whose traders were working their way south from Alaska collecting otter and other valuable fur pelts, and from other European nations sailing into the Pacific, Spain and its Franciscan missionaries began establishing missions, forts (*presidios*) and small villages (*pueblos*) in California. San Francisco, established in 1776, was the sixth of twenty-one.

To build in treeless San Francisco, soldiers came by boat to the base of Mt. Tamalpais, where they cut redwoods growing near the bay. In 1817, Mission San Rafael was founded to provide both another bulwark against the Russians and a healthier environment for the native people of Mission San Francisco de Asís, who were dying in the fog-shrouded city. (Nothing of the original structure remains.) Four years later, Mexico achieved independence from Spain and assumed sovereignty over California.

Mexico secularized the California missions and began awarding mission and former Crown lands to soldiers and other favored settlers, many of them not Hispanic. Mt. Tamalpais was carved into six huge land grants, four of which met at a single point: Knob Hill, above today's Kent Woodlands. These six grants, which have an impact on the mountain to this day, were as follows:

- *Rancho Corte Madera del Presidio*: 8,878 acres, including the southern slope of Tamalpais, to John Reed, 1833.

- *Rancho Saucelito*: 19,571 acres, including the southwest and west slopes of Tamalpais, to William Richardson, 1835.

- *Rancho Tomales y Baulines*: 23,050 acres, including much of the north side of Tamalpais, to Rafael Garcia, 1836.

- *Rancho Cañada de Herrera*: 6,658 acres, including the northeast slope of Tamalpais, to Domingo Sais, 1839.

- *Rancho Punta de Quentin*: 8,877 acres, including the east slope of Tamalpais, to John Cooper, 1840.

- *Rancho las Baulines*: 8,911 acres, including the west slope of Bolinas Ridge, to Gregorio Briones, 1846.

Ranchos Saucelito and Tomales y Baulines, which met along the mountain's summit ridge, covered most of Tamalpais.

Marin's Mexican era lasted just twenty-five years, effectively ending when Americans seized control of California in 1846; it formally ended in 1849 with the treaty of Guadalupe Hidalgo, which ceded California (as well as modern-day Arizona, New Mexico, Nevada, Utah, and parts of Wyoming and Colorado) to the United States and marked the end of the Mexican–American War.

When gold was discovered in the Sierra foothills in 1848, the subsequent Gold Rush transformed the region's sleepy settlements. Those granted land by Mexico had to prove their claim before a United States Land Commission that began holding hearings in San Francisco in 1852. The legal costs, which invariably involved appeals stretching over decades, forced most grantees to sell or otherwise lose their claims long before final settlement.

The American Period
From Gold Rush days until attitudes began to shift at the turn of the twentieth century, Mt. Tamalpais was essentially viewed as an exploitable resource. Each of the original Tamalpais land grantees had grazed cattle on their lands, and cattle drove the economy. But immediately after the Gold Rush, activity on Tamalpais increased drastically.

Logging
Basically all of Mt. Tamalpais, with rare exceptions that include today's Muir Woods National Monument, was logged in the frenzy to provide building materials for a burgeoning San Francisco. Frequent fires in the city created even more demand. Many logging operations were small, and not all were authorized by landowners, so records are scarce. The Baltimore & Frederick Lumber Co., a syndicate organized in Maryland, is well documented, however. Sailing around Cape Horn, its members brought a sawmill to the area in 1849, reassembled it on the bay shore of today's Larkspur (on lower West Baltimore Avenue), and began cutting the great stand of redwoods lining Larkspur Creek, in what came to be called Baltimore Canyon. Some of the redwoods were said to be 300 feet tall. The firm disbanded when the canyon was denuded. Shaver Grade was used to bring logs from Tamalpais to Isaac Shaver's mill in San Rafael. Swede George, one of Tamalpais's strongest creeks, and Tucker Trail are named for early woodcutters.

Some of the logged forests returned, and were logged a second, even a third, time. Some areas were kept cleared as grassland for pasture. Many of these grassy former grazing lands are today being colonized by Douglas-firs.

Cattle and Dairy Ranching
Cattle were of paramount importance during the Mexican era. Their meat fed the region's residents, and hides and tallow were traded for goods brought in by merchant sailing ships. Grazing cattle remained a feature of the Tamalpais landscape for another century after the Gold Rush, although the emphasis switched to dairying. The Rancho Saucelito land grant covering the southwest

slope of Tamalpais was divided into some two dozen dairy ranches, designated by letters of the alphabet. These and other ranches were fenced, with stiles to permit through passage. In the 1930s, runners in the Dipsea Race had to negotiate fifteen such stiles.

Tourism

The 1875 opening of the North Pacific Coast Railroad, which ran from Sausalito into Sonoma County, jumpstarted tourism on Tamalpais (and commerce across Marin). The earliest intrepid hikers came from San Francisco by ferry, exited the train at stations on the mountain's east edge, and set off uphill. All of Tamalpais was privately owned throughout the nineteenth century, but some landowners permitted, or at least tolerated, hikers. By the 1880s, a summit register was installed atop Mt. Tamalpais, and it began filling ever faster.

In 1889, a track was laid from the main line along what is now Mill Valley's Miller Avenue to today's downtown. The Mill Valley-main line junction was called "Almonte," or "to the mountain." A year later, Mill Valley lots were auctioned and the town was born. Many more tourists came to Tamalpais from this new, closer portal. Then, in just seven months in 1896, a private syndicate, using teams of mostly Irish laborers, laid 8.25 miles of track from downtown Mill Valley to what is now the East Peak parking lot. A new tavern at the summit welcomed travelers. Mt. Tamalpais became perhaps the leading outdoor tourism destination in the Bay Area. These ramblers and campers and tourists would become a voice for preserving Tamalpais as a public park.

Road Building

To accommodate expanding commerce and travel in Marin, new roads were built, including on Mt. Tamalpais. Sausalito-Bolinas Road, today's Highway 1, was constructed in just fifteen weeks during 1870 by "100 Chinese and 15 whites." It was then continued north through Olema Valley. San Rafael-Bolinas Road was completed in 1878. A more direct routing from the Fairfax train station, today's Fairfax-Bolinas Road, was added six years later and survives, though altered. Eldridge Grade, a vision of John Oscar Eldridge, opened in 1884 as the first route to the summit for horse-drawn wagons. Muir Woods Road was carved to bring members of the Bohemian Club to their very first summer gathering (the "Jinks") in 1892 in what is now called Bohemian Grove.

Early twentieth-century roads are also worth noting. Ridgecrest Boulevard opened in 1924 as a toll road from Fairfax-Bolinas Road to Rock Spring. A year later, the road was extended to the rail line's upper terminus, opening the summit to automobiles and dooming Mountain Railway. In 1928, the hotly contested Mill Valley-Stinson Beach Road (see the Mt. Tamalpais State Park section), now called Panoramic Highway, was built. In 1930, Pantoll Road connected Panoramic Highway and Ridgecrest Boulevard.

Development and Preservation

In 1887, Charles Wright bought several hundred acres on Tam's eastern slope and began selling off lots in a new community, Larkspur. On May 31, 1890, the Tamalpais Land and Water Co. held a well-advertised auction in what was about to become Mill Valley. More than two hundred lots were sold that day, and the town was born. Another land auction, on April 30, 1892, created San Anselmo's Sunnyside tract, on Tam's northeast corner. The terrible San Francisco earthquake and fire of 1906 drastically increased the pace of home building on Tam.

Among the other commercial activities on Tamalpais was the tapping of its creeks (a story told in the Marin Municipal Water District section). There was also mining. For example, today's Old Mine Trail passes a failed gold claim site. There was a tourmaline mine near East Peak, Coastal Trail skirts remains of a copper mine, and Copper Mine Gulch runs south of McCurdy Trail.

But attitudes were changing. In 1892, John Muir co-founded the Sierra Club to help carry out his life's work of calling attention to, and preserving, the nation's wild places. Some of the club's first hikes were on Mt. Tamalpais. In September 1900, Emma Shafter Howard, whose family, on both sides, owned thousands of acres on the north slope of Tam, wrote a letter to Muir asking for his help in saving the mountain's remaining forests. Muir wrote back, "I would gladly go to Tamalpais and a thousand times farther to stay the ruthless destruction of the forests you refer to. But, alas, all land thereabouts is private property. . . . I hope however that a block of redwoods may yet be saved for a public park."

Such a block of redwoods was indeed about to be saved, largely by one man, William Kent. No book about Mount Tamalpais is complete without tribute to him and the lasting mark he made on the twentieth century, and forever forward.

Everyone who loves and visits Mt. Tamalpais owes an enormous debt to William Kent. He donated the acreage that became Muir Woods National Monument, the first public land on the mountain, to the federal government, as well as today's Mountain Theater. He played much the largest role in the birth of the Marin Municipal Water District. And he was the leading figure in making Mt. Tamalpais State Park a reality. Indeed, he donated its initial acreage, Steep Ravine, the day before he died. His family kept Kent's legacy alive, making major donations to Muir Woods and the state park. All of the thousands of acres Kent once owned on Mt. Tamalpais—by 1905, you could walk from the bay at Kentfield to the ocean at Stinson Beach on his property—became public land, save for Kent Woodlands and Seadrift, subdivisions carved out decades after his death.

Kent's father, Albert (1830–1901), founded a meat packing company in Chicago in 1859. Supplying meat to the Union Army during the Civil War quickly earned him a fortune. Albert married Adaline Dutton in 1856; William Kent, the only one of their three children to survive to adulthood, was born March 29, 1864.

The terrible Chicago fire of October 1871, plus concerns about his health, prompted Albert to move his family to Marin. In 1872, he bought 13 acres in what is now Kent Woodlands and built a grand home. Albert added hundreds of acres adjacent to his original homestead, and hundreds more elsewhere on Tamalpais.

William Kent grew up on Mt. Tamalpais, later describing the experience in his autobiography, *Reminiscences of an Outdoor Life*. He went off to Yale (class of 1877), where he met his wife, Elizabeth Thacher, daughter of the dean of Yale's Department of Latin. They married in 1890 and had seven children: Albert; Thomas; William, Jr.; Sherman; Roger; Adaline; and Elizabeth.

William had moved to Chicago after graduating from Yale, and he was elected an alderman in 1895. But soon after his father's death, he relocated his family to Kentfield, and over the next few years, added to Albert's already considerable holdings by buying huge chunks of the old Rancho Saucelito.

In some ways, September 12, 1903, could be considered the seminal date for the preservation of Mt. Tamalpais. That was when Kent chaired a meeting, which he had called, at the new Lagunitas Country Club in Ross. The purpose was to advance the cause of a Tamalpais National Park. Gifford Pinchot, one of Kent's friends from his Yale days and first chief of the new United States Division of Forestry, represented the government. Also attending were some of the most influential figures in the Bay Area, including the presidents of Stanford (David Starr Jordan) and the University of California, Berkeley (Benjamin Ide Wheeler).

Kent made a stirring speech on the importance of preserving Tamalpais for future generations, and this address was widely distributed as a brochure. The Tamalpais National Park Association was created, with an office in San Francisco. When the 1906 earthquake and fire diverted attention from his quest, Kent felt he had to act on his own. And he did. (The story of the conversion of Mt. Tamalpais from private to public land continues in the discussion of Muir Woods National Monument.)

In 1910, William Kent was elected to the United States House of Representatives as a Progressive Republican and re-elected for two additional terms as an Independent. In 1912, he helped found the Tamalpais Conservation Club (TCC), which held its organizational meeting on land Kent had donated to the public; today, the College of Marin campus occupies this land. In 1913, Kent opposed John Muir when he played a key role in passage of the Raker Act, which permitted a dam in Yosemite National Park's Hetch Hetchy Valley to supply water to San Francisco. But he also helped draft the National Park Service Organic

Act of 1916, creating the National Park Service to make sure there would never again be such an intrusion. In 1914, Kent deeded a natural amphitheater high on Tam to the new Mountain Play Association.

William Kent served on the United States Tariff Commission from 1917 to 1920, when he resigned to make an unsuccessful bid for the United States Senate. In 1918, he was one of the founders of, and biggest donors to, Save the Redwoods League. He then championed creation of a California State Park system. There is today a William Kent Campground and beach on the shore of Lake Tahoe.

William Kent, 1913

In 1927, William Kent suffered a debilitating stroke. He died March 12, 1928, the day after he donated his beloved Steep Ravine to the brand-new Tamalpais State Park. The TCC promptly dedicated the largest tree in Muir Woods National Monument to him. (This Douglas-fir fell in 2003 but the plaque is still there.) Kent's family continued his legacy, donating, or selling at vastly below-market rates, lands on Mt. Tamalpais as additions to Muir Woods National Monument and the state park.

Kent's vision of Mt. Tamalpais as a public park did not happen in a single grand step, as he perhaps hoped. But it did happen. The story of the transformation of Tamalpais during the twentieth century from all-private to today's public open space, under several independent land managers, follows.

Upper left: Virtually all Marin's virgin redwoods—save those in what is now Muir Wood National Monument and a few others—were logged in the decades immediately following the Gold Rush.

Upper right: In 1892, the Bohemian Club held its first summer camp in what is now Bohemian Grove in Muir Woods National Monument.

Center: The original Muir Inn, built in 1907 at what is now Camp Alice Eastwood.

Bottom: Mt. Tamalpais & Muir Woods Railway gravity car runs from Mesa Station down Redwood Canyon toward Muir Woods, 1927.

PUBLIC LAND ACQUISITIONS

The very first public lands on Mt. Tamalpais were the original few acres of Old Mill and Cascade Parks in Mill Valley. The Tamalpais Land and Water Company "reserved" them from sale in the 1890 land auction, then donated them to the newly incorporated town a decade later. Muir Woods National Monument followed in 1908. Today, essentially all of Mt. Tamalpais above the residential streets is public open space. Four agencies—Marin Municipal Water District, the federal government (Golden Gate National Recreation Area and Muir Woods National Monument), the State of California (Mt. Tamalpais State Park), and the County of Marin (Marin County Parks) manage almost all of this public land.

In March 2014, these four agencies formed, with the Golden Gate National Parks Conservancy, the Tamalpais Lands Cooperative (TLC). Under the motto "One Mountain, One Vision," the TLC partnership aims to achieve a more unified approach to large-scale projects on Mt. Tamalpais, many of which cross jurisdictional lines, and to secure increased funding for those projects.

Here are brief histories of how these agencies acquired their Tamalpais lands. A more thorough account is found in my book, *To Save a Mountain: The 100-Year Battle for Mt. Tamalpais*, published by the Tamalpais Conservation Club in 2012 to commemorate their centennial anniversary.

Muir Woods National Monument (1908)

While virtually every mature redwood (and other tree) on Mt. Tamalpais had been logged in the decades after the Gold Rush, the magnificent stand lining lower Redwood Creek remained untouched. (In 1892, the influential Bohemian Club held its summer "Jinks" in the pristine canyon, before buying an even larger redwood grove in Sonoma County as a permanent site.) Geography was an ally, making logging there uneconomical: Redwood Creek emptied into a non-navigable shallow lagoon and was otherwise surrounded by steep hillsides.

But as the population of Marin grew, what was then called Sequoia Canyon (the scientific name for the redwood is *Sequoia sempervirens*) was increasingly eyed as a reservoir site. The trees would, of course, be logged prior to flooding the canyon. In 1903, Lovell White, president of the Tamalpais Land and Water Co., which owned the land, offered to sell the canyon and hillsides, 611 acres in total, to his friend William Kent. A below-market price of $45,000—the perceived preservation, rather than economic, value—was fixed. (Lumber from the redwoods, Douglas-firs, and tanoaks had an estimated worth of $160,000.) Of the price, Kent famously said to his wife, "If we lost all the money we have and saved those trees it would be worthwhile."

Kent intended opening the woods as a tourist attraction, and began planning a rail line and inn (both opened in 1907). In 1910, Kent upgraded an old wagon grade for automobiles, and Muir Woods Road remained a toll road until 1939.

But the redwoods were not yet saved. The terrible 1906 San Francisco earthquake and fire brought a new influx of residents to Marin and even more calls for a new reservoir to serve both Marin and San Francisco. Kent feared he would lose the canyon in the courts through condemnation. Providence came in June 1906 with passage of the Antiquities Act. Congress gave the president unprecedented authority to designate, without legislative review, unique sites as national monuments. Within months, President Theodore Roosevelt created five national monuments, all in the rugged Southwest.

On December 23, 1907, Kent wrote a letter to Interior Secretary Garfield offering to donate 295 acres of the canyon floor to the United States. The offer was accepted and just seventeen days later, on January 9, 1908, President Roosevelt signed the document creating Muir Woods National Monument. (Grand Canyon became a national monument two days later.) It was the first national monument donated to the American people by a private individual. Roosevelt wanted to name the new park Kent National Monument. Kent declined, saying, "I have five good husky boys . . . if [they] cannot keep the name of Kent alive, I am willing it should be forgotten." He also said, "I deserve no more credit than if I had protected my children from a kidnapper." Kent suggested honoring John Muir, then seventy years old and the dean of American conservationists. Through the generosity of his family, all of Kent's original 611-acre Redwood Canyon purchase ultimately became part of either Muir Woods National Monument or Mt. Tamalpais State Park (which now surrounds the monument).

The monument is managed as a unit within Golden Gate National Recreation Area.

Marin Municipal Water District (1912)

Marin receives a relatively bountiful rainfall, an average of some 40 inches per year, double that of San Francisco. Also, westerly winds drive storms up and over Tamalpais, which drops even more rain on the mountain's eastern and northern slopes. But annual rainfall varies wildly, from lows near 20 inches to highs approaching 100 inches, and it all falls between November and March.

As Marin's population grew, so too did the need for reservoirs. At one point, there were more than two dozen water companies in Marin (Marin Municipal Water District [MMWD] ultimately absorbed twenty-six of them). Marin County Water Company was incorporated in 1871. Its chief organizer was William Tell Coleman, who led the notorious San Francisco Vigilante Committee in the 1850s and later moved to San Rafael (his house, built in 1849, still stands on Mission Street). The company acquired water rights along Lagunitas Creek, Marin's main "river," and built a dam where its three headwater streams meet at an elevation of 780 feet on Mt. Tamalpais. Lagunitas Dam created Lake Lagunitas, the first reservoir on Tamalpais. In 1886, Marin County Water Company placed a small dam (still evident on the Bill Williams Trail) across Bill Williams Creek to create another reservoir. In 1905, a reorganized successor to Coleman's company, Marin Water and Power Co., built a dam at the confluence of Phoenix and Bill Williams Creeks to create Phoenix Reservoir.

North Coast Water Company, another major pre-MMWD company that owned land on Tamalpais, held 2,000 acres. It was a spinoff of Tamalpais Land and Water Co., which acquired the Rancho Saucelito land grant through foreclosure in the 1880s. North Coast supplied Mill Valley out of Cascade Reservoir (dating from 1895, and no longer in use). In 1903, it won a contract to supply water to Belvedere Island and built the then-open air (now enclosed) Belvedere Reservoir on Sequoia Valley Road in Mill Valley. Water was gathered from several streams on the south side of Mt. Tamalpais; the old pipe and intakes are still visible along the Troop 80 and Pipeline Trails.

Also important was the Lagunitas Water Company, which controlled thousands of acres on the northern slopes of the Tamalpais watershed. The company started to build Tamalpais Dam in 1903, but the project was not completed. Remnants are visible, when the water level is low, beside Alpine Lake just downstream from Bon Tempe Dam.

As Marin's population surged, water supplies proved inadequate. Rationing and other water restrictions were commonplace, rates were considered high and complex (for example, residents of upper floors and at higher elevations paid more than others), and no single water company had the resources for a comprehensive solution. So when a progressive California legislature passed the Municipal Water District Act in October 1911, enabling public water districts, Marin was quick to take action. On April 13, 1912, the Marin Municipal Water District—the state's first such district—was created by a vote of 2,130 to 391.

The new district had neither land nor capital. To remedy this, it began condemnation proceedings against the major Tamalpais water companies: Marin Water and Power, North Coast, and Lagunitas. After lengthy hearings, at which Los Angeles water czar William Mulholland was one of the eminent witnesses, the court fixed values on the condemned lands. The decisions were appealed, but the rulings held. MMWD then needed money to buy the land. A $3 million bond measure went to voters on August 28, 1915. The private water companies lobbied vigorously against the bond, and many voters were concerned about the taxes required to pay for it. But William Kent, Marin's representative in the US Congress and the principal landowner affected, spoke forcefully in favor of the bond measure. He was to receive the largest share of the condemnation money but pledged to accept none of it, and to donate additional land to MMWD. The bond measure passed 3,692 to 1,090. The *Marin Journal* called it "the greatest achievement in the history of the county."

With the bond money in hand, MMWD immediately moved forward with plans for a dam at the confluence of Lagunitas and Cataract Creeks, a spot called Alpine. Some thought Alpine Dam (completed in 1919) and Alpine Lake would solve Marin's water needs forever. Indeed, there was so much surplus water that MMWD began selling to the water-thirsty C & H sugar refinery in Crockett.

But it was not be. Within a few years, MMWD began new condemnation proceedings against landowners downstream from Alpine Lake. This time, the price set by the court was too high for MMWD to pay. (One of the owners was Stanford University, which had acquired more than 2,000 acres when James Shafter defaulted on a loan from the school's founder, Leland Stanford. Stanford's widow, Jane, donated the land to the then-new university.) The condemnation suit was reopened after World War II; the case of "MMWD vs. Stanford University, et al." was on the docket of the Marin Superior Court for May 10, 1946. In the end, the matter was settled without a trial; MMWD paid $27 an acre for 6,282 acres. Peters Dam, which created Kent Lake on this land, was completed in 1954.

MMWD also has two reservoirs, Nicasio and Soulajoule, outside the Tamalpais watershed. After two drought years in the mid-1970s, the district began importing water from Sonoma County. These imports now account for up to 25 percent of total usage.

The water district is governed by a board of five members, elected by district. (A completely separate North Marin Water District serves Novato.)

Mount Tamalpais State Park (1928)

With the creation of Muir Woods National Monument in 1908 and Marin Municipal Water District in 1912, hikers and other outdoors lovers began dreaming of a park to join these two public open spaces into a vast preserve across Mt. Tamalpais. Leading the effort was the Tamalpais Conservation Club (TCC).

TCC was born on February 18, 1912, at a meeting at Kentfield's Tamalpais Centre—now part of the College of Marin campus—donated by the Kent family to the citizens of Marin. TCC lore holds that the organizers were moved to action after seeing hunters kill and skin a deer on Kent land near Rifle Camp; one of TCC's first accomplishments was helping to pass legislation creating the Mt. Tamalpais Game Refuge in 1917. After a terrible 2,000-acre fire on Tam in 1913, William Kent and TCC also played leading roles in creating the Tamalpais Forest Fire District (1917). Members of TCC carved and maintained trails, built camps (such as Bootjack), organized litter cleanup days, erected signs, and helped patrol the mountain.

In 1902, California created its first state park, Big Basin Redwoods. (President Lincoln had placed the heart of today's Yosemite National Park into California's hands in 1864, where it remained until taken over by the federal government in 1890.) A second state park, Humboldt Redwoods, followed in 1921, despite the fact that there was still no state park department.

In November 1925, Marin voters overwhelmingly approved (with an 88 percent "yes" vote) a $1,250,000 bond measure to build and improve the county's roads. One of the proposed projects was a Mill Valley-Stinson Beach road. The only existing connection between Mill Valley and the coast was what is now Highway 1: long, twisting, and dangerous. It sometimes took students living in Stinson Beach and Bolinas two hours to get to Tamalpais High School. The road was considered so essential that residents of the Homestead district voted 126-1 for the bond measure.

But the planned road would cut right through land that TCC hoped would join Muir Woods and the Marin Municipal Water District. James Newlands and William Magee jointly owned much of that land, some 580 acres that had provided southern Marin with water in pre-MMWD days. TCC feared that once Newlands and Magee began planning for residential development along the road—which they did—land values would escalate and public acquisition costs would become prohibitive. (William Kent also owned land along the road's proposed route, but he wanted no payment and remained a staunch ally for a park.)

TCC, together with the Sierra Club, California Alpine Club, Tourist Club, and others, began a vigorous "Save Our Mountain" campaign to both block the road and create a Tamalpais state park. What ensued was the most contentious preservation vs. development debate yet waged in Marin County. TCC lawyer Sidney Van Wyck (today honored on Tam by both Van Wyck Creek and Van Wyck Meadow) became the leading public (and behind the scenes) spokesman for the park effort. Eventually, TCC succeeded in delaying the road project while advancing a park bill through the state legislature.

Finally, Assembly Bill No. 677, authorizing a Tamalpais state park and the road, plus three companion bills that created a state parks department (California Department of Parks and Recreation, better known as California State Parks), a survey of other potential park sites, and a funding mechanism were signed into law on May 25, 1927. A condemnation hearing held in San Rafael fixed $52,000 as the amount Newlands and Magee were to be paid for their land. There was an urgent deadline to raise the money, to supplement the state's $20,000 contribution.

Again, TCC took the lead. Benjamin Schlesinger, who owned City of Paris department store in San Francisco and loved to take his family on hikes on Tamalpais, was the largest individual donor.

On March 12, 1928, William Kent donated 204 acres of Steep Ravine as the new Tamalpais State Park's initial parcel. Construction of the road, renamed Panoramic Highway and indeed running right through the park, began in the summer of 1928.

Over the ensuing decades, Mt. Tamalpais State Park expanded to its present 6,300 acres. Several of the acquisitions were directly due to the generosity of the Kent family. These include buffer tracts surrounding Muir Woods, land along the abandoned Mountain Railway route, Mountain Theater, 240 acres of the Steep Ravine cabins area, and 256 acres surrounding O'Rourke's Bench near Rock Spring. Several hundred acres between Ridgecrest Boulevard and Stinson Beach were purchased from George and Wilma Leonard in the 1950s. In 1960, 376 acres of the former Dias Ranch were purchased from a developer. That same year, 30 acres atop Lone Tree Hill, already being graded for subdivision, were acquired. In 1962, Joe De Ponte sold his two dairy ranches, totaling 286 acres, above Redwood Creek to the state park. (He died of a heart attack on the day he was to move off his land.) Fifteen acres slated for development where the Dipsea Trail crosses Panoramic Highway were bought in 1965. The largest single expansion was the former 2,150-acre Brazil Ranch, in 1968. It was only achieved after the supposed church group that bought it first was unmasked as a front for a developer.

The state park has an official volunteer support organization, Friends of Mt. Tam (originally, the Mt. Tamalpais Interpretive Association). Friends members lead hikes that are free and open to all, staff the visitor center at the East Peak parking lot, organize popular astronomy nights in summer at Mountain Theater, and help fund state park needs.

Audubon Canyon Ranch (1962)

In 1932, Martin Griffin, then thirteen, visited Bolinas Lagoon with his Boy Scout troop and saw the egrets that nest there. The trip made a lasting impression.

In the 1960s, the rookery and the lagoon, essential to the birds' survival, were threatened. Bolinas Lagoon was about to be turned into a marina and resort complex. Two highways, one across Bolinas Ridge, the other, a widened Highway 1, would provide access. Griffin, Stan Picher, Aileen Pierson, and others led an effort to save the rookery and lagoon, and the Marin chapter of the Audubon Society (which Griffin had co-founded in a successful effort to thwart filling and residential development of Richardson Bay) joined with the Golden Gate chapter to form Audubon Canyon Ranch (ACR). Griffin wrote a personal check to secure ACR's first land purchase. The Kent family offered Kent Island, essential to the marina plan, to Marin County at a low price, and the transaction was sealed literally hours before a key deadline.

Today, ACR's Martin Griffin Preserve covers 1,000 acres on the northwest slope of Mt. Tamalpais and is an important nature education center. The preserve encourages visitors, and all Mt. Tam lovers should explore the several trails lacing the property. But as the preserve is privately owned and open to the public only seasonally, primarily weekends during the March to mid-July breeding season, these trails are not separately described in this book. They do, however, appear on the accompanying map. Permission to enter at other times should be obtained from Audubon Canyon Ranch.

Golden Gate National Recreation Area (1972)

William Kent had been lobbying for a Tamalpais National Park since at least 1903, when he gathered many of the region's most influential figures at a meeting in Ross to try to make it happen. In 1908, he gave a virgin stand of redwoods to the federal government (see the Muir Woods National Monument section). Over the ensuing sixty-five years, the federal government expanded the monument's boundaries, again largely due to Kent family donations. Then, during World War II, the government took control of parts of Tamalpais for military purposes.

The creation of Golden Gate National Recreation Area was sparked by several almost-simultaneous catalysts. One was the pending decommissioning of San Francisco's sprawling Presidio, a military base with a two-hundred-year history under three flags (Spain, Mexico, and the US). Another was the Native American occupation of Alcatraz Island for nineteen months in 1969–1971, six years after the island's federal prison had been closed.

In Marin, a proximate cause was the battle over a planned development called Marincello. In 1964, Gulf Oil's real estate division, which had just developed Reston, Virginia, purchased 2,138 acres of dairy land in and above the southernmost valley of Marin. Developer Thomas Frouge unveiled plans for a multi-use project, Marincello, on the site. It would include housing for more than 25,000 residents in some fifty high-rise buildings, plus a hotel, a mile-long shopping mall, churches, five schools, and light industry.

Although there was opposition, the project, slightly scaled down, was approved by the Marin County Board of Supervisors by a three-to-two vote on November 12, 1965. Some construction work actually began, including stone entry portals at the foot of a new road (now Marincello Fire Road) out of Tennessee Valley. But the tide quickly began to turn.

The City of Sausalito sued to stop the project, and won. Also suing was George Wheelwright, a co-founder of Polaroid who owned adjacent property (most of which is now within GGNRA). San Franciscan Amy Meyer, who became an activist when plans to turn the VA hospital near her home into a subdivision surfaced, led a grassroots fight. Sierra Club head Edgar Wayburn, who had dreamed of a southern Marin park for decades, marshaled considerable resources. San Francisco's Phillip Burton (D-California) ably guided the complicated legislative process through the House of Representatives and gathered allies in the Senate.

After Frouge died of a heart attack in 1969, Gulf, which had been subject to local boycotts and criticism, abandoned the effort. The Nature Conservancy, headed by Mill Valley resident Huey Johnson, purchased the 2,138 acres from Gulf in 1972 for $6.5 million; Martha Gerbode, for whom a valley is now named, made a sizable financial contribution. Legislation to create Golden Gate National Recreation Area along the coasts of three counties—Marin, San Francisco (with Alcatraz and the Presidio), and San Mateo—was signed by President Richard Nixon on October 27, 1972.

GGNRA initially drew its boundary on Mt. Tamalpais north to Stinson Beach. The recreation area has since expanded, starting in the mid-1970s when thousands of acres of ranch land on the west slope of Bolinas Ridge extended GGNRA land to Olema and beyond. In 1974, through Nature Conservancy efforts, Slide Ranch and Green Gulch were added. Stinson Beach itself was transferred from the state to GGNRA in 1977. Muir Beach State Park, created in 1969, became part of GGNRA in 1976. So too did the short-lived (barely ten years old) Marin Headlands State Park. The Banducci flower farm above Muir Beach was added in 1980. (Land in San Francisco and San Mateo Counties has also been incorporated over time.)

GGNRA is a unit of the National Park Service, within the Department of the Interior; its headquarters is at Fort Mason in San Francisco.

Marin County Parks/Marin County Open Space District (1972)

The opening of Golden Gate Bridge to automobiles on May 28, 1937, made Marin vastly more accessible. Between the 1930 and 1950 censuses, Marin's population more than doubled, to 53,000. During the 1950s, it increased another 71 percent. In the '60s, the growth was an additional 40 percent (In contrast, Marin's population has grown 40 percent over the past 45 years.)

Former dairy ranches in and along the Highway 101 corridor were being rapidly converted into subdivisions: Enchanted Knolls, Warner Canyon, Alto and Scott Valley in Mill Valley, the entire formerly pastoral Strawberry peninsula, Meadowsweet in Corte Madera, Greenbrae, Sleepy Hollow, Peacock Gap, Terra Linda, Santa Venetia, Marinwood, and others. Richardson Bay (which was slated to be filled) and Angel Island barely escaped a similar fate.

New, multi-lane highways across Mt. Tamalpais were being planned to open agricultural West Marin to development. One road was to run from Golden Gate Bridge straight over Tamalpais's west shoulder to the ranches of Point Reyes peninsula (itself saved from development when Point Reyes National Seashore was created in 1962). A freeway would run from the new (1957) Richmond–San Rafael Bridge, through central Marin, then to a large-scale subdivision and marine recreation area planned for Bolinas.

But development sentiment began to wane. Pro-growth supervisors were voted out of office, replaced by more environmentally friendly officials; Peter Behr was the most influential. Audubon Canyon Ranch, the Kent family, and the voters of Bolinas killed the Bolinas marina project and its proposed roads. County zoning changes preserved West Marin as agricultural.

In 1965, the Marin County Parks and Recreation Department was formed. A landmark 1971 countywide planning document subtitled "Can the Last Place Last?" called for protecting remaining open space. Adding to the wave of environmental advocates, local residents began to fight a plan for development on pristine ridges, collectively called Northridge, which connect Mill Valley with Corte Madera and Larkspur.

On November 7, 1972—just eleven days after President Nixon signed the legislation that created Golden Gate National Recreation Area—Marin County citizens went to the polls to vote on Measure A. It succinctly read, "Shall the Marin County Regional Park District be created and established?" Sixty-five percent of the voters answered "yes." The new district set a property tax rate of 10 cents per $100 of assessed value and began purchasing properties. Many of the first acquisitions focused on Northridge and nearby parcels on the eastern slope of Mt. Tamalpais. Today, these properties are known as the Alto Bowl, Baltimore Canyon, Blithedale Summit, Camino Alto, and King Mountain Preserves (trails within these preserves are included in this book).

In 1974, a new name was adopted: Marin County Open Space District (MCOSD). Today, MCOSD is an entity within Marin County Parks and manages 16,000 acres in thirty-four preserves across the county. By policy, MCOSD does not enhance trailheads, which are mostly in residential neighborhoods, so do not expect bathrooms, fountains, or parking areas. The department is overseen by the county's five elected supervisors and an appointed commission.

HOW TO USE THIS BOOK

This book describes all Mt. Tamalpais trails and roads that are at least ¼ mile in length, entirely on public land, and closed to non-official motorized vehicles.

Defining just what Mt. Tamalpais is can be a challenge. It is generally considered as a three-peaked summit ridge, sometimes called Tamalpa or Temelpa Ridge, and the ridges that descend from it. The mountain's boundaries are clear only to the west, where Tamalpais drops steeply to the Pacific Ocean, and to the east, where it descends to San Francisco Bay (or did, until the Highway 101 corridor saw extensive landfill).

Things get tricky north and south, where its long ridges extend for miles. Bolinas Ridge, for example, runs more than 20 miles from Rock Spring before dropping to Lagunitas Creek near Point Reyes Station. But few of its visitors consider themselves on Tamalpais. Likewise, Throckmorton Ridge to the south runs into the Marin Headlands.

The boundaries used in this book correspond to those of the Tamalpais Lands Collaborative. (Four City of Mill Valley trails are included as well): essentially, the Pacific Ocean to the west, Highway 1 to the northwest, the boundaries of the Marin Municipal Water District to the north, Sir Francis Drake Boulevard to the northeast, the old State Highway corridor (Camino Alto and Corte Madera, Magnolia and College Avenues) to the east, and Coyote Ridge to the south.

Four Marin County Parks preserves on the eastern edge of the TLC map—Horse Hill/Alto Bowl, Cascade Canyon, White Hill, and Gary Giacomini—are excluded for space reasons. Also excluded are trails within the Homestead Valley Land Trust; most are presently overgrown with poison oak. Trails within these areas (and Audubon Canyon Ranch) do appear on the accompanying maps.

Trail Names

There is no single authority for names of trails and roads on Tamalpais, and the variety of names is part of the mountain's charm. You'll find many disparities among the several Mt. Tam maps printed over the decades; various user groups may have their own special names, and there are still trails with different names on the signposts at each end! Land managers are working on coordinating names—it would certainly be helpful for first responders—but the effort is far from complete, and may never be.

In this book, names used by the managing jurisdiction on maps and signs take precedence. When there is some confusion, I defer to the name used on the map meticulously researched by Ben Pease. In a few cases, colorful, historic names trump all. If there are name variants, they are noted.

Jurisdictions are now designating broad, unpaved routes wider than trails as "roads." But, in the text, I will continue to use the more traditional term "fire road," as it seems more evocative of an outdoors experience and avoids any confusion with paved roads. In general, across all jurisdictions, fire roads are open to bicycles and trails are not (exceptions are noted in the description heading). There are also a handful of routes, such as Coast View, that have been reworked into multi-use trails, wide enough for cyclists as well as hikers. A critical caveat: **rules change** and **posted signs** always prevail.

Closed/Overgrown/Social Trails

Even the most casual visitors soon notice that many routes lace their way across mountain in addition to the named trails. In this book, they are called "paths." Some were trails that land managers have closed and returned to nature. Some were never on maps but long used by mountain veterans. Some are routes cut without authorization, a practice always illegal in all jurisdictions. Some are environmentally dubious shortcuts. Some are deer paths. Some lead to favored view spots or other landmarks. (Many, particularly in the MMWD, have generic "Citations Issued" signs at their entries.)

While it is not illegal for hikers to go off trail—except in Muir Woods National Monument and in areas posted as closed—these paths are only noted when not doing so might cause confusion. Among other things, paths usually do not meet minimum safety standards and pose added risks such as getting lost, slipping on rough or steep terrain, or wading through poison oak. Additionally, rare and endangered plant species on Tamalpais face the threat of being trampled and resident fauna require seclusion to breed. (In the Mt. Tamalpais watershed, seventy-seven species of plants and animals are listed as rare, threatened, or endangered.)

The entire ecosystem of Mt. Tamalpais, part of a metropolitan area populated by many millions, needs protection to survive. On a practical note, this book would weigh several pounds if even a fraction of these unofficial routes were described. All jurisdictions encourage visitors to stay on marked trails.

Signs

Soon after its founding in 1912, the Tamalpais Conservation Club began placing signs for hikers across the newly acquired (1916) lands of the Marin Municipal Water District and private lands (mostly those owned by William Kent) that had been opened to the public. Some were simply arrows attached to trees, others were more elaborate and descriptive, and encouraged proper behavior, such as carrying out litter. In the "golden" decade of hiking in the 1920s, before Panoramic Highway and Ridgecrest Boulevard opened the way for automobiles, there were color-coded signs designating long routes and east-west and north-south directions. Virtually none of these signs remain in place, although several classic MMWD and state park versions survive.

When I began working on *Tamalpais Trails* in the late 1980s, many intersections were well signed, but others either had no signs or the signs they had were potentially confusing; for example, sometimes, they did not match as to trail name or distance. In recent years, all jurisdictions have been upgrading their signs.

With funds generated in part by increased entry fees at Muir Woods, the National Park Service is financing a joint project with Mt. Tamalpais State Park to add and replace scores of signs, each showing the trail the hiker is on (color coded by jurisdiction) and distances to the next intersections. A few of the new MMWD signs enable visitors to download trail maps and district rules onto smart phones. Newer Marin County Parks signs give precise coordinates, to the thousandth of a degree, for GPS users. All in all, those paying attention to the new signs are far less likely to get lost than in olden days.

Descriptions

The trails and fire roads in this book are grouped into thirteen trailheads, representing the nearest popular access point. (Several routes may be reached with roughly the same effort from more than one trailhead.) The accompanying maps show routes within the trailhead, and the maps overlap.

Background on the trailhead is followed by a few suggested loop walks, nearly sixty in all (plus many more in the individual trail descriptions). But the philosophy and essence of this book are that, with a bit of effort, readers can create thousands of different walks and rides for themselves and know the exact distance and elevation changes of each.

The heading for each trail and road description gives the route's "official" name and any widely used variations. The second line has the route's end points, in the direction of the description. Obviously, trails can be taken in either direction; the choice here is based on the more commonly traveled way or safety considerations, or to complete a loop route. A few trails have a "spur," or short, third entry, and this is noted as well. Also given is the trail's total distance, as determined by a hand-held measuring wheel, to the hundredth of a mile.

The third line, "Terrain," briefly notes the dominant vegetation encountered. The managing jurisdiction(s)—Mt. Tamalpais State Park (MTSP); Marin Municipal Water District (MMWD); Golden Gate National Recreational Area (GGNRA); Marin County Parks (MCP), which includes Marin County Open Space District (MCOSD); Muir Woods National Monument (MWNM); and City of Mill Valley—is also cited here.

The next line shows the elevation, in feet, of the start and end points, and of highs and lows in between if the route is particularly up and down. (Most elevation figures were gleaned by squinting at topographical lines, so should be viewed as approximate.)

This is followed by a word or two on the gradient. "Level" means the route is fairly flat. "Gradual" means the gradient should be easy for all users. "Steep" indicates there may be travelers who find all or part of the route taxing. "Very steep" will present a challenge for all but the fittest visitors, going both up and down. A few trails merit "extremely steep," perhaps only for a section, and some users may wish or need to avoid these. The last line gives intersecting trails, if any, with distance (in tenths of a mile) from the trailhead.

Abbreviations

ACR: Audubon Canyon Ranch

CCC: Civilian Conservation Corps

FR: Fire Road

GGNRA: Golden Gate National Recreation Area

MCP: Marin County Parks, including Marin County Open Space District/ MCOSD

MMWD: Marin Municipal Water District

FMT: Friends of Mt. Tam, formerly Mt. Tamalpais Interpretive Association/ MTIA

MTSP: Mt. Tamalpais State Park

MWNM: Muir Woods National Monument

TCC: Tamalpais Conservation Club

TLC: Tamalpais Lands Collaborative

The terms *Tamalpais, Mt. Tamalpais, Mt. Tam, Tam,* and *the mountain* are used interchangeably.

Contact information for the various entities referenced in the book—phone numbers, URLs, and related details—can be found on p. 351, arranged in alphabetical order.

Each trailhead is prefaced with a detailed map; flip to the end of the book (p. 356) for the legend.

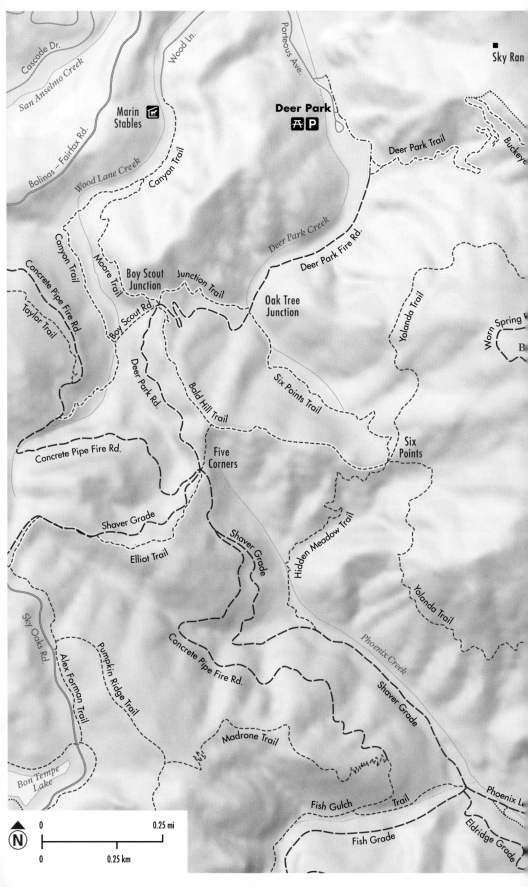

Deer Park FR toward Boy Scout Junction

TRAILHEAD ONE: DEER PARK

Directions
Highway 101—Sir Francis Drake Blvd. (exit) west to San Anselmo—Center Blvd. to Broadway, Fairfax—left on Bolinas Road—left on Porteous Ave. to end

---

Deer Park is a delightful picnic area flanking both banks of Deer Park Creek. It sits on the border of MMWD land, and all trails are within the water district. The adjacent former Deer Park School is owned by the Ross Valley School District and leased to the Fairfax-San Anselmo Children's Center. (At press time, the school district was considering selling the five-acre site.) Pass to the left of the school to enter the trail network. Parking nearest the school is reserved for school use on weekdays. Bathrooms and a fountain can be found near the parking lot.

Deer Park Fire Road and Deer Park Trail leave directly behind the school. The fire road is well used. It passes two key junctions. The first, in $^1/_3$ mile, is Oak Tree Junction. The spokes, clockwise, are Six Points Trail up to Six Points, Deer Park FR (now beginning to climb), and Junction Trail to Boy Scout Junction. The second big intersection, in $^2/_3$ mile, is seven-way Boy Scout Junction, the nexus of the Deer Park area. The routes meeting there, clockwise, are Bald Hill Trail, Deer Park FR continuing up, a broad connector (Boy Scout FR) dropping to Canyon Trail, Moore Trail, a path, and Junction Trail.

A second nearby public access to the mountain is through Marin Stables at the far end of Wood Lane, passed when driving in on Porteous Avenue. Walk quietly through the stables so as not to startle the horses.

There is a completely separate Deer Park, originally called Kent's Deer Park, high on the southwest slope of Tamalpais.

Suggested Loops from Deer Park (elevation 190 feet)

1. Deer Park Trail, .8 mile, to Worn Spring FR—right, .4 mile to Yolanda Trail—right, .9 mile, to Six Points Junction—right, .4 mile, on Bald Hill Trail and fire road connector to Five Corners—right, 1.1 miles, on Deer Park FR to start. **3.6 miles total**

2. Deer Park FR, .4 mile, to Junction Trail—right, .3 mile, to Moore Trail—right, .5 mile, to Canyon Trail—left, .7 mile, to Concrete Pipeline FR—left, .6 mile, to Five Corners—left on Deer Park FR, 1.1 miles, to start. **3.6 miles total**

3. Deer Park FR, 1.1 miles, to Five Corners—left on Concrete Pipeline FR, 1.4 miles, to Fish Gulch Trail—left, .4 mile, to Phoenix Junction—left on Shaver Grade, .4 mile, to Hidden Meadow Trail—right, .8 mile, to Six Points Junction—left on Bald Hill Trail, .7 mile, to Boy Scout Junction—right on Deer Park FR, .7 mile, to start. **5.5 miles total**

■ Bald Hill Trail

Boy Scout Junction to Six Points Junction: .71 mile

TERRAIN: Madrone woodland, parts through redwoods and grassland; horses permitted (MMWD)

ELEVATION: From 380 to 550 feet; gradual, short part very steep

INTERSECTING TRAIL(S): Connector fire road to Five Corners (.4 mile)

This delightful trail begins at a seven-way intersection, passes a connector to Five Corners (which has six options), and ends at a five-way junction called Six Points! We'll try to untangle things.

When arriving at Boy Scout Junction on Deer Park Fire Road from Deer Park, Bald Hill Trail is the first fork left. It starts steeply uphill on the western flank of Bald Hill. The sunny opening yards are particularly rich with spring wildflowers, among the best displays anywhere on Tam. Ahead, up into the light forest cover, irises are abundant. Note that early on, the irises are mostly deep blues and purples. Farther along the trail the shadings are more pink and white.

In just under .4 mile, the trail hits the ridgeline at a T intersection. To the right, a connector fire road drops .1 mile to Five Corners. There are magnificent views of Mt. Tamalpais.

Bald Hill Trail continues left, along the spine of what is sometimes called Kentucky Ridge. It skirts an area now blocked for erosion control, then veers left into a redwood forest at another rerouting. Bald Hill Trail re-emerges onto the ridge. A former spur of Hidden Meadow Trail here is now closed.

In another .1 mile, the trail ends at Six Points on the western flank of Bald Hill. The four other trails are, clockwise, Six Points dropping to Deer Park FR, Yolanda going to Worn Spring FR, Yolanda toward Phoenix Lake, and Hidden Meadow Trail dropping to Hidden Meadow. Decades ago, there was a sixth option up Bald Hill.

◾ Buckeye Trail

Deer Park to Worn Spring FR: .25 mile

TERRAIN: Grassy hillside; narrow and uneven (MMWD)

ELEVATION: Around 540 feet; almost level

INTERSECTING TRAIL(S): None

This ¼-mile trail cuts off a short uphill on loops tying Deer Park Trail to Worn Spring Fire Road and Yolanda Trail.

Buckeye's northern end is 100 feet above the top of Deer Park Trail. The trail is quite narrow throughout. Pause to enjoy the views of Bald Hill and of the many miles of open space. In fall, the trail remains colored by late-blooming wildflowers, pink from willow herbs and yellow from madias, a daisy-like plant.

Except for an oak or two, all the trees passed along the way are buckeyes. Several nearly uprooted trees cling to life. The buckeye's fragrant, candlelike blossoms and palmate leaves in spring and summer; its big brown seed pods in fall; and its bare limbs in winter are all highly distinctive.

Aptly named Buckeye Trail ends at Worn Spring FR in a saddle. To the right, the fire road passes the north end of Yolanda Trail and continues up Bald Hill. Left returns to Buckeye's start. (The path straight ahead winds across private property into San Anselmo.)

■ Canyon Trail

Marin Stables to Concrete Pipeline FR: .74 mile

TERRAIN: Riparian; woodland; muddy in winter; horses permitted (MMWD)

ELEVATION: 190 to 480 feet; gradual, last part very steep

INTERSECTING TRAIL(S): Moore (.1 mile), connector fire road to Boy Scout Junction (.6 mile)

Canyon Trail begins directly behind Fairfax's Marin Stables, founded in 1937. The stables, although on MMWD land, are privately run; Jim McDermott was the leaseholder from 1980 to 2007, when the nonprofit Marin Stables & Trails was organized to restore and preserve the site. Be quiet as you pass through so as not to disturb horses boarded here. Canyon Trail is used principally by riders from the stables, but is now closed to horses in winter to minimize mud and sediment erosion into the creek.

The opening ½ mile parallels a stream (called Deer Creek by some) through a peaceful, tree-lined canyon. Less than 100 yards past the stables, at a signed junction, the (Ethel and Harry) Moore Trail forks left and up. Canyon Trail continues beside the stream. In ⅙ mile, a newer routing (opened in 2004) takes Canyon Trail to the right, avoiding a former crossing of the stream. Now the trail goes over the creek and a feeder on new Boy Scout–built bridges. The trees in this wonderful woodland are mostly laurels, with some madrones. Farther in, redwoods prevail.

At ½ mile, the rerouted Canyon Trail returns to the creek. Across, Boy Scout FR rises to Boy Scout Junction. Canyon Trail continues straight.

This last section of Canyon Trail is very steep, with switchbacks barely easing the climb. It ends at Concrete Pipeline FR. Just to the right is Taylor Trail, with Fairfax-Bolinas Road .7 mile distant. To the left, it is .7 mile to Five Corners.

The trail likely dates to the founding of the stables, when it was simply known as "Horse Trail."

■ Deer Park Fire Road

Deer Park to Five Corners: 1.13 miles

TERRAIN: Wooded; riparian; heavily used (MMWD)

ELEVATION: From 190 to 520 feet; first half level, second half very steep

INTERSECTING TRAIL(S): Six Points (.3 mile), Junction (.3 mile), Bald Hill (.7 mile), connector fire road to Canyon (.7 mile), Moore (.7 mile), Junction (.7 mile)

Deer Park FR is the principal route out of Deer Park trailhead. It is popular for short out-and-back jaunts and as an entry to more distant trips.

The fire road begins at a gate across the playing field behind the old Deer Park School, now leased by the Ross Valley School District to the Fairfax-San Anselmo Children's Center. Deer Park Trail goes left from the near side of the field.

The fire road is level at first, through lovely oak woodland, with several stately monarchs. Deep rows of poison oak, among the densest on Tam, line the margins. You will pass an entry to what was once called School Trail.

In just over .3 mile is four-way Oak Tree Junction, presided over by a huge, old oak. To the left is Six Points Trail, rising to Six Points. To the right, beside this landmark oak, is Junction Trail, a pedestrian-only alternate route up to Boy Scout Junction.

Deer Park FR then begins climbing steeply under a madrone-laurel canopy. After a stiff rise, the fire road briefly levels and opens as it meets seven-way Boy Scout Junction (see trailhead description).

Deer Park FR continues to climb, but less steeply, through woodland, ending at six-way Five Corners. The options meeting here are, clockwise: a connector fire road uphill to Bald Hill Trail, the combined Shaver Grade and Concrete Pipeline FR going downhill, Elliott Trail going uphill, Shaver Grade going uphill, and Concrete Pipeline toward Fairfax-Bolinas Road.

The fire road was built by the Marin County Fire Department in 1948. MMWD undertook major work on the fire road in 2002–2003 to reduce erosion. (At press time, MMWD has plans to build a large water storage tank just above Five Corners, and there will be some changes.) There is a second, longer Deer Park FR between Muir Woods Road and Pantoll.

◾ Deer Park Trail

Deer Park School to Worn Spring FR: .84 mile

TERRAIN: Lower part riparian and wooded, upper part grassland; horses permitted (MMWD)

ELEVATION: From 190 to 520 feet; steep

INTERSECTING TRAIL(S): None

Deer Park Trail offers serenity within minutes of the trailhead. Its warm southern exposure makes it outstanding for wildflowers. It is also part of the main Deer Park–Bald Hill summit route.

To reach the trail from Deer Park, go left of the buildings. You enter an open playing field. Deer Park Trail rises from it, signed (along with a warning about mountain lions), to the left, by a black oak. Directly across the field, behind the gate, is the start of Deer Park FR.

After a short stretch in woodland, the trail enters a rocky, south-facing, grassy area, with a stream running below. You can count on white milk maids and blue-purple hound's tongue to lead the rich annual wildflower parade in January. Dozens more species follow.

The trail winds its way steadily up the pastoral northwest flank of Bald Hill. Buckeyes and laurels are the common trees. Deer paths cut through the area. Views open as the trail nears the ridge; look back to see it snaking up the hill.

Deer Park Trail ends at Worn Spring FR. Another path, straight across, leaves water district land and goes into private property. To the right, Worn Spring FR rises past Buckeye Trail (30 yards uphill) to the ridgeline, then continues to the top of Bald Hill.

■ Elliott Trail

Five Corners to Sky Oaks-Lagunitas Trail: .48 mile

TERRAIN: Madrone woodland; horses permitted (MMWD)

ELEVATION: 520 to 700 feet; gradual, parts steep

INTERSECTING TRAIL(S): Shaver Grade (.3 mile)

Elliott is the only trail option at the Five Corners junction; the other spokes are broad roads. It winds its way uphill as an equestrian and pedestrian bypass of Shaver Grade.

Elliott starts up a few wooden steps, between the two arms of Shaver Grade. It ascends through madrone woodland, becoming steep for a stretch. Shaver Grade, running roughly parallel to the right, is visible.

In ⅓ mile, Elliott crosses Shaver Grade at a marked junction. The trail continues climbing through quintessential California oak woodland. At a crest, a path forks right to an isolated grassy knoll. Elliott continues to the left, descending to again meet Shaver Grade.

Elliott continues up on the other side of Shaver. This uppermost section of Elliott was posted as closed during the 1990s for erosion control, but has been improved and reopened. It climbs steeply, ending in deeper woodland at Alex Forman Trail. Shaver Grade is still nearby, its top just to the right.

Walter Elliott, an ex-mule skinner, and his wife, Harriet, built the nearby Marin Stables in 1937, and were guiding forces among the Tamalpais Trail Riders. Walter died while riding in 1962; the trail was built soon after.

64

Junction Trail

Oak Tree Junction to Boy Scout Junction: .25 mile

TERRAIN: Lightly wooded hillside; narrow and rocky (MMWD)

ELEVATION: From 200 to 380 feet; steep

INTERSECTING TRAIL(S): None

This trail permits hikers to travel between Oak Tree and Boy Scout free from any bicycle traffic. It rises from Oak Tree Junction, the four-way intersection on Deer Park FR just before the uphill when coming from Deer Park. Junction Trail sets off to the right. Across is the base of Six Points Trail.

Junction Trail immediately passes the huge (and, unfortunately, dying) oak that gives the junction its name. It then rises steeply, with some rocky sections. The trail's southern exposure allows wildflowers, including a mass of baby blue eyes (*Nemophila menziesii*) near the top, to bloom early. The trail is particularly lovely on warm summer evenings, when it catches the last sunlight in the canyon. Junction Trail ends at Boy Scout Junction.

(Ethel and Harry) Moore Trail

Canyon Trail to Boy Scout Junction: .43 mile

TERRAIN: Laurel-dominated woodland; muddy in winter; horses permitted (MMWD)

ELEVATION: 220 to 380 feet; gradual

INTERSECTING TRAIL(S): None

Canyon Trail sets off behind Marin Stables. In 100 yards, it meets a fork. Canyon continues to the right, while Moore Trail sets off uphill left. A pair of signs here names the trail for Ethel and Harry Moore.

Moore Trail climbs steadily through light woodland of mostly laurels, with some madrones. Steps aid the way, keeping the grade gradual. In winter, when horses are directed off Canyon Trail to Moore Trail, mud can be an issue. In summer, expect dust. Recent trail work has ameliorated these problems.

Views open to Bald Hill over the final yards of Moore Trail. A sign reads "Ethel Moore Trail." The "Harry Moore" mate had been missing for years but is now restored. Moore Trail ends a few yards below at Boy Scout Junction.

The Moores were horse lovers closely associated with Marin Stables, and were also charter members of Tamalpais Trail Riders. Harry Moore died in 1944. The trail was built a few years later and named for him. Ethel Moore, then 86, attended the dedication ceremony.

■ Six Points Trail

Deer Park FR at Oak Tree Junction to Six Points Junction: .57 mile

TERRAIN: Deeply wooded; riparian; horses permitted (MMWD)

ELEVATION: From 220 to 550 feet; steep

INTERSECTING TRAIL(S): None

Six Points Trail plays a role in many loops out of Deer Park. It runs alongside a stream through deep woods.

The trail rises to the left (south) of Deer Park FR, .3 mile from the fire road's start. On the opposite side of the four-way intersection (Oak Tree Junction) is Junction Trail.

Six Points Trail heads off into a quiet, creek-side woodland. Redwoods, madrones, and laurels line the way. The route begins ascending steeply alongside Deer Park Creek, but switchbacks ease the climb.

The cool, wet forest—which rarely sees sunshine in winter—supports lush vegetation. Ferns are abundant. In summer, you may be lucky enough to spot the small greenish-white flowers of the rein orchid (*Piperia unalascensis*). It is one of ten or eleven orchid species to be found on Mount Tamalpais by observant searchers.

Near the top, the trail veers right, away from and above the headwaters of the creek. It ends at five-way Six Points Junction, on a ridge with striking Mt. Tam views. The other four trails are, clockwise: Yolanda heading to Worn Spring FR, Yolanda toward Phoenix Lake, Hidden Meadow downhill, and Bald Hill Trail on to Boy Scout Junction. The missing sixth point is a now-overgrown path up Bald Hill.

The trail has also been known as Redwood Trail, particularly among equestrians.

Junction Trail is a pedestrian-only alternative route up to Boy Scout Junction.

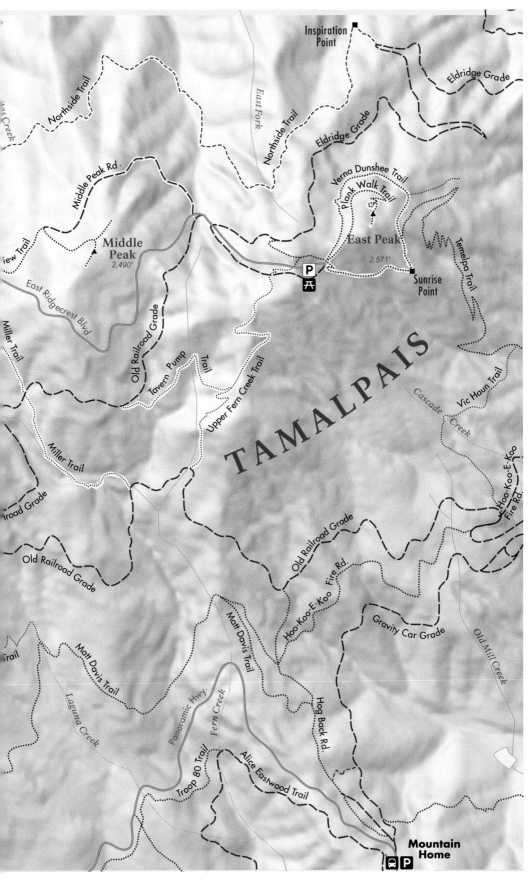

The hiker's path to the East Peak parking lot, atop Upper Fern Creek Trail.

TRAILHEAD TWO: EAST RIDGECREST BOULEVARD

Directions

1. From the south: Highway 101—Highway 1—Panoramic Highway—Southside (Pantoll) Road to Rock Spring

2. From the north: Fairfax-Bolinas Road, from either Fairfax (where it is called Bolinas Road) or Highway 1 at Bolinas—West Ridgecrest Boulevard to Rock Spring

---

Ridgecrest Boulevard runs 6.6 miles from Fairfax-Bolinas Road to the East Peak parking area. The 3.7-mile stretch between Rock Spring, where Pantoll Road joins, and Fairfax-Bolinas Road is described in the West Ridgecrest trailhead, where there is also background on the road's history.

The East Peak parking area, from which the summit is a short (but very steep) walk, has long been a popular destination. It was also the high point of the Mill Valley & Mt. Tamalpais Scenic Railway, which ran from 1896 through 1929. There are bathrooms, fountains, and some spectacularly located picnic tables. A parking fee was introduced in the late 1990s.

The level area beside the parking area, site of the railway's Tavern of Tamalpais, has seen changes over the last decade or so. The old East Peak Snack Bar and adjacent soda machines are gone. The Mt. Tam Visitor Center, a one-time restroom refurbished by the Mt. Tamalpais Interpretive Association (now known as Friends of Mt. Tam), has again been renovated. The center is staffed by volunteers and open on weekends. Inside are informative displays, snacks, books, maps, and Tam-logo clothing. In 2014, the Friends added a bicycle repair station. New too is the Gravity Car Barn, another Friends project. It was built in anticipation of housing the last surviving Heisler engine from Mountain Railway days, which is currently in Scotia, California. (Negotiations to acquire it are underway at press time.) A rebuilt gravity car is brought out on weekends. Near the barn and track are informative panels on the railway's colorful past.

The trails that intersect East Ridgecrest are, in order eastward from Rock Spring: Rock Spring, Mountain Top, Rock Spring-Lagunitas FR, Arturo, Eastwood (now closed), International, Miller, Lakeview, Middle Peak FR, Old Railroad Grade, Eldridge Grade, Upper Fern Creek, Verna Dunshee, and Plankwalk. There are a few parking spots near each of these junctions.

Gates bar vehicular access to East Ridgecrest Boulevard at night. The Fairfax-Bolinas gate opens at 9 AM all year. The Pantoll gate opens as early as 7 AM in summer. Call the ranger station to check.

Suggested Loops from East Peak Parking Area (elevation 2,360 feet)

1. Verna Dunshee Trail. **.7 mile**

2. Upper Fern Creek Trail, .7 mile, to Old Railroad Grade—right, .1 mile, to Miller Trail—right, .7 mile, to across Ridgecrest Road—right on Lakeview Trail, .2 mile, to Middle Peak FR—left, .7 mile, to Ridgecrest Boulevard and up to start. **2.4 miles total**

3. Verna Dunshee (counterclockwise), .3 mile, to Temelpa Trail—down, 1.1 miles, to Vic Haun Trail—down right (Vic Haun), .5 mile, to Old Railroad Grade—right and up on Old Railroad, 1 mile, to Upper Fern Creek Trail—right and up, .8 mile, to start. **3.7 miles total**

4. Eldridge Grade, 1.2 miles, to Northside Trail—left, 1.6 miles, to Colier Trail—left (uphill), .4 mile, to International Trail—left, .1 mile, to Ridgecrest Blvd.—cross Ridgecrest to Miller Trail, .3 mile, to Old Railroad Grade—left, .8 mile, to Ridgecrest Boulevard and up to start. **4.4 miles total**

▦ Arturo Trail

FAA gate off East Ridgecrest Boulevard to Rifle Camp: .49 mile

TERRAIN: Deep woodland (GGNRA, MMWD)

ELEVATION: 2,360 to 2,000 feet; very steep

INTERSECTING TRAIL(S): None

The reopening of Arturo Trail in 1985 was a source of joy to mountain veterans. Long part of a popular route between Tam's north and south sides, the trail was closed in 1951 after construction of the Mill Valley Air Force Station. It is now again a key north-south link, and as hauntingly lovely as ever.

To reach the upper end of Arturo, enter the main Federal Aviation Administration (FAA) entry gate off Ridgecrest Road. Veer left through a gap in the fence and follow the hiker symbol sign down the left fork of the paved road. In a few yards, veer sharply right at another hiker sign, under an oak, to begin on Arturo Trail. (Left and straight both quickly meet fences.) The trailhead can also be reached via Mountain Top Trail.

Arturo immediately passes through the USAF base's old fence, and borders it. The trail then veers off downhill into the forest, where it remains throughout. Quiet is assured.

There are oaks, tanbarks, and bays. A small grove of rare bitter cherry trees *(Prunus emarginata)* is dedicated to the late Tam historian Lincoln Fairley. But dominating are Douglas-firs. More than a century ago, this area was rather open, the aftermath of logging and fire. Manzanitas came in, enjoying full sunlight. Then Douglas-firs invaded, crowding out the manzanitas, whose skeletons remain.

Some of the huge, older Douglas-firs, which grew here first without competition for light, have sizable lower limbs. These monarchs are called "wolf trees" because they supposedly choke out competing plant growth. An impressive pair halfway down has been named Romulus and Remus. The old Potrero Cutoff here is now off-limits as MMWD has designated the area as environmentally sensitive and has prohibited off-trail travel. Lower Arturo is the only place on Mt. Tamalpais that the small bitter cherry tree can be found.

Arturo Trail reaches a few steps and ends at Northside Trail, near Rifle Camp on the Rock Spring-Lagunitas FR. Right, Northside Trail departs on its 2.7-mile journey to Eldridge Grade. Directly across the fire road, Azalea Meadow Trail begins its descent to Cross Country Boys Trail. Immediately left, across a bridge dedicated in May 2000 to long-time Tamalpais Conservation Club volunteer trail workers Jack and Janet Walker, is Rifle Camp. Just beyond is Potrero Meadow, a must-visit.

Arthur, or Arturo, Oettl, a member of the Cross Country Boys Club, built the trail in the 1920s. It was a partial reroute of the old Coyote Trail, the first ever constructed by Tamalpais Conservation Club after its founding in 1912. Marin Conservation Corps, GGNRA, MMWD, and the Mt. Tamalpais History Project all played roles in Arturo's reopening.

Azalea Meadow Trail

Rock Spring-Lagunitas FR at Rifle Camp to Cross Country Boys Trail: .31 mile

TERRAIN: Riparian; heavily wooded (MMWD)

ELEVATION: 2,000 to 1,730 feet; steep

INTERSECTING TRAIL(S): None

Azalea Meadow Trail did not appear on early Tam maps; it was only signed after the MMWD and Tamalpais Conservation Club did extensive work on it in 2010. It runs through deep forest, beside a lively, azalea-edged creek.

The trail begins off Rock Spring-Lagunitas FR at Rifle Camp, directly across from the steps to the Arturo-Northside trail junction. It descends through woodland of mostly Douglas-firs, with a few struggling madrones. The nearby stream, followed closely throughout but not crossed, is the East Fork of Swede George Creek. An impressive stand of giant chain ferns grows where the trail passes through a seep.

Azalea Meadow Trail ends at its junction with Cross Country Boys Trail, just above Azalea Meadow (or Azalea Flat) itself. Cross Country goes right, up to Rock Spring-Lagunitas FR and left, down to High Marsh Trail. Azalea Meadow Trail formerly continued another ½ mile to Willow Meadow, by the intersection of Kent and High Marsh Trails. This section is still evident, but not designated by MMWD.

Azalea Meadow is one of the mountain's special places. Western azaleas are usually in full bloom in May and June. As John Thomas Howell wrote in his *Marin Flora*, "The beauty of the western azalea is not restricted to what is seen in graceful shrubbery but when in flower its beauty pervades the mountain or canyon with a most agreeable fragrance." I've seen bees swarm above the creamy white flowers in such numbers they created a low roar as they pollinated the next generation of azaleas.

▦ International Trail

East Ridgecrest Road to Northside Trail: .52 mile

TERRAIN: Forest; lowest yards, open serpentine (MMWD)

ELEVATION: From 2,300 to 2,060 feet; gradual, parts steep

INTERSECTING TRAIL(S): Colier (.1 mile)

International Trail starts at one of Tamalpais's best view spots and ends at another. The signed trailhead is on the north side of Ridgecrest Road, 1.9 miles from Rock Spring, at a turnout. Here, in the dip between West and Middle Peaks, is a rare vista to both the north and south of Tam. A few yards up Ridgecrest is the west end of Lakeview Trail. Across the pavement (south) is the upper end of the Miller Trail.

International Trail immediately enters woodland. In 100 yards, the top of extremely steep Colier Trail, which drops all the way to Lake Lagunitas, enters on the right.

After a short uphill, International begins its long descent. Parts are steep, including a haunting stretch through a stand of dead manzanitas. (TCC eased the grade a bit with some trail work in 2002.) International continues down, less steeply. It leaves the forest, which is replaced by serpentine rock and chaparral. There are more long views. International ends at Northside Trail. Left leads to Rifle Camp, right to Colier Trail and a loop option.

International was built in the 1940s as a replacement north-south route over the mountain's summit ridge for Arturo Trail, which was closed during World War II. One story contends that it was named in a spirit of harmony to reflect the many ethnic backgrounds of those who worked on it. Another story has it that MMWD patrolman Joe Zapella remarked—when planning to talk to those responsible for the trail's unauthorized construction—that there would be an "international situation" because of the many nationalities of the builders.

▦ Lakeview Trail

East Ridgecrest Boulevard to Middle Peak FR: .25 mile

TERRAIN: Light woodland and chaparral (MMWD)

ELEVATION: From 2,300 to 2,400 feet; gradual

INTERSECTING TRAIL(S): None

Lakeview Trail (different from much-lower Lakeview FR, which connects Lake Lagunitas to Eldridge Grade) is one of Tamalpais's oldest. It once ran from Old Railroad Grade, over today's upper Miller Trail, to the saddle between Middle and East Peak.

Today's shortened Lakeview Trail sets off on the north side of Ridgecrest Road at the splendid vista point in the West Peak-Middle Peak saddle, 1.9 miles from Rock Spring. The top of International Trail is a few yards below Ridgecrest. Miller Trail descends from the opposite, south side of the road, where there are some parking spots.

Lakeview gently but steadily rises along the northern face of Middle Peak. Between the shrubs and trees are occasional long views, but not as sweeping as years ago, when fires and trimming kept foliage lower. Lake Lagunitas, the closest of the three visible lakes and the "view lake" that gave the trail its name, can now just barely be glimpsed. Bon Tempe Lake is more prominent, with a bit of Alpine Lake visible beyond Bon Tempe Dam.

Lakeview Trail ends at its junction with Middle Peak FR. Straight ahead, the fire road, over the original Lakeview Trail route, descends to Ridgecrest Road by the tops of both Old Railroad and Eldridge Grades. To the right, the fire road rises .2 mile to Middle Peak's summit.

Lower Northside Trail

Colier Spring to Rock Spring-Lagunitas FR: .91 mile

Terrain: Heavily wooded; parts open and rocky (MMWD)

Elevation: From 1,840 to 1,800 feet; almost level

Intersecting Trail(s): None

Lower Northside Trail runs, nearly level, through a remote area high on the mountain's north face. To reach the trailhead, follow Colier Trail down from Ridgecrest Boulevard to the traditional hiker's resting spot of Colier Spring. The other intersecting trails here are, clockwise: Upper Northside, heading west to Rifle Camp; Lower Northside; Colier Trail, descending to Lake Lagunitas; and Northside, going east to Eldridge Grade. A classic old sign pointing the way to Lower Northside disappeared in 1992.

Lower Northside, which was built in the 1930s, begins amidst towering redwoods. There is a brief opening, another redwood grove, then a somewhat rocky stretch. The trail gently rises to a view site, with Pilot Knob and Bald Hill framed between the trees. A short rise brings Lower Northside to another stand of redwoods and a bridge crossing the West Fork of Lagunitas Creek.

Just about all the most common trees of Tam are to be found in the woodland ahead: huge Douglas-firs and redwoods along with bay, madrone, live oak, tanbark oak, and California nutmeg. The trail leaves the forest to enter an open area of serpentine rock. Here, only shrubs and stunted Sargent cypress grow. The views to the north and west are outstanding. In 1997, Lower Northside was cleared an additional 100 yards to meet Rock Spring-Lagunitas Fire Road.

■ Middle Peak Fire Road

Ridgecrest Boulevard to Middle Peak: .62 mile

TERRAIN: Mostly chaparral; short part paved (MMWD)

ELEVATION: From 2,240 to 2,480 feet; gradual

INTERSECTING TRAIL(S): Lakeview (.4 mile)

Middle Peak FR starts on the north side of Ridgecrest Road, in the saddle between Middle Peak and East Peak, 2.5 miles from Rock Spring. This saddle and its trees are quite visible from the Ross Valley, miles below. (The area was once known as Pieville.) A funicular—cable railroad—from here to Middle Peak was built in 1905; its route up the peak's face is now overgrown. Opposite the trailhead is the top of Old Railroad Grade. Just uphill is the top of Eldridge Grade.

Middle Peak FR begins rising gradually beyond the gate. (You may encounter vehicles servicing the communication facility at the summit.) There are views to the north between gaps in the foliage. Be patient; the vistas will soon open completely.

The fire road, paved for a short stretch, bends sharply to the left. Lakeview Trail sets off straight ahead, to Ridgecrest Road in the saddle between Middle and West Peaks. Middle Peak FR continues uphill.

The fire road again forks to two summit areas. The route straight ahead, to the true summit at 2,490 feet in elevation, is off-limits behind a locked fence. Radiation levels from all the communications apparatus make it unsafe for visitors. (The prominent green, geodesic-shaped building dates from 1981.) Veer right to buildings and towers operated by the Federal Aviation Administration. Cameras monitor the site.

Use of Middle Peak for communications has a long history. In 1905, two 300-foot-tall wooden radio transmission towers were constructed, using the funicular. Not surprisingly, they blew over the following year. Middle Peak FR was built over the eastern half of the older Lakeview Trail to access the facilities on the summit.

▉ Miller Trail

East Ridgecrest Road to Old Railroad Grade: .68 mile

TERRAIN: Upper half chaparral, lower half riparian and wooded; rocky in parts (MMWD)

ELEVATION: From 2,300 to 1,580 feet; very steep

INTERSECTING TRAIL(S): Old Railroad Grade (.3 mile)

Miller Trail has two completely different characters. Its upper half travels through chaparral, with sweeping views from high on the mountain. The lower half is heavily wooded, alongside a stream in a deep canyon. Each part contributes to make Miller one of Tamalpais's lovelier trails.

East Ridgecrest Road drops to a saddle, or dip, between West and Middle Peaks, 1.9 miles from Rock Spring. There are paved parking turnouts and splendid views on both sides of the road. To the north is the top of International Trail, with Lakeview Trail just to its right. On the south is the signed top of Miller Trail.

Miller starts with a few downhill steps over a pipe, and continues dropping steeply. The canyon, with headwaters of the West Fork of Fern Creek, is to the right. Chaparral shrubs line the trail as it passes over serpentine rock. A few pioneering Douglas-firs stand out; they may one day cover the canyon.

In ¹/₃ mile, Miller hits Old Railroad Grade; the last few yards before the junction are quite rocky and steep. A wooden signpost, and the remains of an older metal one, mark the intersection. West Point Inn is .7 mile to the right.

Miller continues directly across Old Railroad Grade. It offers a 1-mile shortcut downhill compared to the less steep grade. Miller again is steep and rocky. In summer, the highly fragrant pink-purple flowers of western pennyroyal (*Monardella* spp.), in the mint family, dot the serpentine rocks. In .1 mile, the trail enters woodland, then crosses a rivulet and the West Fork of Fern Creek.

Miller Trail continues, in parts quite narrow, down the edge of the lively creek. Chain ferns and elk clover grow densely in the creek bed, perhaps in greater profusion than anywhere else on Tam. This is a lovely, quiet, haunting area. Soon, the trail crosses back to the creek's left bank over a bridge.

The trail encounters a slide from a huge storm in January 1982; redwoods lie across the creek, while other massive trees tower above. When the trail was repaired in 1989, dozens of steps were added to ease the remaining descent, but the going is still very steep. A pipe that carried water from a dam on the creek lies broken off at both ends.

Miller ends at a second junction with Old Railroad Grade, marked with an MMWD trail signpost. Old Railroad Grade now actually rises on both sides of the redwood-lined bend. This rarity on the grade also dates from January 1982. The raging creek tore off 40 feet of the grade, which was then refilled. Note a redwood stump spouting young trees from its top. Fern Creek Trail is .1 mile to the left and West Point, 1 mile to the right.

John Miller was a native of Canada who came to San Francisco in 1895, when he was twenty-nine. He joined Tamalpais Conservation Club in 1921, and worked tirelessly on the mountain's trails until his death in 1951. When he was eighty, he badly injured his back trying to pry loose a boulder on this trail, an accident that left him bedridden for most of the final three years of his life. The trail was named in his honor. He left a sizable bequest to TCC, which was used to help purchase additions to the state park, notably the Scott property around O'Rourke's Bench. To Miller is attributed the wonderful quote, "Why should I deserve praise? Hasn't the mountain always repaid whatever work I did on it, giving me health, happiness, and friendships?"

▦ Mountain Top Trail

East Ridgecrest Blvd. to former USAF base on Tamalpa Ridge: .54 mile

TERRAIN: Lightly wooded (MMWD, GGNRA)

ELEVATION: From 2,100 to 2,400 feet; steep

INTERSECTING TRAIL(S): None

Mountain Top Trail originally went to the highest point on Tam, the 2,604-foot summit of West Peak. But in 1951, West Peak was leveled for a helipad, losing 30 feet in elevation, during construction of the Mill Valley Air Force Station. California Alpine Club's Great War memorial rock cairn at the summit was lost, and a fence blocked Mountain Top Trail and all other access points.

The surviving Mountain Top Trail, newly signed, begins at a gate on the north side of Ridgecrest Road, across from a parking area for Mountain Theater and .4 mile from Rock Spring. Rock Spring-Lagunitas Fire Road also begins here. The trail climbs parallel to, and above, Ridgecrest Boulevard.

The route is lined with trees, now mostly Douglas-firs, but there are enough openings to enjoy magnificent views of the San Francisco skyline and the Pacific. At .4 mile, the trail passes through the base's old fence line. The remaining route was narrow and rough before it was upgraded and slightly rerouted in 2012. Mountain Top Trail ends on the summit ridge, amid what is left of the old military base. The ridge has been called West Peak Ridge; Tamalpa Ridge; and, earlier, Bill Williams Ridge.

During World War II, the military secured long-term leases to 277 acres of water district and private land high on Mt. Tamalpais. Soldiers lived in a camp at Mountain Theater and at the old Mountain Railway tavern, and large parts were closed to the public. After the war, Mill Valley Air Force Station, a radar tracking facility, was built on a 106-acre parcel atop West Peak.

Among the sixty-two new buildings were residence halls; up to three hundred servicemen and their families enjoyed the best views in the Bay Area—and endured fog and wind—as well as a gymnasium, movie theater, and bowling alley. The 666th Radar Squadron was deactivated in 1980. In 1983, the base was transferred to the National Park Service. Work began on tearing down the structures, but the effort stalled over asbestos problems and lack of funds. A further effort in 1996 also stalled. In 2005, the federal leases ended and the area was returned to the Marin Municipal Water District. Gary Yost's 2014 documentary film, *The Invisible Peak*, has helped revive a push, led by the new Tamalpais Lands Collaborative, to restore the site.

Venture right to enjoy the unsurpassed views. Beyond the derelict tennis court, veer left to pick up the top of Arturo Trail, which descends to Rifle Camp. Straight ahead is a fenced, off-limits aviation facility with its prominent white dome (formerly two domes).

A trail called Bill Williams (separate from the Bill Williams Trail that connects Phoenix Lake to Tucker Trail) ran atop Bolinas Ridge to West Peak from the late 1800s. A parallel fire trail, just to the south of Bill Williams, appears on the 1914 map published by the Tamalpais Fire Association. It is apparently this fire trail that survives as Mountain Top Trail.

Northside (and Upper Northside) Trail

Rifle Camp to Eldridge Grade: 2.66 miles

TERRAIN: Mostly wooded; parts in chaparral, rocky; horses permitted (MMWD)

ELEVATION: Around 2,000 feet; almost level

INTERSECTING TRAIL(S): International (.6 mile), Lower Northside (1.1 miles), Colier (1.1 miles)

Note: The section of Northside Trail west of Colier Spring is called Upper Northside on the accompanying map, to distinguish it from what was always known as Lower Northside Trail. I'll keep the older designation of Northside for the entire route from Rifle Camp to Eldridge Grade, as it was built as one trail.

No trail in Marin runs longer above 1,800 feet than Northside. It also plays a role in most circuit routes of Tam. Follow Rock Spring-Lagunitas FR down 1.1 miles from Ridgecrest Boulevard to Rifle Camp. Here also is the base of Arturo Trail and, across the road, the top of Azalea Meadow Trail.

Douglas-fir dominates in the deep woodland. Soon, bays become the principal forest tree. In $^1/_3$ mile, the trail enters an open serpentine rock area. The views from this short section, just above 2,000 feet, are spectacular. They sweep from Point Reyes across Marin into Sonoma and Napa Counties. The only trees that grow in this calcium-poor, heavy metal–rich soil are Sargent cypress, and even they are shrublike.

Northside continues across at a wood signpost. In 120 yards, still on the open serpentine, International Trail comes in from the right. It rises to Ridgecrest Road.

Northside returns to woodland and gently descends. It passes through a grove of short redwoods (in the next grove, near Colier Spring, the redwoods are towering). Colier Spring was once a reliable source of water, but since a storm shifted its underground source away from the outlet pipe, it is usually dry. Still, it is one of the best-loved resting spots on the mountain. Five routes converge. Clockwise from Northside, they are: Lower Northside, dropping to Rock Spring-Lagunitas FR; Colier, descending extremely steeply to Lake Lagunitas; Northside, continuing; and Colier, uphill to International Trail.

Northside Trail rises slightly as it leaves the redwood forest. At ¼ mile past Colier is another pipe, tapping a more reliable spring. (MMWD discourages drinking untreated water.) Chain ferns mark the damp site. Within a short distance are azalea bushes on both sides of the trail. Irises also abound here. Back in the chaparral, the closed, extremely steep Lagunitas Fire Trail crosses Northside.

The last mile of Northside offers many vista points. Attention to footing also becomes important as the trail passes through a ¼-mile band of loose, broken rocks. Northside crosses the East Fork of Lagunitas Creek. The trail has now passed all three forks of Marin's most important creek, and madrone and California nutmeg become the most abundant trees. A clearing offers a view down the canyon to Pilot Knob and beyond.

Northside then hits Inspiration Point, a rock ledge with a splendid northern panorama and goes on, wider, for another 100 yards. It ends at a bend in Eldridge Grade, .6 mile above the Wheeler Trail intersection and 1.2 miles below Ridgecrest Boulevard. A classic old sign marks the spot.

Mountain veterans Ted Abeel and Earl Parks began working on Northside in 1926 to improve hiking options over the mountain's less-visited north face. Other sources credit Sierra Club and Civilian Conservation Corps as playing key roles.

◼ Plankwalk Trail

East Peak parking area to East Peak: .32 mile

TERRAIN: Chaparral; loose rock; heavily used (MTSP)

ELEVATION: From 2,390 to 2,571 feet; very steep

INTERSECTING TRAIL(S): None

Plankwalk Trail rises to Tam's 2,571-foot East Peak. The lure of reaching the summit makes Plankwalk one of the most-used trails on the Mountain.

Plankwalk derives its name from the wood planks, placed for surer footing, that once covered it. The planks have been restored on the lower section, while the upper section is extremely rocky and a challenge to navigate, particularly when wet and slippery.

Plankwalk rises from the Verna Dunshee Trail loop near the bathrooms and Gravity Car Barn. In 150 yards, where the planks end, is an old, eroded route right. It was closed by MTSP in 1989 after a visitor, shod in inappropriate footwear for the terrain, slipped and subsequently filed a lawsuit.

Plankwalk, narrower, continues on the north, then the east side of the peak, where the views are magnificent. It then bends right. At the final bend (left), near the lookout, an overgrown and precipitous "path" continues straight, following a pipe a few yards to one of the mountain's hidden treasures, an old bench and plaque just yards below the northwest corner of the lookout tower. The plaque reads: *Beneath this plate are the names of those heroes of the air who have fallen in the pursuit of the science of aviation, erected by the citizens of Mill Valley, May 30, 1915.*

One "hero" was Lincoln J. Beachey, a San Francisco native who achieved several aviation firsts, including the first to fly over Niagara Falls. He died in view of roughly 250,000 spectators on March 14, 1915, when his monoplane plunged into San Francisco Bay during an air show at the Panama–Pacific International Exposition. Another was Weldon B. Goode, apparently the first person to fly over Mt. Tamalpais, who died in 1914. The plaque's centennial was celebrated with a ceremony in 2015.

Return to the stone steps for the final yards up Plankwalk, to the door of Gardner Lookout atop East Peak. Strong winds are common, but there are perfectly calm days as well; you'll want to linger in any case. Nectar feeders draw numerous hummingbirds.

The panorama is now complete. It is interesting to compare what the famed surveyor George Davidson recorded as visible from here during his visits, dating from 1858. (See the list in Lincoln Fairley's *Mount Tamalpais, A History*, pp. 8–9.)

Many of the natural landmarks he observed are still often, or occasionally, visible. They include (clockwise, with his marginally overstated distances in parentheses): Point Reyes Head (24 ¾ miles), Bodega Head (37 ½ miles), Mount St. Helena (51 ⅔ miles), Mt. Diablo (36 ⅔ miles), Mt. Hamilton (65 ½ miles), San Bruno Mountain (17 ⅔ miles), and Montara Mountain (26 miles). The 56-mile-long chain of Sierra peaks he saw, at a distance of 158 miles, are now only partially visible on the clearest winter days. Davidson also notes that the ocean horizon is 67 miles distant, with the Farallon Islands some 28 miles away. Other landmarks that Davidson recorded—such as the golden dome of the State Capitol building in Sacramento—can no longer be seen.

Gardner Lookout atop East Peak was built by the Civilian Conservation Corps in 1935–1936. The lookout in residence (since the early 1990s, it has been staffed by volunteers) plays an important role in spotting fires on the mountain and elsewhere in the county. An earlier structure, built in 1901 through financing by the *San Francisco Examiner*, was used for marine communications until 1919, and as a fire lookout from 1921. It was blown down by high winds in the early 1930s. Edwin Burroughs Gardner (1880–1935) was the first chief warden of the Tamalpais Fire District. East Peak itself is an erosion-resistant block of the metamorphic rock quartz tourmaline.

▊ Tavern Pump Trail

Old Railroad Grade (below Mile Marker 8) to Fern Creek Trail: .33 mile

TERRAIN: Chaparral and light woodland (MMWD)

ELEVATION: From 2,080 to 1,920 feet; steep

INTERSECTING TRAIL(s): None

To reach Tavern Pump Trail, descend Old Railroad Grade ½ mile from Ridgecrest Boulevard. If ascending the grade, Tavern Pump Trail is ¼ mile above the top of Miller Trail.

The trail begins in a forest of laurels and tanbark oaks. A bit lower, manzanitas line the way. Halfway down, Tavern Pump Trail crosses a pair of seeps supporting a clump of giant chain ferns. Just below, a newer bridge carries the trail over Fern Creek.

The trail drops toward a water tank and a building. It ends there, at a signed junction with Fern Creek Trail, which rises left to the East Peak parking lot and drops right to Old Railroad Grade. Azaleas impart fragrance here in late spring and early summer.

Steps lead down to the tank and the blue building housing the "tavern pump." Water from Fern Creek was pumped up to the Tavern of Tamalpais, which stood at today's East Peak parking area. The tavern was built in 1896 as part of the Mountain Railway project, and rebuilt, smaller, in 1923 after a fire. It remained open, offering light fare, after the railway ceased operating in 1929.

During World War II, it housed soldiers stationed on the mountain. It was in total disrepair when MMWD razed it 1950. The pump, meanwhile, still delivers water up to the East Peak area.

Upper Fern Creek Trail

Ridgecrest Boulevard to Old Railroad Grade: .77 mile

Terrain: Upper half through chaparral with loose rock; lower part riparian, wooded and rocky (MMWD)

Elevation: From 2,340 to 1,580 feet; extremely steep

Intersecting Trail(s): Tavern Pump (.4 mile)

Fern Creek descends some 2,000 feet before flowing into Redwood Creek in Muir Woods. What is now designated as Upper Fern Creek Trail—the "upper" is new—follows the creek's higher reaches. Lower Fern Creek Trail (formerly Fern Canyon Trail) is separated from it by nearly 2 miles and borders the creek on its final stretch.

Fern Creek Trail is historic, appearing on the first published hiking map in 1898. It is also fairly well used as a hiker's shortcut to and from the top of the mountain, bypassing 3 miles of Old Railroad Grade. But in 2000, concerned about safety and erosion issues, MMWD closed the trail, with no plans to reopen it. Then, in 2002, prompted by pressure from the hiking community and aided by funds from Proposition 12 (the Safe Neighborhood Parks, Clean Water, Clean Air and Coastal Protection Bond Act), the water district undertook a major repair project. Marin Conservation Corps crews "improved 1,100 linear feet of the trail, rebuilt 10 staircases, installed 136 crib stairs [two-sided stair structures] and used 160 eight-foot salvaged railroad ties." Still, be careful; many hikers, weary on their way down from a trip to the summit, still stumble here.

Since the top of Upper Fern Creek Trail is accessible by car, it will be described downhill. It starts southbound from just below the East Peak parking lot. The topmost 125-yard section, between the one-way upper and lower arms of Ridgecrest Road, is little used. The Ridgecrest crossing is marked by white lines and an MTSP sign.

Upper Fern Creek Trail then descends very steeply through chaparral. There are southern views over the canyon. After a plunging bend left, the drop becomes somewhat more gradual. The trail passes beneath a telephone line, and a water pipeline joins on the left.

In .4 mile, the trail meets a water tank and the building that houses the Tavern Pump. The pump sends water through the pipeline (on a narrow sliver of MTSP property in the midst of MMWD lands) to the East Peak area, where the Tavern of Tamalpais once stood. Steps lead down left to the pump, and to a stand of azaleas. Tavern Pump Trail, rising to Old Railroad Grade, sets off, signed, to the right.

Upper Fern Creek Trail continues straight. From the middle of the next bend left, a path (now blocked) once set off straight ahead. Around the bend, the trail drops to cross Fern Creek. A newer bridge carries the trail to the creek's left bank, where it remains.

Framing the bridge is a stand of chain ferns, one of several fern species encountered along the creek. The largest of Marin's ferns, they often reach 9 feet in height. Look on the undersides of the fronds (leaves) and you might see the spore clusters (sori) arranged in chainlike formations, which give the fern its name.

The trail follows the creek down through the lovely, forested canyon. Several short but tricky drops over boulders and roots must be negotiated. A long series of steps now covers almost all of the lower route.

Upper Fern Creek Trail ends at a bend in Old Railroad Grade, amidst some huge redwoods. Hogback FR is .4 mile to the left. Right leads to Miller Trail (.1 mile) and the West Point Inn (1 mile). Fern Creek itself continues under the grade through a culvert.

■ Verna Dunshee Trail

Loop around East Peak: .71 mile

TERRAIN: Chaparral and rock; asphalt; heavily used (MMWD, MTSP)

ELEVATION: Around 2,400 feet; almost level

INTERSECTING TRAIL(S): Temelpa (.3 mile)

Over the decades, millions of visitors who have taken this loop trail have been rewarded by its unsurpassed views. A self-guided trail-walk brochure keyed to numbered stops along the loop is sold at the Friends of Mt. Tam's Interpretive Center, and the group conducts guided loop walks on weekends. (The late Otto Reutinger also wrote a guide to the trail [1986, reprinted in 1992].)

In 2004, Verna Dunshee Trail underwent improvements to make it compliant with the Americans with Disabilities Act (ADA). Low stone curbs; additional benches; and a resurfaced western section, which formerly went over railroad ties, now make Verna Dunshee truly wheelchair accessible.

We'll follow the Verna Dunshee loop counterclockwise from the bathrooms. This level clearing was the terminus of the famed Mountain Railway, in operation from 1896 to 1929. Here, too, stood—its foundations still evident—the railroad's Tavern of Tamalpais. After falling into extreme disrepair, it was razed by the water district in 1950. A plaque at the start of the loop identifies Verna Dunshee: *The First Lady of the State Park System, She Did So Much for So Many.*

Stop 1 is by an interpretive sign that calls out features that can be seen to the southeast on clear, fogless days. Distant landmarks include the Diablo Range east of Hollister (120 miles away, and now very rarely visible), Sutro Tower in San Francisco (14 miles), Montara Mountain on the San Mateo coast (26 miles), and the ocean horizon (58 miles). Alas, the pay telescope has been removed. The four choice tables here each carry dedications. One says, *In Loving Memory of Joyce & Ron Lake* (I worked with Ron at the Federal Home Loan Bank of San Francisco in the 1970s).

Shrubs have been cleared to open the views at Stops 2 and 3. At .2 mile (Stop 4), a railing surrounds Sunrise Point. This was the site of the famous Tamalpais Locator, a spotting scope that helped visitors identify distant landmarks. A stone bench carved with the words "Sunrise Point" provides a place to sit and enjoy the views. Three Bay Area peaks taller than Tam—Mount St. Helena to the north, Mount Diablo to the east, and Mount Hamilton to the south—may be visible. On a sparkling winter day, the snow-covered Sierra, some 160 miles away, can be discerned. A few feet beyond Sunrise Point, the trail edges beneath Profile Rock (Stop 5), named for its resemblance to a face in profile.

At .3 mile, Dunshee meets the signed top of Temelpa Trail. After a rerouted, gradual start, Temelpa drops precipitously to Hoo-Koo-E-Koo FR and Mill Valley's Summit Avenue. Only nimbler hikers should attempt its full length.

Some 100 feet beyond is a bench and Stop 6. Just past, a slide shored by railroad ties has been dubbed the "Great Wall of Mt. Tam." (You have to lean over to read the sign.) The "wall" was built in February 1982, a month after a massive slide triggered by Marin's heaviest rainstorm in decades came to rest in a redwood grove just above Hoo-Koo-E-Koo FR.

Next, no longer signed, is the upper end of Indian Fire Trail. Lower entry points to this extremely steep trail are closed for erosion and safety reasons, and to give vegetation a chance to cover the scarred landscape. Nonetheless, visitors sometimes venture on its uppermost, mildly sloping section to visit the quartz tourmaline rock outcropping known as North Knee.

Views open north (Stops 7 to 10) to Mendocino County on clear days. Much nearer are Bon Tempe and Lagunitas Lakes. The new benches make great rest stops to enjoy the long vistas. At .6 mile (Stop 10), a plaque on a rock to the right carries the inscription: *Back to the Mountain in the Fullness of Life*. It is dedicated to George Grant, who died at seventy-two in 1914, and his wife, Grace Adelaide, who passed away the following year. George Grant was a former "Cariboo" (Klondike) gold miner who came to be called the "old man of the mountain." His signature appears on the East Peak summit register of 1887. Old maps show a Grant Trail up from West Point.

The repaved section of Dunshee begins immediately beyond the Grant plaque. Though there's a noticeable descent, it's far better for wheelchair users than the former dirt/railroad tie trail bed. Dunshee's original, more level routing was abandoned after a slide; the closed route is still evident to the left.

Back on level terrain, Dunshee passes a section of railroad track laid in conjunction with the 1996 centennial gala celebration of Mountain Railway, when, in a recreation of the tavern era, guests dined elegantly in a tent. Mount Tamalpais Interpretive Association (now Friends of Mt. Tam) erected the adjacent Gravity Car Barn, which is open on weekends. Don't miss the descriptive panels on the railway's history. At the end of the loop, Plankwalk Trail rises .3 mile to the lookout tower atop East Peak.

Verna Dunshee first hiked on Tam in 1913 while a student at the University of California, Berkeley. After she and her husband, Bertram, moved to Ross in 1920, both became activists for preserving Marin's open space within state and county parks; Mrs. Dunshee served as president of the Tamalpais Conservation Club in 1950–1951. The trail was dedicated to her by the California State Parks Rangers Association in 1973, the year she died. The loop is sometimes called "Twenty-Minute Trail," for the length of the walk (the brochure now suggests 30 minutes). It was also once known as Race Track Trail.

Gardner Lookout atop East Peak was built by the Civilian Conservation Corps in 1935–1936.

The view from the Verna Dunshee Trail: Mill Valley, Richardson Bay Bridge, and beyond.

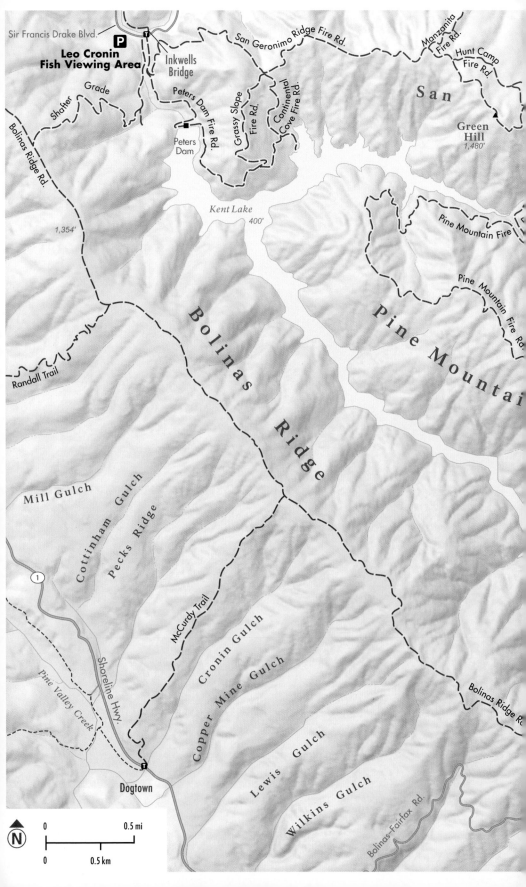

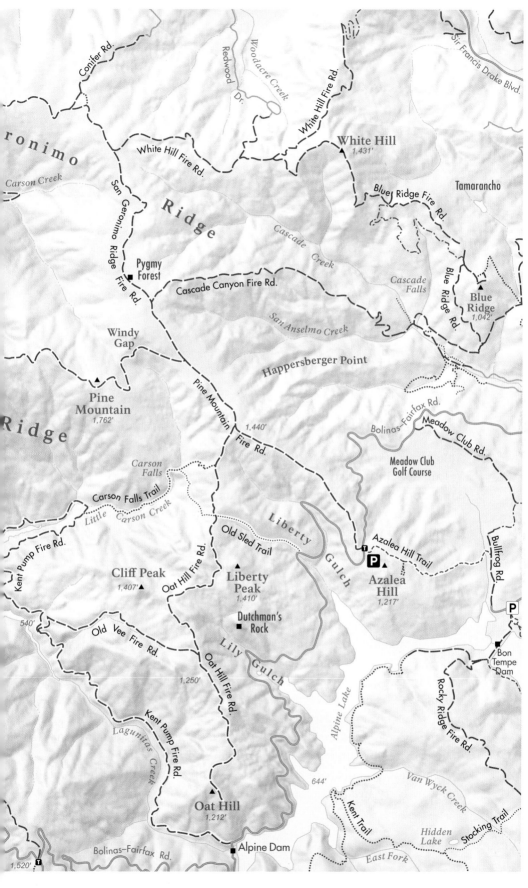

Kent Lake, largest of the MMWD's five reservoir lakes on Mt. Tamalpais.

TRAILHEAD THREE: KENT LAKE/PINE MOUNTAIN

A huge tract of completely pristine, relatively little-visited open space is bounded by Fairfax-Bolinas Road on the south, Sir Francis Drake Boulevard to the north, San Geronimo Ridge on the east, and Bolinas Ridge to the west. It is part of the Mt. Tamalpais watershed, and MMWD acquired almost all of it after World War II in preparation for creating Kent Lake, Marin's largest reservoir. Some call the area Pine Mountain for its highest peak (third tallest in Marin, after Tamalpais and Big Rock Ridge), or Kent Lake. (Carson Country, for Little Carson and Big Carson Creeks, which flow into Kent Lake, is used in *Marin Flora*.)

One reason the area remained untouched is that it was long the domain of private hunting clubs. These clubs—including Lagunitas Rod and Hunting, Big Trees, and Redwood—maintained isolated hunting camps for members. In 1946, MMWD began condemnation proceedings to purchase more than 6,000 acres in the Carson watershed. Stanford University was paid $55,000 for its roughly 2,000 acres, which had been acquired in 1892 after a personal loan made by Leland Stanford to James Shafter went unpaid. The acquisition process was finally completed in 1977, when MMWD swapped the Meadow Club Golf Course for 2,200 additional acres of Carson Country.

There are several access points to the vast area. None have water fountains, so always carry an adequate supply during visits.

1. Azalea Hill—The Azalea Hill parking lot, at the highest point of Fairfax-Bolinas Road (Mile Marker 3.75) and a mile above the Meadow Club Golf Course, is a popular trailhead. Directly across the road (west) is Pine Mountain FR, the longest route in this book.

2. Leo T. Cronin Viewing Area—This is the closest parking to Kent Lake. It was dedicated on October 21, 1995, to Leo T. Cronin, an MMWD director who championed fish and fisheries across California and who died earlier that year. The lot, beside Sir Francis Drake Boulevard (Mile Marker 15.25) at the Shafter Bridge, is jammed when the salmon return but is otherwise quiet. There is a one-hour parking limit, and the nearest alternate spots are ¼ mile west on Drake. There is also an outhouse. Across Drake, a bridge over the junction of San Geronimo and Lagunitas Creeks leads to the Cross Marin Trail through Samuel P. Taylor State Park.

3. Alpine Dam—Kent Pump FR sets off from Alpine Dam past Mile Marker 7.80 of Fairfax-Bolinas Road. Across the dam, where the road makes a hair-pin turn and begins to climb, is the foot of Cataract Trail. Earlier on Fairfax-Bolinas Road are the base of Old Sled Trail (Mile Marker 4.83) and an entry to charming Lily Lake (Mile Marker 5.98).

4. Fairfax-Bolinas Road/Ridgecrest Boulevard junction—Directly access Bolinas Ridge FR and the Coastal Trail from the junction of Ridgecrest Boulevard and Fairfax-Bolinas Road, where there are a handful of parking spaces.

5. Marin County Parks—San Geronimo Ridge and Carson Country can also be approached through Cascade, White Hill, Summit, Conifer, Sylvestris, and Manzanita Fire Roads in MCP's Cascade, White Hill, and Giacomini Preserves.

Suggested Loops from Azalea Hill
1. Pine Mountain FR, 1.1 miles to Oat Hill FR—left, .2 mile, to Carson Falls Trail—right, 1.1 miles, to Little Carson Falls then Kent Pump FR—left, 1.4 miles, to Old Vee FR—left, 1.2 miles, to Oat Hill FR—left, 1.7 miles, to Pine Mountain FR—right, 1.1 miles, to start. **7.8 miles total**

2. Pine Mountain FR, 8.8 miles, to end at second San Geronimo Ridge FR junction—right, 4.4 miles, on San Geronimo Ridge FR and Pine Mountain FR, to start. **13.2 miles total**

Suggested Loop from Leo Cronin Viewing Area
Peters Dam FR, .2 mile, to San Geronimo Ridge FR—left, 1.2 miles, to Grassy Slope FR—right, .8 mile, to Peters Dam FR—straight, 1.8 miles, to start. **4.0 miles total**

◼ Azalea Hill Trail

Fairfax-Bolinas Road to Bon Tempe Creek: .85 mile

TERRAIN: Part grassland, part woodland (MMWD)

ELEVATION: From 1,080 to 1,180 to 650 feet; steep, extremely steep in parts

INTERSECTING TRAIL(S): None

Note: Azalea Hill Trail is in extremely poor condition, with sections dangerous and indistinct.

Azalea Hill Trail sets off directly from the Azalea Hill parking spaces. Across Fairfax-Bolinas Road is Pine Mountain FR. The opening uphill is fire road–width, but with deep gullies. A sign warns that MMWD lands are open only sunrise to sunset; previously, Azalea Hill was a popular locale for stargazing.

Just about every step upward brings new landmarks into view. In rapid order, Pine Mountain, White Hill, Loma Alta, Big Rock—four of the tallest peaks in Marin—become visible. There is then a view down to the Meadow Club Golf Course and, well beyond, San Pablo Bay. At a path left is the first glimpse of Tam's East Peak summit.

Next, Bald Hill, the ridges above China Camp, the Richmond-San Rafael Bridge, and Mt. Diablo, 40 miles east, are added. Hundreds of introduced daffodils bring even more color in late winter to the rich native wildflower display.

At .2 mile, the fire road crests. Bicycles are not permitted beyond. (Mountain bikers have long called for improving a continuing route over the eastern slope of Azalea Hill as an off-road connection between the lakes and Pine Mountain.) A path at the crest leads to the 1,217-foot top of Azalea Hill (noted by a survey marker), a side trip definitely worth taking. Wade through the shrubby leather oak and manzanita and over the serpentine rocks to check out even broader views.

Continuing east on the trail, Bon Tempe Lake, 500 feet below, suddenly becomes visible in one of Tam's classic vistas. This lovely meadow, laced by paths, is special to many. (I was once best man at a wedding there.)

The route may be said to end where the fire road narrows, and those leery of slippery, rugged terrain should go no farther. The traditional Azalea Hill Trail continues straight, down through a maze of serpentine. An unusual fern at the base of many of the rocks is serpentine fern. Descend with care. As the trail crosses dark, often wet rock, look right for azalea bushes, the showy, fragrant shrub that gives the hill its name. Poison oak intermingles with azalea.

The roughest patch of the trail appears next, but it is quickly followed by a clearer route, left, through a pleasing grove of black oaks and madrones. Still, be cautious of slippery conditions and more poison oak. Isolated rest sites, with views of Mt. Tamalpais across Bon Tempe Lake, beckon.

The trail makes its final descent over a steep, grass- and bracken-covered hillside to a path crossing left and right. Left goes through a boggy area to a crossing (not always dry) of Bon Tempe Creek onto Bullfrog FR. Right leads to the edge of Alpine Lake, so is used by fishermen, and the lower end of the former Liberty Gulch Trail.

▦ Carson Falls (Little Carson) Trail

Oat Hill FR to Kent Pump Road: 1.11 miles

TERRAIN: Light woodland (MMWD)

ELEVATION: From 1,320 to 450 feet; upper half gradual, lower half very steep with parts extremely steep

INTERSECTING TRAIL(S): Old Sled (.3 mile)

The upper part of this trail was carved in 2010 to replace an earlier, deeply eroded, and extremely steep (and now closed) access path to Little Carson Falls. As the main route to the popular falls, it is well traveled.

Carson Falls Trail begins its descent from Oat Hill FR at a signpost ¼ mile below Pine Mountain FR. The trail quickly enters a light forest canopy. Switchbacks are a welcome relief from the treacherous plunge of the old days.

The trail exits the woods into grassland. Willows line Little Carson Creek just above the famous falls. On the left, through a pile of serpentine boulders, unsigned Old Sled Trail sets off uphill back to Oat Hill FR. Fifty yards later is the bridge carrying Carson Falls Trail over the creek, a sign about the endangered foothill yellow-legged frog, and the falls themselves.

Pools here are one of two remaining breeding sites in the MMWD watershed of the foothill yellow-legged frog, a listed species of "special concern" in California. In 2004, MMWD began recruiting docents to be in attendance here on weekends during breeding season, March to early June.

Carson Falls Trail continues right over the bridge, which dates to the 2010 project (though it was designed to look older). Virtually every visitor first goes the few yards left to the rocks looking over Little Carson Falls. In winter, the falls roar. By spring, a riot of wildflowers, with red larkspur most vivid, adds more color. No one is disappointed here any time of the year.

Those continuing on Carson Falls Trail face .1 mile of very difficult going as they descend precipitously on rock stairs along the creek's right bank, at the edge of the falls. Make sure to look back. There are several vantage points of the falls that rival or surpass those above. (Please do not step into the water.)

The route next enters the deep riparian woodland of Little Carson Creek, and is easier to follow. Still, mud, loose rock, and fallen leaves demand caution. This much-less-visited stretch of trail is among the loveliest in the watershed. In winter, the creek roars. At other times, complete quiet reigns. Azaleas are abundant at rivulet crossings; their showy white flowers peak in late spring, exuding a delightful fragrance.

Carson Falls Trail levels as it meets a grove of towering redwoods, several of which are more than 200 feet tall. As this was long a hunting camp, the redwoods here weren't logged. All show burn scars from the big fire of 1945.

Camp Reposo was an early name for the camp. It was also called Big Trees Camp when it was headquarters for the Big Trees Club, whose members held a hunting lease to more than 5,000 acres of Carson Country. This lease was cancelled by MMWD in 1971. The club was criticized for its efforts to bar the public from the lands, its exclusive membership, and its low annual lease payments (11 cents per acre). There were also concerns about pollution of Kent Lake downstream. MMWD tore down the camp in 1972.

Cross the redwood plank bridge to continue. Just into the grassland, a path sets off to the left. The final ¼ mile of Carson Falls Trail was formerly known as Big Trees Road. The rebuilt route is wide as it drops through deep woodland.

The trail meets Kent Pump FR and Kent Lake at a pair of MMWD pump buildings. To the right, 200 feet, is the start of the Pine Mountain Tunnel. It is 3.4 miles left on Kent Pump FR to Alpine Dam and the Fairfax-Bolinas Road. Right, Kent Pump goes 1.1 miles to a dead end at the edge of Kent Lake.

The "Carson" of the name remains unknown, although Kit Carson did pass through Marin in 1846. In an incident that remains shrouded in uncertainty, some accounts say it was Carson who shot and killed three unarmed Mexicans in San Rafael in an infamous Bear Flag Revolt skirmish. Little Carson Falls Trail and Little Carson Trail are alternate names, and perhaps better, as Big Carson Creek has its own waterfall (but no trail to it).

▋ Continental Cove Fire Road

San Geronimo Ridge FR to Continental Cove, Kent Lake: .65 mile

TERRAIN: Light woodland above, deep forest lower (MMWD)

ELEVATION: From 840 to 400 feet; very steep

INTERSECTING TRAIL(S): Peters Dam FR (.5 mile)

To reach Continental Cove FR, take Peters Dam FR from the Shafter Bridge, then stay on either it or San Geronimo Ridge FR where they split. Where the two routes meet again, at a newly signed four-way intersection well higher, Continental Cove FR departs down to Kent Lake.

The upper section of Continental Cove FR is open, dominated by baccharis, a shrub also called coyote brush or dwarf chaparral broom. In winter, female plants produce white crowns of filaments ("pappus," plural, "pappi") that wind-disperse the seeds. At .2 mile, left at a bend, is an impressive Douglas-fir with an unusual heavy growth of foliage 15 feet up.

Continental Cove FR enters deeper woodland, where it remains the rest of the descent. The grade is fairly even, always down. Several shrubs are abundant and showy in fall. Coffeeberry bears clusters of black drupes (drupes, unlike berries, have stones, seeds encased in a hardened ovary wall). Bright red hips adorn wood rose (*Rosa gymnocarpa*). Hazel produces an edible gourmet nut, but birds and squirrels usually find them first. Poison oak leaves seem to glisten particularly red here.

At .5 mile, Peters Dam FR joins on the right. It leads back to Peters Dam. Continue down 300 yards to the shore of Kent Lake. The long lake has numerous coves, but few are named; Continental Cove got its name from the abandoned car that was found here. Dead Douglas-firs, drowned when Kent Lake was raised in 1982, stand eerily in the lake, riddled with woodpecker holes. Tempting as it may be, there is no swimming in this, or any other, reservoir.

■ Grassy Slope Fire Road

Peters Dam FR to San Geronimo Ridge FR: .82 mile

TERRAIN: Mostly Douglas-fir forest; section grassland (MMWD)

ELEVATION: From 400 to 840 feet; steep

INTERSECTING TRAIL(S): None

To reach Grassy Slope FR, follow Peters Dam FR another .7 mile above the dam, to the first intersection (presently unsigned). There is a view of Kent Lake here. Grassy Slope FR sets off uphill left, while Peters Dam FR continues down right.

Immediately, you pass beneath the steep, imposing, grassy slope that gives the route its name. In the early 1950s, this hillside was a "borrow pit," from which dirt was removed to build Peters Dam. (Another such site, its terraces still plainly visible, is just above the dam's spillways.) The hillside has been revegetated, both naturally and by MMWD.

After a horseshoe curve left cutting through the grassy slope, the fire road rises into light woodland. Many of the Douglas-firs have multiple low branches, indicating that they grew before there was competition for sunlight.

A prominent slide, shored up to prevent further collapse, is the reason vehicles are no longer allowed through. Baccharis narrows the way, and you may have to push aside coffeeberry shrubs.

The route crests and Grassy Slope's final descent is lined with broom. Unless you visit after it has been cleared, you may wonder if you are on what is called a fire road. But you are, and there are no side routes upon which to get lost.

Grassy Slope ends at a newly MMWD-signed four-way junction. Left, San

Geronimo Ridge FR drops to Peters Dam FR for a loop option. Straight, San Geronimo Ridge FR continues its long journey to Fairfax-Bolinas Road. Right, Continental Cove FR drops to one end of Peters Dam FR (another loop option), then further down to the shores of Kent Lake.

◾ Kent Pump Fire Road

Fairfax-Bolinas Road/Alpine Dam to Kent Lake: 4.53 miles

TERRAIN: Riparian woodland (MMWD)

ELEVATION: From 640 to 400 feet; almost level

INTERSECTING TRAIL(S): Old Vee FR (2.2 miles), Carson Falls (3.45 miles)

Kent Pump FR (also Alpine-Kent Pump FR) is the longest, uninterrupted, basically level fire road in the Mt. Tamalpais watershed. ("Level" is a relative term on Tam. The pump fire road descends 240 feet, but mostly in the first .3 mile.) It is also tree-lined the entire way, and leads to one of the most remote spots in the Bay Area. Still, the fire road is little visited as its trailhead is 8 winding, up-and-down miles from downtown Fairfax, and the few loop options are arduous.

Kent Pump FR begins directly off Fairfax-Bolinas Road on the near side (from Fairfax) of Alpine Dam. The dam, built in 1918, flooded a tranquil valley and was the centerpiece of the newly formed Marin Municipal Water District. The reservoir provided Marin with so much excess storage capacity that water was sold to the C&H Sugar refinery in Crockett. (C&H helped pay the cost of raising Alpine Dam 8 feet in 1924, to increase capacity.) A pipeline, dubbed the Sugar Line, was laid along today's Sir Francis Drake Boulevard to a pier—which collapsed on the first day of use—at Point San Quentin, where barges were loaded. (During Marin's drought of 1976–1977, the sugar-line system was used in reverse, carrying water from the East Bay over the Richmond-San Rafael Bridge.) In 1941, following the 1937 opening of the Golden Gate Bridge, the dam was raised another 30 feet.

When Alpine Dam overflows, which it occasionally does after heavy rains during wet winters, the waterfall is among the most impressive in the county. (Note that the dam's slippery steps are posted as off limits.) Remnants of stone works, including an old fountain, show that entry to the fire road was once grander. Now, you need to bend low under the gate to start. An MMWD signpost says it is 4.8 miles to the end; my measurement came out a bit shorter, 4.53 miles.

The broad fire road begins with a steep ¼-mile drop. At the end of the descent, an MMWD service road comes in from the left. It goes .2 mile to a pair of pump buildings, and offers a head-on view of the dam, worth a visit when water is spilling over.

Now settle in for a long, level walk or bike ride in the woods. Six species, all encountered right at the start, account for virtually all the trees. Tallest, with straight trunks, are redwoods, Douglas-firs, and tanbark oaks. Some of the oldest trees still bear black scars from the big fire of 1945. Laurels, trunks twisting to the sunlight, are perhaps most numerous. Maples drop their leaves in winter after a fall foliage color display. Madrones are found more in the less dense, sunnier, later miles. Shrubs such as ceanothus; several species of ferns; and, of course, wildflowers, add to the lushness. Look closely at the many small holes on the road's right edge and you may see spiders quickly retreating.

Lagunitas Creek flows freely in the canyon at left, released for the first time after the succession of Lagunitas, Bon Tempe, and Alpine Dams. Above the creek's far side rises the densely treed, trailless northeast wall of Bolinas Ridge. Enjoy the serene landscape, apart from civilization's noises.

The few landmarks are man-made, placed by MMWD. The pair of old pipelines that run under the fire road are visible in the bigger bends, supported by stone trestles. Numbered green MMWD markers, the "KP" referring to "Kent Pump," mark culverts. Blue numbered posts with "A" are found at metal drainage covers. At KP9/KP10, a seep nourishes the lovely, and uncommon, scarlet monkeyflower (*Mimulus cardinalis*). Look for its bright red flowers in early summer.

Though trees line the entire way, sunlight increases, and sections of the fire road can be hot in summer. At 1.7 miles, pavement on the left shores up a slide. Just past, on rocks on the right, look for bright spots of color: in fall, the vibrantly red California fuchsia, and in summer, the tall, spectacular leopard lily (*Lilium pardalinum*).

The first of Kent Pump's two intersections is at almost 2.2 miles (or 100 yards past the blue marker A7). Old Vee FR, marked by a signpost, rises very steeply to Oat Hill FR. A tough loop can be made by going left on Oat Hill FR, then left again on Carson Falls Trail, which returns to Kent Pump FR, 1.35 miles ahead.

There are glimpses of the pump buildings at the road's end, not far off across the water. But Kent Pump FR, which had been trending northwest, now begins a long meander northeast, following the arm of Kent Lake fed by Little Carson Creek. The grass- and chaparral-covered top of Pine Mountain Ridge comes into view high on the left.

At 3.4 miles, a short descent leads to the heart, or raison d'être, of the fire road. First, Carson Falls Trail branches right. It rises gently ¼ mile to historic Big Trees Camp, then very steeply along the creek to Little Carson Falls. Just past is a 200-foot-long connector to the west end of the Pine Mountain Tunnel. Take the short side trip beside Little Carson Creek to see a piece of Marin history.

When Alpine Dam was constructed, lake water was drawn downhill via pipeline to this tunnel; the fire road was built for the pipeline. The tunnel went under Pine Mountain toward Fairfax. The Fairfax outlet is at the far end of Pine Mountain Tunnel FR, a continuation of Concrete Pipeline FR. The old tunnel was abandoned for water conveyance in 1971 but it still used for storage. Eventually, MMWD plans to decommission it entirely.

Though a sign says the dead end on Kent Pump is .5 mile ahead, there is actually a bit over 1 mile remaining. A power line is a companion the remainder of the way.

The fire road bends back, heading almost due west. First, it drops beside the lowest reaches of the Little Carson. Then Kent Lake becomes visible. Long-dead but still ramrod-straight redwoods rise from the lakebed.

The fire road passes a short rise right to a pump building, then continues a few more yards beyond another pump house before simply disappearing into Kent Lake. (The route once went farther, before the dam was raised in 1982.) A sign notes the dead end, with no continuation possible.

Though pumps and power lines make the spot less than pristine, this is still a magical place. The nearest paved road is miles away, and the effort required to get here all but guarantees a private visit. Look atop the dead redwoods—killed by the rising waters of Kent Lake—for osprey nests. Ospreys, once severely imperiled by DDT spraying, made a comeback once the spraying was banned. In recent years, more than a dozen nests have been observed near here, making Kent Lake one of California's major osprey breeding grounds. The nests, which can hold two to four young, are active in late winter and early spring. (An interesting bit of information: when an osprey pulls a fish from the lake, it shifts the fish in its claws to carry it head-forward.)

▦ Oat Hill Fire Road

Pine Mountain FR to Oat Hill: 2.70 miles

TERRAIN: Serpentine chaparral, occasional light woodland (MMWD)

ELEVATION: From 1,400 to 1,300 feet; rolling

INTERSECTING TRAIL(s): Carson Falls (.2 mile), Old Sled (.6 mile), Old Vee FR (1.7 miles)

Because Oat Hill FR is a dead end, most visitors only travel the section to Carson Falls Trail. But the fire road continues well past, and offers great views and solitude.

Entering Pine Mountain FR from Fairfax-Bolinas Road, Oat Hill is the first fire road intersection, after 1.1 miles of climbing. A shortcut path goes left at the first summit; the true start of Oat Hill FR, marked by a signpost, is a few yards down.

Oat Hill FR opens downhill, with the rest of the route rolling gently along the ridge. In ¼ mile on the right is Carson Falls Trail. It descends to Little Carson Falls, so most Oat Hill travelers depart here. Now comes the less-visited section of the fire road.

At .6 mile, just beyond power poles perched on a knoll, the historic Old Sled Trail, unsigned and faint, crosses. Left, over the fire road's edge, leads down to Fairfax-Bolinas Road at Mile Marker 4.83.

In another ⅓ mile, again near a line of power poles, there is a dramatic shot of Bon Tempe Lake. Beyond the power line knoll is another stunning vista, the distinctive outcropping called Dutchman's Rock. Behind is the whole north face of Mt. Tamalpais. Alpine Lake also comes into view. In fall, when the water level is low, Cheda Island, submerged the rest of the year, stands out.

The hills left and right are among Marin's tallest. Left is chaparral-crowned, 1,410-foot Liberty Peak. It is named for the Liberty family, who ran a dairy on these slopes in the late 1800s. Just ahead on the right is Cliff Peak, 1,407 feet.

Climb out of the saddle (long called Bathtub Gap, for an old tub there). To the left, just before the crest on the shoulder of Liberty Peak, is Lily Gulch. Dutchman's Rock rises above it.

Just around the bend, the fire road passes a band of serpentine, and new perspectives open. The route descends gently. Just under ½ mile past Lily Gulch is a fork. Signed Old Vee FR departs right, descending steeply to near the mid-point of long Kent Pump FR. Signs here note that the remaining mile of Oat Hill FR is a dead end for all users.

Oat Hill FR now passes through woodland. Most of the trees are bay laurels and Douglas-firs. This is remote country. At 2.3 miles, a path left was once a fork of Oat Hill FR, but is no longer cleared. Continue straight.

Oat Hill FR exits the woods onto a grassy plateau. There used to be a breath-taking view down to Alpine Lake, but trees now obscure it. Still, there are sights and places to sit and enjoy them. Signs warn that the area ahead, leading to a ranger residence, is closed to the public.

Oat Hill presumably gained its name from oat grasses (genus *Avena*) across its summit. Mt. Tamalpais's three oat species—*A. barbata* is the most common—were all introduced with the arrival of the first settlers and their livestock in the 1800s.

▪ Old Sled Trail

Fairfax-Bolinas Road to Little Carson Trail at Little Carson Falls: 1.03 miles

TERRAIN: Light riparian woodland; rocky (MMWD)

ELEVATION: From 780 to 1,260 to 1,020 feet; very steep

INTERSECTING TRAIL(S): Oat Hill FR (.5 mile)

This historic trail is one of the oldest on Mt. Tamalpais. During the second half of the nineteenth century, when it was broader, it was used to bring dairy products down, presumably sometimes by sled, from the upper pastures of Liberty Ranch. It is not signed at its ends or single intersection, and is only minimally maintained, yet still appears on all MMWD maps. Old Sled is presently among the more marginal of recognized MMWD trails.

Old Sled sets off from a small parking area by Mile Marker 4.83 on Fairfax-Bolinas Road. (There is more parking across the pavement.) Set off uphill from the signpost; the creek is to your left. The initial few yards are indistinct and very steep. Things improve, but not much.

Old Sled ascends the creek's left bank. It can roar in winter but is otherwise barely noticeable. The trail is on the edge of lightly wooded, riparian terrain (left) and shrubby serpentine (right). False lupine (*Thermopsis macrophylla*) is abundant, its yellow flowers in bloom in spring. As summer approaches, bright red silene, yellow mariposa lily (genus *Calochortus*), and blue brodiaea put on a colorful floral show. Tall azalea bushes thrive in the creek bed.

At ¼ mile, a look back reveals a vista of Mt. Tamalpais. A bit higher, Alpine Lake can also be seen.

The trail passes a grove of Sargent cypress trees. After a short stretch of grassland, Old Sled crests at Oat Hill FR. A view from Bolinas Ridge across Kent Lake to Pine Mountain opens. The intersection is unsigned; there are three utility poles on the knoll just to the right. Oat Hill FR leads right to Pine Mountain FR and left to Old Vee FR.

Old Sled continues directly across Oat Hill FR; the opening here, over a few rocks, is also indistinct. This section, sometimes called Old Spool Trail, is in even poorer repair than the first half. Stretches may be overgrown and there are a couple of short leaps over gullies. The trail alternates between light woodland and grassland. Look for azaleas at rivulet crossings.

Old Sled cuts through an area of barren serpentine and ends at Carson Falls Trail. Several serpentine boulders stand at the junction. Some 50 yards left on Carson Falls Trail are the famous falls and an MMWD sign warning visitors that this is a home for the endangered yellow-legged frog. (Off-trail visitors have imperiled them still further.)

◼ Old Vee Fire Road

Kent Pump FR to Oat Hill FR: 1.09 miles

TERRAIN: Mix of chaparral and light woodland above, forested lower (MMWD)

ELEVATION: From 440 to 1,240 feet; very steep

INTERSECTING TRAIL(S): None

Hardy travelers who make it onto Old Vee will likely have it to themselves. Few visit because of its remoteness, 2 miles or more from any vehicular access point. Old Vee is also very steep, and has no intersections. The shortest loop incorporating it is a hilly 7-plus miles.

The most direct way to Old Vee is via Kent Pump FR, followed 2.1 miles from Alpine Dam. The Old Vee intersection is signed.

The lower half of Old Vee is very steep. Trees provide welcome shade. There are few landmarks other than MMWD signs, where culverts carry rivulets under the road to the stream.

The upper half of Old Vee, above the "OV4" post, is less grueling and a bit more open. Still, there are no downhill steps to relieve the climb. To the left is a chaparral-covered, sunny slope. To the right is one of the densest of the Carson Country's many haunting laurel forests. It beckons across a shallow channel paralleling the fire road. This stream, unnoticed much of the year, roars after winter rains, and has several waterfalls.

Old Vee crests and ends as it meets Oat Hill FR at a signed junction. Right on Oat Hill is, as the sign says, a dead end. Left, it is 1.7 miles to Pine Mountain Road.

The "Old Vee" refers to the late Jim Vitek, long-time MMWD trail builder and one of the most knowledgeable of all Tam's grand old men.

◼ Peters Dam Fire Road

Sir Francis Drake Boulevard at Shafter Bridge to Continental Cove FR: 1.83 miles

TERRAIN: Light woodland, section paved (MMWD); western segment part of Bay Area Ridge Trail

ELEVATION: From 200 to 840 feet; first section level, second half steep up and down

INTERSECTING TRAIL(S): Creek Trail (.1 mile), San Geronimo Ridge FR (.2 mile), connector road to dam (.2 mile), service road (.9 mile), Grassy Slope FR (1.6 miles)

Peters Dam FR is much the easiest entry to Kent Lake. It begins, presently without a sign, behind a gate along Sir Francis Drake Boulevard (Mile Marker 15.25) at the green-painted Shafter Bridge. There are actually two fire roads here, on either side of Lagunitas Creek; Peters Dam FR is to the left when entering (along the creek's right bank). The other route is Shafter Grade.

The opening segment of the fire road, part of the Bay Area Ridge Trail, is level. A sign warns visitors to be quiet so as not to disturb the endangered coho salmon. Lagunitas Creek flows year round, as MMWD releases cold water from Kent Lake to help sustain the salmon and other riparian life. In 100 yards is a second, open gate. Just beyond, the fire road's edge is brightened in May and June by a riot of red ribbons (*Clarkia concinna*), one of the densest concentrations of this showy wildflower in Marin. At $\frac{1}{6}$ mile, San Geronimo Ridge FR and the Bay Area Ridge Trail branch left and up at a gate to begin a long journey toward Azalea Hill.

There is another junction 200 feet later. To the right, an MMWD service road goes to the base of the dam. (There are several such roads in the dam area. None are signed or designated as trails, but are open for exploring.) Beyond, Peters Dam FR is asphalt-covered for a stretch, and begins to climb. Sticky monkeyflower lines the way.

Peters Dam, its slope covered with grass, comes into view. In winter, you might hear water roaring down the spillways.

Keep climbing. A bit below the top of the dam, a rough shortcut path on the left cuts 500 yards off the route. Bend right. You crest the dam at .9 mile. Go a few yards straight toward the spillway to see a boulder with a pair of plaques, one dedicated when the dam was built (1954) and the other when it was raised (1981). Straight ahead is another of the service roads, which can be followed to the other side of the spillway and to Shafter Grade. The dam overflows in only the wettest of winters, when MMWD's Mt. Tamalpais water storage capacity reaches 100 percent. It's a spectacular sight.

Cross the dam. At the far end, a path drops right, to the lake. (I've watched Marin County's water rescue team practice here.) This second half is sometimes called Upper Peters. There is a pump building on the left, then an array of valves on the right.

The fire road begins a steady, mildly strenuous uphill climb. Among the joys are the many shrubs (which may be considered small trees) lining the route. They are *Ceanothus thyrsiflorus*, variously known as blue blossom and mountain, wild, and California lilac; they put on a dazzling display of blue in late winter and early spring. There are several other ceanothus species in Marin, including one unique to the county (*C. masonii*), found only on Bolinas Ridge. Also delightful are views over Kent Lake. It takes some adjusting to realize you are in Marin, not a far more remote setting.

Enjoy another lake view where the fire road was briefly paved to shore up the hillside. Keep climbing. There is an unsigned junction ⅔ mile above the dam. The broad route up left is Grassy Slope Road. Continue straight, or right.

After a short level stretch, Peters Dam FR descends ¼ mile through ever-deepening woodland. The fire road ends when it meets Continental Cove FR at an unmarked intersection. Right, it is 300 yards down to Kent Lake, at Continental Cove. Left is a ½-mile climb to San Geronimo Ridge.

Thomas K. Kent, one of William Kent's five sons, served on MMWD's board of directors for thirty-two years, and was president when the dam was built in 1954. James S. Peters, MMWD's general manager at the time, was the dam's chief engineer.

■ Pine Mountain (Truck) Fire Road

Fairfax-Bolinas Road to San Geronimo Ridge FR (second junction): 8.85 miles

TERRAIN: Serpentine chaparral, light and deep riparian woodland (MMWD)

ELEVATION: From 1,080 to 1,730 to 420 to 1,180 feet; rolling to very steep

INTERSECTING TRAIL(S): Oat Hill FR (1.1 miles), San Geronimo Ridge FR (1.5 miles)

Pine Mountain FR is long, varied, remote, and beautiful. Traveling it is a requisite to fully appreciate the splendor of Carson Country. Bikers and equestrians visit but few hikers make the full crossing. The main obstacle is length.

Covering all Pine Mountain FR requires a total journey of nearly 14 miles from either the Sylvestris FR entry or the more popular Azalea Hill trailhead. (A car shuttle between these two entries shortens the distance to just over 11 miles, but involves long rides.) Also, hikers face two spots (near mile 8) that are regularly overrun by Big Carson Creek after rains.

Pine Mountain Road sets off from Fairfax-Bolinas Road across from the Azalea Hill parking area. The first 1.1 miles are uphill. The views are immediately glorious, and remain so all the way. Turn back for stunning shots of Mt. Tam, Mt. Diablo, San Francisco Bay, the East Bay hills, and Alpine Lake below. To the right are White Hill, Loma Alta, and Big Rock. Near the first crest, .9 mile in, you may see the snow-capped Sierra. The verdant green of the 162-acre Meadow Club Golf Course stands out to the right below.

Serpentine defines the early terrain. Manzanita and chamise are the most abundant shrubs. The showy wildflower, Oakland star tulip (*Calochortus umbellatus*), listed as "rare" in Jepson, is rather abundant here in spring. Its large flowers are white, sometimes with a hint of lavender, and very hairy.

At the first crest, views open north to Mt. St. Helena. The first path left is only a cut for the power poles. Descend a few yards to the true junction with

Oat Hill FR. It is the route to Little Carson Falls, Old Vee FR, and Oat Hill itself.

Pine Mountain FR now descends. The grassy western wall of White Hill is prominent to the right. In a small meadow, covered with yellow goldfields (*Lasthenia* spp.) in spring, a path departs right. A short way in, beside the creek, is what little is left of old Carey Camp.

The fire road bottoms and begins to rise. The first Sargent cypress trees, landmarks along San Geronimo Ridge, begin to appear on both sides of the fire road. There is then a signed fork. Straight ahead is San Geronimo Ridge FR, which can followed more than 6 miles to Sir Francis Drake Boulevard at Shafter Bridge.

Pine Mountain Truck Road heads left, steeply uphill. After 100 yards, the Sargent cypresses are gone. Broad views open on a seemingly untouched landscape. The upper course of Little Carson Creek, from its headwaters to near the falls, is visible in the valley below left.

The uphill eases, briefly. At a low point in the middle of a big bend left is the Saddle (or Windy Gap). It is a Carson Country landmark, visible along many routes and a helpful orientation feature. Through the saddle's indeed often-windy gap, almost all of northwest Marin suddenly opens. Looking straight in, the first major peak is Green Hill, crossed by San Geronimo Ridge FR. Behind is Mt. Barnabe, with its fire lookout, above Samuel P. Taylor State Park. Beyond both is Tomales Bay.

The saddle separates drainages of Little Carson Creek to the south (left), and Big Carson Creek to the north (right). Look up and right to see part of the rock wall built by Chinese laborers 150 years ago to mark the boundary between two Mexican land grants, San Geronimo from Tomales y Baulines. A path goes through the old fence. Well down the creek bed is what is left of Mailliard Camp, once used by hunters. (Adolph Mailliard bought the San Geronimo grant in 1867.)

Continue climbing. The fire road crests .8 mile beyond the San Geronimo Ridge FR split. On the right, an MMWD marker used to note "Pine Mountain Summit." Now, the 50-yard path to the top of Pine Mountain—at 1,762 feet, the third highest peak in Marin—is overgrown The rock wall goes right through the summit. And, sure enough, a few feet away is a lone pine. (Although it may be the grove of older bishop pines encountered later in the fire road that accounts for the name "Pine Mountain.")

A few yards beyond the fire road crest, Kent Lake comes into view and behind it, the forested wall of Bolinas Ridge. The prominent cut on the ridge face was created for a power line. For the remainder of the route, more than 6 miles, no buildings are visible, not even in the far distance.

After passing a stand of laurel (bay) trees, you will encounter several even deeper and more haunting groves. At 3.1 miles, Pine Mountain FR passes under the power line.

In another .2 mile, a short path leads left to a knoll. A more spectacular view knoll is just ahead (3.4 miles), via a steep path up the grass at the edge of the tree line. Take it to its end and you'll understand why the knoll has been dubbed "Sound of Music." (You don't have to veer off to get to a view knoll; one is ahead.)

The fire road passes through another laurel grove, then returns to grassland. At 3.6 miles, a sign notes the short path left to a 20,000-gallon water tank fed by unfortunately named Poison Spring. (There is also a horse hitch and trough, so presumably the water isn't too bad.) The fire road again crests; a red metal post labeled SG 21 marks the spot. This is surely one of Marin's special places.

The prominent path at right is the top of the infamous Paradigm Trail, which descends to lower on Pine Mountain FR. When the illegally cut 2-mile route was discovered by MMWD in 1993, it made front-page news. The builders, one a member of the County Trails Committee, were prosecuted. Warning signs were placed and the route was covered and closed.

Pine Mountain FR now plunges. Be careful, as loose rock and dirt make for slippery footing over the next 2.5 miles. MMWD has even placed signs warning bikers to slow over the steepest sections. There are short stretches of grassland, chaparral, and light woodland. Bracken fern is colonizing the grassland here; it is often a precursor for Douglas-firs to follow. In the woodland are many dying or dead tanbark oaks. Tanoaks were the first of Marin's trees to be diagnosed with Sudden Oak Death syndrome.

At 4.9 miles is a ¼-mile-long stand of bishop pines, the only pine native to Marin. Note the long needles in bunches of two, and tightly closed cones whorled around the branches. The cones open only during fires, reseeding a new generation from the ashes of the old.

Redwoods begin appearing at about 5.4 miles. The fire road then descends very steeply to a seeming fork; take the broad bend right. Huckleberry is abundant, perhaps more so than anywhere else in Marin. Since the area is so little visited, you'll find a plentiful supply of the ripe, sweet, edible, dark berries from mid-August to mid-September to enjoy.

Pine Mountain FR bottoms out at 6.0 miles, just a few yards above Kent Lake. This just may be the most remote spot on any trail or road described in this book. Enjoy the serenity, and 2 fairly level miles. Some of the largest redwoods bear scars from the big 1945 fire. Giant chain ferns grow at rivulet crossings. Look for white clusters of snowberry (*Symphoricarpos mollis*) in fall. At the green PM (Pine Mountain) 11 culvert marker is a cluster of azalea bushes.

Two-tenths of a mile beyond is the first of two (sometimes three) notorious spots where Big Carson Creek floods the fire road each winter. There's no turning back now, so be ready to rock hop. Immediately after a big rain, the route may be impassable. The fire road runs adjacent to the creek to the second tricky crossing. If you make it across here, the third, just ahead, will be easy as it the narrowest.

It's now all uphill. Look up and left as you round a bend to see Green Hill. This can be a bit disheartening, as it is where you need to climb. Serpentine begins glistening in the roadbed, and soon becomes dominant. Sargent cypress trees, which accompany the fire road the rest of the way up, start reappearing by the PM 14 marker. The final slog is tough, particularly given the many miles already covered. But there are occasional trees for shade, and many serpentine-endemic wildflowers to enjoy. Look back and see the saddle, passed 6.5 miles earlier.

Pine Mountain FR ends at a four-way junction. Straight and down is Sylvestris FR, which passes Hunt Camp FR, then drops farther to East Sylvestris Road in San Geronimo. (East Sylvestris Road, an access to Pine Mountain FR, is a very narrow street with parking for only two or three vehicles.) Left and right, both uphill, is San Geronimo Ridge FR. Left leads to the top of Green Hill and on to Peters Dam. Right, it is 2.8 miles back to the eastern San Geronimo Ridge/Pine Mountain FR junction, encountered a long, wonderful journey earlier.

■ San Geronimo Ridge Fire Road

Pine Mountain Truck FR to Peters Dam FR: 6.10 miles

TERRAIN: First half serpentine chaparral, second half light woodland (MCOSD, MMWD); western 4.6 miles is part of Bay Area Ridge Trail

ELEVATION: From 1,390 to 1,530 to 1,170 to 1,400 to 240 feet; rolling, parts steep and rocky

INTERSECTING TRAIL(S): Cascade FR (.4 mile), White Hill FR (1.5 miles), Conifer FR (2.0 miles), Sylvestris FR (2.7 miles), Pine Mountain FR (2.7 miles), Hunt Camp FR (3.6 miles), Manzanita FR (3.8 miles), Continental Cove FR (5.0 miles), Grassy Slope FR (5.0 miles)

Crossing the length of San Geronimo Ridge from Azalea Hill to Shafter Bridge is a wonderful journey, one of Marin's treasures. Mountain bikers may be able to handle a round trip or even a loop—the rolling route is dubbed "17 Knolls" on the Marin County Bicycle Coalition map—but most hikers require a shuttle.

To reach the upper end of San Geronimo Ridge FR, for a one-way, net downhill journey, start west from the Azalea Hill parking area. The fire road here is atop San Geronimo Ridge but usually considered part of Pine Mountain Road (previously described). The first junction, after 1.1 uphill miles, is with Oat Hill FR to the left. Continue straight another ½ mile to the next signed junction, the east end of San Geronimo Ridge FR. Pine Mountain FR branches left here up to Pine Mountain, then down to Kent Lake, then climbs again to rejoin San Geronimo Ridge FR 2.7 miles ahead.

San Geronimo Ridge FR, straight, begins rising over very rocky terrain. Pine Mountain blocks views left, but otherwise, the grand vistas that characterize all of this first half of San Geronimo Ridge FR are in evidence early.

The first junction, right, is with Cascade FR, known as Repack Road in mountain biking lore. At 1,530 feet, this is also the highest point along San Geronimo Ridge FR. Cascade descends very steeply into Marin County Open Space's Cascade Canyon Preserve. (The boundary between MMWD [south] and MCOSD [north] runs down the center of San Geronimo Ridge FR) The fire road is now truly on the ridgeline, the slope of Pine Mountain behind.

While you've likely noticed stunted trees edging the fire road earlier, it is over this next section that Sargent cypresses reach their densest concentration, the famous "Pygmy Forest." This tree grows only in California, virtually always in serpentine soil. Fully mature trees stand here in thickets just 3 to 5 feet high, though many rise 10 to 25 feet. The round, closed cones are distinctive. They open during fires to release their seeds into ashy soil, and long-time visitors tell of hearing cones pop during exceptional heat waves. The lighter green growth is mistletoe, a parasite.

A ½ mile from the Cascade FR junction, San Geronimo Ridge FR meets an open area and briefly descends. Sargent cypresses abruptly disappear, with Douglas-firs, hazels, and laurels taking their place. After a sharp bend left, and more descent, the cypresses return.

At 1.1 miles from the last (Cascade FR) intersection, another MMWD Watershed sign marks the junction with White Hill FR on the right. There are two entries, on either side of a small "tree island." White Hill FR, part of the Bay Area Ridge Trail, meets an access route from Buckeye Circle in Woodacre, then continues over the summit of White Hill. The remaining 4.6 miles of San Geronimo Ridge FR are also part of the Bay Area Ridge Trail.

The fire road trends down to the lovely grassland of Carson Meadow, with views over northwest Marin into Sonoma County. On the right, through a gap in the low fence, a connector down to Conifer FR is marked with an MCOSD "Trail" signpost. Conifer FR itself is just ahead, with a newer signpost. Between the two, a path left through the grass leads to views of the trailless headwaters of Big Carson Creek. Conifer FR goes right, dropping ¾ mile to Conifer Way in Woodacre.

You will pass an old fence line; it long had a California Fish & Wildlife sign warning against poaching. The fire road climbs. This is another rolling section, quite rocky so no fun for runners. Sargent cypresses again line the way. At the next crest, there are views of Mt. Barnabe, the high point of Samuel P. Taylor State Park, and distinctive Black (or Elephant) Mountain. The massive block of Mt. St. Helena, highest peak in the Bay Area, may also be discerned. Next come views of Green Hill, which the fire road will soon pass, and of Pine Mountain Road, coming up from Kent Lake.

San Geronimo Ridge FR bottoms at a four-way junction. Left is Pine Mountain Road. Right, also down, is Sylvestris FR, which drops a mile, passing Hunt Camp FR to East Sylvestris Drive in San Geronimo. Continue straight, and steeply up.

Just up from the junction, pink clarkia flowers brighten the fire road's edge in June and July. The stiff climb up Green Hill is rewarded with a breathtaking vista of Kent Lake, which looks more like a broad river of the Pacific Northwest than a reservoir of Lagunitas Creek. San Geronimo Ridge FR hits its last major high point, just below the 1,480-foot summit of Green Hill. There are still several upslopes ahead, but the route now begins a drop of more than 1,200 feet over the next 3.3 miles. You've done the hard work, now enjoy the descent.

There is a marked change in vegetation. Taller shade trees, particularly Douglas-firs, line the route. There are also many laurels, redwoods, madrones, and tanbark oaks. Sargent cypresses are gone for good. The road's surface is far less rocky here, mostly dirt softened with duff.

It is all downhill to the next intersection, at 3.2 miles. Hunt Camp FR goes right, down to the old Hunt Camp itself before joining Sylvestris FR, a loop option.

A short, roller-coaster section of $\frac{1}{6}$ mile leads to the next junction, with Manzanita FR. It descends over MCOSD land to the northern boundary of the Gary Giacomini Open Space Preserve.

The next section runs 1.2 miles without a junction, thus, one of the more remote parts of Carson Country. It opens with a short climb. The descent brings, briefly, another glimpse straight ahead of Mt. Barnabe, identifiable by the towers and fire lookout on its top. A treeless area owes to a band of serpentine—the last encountered along the long route—running across the fire road, which also opens views. A path drops right, one of several lacing the northeast flank of San Geronimo Ridge over both MCOSD and private lands. Look for the bright yellow flowers of the tree poppy (Papaveraceae family, actually a shrub).

The final intersection along San Geronimo Ridge FR has four spokes, and is now signed. Left is Continental Cove FR, dropping to Peters Dam FR, then the shore of Kent Lake. Straight and up is what may seem to be continuation of San Geronimo Ridge FR but is actually Grassy Slope FR. It too meets Peters Dam FR, and is an alternate, slightly longer route to Sir Francis Drake Boulevard.

San Geronimo Ridge FR and the Bay Area Ridge Trail drop right. This is the most deeply wooded section, and entirely downhill, welcome after the long trek. Shrubs are abundant. Hazel, with its very soft leaves, immediately edges both sides of the road. Currant is common, as is elk clover with its huge leaves. Maples add to the tree list. Look left on the road shelf for showy flowers such as trillium and clintonia.

A ½ mile down, a gated fire road to the right is marked with an MCOSD "No Trail Outlet" sign. Lower, an old fire road left has been returned to nature.

San Geronimo Ridge FR ends when it hits paved Peters Dam FR at a gate. Left leads up to Peters Dam. Right, following Lagunitas Creek, the road meets Sir Francis Drake Boulevard at Shafter Bridge. Across Drake is a bridge over the junction of Lagunitas and San Geronimo Creeks and the Cross Marin Trail. But that's another journey.

▪ Shafter Grade

Shafter Bridge on Sir Francis Drake Boulevard to Bolinas Ridge FR: 1.70 miles

TERRAIN: Redwood/Douglas-fir forest (MMWD)

ELEVATION: From 200 to 1,320 feet; very steep

INTERSECTING TRAIL(S): Lagunitas Creek (.2 mile), maintenance road (.4 mile)

Shafter Grade is a lovely, deeply wooded route that climbs to Bolinas Ridge. Yet few visit more than its opening 300 yards, and even that only in December and January, when it is jammed with people looking for salmon. One reason is that the trailhead lot limits parking to just one hour. (There are a few additional spaces ¼ mile east on Sir Francis Drake Boulevard, but no other options.) Also, the shortest loop option, with the Jewell and Cross Marin Trails, is more than 11 miles. Shafter Grade is very steep, but those who travel it, perhaps with the help of a carpool or by using the West Marin Stage bus that passes right by the trailhead, are well rewarded.

The trailhead parking lot is at the green Shafter Bridge, at Mile Marker 15.25 on Sir Francis Drake Boulevard, west of Lagunitas and just before the Samuel P. Taylor State Park sign. Across the road is the Cross Marin Trail into Samuel P. Taylor Park.

The parking lot for the Leo T. Cronin Fish Viewing Area holds 18 cars. It fills during salmon-viewing season, but is otherwise near empty. (Cronin served on the MMWD Board of Directors and was recognized nationally for his work on restoring fish habitat. He died of a heart attack at age sixty-five at his Fairfax home in 1995.) The lot used to be closed at all times, then was finally opened, partly due to Cronin's efforts, during the salmon migration and spawning winter season. Now it is open year-round, 8 AM to sunset. Make sure to read the informative interpretive signs explaining the life cycle of coho salmon. There is also a portable toilet here.

Shafter Grade begins, signed, behind the gate. (The new sign currently says it's 2.6 miles to Bolinas Ridge. It's actually 1.7 miles.) The level opening yards of Shafter Grade, beside Lagunitas Creek, is one of the best places in the Bay Area to see coho salmon. There aren't many—they are disappearing throughout the central California coast—and are not always easy to spot. Look carefully, or join someone else who appears to be excited about what they're seeing! Lagunitas Creek itself is just emerging from its fourth, and last, dam. As mentioned, MMWD releases cold water from Kent Lake, and thus from Marin's water supply, to help keep Lagunitas Creek viable for coho.

At 200 yards, a strong (in winter) feeder creek goes under the road. At ⅙ mile, signed Lagunitas Creek Trail departs left. It goes just under .2 mile to a dead end at a pool favored by river otters beneath the Kent Lake spillway.

Shafter Grade veers right and up. If the climbing is too stiff, turn back, for it remains tough to the top.

At ⅓ mile is a level area and a junction. The broad, unsigned, unnamed maintenance road left goes to the Kent Lake dam, which you can then cross to connect with Peters Dam FR. Shafter Grade veers right, and up steeply again.

Redwoods and Douglas-firs border the wide route. The largest redwoods are in the earlier going, the largest Douglas-firs a bit farther along. Big-leaf maples color the forest in fall, after which their fallen leaves carpet the duff. Sword ferns line the route. Higher, blackberries—the native California blackberry (*Rubus ursinus*), not the Eurasian import Himalayan blackberry (*R. armeniacus*) with the tasty fruit—crowd the edge. Coffeeberry, hazel, and wood rose are among the other abundant shrubs.

At 1.2 miles is a row of particularly massive Douglas-firs. One has a branch that itself is an enormous tree. Another is of huge girth. Yet another seems tallest of all. You will also have glimpses of the pristine San Geronimo Ridge area and beyond. Ospreys have nested here for years, and if you're lucky, you will hear them calling during the winter nesting season.

Switchbacks carry Shafter Grade ever upward. The redwoods and Douglas-firs are now markedly thinner and shorter.

A bend right and the uphill eases. Just beyond is an old water tank and horse trough, a landmark that tells visitors the summit is near, ¼ mile away. The remaining section of Shafter Grade is more open and sunny.

Shafter Grade ends when it meets Bolinas Ridge FR at a signed junction. The old post says it is 6.5 miles left to Fairfax-Bolinas Road. Another newer sign says it is 6.1 miles. The first trail reached is Randall, in just over 1 mile. To the right, it is 4.6 miles to Jewell Trail and the 11-mile loop back with Cross Marin Trail. Even farther right is Sir Francis Drake Boulevard, also on the West Marin

Stage route for a one-way option. Across Bolinas Ridge FR is a barbed-wire fence; cattle graze the slope down to Olema Valley. Prominent to the west is Inverness Ridge, within Point Reyes National Seashore.

In the late 1850s, Vermont-born brothers Oscar and James Shafter used their legal skills, financial acumen, and political savvy to amass the largest private land holding ever in Marin. Their 1858–1859 property tax bill (25 cents/ acre) listed 93,198 acres—one-quarter of all Marin!—an empire that stretched from the summit ridge of Mt. Tamalpais to Tomales Point.

Oscar Shafter worked for the leading law firm handling Mexican land grant claims, and so had an inside track on opportunities arising in west Marin. He later served on the California Supreme Court, and died in 1873. James Shafter arrived in California in 1855, after a stint in the Wisconsin State Assembly. He was elected to the California State Senate in 1862, became its head, and played a lead role in drafting a new California constitution in 1878–1879. James Shafter was a friend of Leland Stanford and one of the original twenty-three trustees of the college Stanford founded. When Shafter died in 1892, a $45,000 loan from Stanford remained unpaid, and Stanford University gained title to more than 2,000 Shafter acres in the area of today's Kent Lake. (This land was bought by MMWD after a condemnation suit in 1946.) The Shafter family's interests were managed into the twentieth century by Charles Webb Howard, who married Oscar Shafter's daughter, Emma.

Equestrians enjoying an outing above Kent Lake.

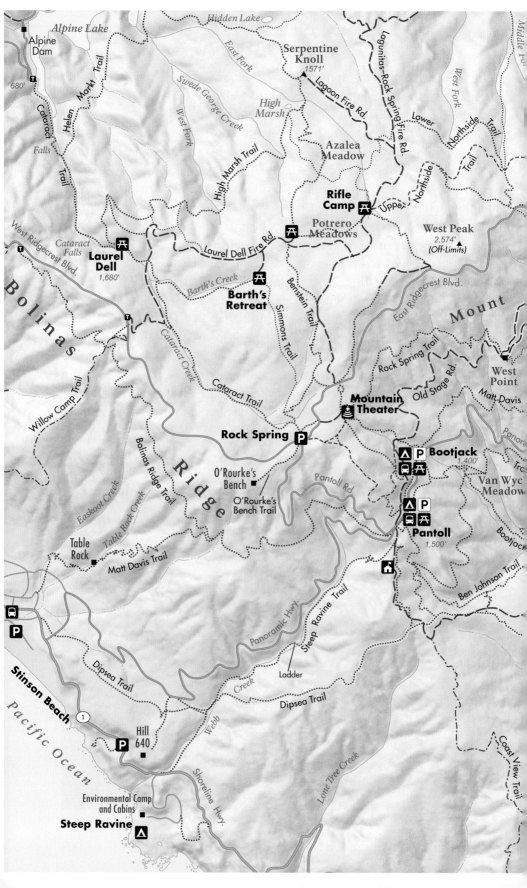

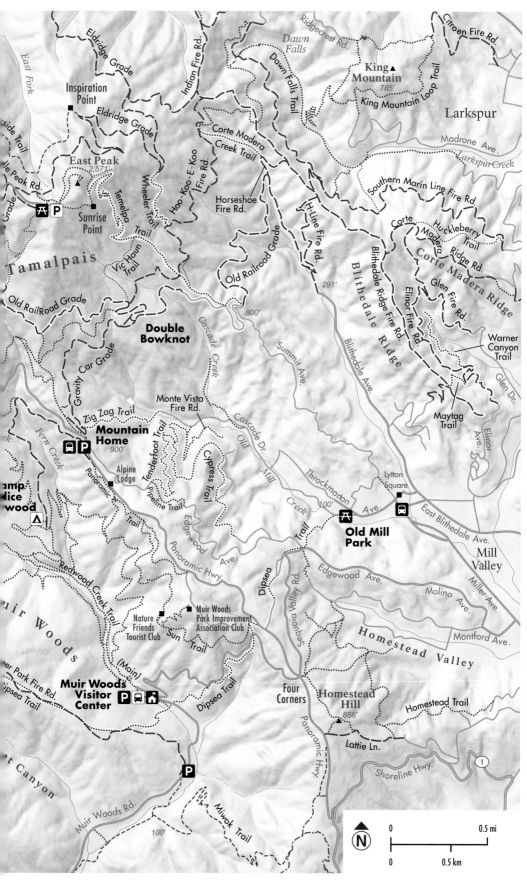

The 7-mile hike on the Dipsea Trail from Mill Valley ends at Stinson Beach.

TRAILHEAD FOUR: MILL VALLEY

Directions
Highway 101—East Blithedale Ave. (exit), Mill Valley—left on Throckmorton Ave., 1 block to Lytton Square, or .3 mile to Old Mill Park.

Much of the Mill Valley area was fenced and off-limits to everyone but invited guests when Samuel Throckmorton owned Rancho Saucelito (from 1856 until his death in 1883). But when the next owners, the Tamalpais Land & Water Co., decided to develop the town and laid a rail line along today's Miller Avenue in 1889 in preparation, Mill Valley immediately became the principal entry to Mt. Tamalpais.

Day visitors and weekend campers from San Francisco and elsewhere took a ferry to Sausalito, rode the main line (part of which is now the Sausalito-Mill Valley multi-use path) to Almonte ("to the mountain"), then transferred to downtown. At that point, they had several options: up Throckmorton Avenue to the Dipsea steps; through Cascade Canyon and up Zig-Zag Trail, then farther up or down to Redwood Canyon; or Temelpa Trail to East Peak.

From 1896 through 1929, the Mill Valley & Mt. Tamalpais Scenic Railway ran from the Mill Valley train depot to near East Peak, opening many more options. There were also horse-drawn-carriage (later motorized) excursions and even burro rides. Passenger rail service into Mill Valley ended in 1940; ridership sunk when driving over then-new Golden Gate Bridge proved too popular.

The former rail depot remains the heart of Mill Valley. It is bordered on the north by Lytton Square, named for Lytton Plummer Barber, the first Mill Valley resident to die in World War I. The popular Depot Bookstore & Cafe occupies the last station (built in 1929). There is a water fountain outside and a public restroom inside.

Other Mill Valley trailheads involve negotiating narrow, winding streets, with little parking and no amenities. One is the start of the surviving Old Railroad Grade, off West Blithedale just past Lee Street. Another is the north end of Cascade Drive, from which Tenderfoot and Zig-Zag Trails set off uphill. Blithedale Ridge and Warner Canyon can be reached from the top of Elinor Avenue. Warner Canyon can also be accessed from the top of Glen Drive. Greenwood Way offers access to Blithedale Ridge. Cypress Trail leaves from the end of Cypress Avenue. Mill Valley's highest trailhead is Fern Canyon Road, a paved section of Old Railroad Grade, reached via winding Summit Avenue.

Mill Valley also has several neighborhood trailheads onto more recently acquired Marin County Parks preserves. Paths set off from Del Casa Avenue, Fairway Drive, Manor Drive, Marlin Avenue, Tartan Road, Val Vista Avenue, and other locations on the east side of Mill Valley.

Suggested Loops

1. Top of Glen Drive (elevation 280 feet)—Glen FR, .4 mile, to Elinor FR—left, .6 mile, to Tartan Road Trail—left, .3 mile, to Tartan Road—left, .1 mile, to Glen Drive—left, .4 mile, to start. **1.8 miles total**

2. Cascade Drive (elevation 270 feet)—Tenderfoot Trail, .4 mile, to Cypress Trail—left, 1.1 miles, to connector to Rose Avenue—left, .5 mile, to Monte Vista FR—straight, .4 mile, to Tenderfoot Trail and start. **2.5 miles total**

3. Old Railroad Grade trailhead (elevation 240 feet)—Railroad Grade, .6 mile, to Horseshoe FR—right, .1 mile, to Corte Madera Trail—left, .6 mile, to Hoo-Koo-E-Koo Trail—right, .5 mile, to Blithedale Ridge FR—right, .5 mile, to H-Line FR—right, .6 mile, to Railroad Grade—left, .1 mile, to start. **3.0 miles total**

4. Old Mill Park (elevation 110 feet)—Dipsea Trail, .5 mile, to Edgewood Ave.—right on Edgewood Ave. and Pipeline Trail, 2.0 miles, to Mountain Home—right on Tenderfoot Trail, 1.1 miles, to Cascade Drive—right, 1.1 miles, to start. **4.7 miles total**

5. Fern Canyon Road (elevation 820 feet)—Temelpa Trail, .4 mile, to Hoo-Koo-E-Koo FR—right, 1.8 miles, to Blithedale Ridge FR—right, .8 mile, to Horseshoe FR—right, .3 mile, to Old Railroad Grade—right, 1.6 miles, to start. **4.9 miles total**

■ Blithedale Ridge Fire Road

Elinor Avenue, Mill Valley, to Indian FR: 2.33 miles

Terrain: Chaparral (MCOSD, MMWD)

Elevation: From 520 to 900 to 650 to 1,040 feet; rolling, parts very steep

Intersecting Trail(s): Connector fire road to Greenwood Way (.1 mile), Maytag (.3 mile), Corte Madera Ridge FR (.9 mile), H-Line FR (1.4 miles), Horseshoe FR (1.6 miles), Hoo-Koo-E-Koo Trail (1.9 miles), Hoo-Koo-E-Koo FR (2.3 miles)

Blithedale Ridge runs down the east-southeast face of Mt. Tamalpais, forming an imposing wall between Blithedale and Warner Canyons. Homes cover the lowest reaches of Blithedale Ridge in Mill Valley, but this fire road tops its pristine upper 2.3 miles. Dramatic Mt. Tamalpais summit views—some say the best anywhere—are on tap most of the way.

In 1989, a gate was placed at the foot of private Via Van Dyke at Elinor Avenue, cutting off access to lower Blithedale Ridge FR. In 1997, an opening around the gate (originally marked with a welcoming sign) was added. Climb the very steep pavement to the first fork, then veer right, passing homes. Behind a barrier is a water tank. Go around the tank right and climb the short, steep, dirt path up to one end of Blithedale Ridge FR (MCOSD plans to improve the entry). Or join from any of seven intersecting routes.

When you reach the fire road, a sign reminds you that the way left is private property. Immediately to the right, a path, a remnant of Maytag Trail, parallels Blithedale Ridge FR in the shade.

The fire road is a rollercoaster, steeply rising and falling (mostly rising!). The first uphill leads to the initial Tam summit view. Just beyond, another fire road drops left, leading to Mill Valley's Greenwood Way, an alternate access.

Broom used to line both sides of the Blithedale Ridge FR, but much of it has been cleared as a fire danger. Oaks and madrones thrive. What is now Maytag Trail enters from the right, marked by an MCOSD "Trail" signpost. It descends to Elinor FR for a short loop.

Just beyond is an old MCOSD "boundary" signpost. There is a stiff rise to a fenced, small water tank. Sixty yards past, also left, is an orange-red gate; beyond is private property, so do not enter. In another 100 yards is a pair of old wood property-line posts, left and right. At the one on the right, the upper end of the former Maytag returns to the ridge.

Another pair of uphills leads to a view north, to Bald Hill and Big Rock Ridge, second-highest peak in Marin after Tamalpais. The canyon to the left is Blithedale, cut by Corte Madera Creek. The canyon right is Warner, carved by Warner Creek.

At .9 mile, at a very wide spot, Corte Madera Ridge FR, which tops the opposite wall of Warner Canyon, comes in from the right. The junction is known to some as "Judy's Corners."

Here, a major descent begins, and the views of Tam are particularly striking. The fire road then enters a redwood forest.

At the base of the descent, H-Line FR drops left to Old Railroad Grade, just up from West Blithedale. The signpost now displays the precise longitude and latitude. Twenty-five yards later, at another fork, Blithedale Ridge FR begins to climb again. Straight ahead, H-Line FR drops to Southern Marin Line (Crown) FR.

The stiff uphill levels atop the ridge. Chinquapin, madrones, and a few redwoods stand amidst the chaparral. A down section of the rollercoaster leads to Horseshoe FR, which drops left, also to Old Railroad Grade.

In another ¼ mile, Hoo-Koo-E-Koo Trail crosses Blithedale Ridge. Right leads down to the Southern Marin Line Road, near Kentfield's Crown Road. Left, Hoo-Koo-E-Koo Trail connects to Hoo-Koo-E-Koo FR. After a stiff uphill, you're rewarded by great views to the south from the head of Blithedale Canyon.

The fire road now leaves MCOSD lands and enters MMWD territory. Just above is the 1,091-foot summit of Knob Hill. Four Mexican-era land grants, covering most of the southern half of Marin, met at this single point. To the left is the top of Hoo-Koo-E-Koo FR. Climb the remaining yards to the end of Blithedale Ridge FR at its junction with Indian FR. Left leads up to Eldridge Grade, right down to Kent Woodlands.

In the 1870s, Dr. John Cushing, a pioneering homeopathic physician, opened a sanitarium, "Blithedale," in what is now Blithedale Canyon. The name stems from the novel *Blithedale Romance*, written by Cushing's Bowdoin College friend, Nathaniel Hawthorne. After Cushing's death in 1879, his son Sidney converted Blithedale, near the present 205 West Blithedale Avenue, into a hotel. Sidney then became the chief mover behind construction of the railway up Mt. Tamalpais, which passed the resort. Mountain Theater is today named for Sidney Cushing. ("Blythedale" is an older spelling.)

■ Corte Madera Creek Trail

Horseshoe FR to Hoo-Koo-E-Koo FR: .37 mile

TERRAIN: Deep redwood forest; riparian; several stream fords (MCOSD, MMWD)

ELEVATION: From 500 to 950 feet; extremely steep

INTERSECTING TRAIL(S): None

Corte Madera Creek Trail follows the upper reaches of Arroyo (or Arroyo Corte Madera del Presidio) Creek, which flows into downtown Mill Valley by the Throckmorton-West Blithedale Avenues junction. The upper half of this lovely trail runs through a dense stand of redwoods. It is, however, extremely steep, narrow, and not always clear, and requires some potentially tricky stream crossings after winter rains.

To reach the lower end of Corte Madera Creek Trail, follow Old Railroad Grade uphill from its start off West Blithedale Avenue. The first fire road on the right is H-Line. A ½ mile later, at a bend and crossing over Corte Madera Creek, Horseshoe FR rises on the right. Follow it .1 mile to an MCOSD sign on the left, which simply says "Trail" and marks the start of Corte Madera Creek Trail.

The trail, rising beside the creek, immediately enters MMWD land. The first of four creek crossings, all without benefit of a bridge, is from the left to the right bank. After a heavy rain, this crossing requires a modest leap. If you make it, you can relax; the others are a bit easier.

In early spring, trillium's showy flowers are abundant here. By late spring, another spectacular lily, clintonia, blooms. The trail passes over a redwood downed in the storm of January 1982 and meets a confluence of two creek forks. The many rocks to the left here are not an accident. In 1988, a young artisan gathered them to build a rock wall. In 1997, a sizable redwood fell, taking down the wall and strewing the rocks. Cross and follow the left of the forks.

Redwoods now dominate. Continue climbing through the beautiful, quiet woodland. There are two more fordings.

A final push brings Corte Madera Creek Trail to its signed top at Hoo-Koo-E-Koo Trail, which goes right to Echo Rock. A few yards of scramble uphill is Hoo-Koo-E-Koo FR, which goes right to Blithedale Ridge FR and left to Wheeler Trail.

As mentioned earlier, redwoods from lower in this watershed were cut to expand San Francisco's Presidio. Antonio María Osio has a charming account of a logging expedition in around 1820. (San Francisco was then virtually treeless.) Corte Madera del Presidio was the name of the first Mexican land grant in Marin, awarded to Irish-born John Reed in 1834. It covered much of Mill Valley, plus Tiburon and Belvedere.

▦ Cypress Trail

Tenderfoot Trail to Cypress Avenue, Mill Valley: 1.56 miles

TERRAIN: Woodland (City of Mill Valley)

ELEVATION: 450 to 660 feet; early part gradual, then almost level

INTERSECTING TRAIL(S): Connector to Rose Avenue (1.1 miles)

This is a surprising trail, so close to central Mill Valley and outside of any larger parkland, yet long, fairly isolated, and deeply wooded. It typifies Mill Valley's charm, and its wisdom in preserving old byways.

Cypress Trail does have drawbacks: it is narrow, poison oak borders much of the route, several low trees menace inattentive travelers, and the southern entry has a somewhat tricky stream crossing. The higher (southern) end of Cypress Trail is accessible by car, but since most users join from the popular Tenderfoot Trail, that is how the route will be described.

Cypress Trail sets off left $\frac{1}{3}$ mile up from the base of Tenderfoot Trail. A sign here says "No Bikes"; they have been barred since 1996.

Almost all of the trail's elevation gain is in this opening section; the route is then nearly level. Redwoods dominate the early going, and are abundant the rest of the way, particularly at the several stream crossings. In some 100 yards is the first of numerous intersecting paths, most leading to nearby homes.

At $\frac{1}{3}$ mile, the upper reaches of Mt. Tam are visible through the tree canopy. At $\frac{2}{3}$ mile, the trail passes just above adjacent houses, skirting a back yard fence. But there are few other signs of civilization in the forest. The trail crosses though a haunting double row of dead manzanita shrubs.

The only prominent intersection is just past 1 mile; Cypress is the upper, right route. Down left is a 125-yard connection (called Cypress Lane on Thomas Bros. maps) to the unpaved 300 block of Rose Avenue. Rose offers a loop option back to Tenderfoot via Monte Vista FR. At the intersection, amidst the deep forest, is an incongruous utility pole, anchored to a redwood.

In another 100 yards, Cypress Trail passes several massive eucalyptus trees and another house. The route is more open, but again returns to dense redwoods. There is also a grove of laurels.

The trail passes one more house, then drops steeply to a last stream crossing and its final yards, exiting on a very narrow easement along the edge of the driveway of 100 Cypress Avenue (the entry is all but invisible when entering from Cypress Avenue). Just inside this entry is another "No Bikes, No Horses" sign.

Cypress Avenue goes to Edgewood Road near the top of the Dipsea steps. The street (and thus trail) is presumably named for its planted Monterey cypress trees.

Dipsea Trail

Old Mill Park, Mill Valley, to Highway 1, central Stinson Beach: 6.96 miles

TERRAIN: Varied; deep and light woodland, grassland, riparian, and coastal scrub; heavily used (City of Mill Valley, private [easement], MTSP, MWNM, GGNRA)

ELEVATION: From 90 to 760 to 160 to 1,360 to 80 feet; mostly very steep, almost no level section

INTERSECTING TRAIL(S): Sun (1.3 miles), Deer Park FR (several times between 2.9 and 4.2 miles), Ben Johnson (3.9 miles), TCC (4.1 miles), Steep Ravine (5.6 to 5.7 miles), Hill 640 FR (5.8 miles)

The Dipsea is likely the most famous trail in the San Francisco Bay Area, and, thanks to its annual footrace, even has a worldwide reputation. Few trails anywhere pack such beauty, ruggedness, variety, and history into so compact a distance.

The Dipsea Trail may well have been used by the Coast Miwoks, and it was certainly popular (under the name Lone Tree Trail) with the county's first pleasure hikers in the 1880s. In 1905, it became the route of the Dipsea Race, now the oldest major cross-country race in the United States, and generations of runners hold it in reverence. In 2010, the Dipsea Trail was added to the National Register of Historic Places.

In 1904, William Kent had William Neumann construct the Dipsea Inn on land Kent owned in today's Seadrift. "Dipsea" was Kent's idea, a corruption from a line in the eighth stanza of Rudyard Kipling's poem, Last Chantey: "May we lift a Deep-sea Chantey such as seamen use at sea?" "Dipsea" was then applied to the entire sandspit north of Willow Camp (now Stinson Beach), as in, "going to Dipsea."

Within days of the inn's opening, a group of long-distance hikers from San Francisco's venerable Olympic Club got off the train in Mill Valley for a visit. A friendly wager on who could reach the inn first sparked an idea. On November 19, 1905, a group of Olympians calling themselves the Dipsea Indians staged the first Dipsea Race, from the train station in Mill Valley to the inn. (In 1906, the final trek over the sand to the inn was eliminated; the beach stretch was dropped altogether the following year.) Runners were free to take any route, and the race was handicapped, meaning slower runners were sent off first. Thus, the race has been won by an eight-year-old girl (women were officially admitted in 1971, although a competitive and pioneering Dipsea Women's Hike was held 1918–1922) and a seventy-two-year-old man. No race was held in the Depression years of 1932–1933 or during the war years of 1942–1945, when much of Tamalpais was closed by the military. The Dipsea celebrated its 100th running in 2010. It is now held the second Sunday of June.

The Dipsea Trail is arduous, with more than 2,300 feet each of steep uphill and downhill, most of it over a narrow, root-covered pathway. (It is considerably more treacherous on race day, when hundreds of speedier, younger runners attempt to pass older runners with greater head starts; there are many injuries.) Also note that the Dipsea Trail is a one-way affair. If you can't arrange a car shuttle, or are not up for a "double," West Marin Stagecoach Route 61 offers rides from Stinson Beach back to Bayview Drive on Panoramic Highway, where it is then 1 downhill mile to the start of the Dipsea Trail.

The Dipsea Race itself begins at Lytton Square in downtown Mill Valley. Contestants run up Throckmorton Avenue and cut diagonally through Old Mill Park. The park, which has a bathroom and water fountain, was the site of John Reed's 1834–1835 mill. The current mill is a precise replica, built after a tree crashed though the original in 1968.

Cross Old Mill Creek over the bridge. Continue straight across the street (Cascade Drive is to the right, Molino Avenue to the left) and up the pavement to encounter the Dipsea steps. (Don't take the first steps to the left, as they lead to a house.) The steps, technically Cascade Way, .3 mile into the race, mark the start of the Dipsea Trail. White Dipsea arrows, sometimes faint, are painted on the pavement here and elsewhere.

No part of the Dipsea Trail is better known than these three flights of both dreaded and beloved 685 steps. Originally constructed of logs, they were all replaced in 1936, then subsequently as needed (plaques were sold to finance the latest step-rebuilding project). Private homes border the whole way; the first two are only accessible via the steps. The first flight, to Millside Lane, is the longest: 313 steps. Its topmost 33 rock steps are the steepest.

At the pavement, go right, then immediately left on Marion Avenue. Just around the bend is the second flight, scheduled for a rebuild: 222 steps. At the top, go left on Hazel Avenue a few yards to the third and shortest flight: 150 steps, sometimes called Hale Lane. Think of the runners who jam the steps to over-capacity, fatigued yet still short of the 1-mile mark. According to a famous quote by Jack Kirk, the legendary "Dipsea Demon" who finished every race from 1930 through 2002, "Old Dipsea runners never die. They just reach the 672nd step." (There were 671 steps until a rebuilding project in 1993.)

The steps top out at the intersection of Edgewood Avenue and Sequoia Valley Road at a junction once known as Inspiration Point for the views. Victorino's refreshment stand refreshed hikers here. Across the road is Cowboy Rock Trail, part of the Homestead Valley Land Trust network. It descends a very steep .3 mile past Cowboy Rock to Tamalpais Drive and Stolte Grove in Homestead Valley. (Homestead Valley trails are not separately described in this book.)

Runners go right for 100 yards up busy Sequoia Valley Road, but it is far safer to use the parallel hiker's path to its right. The Dipsea then rises through the gates of the old Flying Y Horse Ranch, on what is now Walsh Drive, named for its developer. Climb the paved street. There is a water fountain by 5 Walsh Drive.

A gate marks the first dirt section of the trail. A marker, Milestone 1, is on the right. It is the first of seven mile-markers, as measured from the start of the race in downtown Mill Valley. A few feet past is a Monterey cypress. In the early 1970s, the words "One Mile Tree" were carved where an overhanging branch was cut. The bark has now completely overgrown the words.

The trail rejoins pavement as residential Bayview Drive. At its top, cross Panoramic Highway and veer right. This is Windy Gap, the first of the route's two main summits. In less than 50 yards, go left off the pavement at a Dipsea Trail signpost. The trail is now in Mount Tamalpais State Park, and remains on public land the rest of the way.

The next section is known as "Hauke Hollow" for Jerry Hauke, who directed the Dipsea race for more than thirty years. After the first big bend left on the downhill, a few yards past a wooden bridge, is the signed Sun-Dipsea Trail junction. Sun Trail goes right to the Tourist Club. The Dipsea takes the left fork and drops steeply over steps often wet from an adjacent spring to paved Muir Woods Road.

All Dipsea racers go right here, flying down the road. Hikers use a newer (1981) Dipsea Trail section, marked by a signpost, directly across the road. Never far from the road, it follows a stream down, under a light forest canopy. This section, closed for years by a slide, finally reopened in 2012 with a new bridge dedicated to Earnest Emig (president of the Tamalpais Conservation Club from 1972 to 1974) over the slide area. In 2013, the California Highway Patrol insisted that runners use this section of trail in the Dipsea Race. (It had earlier become mandatory in the Double and Quadruple Dipsea Races, but was never used in the Dipsea Race.) The County Board of Supervisors helped craft an agreement to keep the Dipsea Race on the road instead of the trail, which is narrow, twisty, and has a slight uphill at the bridge.

The trail and race route meet at a dirt road, Camino del Canyon, marked by a row of mailboxes. Camino del Canyon is an unpaved access road down to old cabins, some dating back to Camp Monte Vista, first subdivided in 1908. Starting in the 1950s, the area blossomed as a bohemian enclave, with Zen guru Alan Watts perhaps its most famous resident. (His house still stands.) By 1984, the area had passed entirely into federal hands, though it is not technically part of Muir Woods National Monument.

The Dipsea continues to the right off this dirt road at a sign. This next section of the Dipsea Trail was built in the late 1970s to replace a precipitous, 45-degree descent known as Suicide. Beware of poison oak, particularly in late winter and spring (good samaritans usually cut it back just before race day). After a short descent, there is a fence on the left with a removable section that is off-limits to hikers; it is opened only for Dipsea racers.

The trail meets a service road (Milestone 2). This was the site of a snack bar and dance pavilion called Joe's Place, popular in the 1920s and '30s. To continue, cross Muir Woods Road into the monument's overflow parking lot. In the summer of 2001, a water fountain was added here (partly at the suggestion of this writer). The main entrance to Muir Woods National Monument (and restrooms) is to the right.

The Dipsea Trail then descends a few steps to cross Redwood Creek on a plank footbridge. This crucial bridge is now only moved into place in spring, sometimes as late as May, severing the Dipsea Trail. To regain the Dipsea Trail when the bridge is out, go left ½ mile on Muir Woods Road, then right, uphill, on Deer Park (or Dipsea) FR. Dipsea Race officials, the National Park Service, and the TCC are exploring options for a permanent bridge.

Across Redwood Creek, the Dipsea Trail begins an almost continuous climb to its highest point. The first part, called Lower Dynamite, is the steepest long section, around ½ mile. It traverses a lush, fern-lined forest in the southwest corner of Muir Woods National Monument, replacing an even steeper, more direct route known as Butler's Pride, which is now off-limits. Here, too, poison oak is abundant.

Deer Park FR—the wet-weather bypass—joins from the left. The climb eases a bit over the section known as Upper Dynamite. Once grazing ceased here around 1970, the grassland began giving way to ferns, then shrubs, and now, ever more and taller Douglas-fir trees. The trail leaves Muir Woods National Monument to again enter Mount Tamalpais State Park.

Deer Park FR is a few feet to the left. The trail first runs to the right of the fire road. The two then merge before the trail departs left at a marked Dipsea sign. The trail and fire road crisscross for the next 1.5 miles; Milestone 3 is at one junction.

The uphill eases a bit more through the grassland called the Hogsback, named for its appearance in profile. Beside the trail, on the left next to a telephone line, is a prominent boulder dubbed by Dipsea Hall of Famer Russ Kiernan as "Halfway Rock" because he reaches it about halfway into his total race time. Panoramas open, including the Pacific and (although now largely blocked) the three summits of Tam. The trail then again merges with and crosses Deer Park FR.

After passing through a small grove, the trail leaves the grassland left of the fire road. This next heavily wooded mile, back in Muir Woods National

Monument, is called the "rainforest"; in summer, water drips off the fog-laden Douglas-firs and redwoods. Another special stretch of the Dipsea, this is one of the best places on Tam to see orchids.

Ben Johnson Trail, which also rises from Muir Woods, meets the Dipsea on the right. Veer left. The Dipsea Trail joins the fire road for the last time by Milestone 4. Go left some 100 yards on the merged pair, then right as the trail branches off.

This final, stiff, 300-yard uphill is called Cardiac, not because it is that much steeper or longer than what has come before, but because by this point, runners are already fatigued from the continuous climb out of Muir Woods. TCC Trail, from Pantoll, comes in on the right and the Dipsea re-enters Mt. Tamalpais State Park.

There is a last push to the summit, one of the loveliest places on the mountain. The top of Cardiac Hill (formerly known as the Sugar Lump) is 1,360 feet and the highest point on the Dipsea Trail. The vistas of San Francisco and the Pacific are dramatic. It's a welcome sight for all Dipsea veterans: the trail, which is now almost all downhill, is fanned by the usual cooling ocean breezes; the views are gorgeous; and on race day, there's a water station here. The stone fountain, in the style of others designed by William Penn Mott, Jr., and built on Tamalpais by the Civilian Conservation Corps during the 1930s, was dedicated June 7, 2013. Runners have dubbed it "Sam's Fountain of Youth" in memory of Sam Hirabayashi, who raced the Dipsea until he was eighty-three.

The Dipsea crosses broad Deer Park FR. Just downhill to the left is the new (2005) Coast View Trail. Up to the right is Old Mine Trail and Pantoll Ranger Station.

The next .2-mile stretch is almost flat, dipping slightly at the start, then rising slightly at the end to a point only 5 inches lower in elevation than at the top of Cardiac. This section is known as Farren's Rest, for Dipsea-lover James Farren, Jr., whose ashes were scattered here. Early photos of this area show a single redwood, the "Lone Tree" that once gave its name to the Dipsea Trail. The redwood still stands, but the hillside above it is covered with Douglas-firs. Beneath the redwood, up a short path to the right, is a stone cairn. A pipe tapping into Lone Tree Spring here long provided the only drinking water (albeit untreated) on the Dipsea. The Tamalpais Conservation Club built the fountain in 1917.

In 2005, California State Parks bulldozed and obliterated historic Lone Tree Trail, which joined the Dipsea Trail here and ran with it and west across it before finally departing to Highway 1. This led to a rerouting and lengthening (by some 300 feet) of the Dipsea Trail over the next ½ mile.

The next section, generally downhill but with one rise, is open grassland offering ocean views. Milestone 5 is passed. Around .1 mile beyond, the Dipsea Trail veers right at a post. The hill and overhanging foliage cut off views.

At a wooden fence, less than .1 mile down, Dipsea racers veer left (or straight) and leave the regular Dipsea Trail to plunge down the near vertical Swoop Hollow, so named by Jack Kirk. The official Dipsea Trail, right, is a section built in 1977 by the Youth Conservation Corps. Racers have dubbed it "the Gail Scott Trail" for the 1986 champion who accidentally took it while leading the '87 race, likely costing her a repeat win (she finished second). It is one of the loveliest parts of the route, deeply wooded and quiet. The redwoods and bent laurels form distinct, magical forests. A few of the Douglas-firs rise to enormous heights. The shortcut and trail meet again ¼ mile below.

A short passage through grassland brings the Dipsea Trail to the cool, wet forest of Steep Ravine. The trail here is extremely steep as it descends into the fern-lined canyon, with protruding rocks and roots. Hundreds of stone and wooden steps, which Dipsea champions have been known to take several at a time, help moderate the descent, but caution is very much in order. Only racers have reason to rush through this pleasing area.

The Dipsea meets Milestone 6 and crosses Webb Creek over a bridge. On the other bank, going right, is Steep Ravine Trail rising to Pantoll. The combined Dipsea and Steep Ravine Trails go left, passing a small reservoir that was once part of Stinson Beach's water supply.

The short, stiff uphill now encountered is called Insult. It is the last uphill on the racer's route (but not on the regular Dipsea Trail), the course's final "insult" to those who thought it was all downhill to the finish line. Steep Ravine Trail branches left, to Highway 1.

Old-timers refer to the area at the top of the hill as White Barn, part of the old White Gate Ranch. The barn was torn down shortly after GGNRA assumed stewardship of the land from here westward in 1972.

Knowledgeable Dipsea competitors depart the trail to the right for the first of two stretches on Panoramic Highway. These well-known shortcuts bypass the trail's remaining uphill, but also cut off one of the most attractive sections.

The marked Dipsea Trail rises a few more yards left. It then descends through rolling grassland known as the Moors, for its appearance during frequent summer fogs. When the weather is clear, there are striking views of Stinson Beach, tantalizingly close below. Hill 640 FR is crossed; it goes right to Panoramic Highway and left to a dead end at a series of old military bunkers.

The trail now drops steadily. It bends sharply right at a fence line, then re-enters woodland. Here, the Panoramic Highway shortcut route rejoins. Veer left. The ocean's influence grows stronger. A boardwalk crosses a boggy area.

A short descent through grassland passes Milestone 7 and brings the Dipsea

Trail to Panoramic Highway, just above Highway 1. There is a large trail sign. (On race day, runners are routed left off the trail a few yards above and have to make a perilous leap over a stile down to Highway 1. They go right, then left on Marine Way, then left again to finish at the southernmost Stinson Beach parking lot.) In 2002, a new, final stretch of trail across Panoramic Highway was opened to provide hikers safer off-road passage to central Stinson Beach.

The Dipsea Trail is a special experience, among the best the mountain has to offer, any time of year. It gets a trifle crowded with runners practicing on weekends before the race. Come on race day to cheer the runners on. The race record is 44 minutes, 49 seconds, by Ron Elijah in 1974—hard to believe, even though the course was a bit shorter then. The women's record is 55 minutes, 47 seconds, by Peggy Smyth in 1988. The Double Dipsea, from Stinson Beach to Mill Valley and back, is held thirteen days after the Dipsea, and the Quadruple Dipsea—four crossings starting in Old Mill Park—is run the Saturday after Thanksgiving.

For a more detailed description of the Dipsea Trail and Dipsea Race, see my book, *Dipsea: The Greatest Race*.

■ Elinor Fire Road

Elinor Avenue, Mill Valley, to Glen FR: 1.20 miles

TERRAIN: Lower part redwood forest; upper part chaparral (MCOSD)

ELEVATION: From 360 to 580 feet; lower part steep, upper part gradual

INTERSECTING TRAIL(S): Tartan Trail (.2 mile), Warner Falls (.3 mile), Maytag (.4 mile)

To reach Elinor FR, follow Mill Valley's winding and narrow Elinor Avenue uphill. When the paved road ends, veer right at the next intersection (left goes up to private residences). In 30 yards, a gate marks the start of Elinor FR, sometimes called Warner Canyon FR. The opening yards of the fire road abut private property; the rest of the way is through MCOSD lands.

Within 30 yards, a rough path drops right to Bay Tree Lane. The fire road is initially level. Redwoods line the way and run down the creek beds, providing shade. At .2 mile, MCOSD-signed Tartan Trail branches right and drops 300 yards to Tartan Road.

In another 100 yards, in the middle of a sharp bend left amidst redwoods, Warner Canyon Trail departs to the right. It runs ½ mile to a seasonal waterfall.

At this bend, the uphill begins in earnest. One hundred yards above Warner Canyon Trail, at a bend right, a few steps on the left mark the start of Maytag Trail. It rises to Blithedale Ridge, and offers a loop option.

Elinor FR passes in and out of redwood groves. The grade lessens, and there is even a short downhill. After the last ¼-mile stretch of redwoods, the fire road opens. There are views of the Mill Valley Municipal Golf Course and the San Francisco skyline. Beyond the big bend right, at another vista point, a delightful little "shrine" was cut into a rock on the hillside left.

Elinor FR ends at its junction with Glen FR. Downhill leads, in .4 mile, to Mill Valley's Glen Drive. A ½ mile uphill is Corte Madera Ridge FR and Huckleberry Trail.

Elinor Burt (1899–1973) was a granddaughter of one of Mill Valley's first settlers, Jacob Gardner, who managed the Throckmorton Ranch. Her father, John Burt, worked for the Tamalpais Land & Water Co., which opened Mill Valley for development in 1890. In 1916, John Burt became the first superintendent of the Marin Municipal Water District. Gardner and Burt developed the Bolsa tract through which Elinor Avenue runs. Elinor Burt was a teacher; a dietitian for the US Air Corps during World War II; and author of two cookbooks, *Olla Podrida* and *Far Eastern Cooking*. Her oral history is in the Mill Valley Public Library.

Glen Fire Road

Glen Drive, Mill Valley, to Corte Madera Ridge FR at Huckleberry Trail: .87 mile

TERRAIN: Broom-lined hillside (MCOSD)

ELEVATION: From 280 to 860 feet; very steep

INTERSECTING TRAIL(S): Elinor FR (.4 mile)

Fire roads rise on both sides of Mill Valley's Warner Canyon, from Elinor Avenue on the west and from Glen Drive on the east. These two fire roads merge and continue up the canyon to Corte Madera Ridge.

Glen FR starts from a gate at the upper end of Glen Drive. An MCOSD sign reads "Northridge-Blithedale Summit." The early going is quite steep but the grade soon eases. Broom, both French and Scotch, lines the fire road's edge. Sage and monkeyflower are among native shrubs holding out. Oaks also border the route, but provide little shade.

Elinor FR, across deep Warner Canyon, is visible most of the time. It joins Glen FR at .4 mile. A lone oak stands sentinel in the middle of the junction. Left leads, in 1.2 miles, to Elinor Avenue in Mill Valley. The continuation straight and uphill is considered to be Glen FR here. Look back for views of the San Francisco skyline.

Glen FR ends atop Warner Canyon at a four-way intersection. Corte Madera Ridge FR goes left to Blithedale Ridge and right to Summit Avenue in Corte Madera. Huckleberry Trail, straight ahead, drops to the Larkspur end of Southern Marin Line FR. Be sure to go up a few yards left for an outstanding view of Tam's East Peak.

When lower Warner Canyon was subdivided after World War II, the streets were given Scottish-themed names, such as Heather, Barrie, Tartan, and Glen. Warner Canyon was dairy grazing land into the 1900s, and a wild area for Mill Valley youth to explore. The golf course in the lower part of the canyon opened in 1919.

■ H-Line Fire Road

Old Railroad Grade to Southern Marin Line FR: .89 mile

TERRAIN: Chaparral (MCOSD)

ELEVATION: From 320 to 660 to 510 feet; very steep

INTERSECTING TRAIL(S): Blithedale Ridge FR (.6 mile)

H-Line is a surprisingly easy connection between Mill Valley and the Larkspur-Corte Madera side of Tam. It is the first fire road to rise from Old Railroad Grade, 200 yards up from West Blithedale Avenue. H-Line quickly leaves the canyon's forest canopy to enter chaparral. In .1 mile, there is some asphalt at the first big bend.

The fire road climbs relentlessly. At a bend left are two water tanks. In 1998, the bigger one (right), holding 500,000 gallons, replaced an older tank. "Two Tanks Road" is a traditional name for the Mill Valley half of the route. The tough uphill forces pauses—time to enjoy the vistas.

There is a last bend, then a level stretch. H-Line crosses Blithedale Ridge FR at a newly signed intersection. Blithedale rises on both sides, to the left toward Indian FR and to the right toward Corte Madera Ridge. Between these two branches, H-Line FR continues, now downhill.

The remaining steep ¼-mile descent is lined with madrones and manzanita. H-Line FR ends at its junction with Southern Marin Line FR, by a drinking fountain and fenced pump station. It is 1.2 miles left to Crown Road in Kentfield, 1.6 miles right to Sunrise Lane in Larkspur.

H-Line was built just after World War II as part of the Southern Marin Line project, which brings water from the lakes on the north side of Tamalpais, through the Bon Tempe treatment plant, and on to users in southern Marin. From the pump station at the H-Line/Southern Marin junction, water is sent over Blithedale Ridge, where it then drops to the two storage tanks and on to Mill Valley.

The name H-Line, used by water district personnel, arose when sections of the Southern Marin Line pipeline were marked by a grid; A-Line, B-Line, and so forth. This fire road straddled the H-Line.

Horseshoe Fire Road

Old Railroad Grade to Blithedale Ridge FR: .28 mile

TERRAIN: Chaparral (MCOSD)

ELEVATION: From 440 to 700 feet; extremely steep

INTERSECTING TRAIL(S): Corte Madera Creek (.1 mile)

Horseshoe is the second of the two fire roads that connect Old Railroad Grade with Blithedale Ridge. It sets off .5 mile above the first, H-Line (Two Tanks), and .6 mile from the grade's dirt start at West Blithedale Avenue.

The fire road rises from a rare downhill (the result of storm damage) on Old Railroad Grade, where the grade crosses over Corte Madera Creek. In railroad days, this bend, called Horseshoe Curve, was well known, as it was the sharpest of all the 281 curves on the entire 8.25 miles of track. Signs at the bend mark the demarcation between MCOSD and MMWD lands.

The uphill is a tough one. In .1 mile, at a green MCOSD "Trail" signpost, Corte Madera Creek Trail departs left to begin its very steep climb to Hoo-Koo-E-Koo FR. Horseshoe FR has its own horseshoe bend, then it is straight up, leaving the redwood forest and moving into chaparral. Views open of Mt. Tamalpais and the San Francisco skyline. The grade steepens.

Horseshoe ends when it hits Blithedale Ridge FR, which goes left to Hoo-Koo-E-Koo Trail and right to Mill Valley.

Maytag Trail

Elinor FR to Blithedale Ridge FR: .33 mile

TERRAIN: Redwood forest (MCOSD)

ELEVATION: From 440 to 730 feet; steep

INTERSECTING TRAIL(S): None

This is a newer trail, cut by MCOSD in the 1990s. Need for the trail arose after there were threats to public access onto Blithedale Ridge from the entry off Elinor Avenue at Via Van Dyke. While access up Via Van Dyke remains open, this lovely trail is a more gradual and attractive alternative, and opens loop options.

Follow upper Elinor Avenue to beyond the pavement. There is a final driveway left for three homes, then a gate marking the start of Elinor FR. Follow this fire road up. At a big bend left, Warner Falls Trail branches right. Climb another $1/8$ mile to the next bend, where Maytag Trail begins, signed, to the left, up five steps.

Maytag Trail immediately enters redwood forest, where it remains its full length. Blithedale Ridge, like other Tam ridges and hills, has a sun-baked, drier south slope and a shaded, wetter north slope. This is peaceful woodland, very near a residential area. The redwoods here were logged, perhaps more than once, but are returning nicely.

Maytag was built to newer trail guidelines, with switchbacks easing the gradient. The lower section parallels Elinor FR, which remains visible below before heading into the heart of the forest. Typical early-blooming (beginning in February) redwood forest flowers of the lily family—including fetid adder's tongue, Solomon seal (*Maianthemum stellatum*), fairy bells (*Prosartes hookeri*), trillium, and mission bells (*Fritillaria affinis*)—are found along the way. Higher, the coffeeberry shrub, so named because its berries resemble coffee beans, becomes common.

Just below Blithedale Ridge, Maytag rises over several steps to meet the original incarnation of Maytag Trail, which goes .2 mile to the end of the public part of Blithedale Ridge FR and the Via Van Dyke connector path.

Go right on Elinor. In roughly 50 yards, bend left and climb the short, final section to Blithedale Ridge FR. The junction is marked by an MCOSD signpost. It is then .6 mile right to the Corte Madera Ridge FR intersection.

When upper Blithedale Ridge was acquired as public open space in the 1970s, a local Boy Scout troop cleared a narrow parallel path in the shaded woodland just below the fire road. The path ran from the private property boundary before petering out in the forest. During the clearing, a discarded Maytag appliance was found (and removed)—hence the name. MCOSD later built a trail from Elinor FR to Blithedale Ridge, incorporating part of Maytag Trail. This new route was dubbed the Elinor Trail by some. But when the MCOSD signs were upgraded, they read "Maytag Trail," so that name prevails. It is also sometimes called Hazel Trail, for the shrub that is abundant along the route.

▓ Monte Vista Fire Road

Tenderfoot Trail to Monte Vista Avenue, Mill Valley: .32 mile

TERRAIN: Redwood forest (City of Mill Valley)

ELEVATION: From 240 to 350 feet; gradual

INTERSECTING TRAIL(S): None

Though broad, this route is called Monte Vista Trail on the semi-official *Mill Valley Steps, Lanes, and Paths* map. It also appears as a street, the lower end of Monte Vista Avenue, on older road maps.

The lower trailhead is the same as for Tenderfoot Trail, beside 477 Cascade Drive. Enter quietly, respecting the adjacent homeowner's privacy. In 100 yards, there is a fork. Tenderfoot, heading toward Mountain Home, branches off sharply right. Monte Vista FR rises left (straight) up the creek canyon.

130

At once, you are in redwood forest. A particularly striking redwood stands 100 yards in, on the left. Two trunks split about 20 feet up, then twist around one another. An aged laurel leans against the tree.

Monte Vista bends left over and around the creek at .2 mile. Another huge, double-trunked redwood stands sentinel at the crossing. At the far end of the bend, a rock suitable for sitting has been placed in what is often the fire road's lone sunny spot. A plaque, placed December 15, 2003, honors *The donation of Paul A. and Eva J. Johansson Griffin of the Griffin Open Space Preserve to the City of Mill Valley for conservation and open space purposes.*

The uphill is gentle. California hazel, with its velvety-soft leaves, is common here. Where the forest thins, look left for the views of Mt. Tamalpais that gave the fire road its name.

The route may be considered to end at the "Mill Valley Steps, Lanes, and Paths" sign. If you continue on, you will come to Monte Vista and Rose Avenues. There is a connector up from Rose Avenue to Cypress Trail, which can then be taken right, back to Tenderfoot, for a loop.

Old Railroad Grade

West Blithedale Avenue, Mill Valley, to Ridgecrest Boulevard: 6.72 miles

TERRAIN: Lower part wooded, upper part mostly chaparral; heavily used (MCOSD, MMWD)

ELEVATION: From 240 to 2,220 feet; gradual

INTERSECTING TRAIL(s): H-Line FR (.1 mile), Horseshoe FR (.6 mile), Temelpa (1.8 miles, 2.2 miles), connector to Hoo-Koo-E-Koo FR (2.6 miles), Gravity Car Grade (2.9 miles), Hoo-Koo-E-Koo Trail (3.1 miles), Hoo-Koo-E-Koo FR (3.2 miles), Vic Haun (3.2 miles), Hogback FR (3.8 miles), Fern Creek (4.2 miles), Miller (4.3 miles, 6.0 miles), Nora (5.3 miles), Old Stage Road (5.3 miles), Rock Spring (5.3 miles), Tavern Pump (6.2 miles)

Incredibly, the original 8.25 miles of Old Railroad Grade were cleared, graded, and covered with track within just seven months (February to August) in 1896. The Mill Valley & Mt. Tamalpais Scenic Railway (changed to Mt. Tamalpais & Muir Woods Scenic Railway in 1907), which proclaimed itself "the World's Crookedest Railroad," carried hundreds of thousands of riders to the summit and to Muir Woods, and brought the grade and the mountain worldwide fame.

The grade remains the most heavily used base-to-summit route on the mountain, particularly for mountain bikers. No route has more intersections: fifteen designated and several more now closed.

Uphill trains departed the downtown Mill Valley train station (now the Depot Bookstore & Cafe) shared with the commuter line from Sausalito. The

8.25 miles of single track up the mountain rounded a total of 281 curves, the equivalent of 42 full circles. The longest straight section, which occurs in the middle of the celebrated series of turns known as Double Bow Knot, was only 413 feet. The uphill never exceeded a modest 7-degree grade. There were originally 22 trestles, all later filled. The last trains ran in October 1929; service did not restart for the 1930 season.

Most of the line's first 1.3 miles run beside Corte Madera Creek along Corte Madera Avenue. The surviving Old Railroad Grade begins off West Blithedale Avenue, some 50 yards beyond Lee Street. (From 1905 to 1927, a local commuter service operated on Mountain Railway track between Lee Street and the downtown depot.) The MCOSD sign on the gate does not mention the route's famous name or past, only the designation "Northridge, Blithedale Summit." There is also a sign about the watershed's salmon.

This lower section skirts private property, with homes visible across Arroyo Corte Madera Creek. The area is well wooded, and the many big leaf maple trees bring a taste of New England-like colors in fall. In 200 yards, the steep H-Line FR (also called Two Tanks Road) rises on the right to Blithedale Ridge. Farther along, a fence adjoins the grade on the left. Surprisingly, two trees—a bay laurel and a redwood—stand in the middle of the fire road. MCOSD rerouted the old railroad bed here for better drainage.

The grade reaches a bend called Horseshoe Curve, the sharpest on the entire route, over Corte Madera Creek. (This was the eighth, and last, crossing for the rail line.) On the near side of the creek, Horseshoe FR, also going to Blithedale Ridge, sets off uphill to the right. Corte Madera Trail splits from Horseshoe FR some 100 yards higher. Damage from the storm of 1982 created a rare dip—the original route had no such dips—in the grade at Horseshoe Curve. Here, Old Railroad Grade leaves MCOSD lands to enter the jurisdiction of the MMWD, where it remains virtually all the rest of the way.

There is a marked change in vegetation as the grade climbs the hotter, drier, south-facing slope. Chaparral largely replaces the redwoods, except at creek crossings. The site of an old wood Mile Marker 2 marker (as calibrated from the Mill Valley depot; deduct 1.3 miles to match our start) is passed. All the old mile markers, which stood until only a few years ago, are now gone.

A fence line on the left marks the upper boundary of the private, 43-acre Ralston L. White Memorial Retreat Center. Ralston White (1877–1943) built his dream home here and named it the Garden of Allah, after a book popular at the time. Building materials came over the Mountain Railroad track and were dropped at the still-evident White Siding. The huge, steel-framed, concrete-walled main house, which was completed in 1917 and is now hidden by trees, was so sturdily built that it survived the terrible 1929 Tam fire that started nearby. In 1957, Mrs. Ralston White deeded the estate to the United Church of Christ for a period of 100 years; it is now available for rental for weddings and other occasions. Just beyond the start of the fence is a fire hydrant beneath a madrone, then a locked gate. The terrain is more open here, characteristic of upper Old Railroad Grade.

From a water tank left, a pipeline is visible, embedded in the grade. A path branches left, then winds down through the private property of the Garden of Allah. In another 150 yards is a big bend left, where the grade goes over a creek. The pipeline in the creek bed supplied water to the Garden of Allah.

Seventy-five yards before Mile Marker 3 (elevation 700 feet), the grade enters its largest road cut, the McKinley Cut. At its start, look for a boulder on the left with the words "McKinley Cut." President William McKinley was scheduled to ride on the railroad in 1900 and the Mill Valley depot was properly festooned, but his wife became ill and the trip was cancelled. Over the years, people have maintained the lettering, but it is presently faded.

Around .3 mile, the grade reaches an MMWD gate and, immediately after, a private residence. Just higher, 10 yards before the grade meets the junction of Summit Avenue and Fern Canyon Road, Temelpa Trail sets off uphill toward the mountain's summit. There is also a connector some 50 yards ahead. A bench with a great view has been added at the intersection.

The grade is paved and open to auto traffic for .7 mile along Fern Canyon Road. Views, including of the San Francisco skyline, compensate. The grade can be reached by car here via Summit Avenue, off Lovell Avenue. Temelpa Trail again touches Fern Canyon Road, on the right. A restored sign in the old style marks the junction.

Once the grade reenters woodland beyond a gate at the upper end of Fern Canyon Road, its surface is again dirt. A fence on the left marks the boundary of a private estate. In 1927, W.H.R. Nostrand purchased 17 acres from Ralston White. In 1930, after the railway ceased operating, MMWD sold 10 additional acres to Nostrand but retained through rights.

Just past Mile Marker 4, the grade crosses the East Fork of Cascade Creek. Steep, rough, shortcut paths to Hoo-Koo-E-Koo FR climb both banks. The second one used to be known as Murray Trail, named in honor of Frank Murray upon his death in 1922. One of the first trail chairs of the Tamalpais Conservation Club, he signed the East Peak summit register in 1881 as a fourteen-year-old.

The grade leaves tree cover for the chaparral that characterizes much of the rest of the climb. (Early Tam photos show this whole upper part of the grade as treeless.) Views to the east, south, and west become ever more expansive.

The grade then enters the famous Double Bow Knot (a name that also appears as Bow-Knot and Bowknot, and without the "Double"). Here, the tracks ran parallel to themselves five times over a straight-line distance of just 600 feet, to gain 168 feet of elevation. It used to be easy to go wrong in the maze here, losing the grade by not bending right and ending up on Gravity Car FR toward Mountain Home. New signposts ease the problem.

The grade passes the stone platform remnant of Mesa Station, at 4.5 miles, elevation 1,120 feet. (A shortcut path, with steps, goes to Mesa Station from just lower in the grade. Other paths within the Bow Knot, originally worn by railway employees hopping on and off the train to change signals, are now posted as closed.) In 1907, track was laid from here to the new Muir Inn, above what was soon to become Muir Woods National Monument. Passengers left the main line for the descent, often on engineless gravity cars. Also at Mesa Station, returning Muir Woods visitors could catch a train up Tam or back to Mill Valley. The grade bends left. There is a stand of introduced Coulter pines, which produce the world's heaviest cones.

Just before the Bow Knot's final bend, Hoo-Koo-E-Koo Trail branches sharply left to Hogback FR. One hundred yards beyond on the grade, Hoo-Koo-E-Koo departs right as a fire road. The top of the former Murray Trail is 15 yards along, on the right. The grade itself bends left here. In this bend, Vic Haun Trail sets off uphill to Temelpa Trail.

The grade is now on a steady course west. Past Mile Marker 5 is the intersection with Hogback FR, which drops directly to Mountain Home. To the right is the long-closed, precipitous, and rocky Throckmorton Trail, a once-popular route to East Peak.

The grade re-enters woodland as Upper Fern Creek Trail rises to the right at the bend over Fern Creek. This was one of the few flat spots on the original railroad grade, a problem for descending gravity cars. Brakemen would either warn downhill passengers they would be gaining extra speed approaching this curve, or face stopping and pushing. Just ahead, a reliable spring flows down a rock on the right.

At the next big bend, rebuilding after the January 1982 storm introduced a second short, but noticeable, downhill to the grade (Mile Marker 6 was a victim of the storm). Here, Miller Trail begins its very steep climb as a shaded shortcut to higher on the grade.

The grade climbs nearly a mile through the chaparral without another trail intersection. Finally, the cluster of buildings of West Point Inn appears. The inn sits at the westernmost edge of Old Railroad Grade. It was built by the railroad in 1904 in anticipation of a new rail line—never constructed—from West Point to the coast.

West Point remained the transfer point for rail passengers continuing to Bolinas via stagecoach. The rustic guest cottages—there is no electricity—were added a few years later (they're open to visitors; phone well in advance for reservations). The inn's famous "honeymoon suite" was built in 1918 by Dr. Henry Washington Dodge, a survivor of the *Titanic* disaster and member of the Tamalpais Conservation Club.

The inn is run, under lease from MMWD, by the West Point Inn Association. The association also hosts a series of popular Sunday pancake breakfasts open to all. A public bathroom; picnic tables (including some sheltered and shaded under the veranda) with great views; and exhibits on the mountain's geology, flora and fauna, and history are all available here. The long-time water fountain in front of the inn was shut off by MMWD in April 2003 due to stricter federal quality standards, though the spring-fed, filtered water had always been considered safe. (Ironically, in the 1990s, MMWD considered bottling and marketing this same water!)

Three routes meet the grade at West Point: Nora Trail, dropping steeply left to Matt Davis; broad Old Stage Road, descending to Pantoll; and Rock Spring Trail, heading to Mountain Theater. West Point also was the site of a siding for the extra railway cars used on Mountain Play weekends; playgoers then walked Rock Spring Trail to the theater.

The grade rounds the inn and soon passes Mile Marker 7. The final stretch is largely treeless, and often hot in summer. Miller Trail crosses the grade, and continues left uphill to Ridgecrest Boulevard and International Trail.

Soon after, Tavern Pump Trail joins from the right. It descends to Fern Creek Trail. Mile Marker 8 is passed.

The grade ends at paved Ridgecrest Boulevard in the saddle between East and Middle Peaks. Across the pavement is Middle Peak FR and, to the right, the top of Eldridge Grade. The track once continued up to the famous Tavern of Tamalpais, or Summit Tavern, at the far edge of today's East Peak parking lot. The original tavern was built in 1896 as part of the railway project; it was instantly popular, which led to its expansion not long after opening. It offered gracious dining, dancing, and overnight accommodations. The tavern burned to the ground in 1923, was rebuilt, and survived the mountain's 1929 conflagration. It continued as a commercial enterprise until 1942, when it was leased to the army for use as a barracks. The structure fell into such disrepair that it was deliberately burned down by MMWD in 1950. Its foundation now blends into the overlook picnic area.

Among the private railway's principal financial backers were Sidney Cushing, who owned the Blithedale Hotel near the starting point; William Kent, who went on to donate land for Muir Woods, Steep Ravine, and other sites to the public; and the Tamalpais Land and Water Co., which was then developing its Mill Valley holdings.

The railway was beloved, and popular; in 1915, the year the Panama–Pacific International Exposition was held in San Francisco, more than 100,000 people took the ride to the top. Later, it fell victim to the increased popularity of the automobile, particularly when the construction of Ridgecrest Boulevard and Panoramic Highway in the 1920s made it possible to drive to the top. The fire of 1929 was a final blow. The tracks were pulled in 1930 but it is still possible, if you're sharp-eyed and lucky, to find old spikes along the grade.

The story of the railway is one of the mountain's most colorful. It is well told in *The Crookedest Railroad in the World*, by Ted Wurm and Al Graves. The railway's flavor is also charmingly recaptured in Cris Chater's 1988 award-winning film, *Steaming Up Tamalpais*.

■ Temelpa Trail

Old Railroad Grade at Fern Canyon Road, Mill Valley, to Verna Dunshee Trail: 1.76 miles

TERRAIN: Chaparral, very rocky (MMWD)

ELEVATION: From 820 to 2,380 feet; very steep, middle section extremely steep and dangerous to descend

INTERSECTING TRAIL(S): Old Railroad Grade (.2 mile), Hoo-Koo-E-Koo FR (.5 mile), Vic Haun (.7 mile)

Temelpa was built to be the most direct route from Mill Valley to the top of Mt. Tamalpais. Needless to say, that also made it Tam's steepest trail. Now, the lower part of Temelpa is gone, cut off by private property. What is currently its lower section has been improved with steps, and the section above Vic Haun Trail has been significantly eased (and lengthened) with gentle switchbacks.

Still, Temelpa is a formidable route. The surviving untouched section, between Hoo-Koo-E-Koo FR and Vic Haun, will test anyone, uphill or downhill (which is treacherous and not recommended). But the rewards, including a visit to the little-known treasure of the Sitting Bull plaque, make Temelpa a must for all hardy Tam lovers.

Temelpa Trail presently starts uphill, unmarked, off Old Railroad Grade a few feet below the junction of Summit Avenue and Fern Canyon Road. Not many years ago, it commenced by the bridge on Summit Avenue, before upper Summit was paved. Originally, Temelpa started even lower, in Blithedale Canyon.

Temelpa Trail meets an access path coming from Fern Canyon Road to the left. After another 100 yards, Temelpa briefly touches Fern Canyon Road, which is a paved section of Old Railroad Grade. The junction is identified by a restored sign and yellow fire hydrant (and may be considered the true start of today's Temelpa).

The next section, to Hoo-Koo-E-Koo FR, was greatly improved in 1997. An old 2-inch pipeline that cut a gully through the trail was removed, dozens of wood steps added, and brush cleared. Much of the work was done by local Eagle Scouts under MMWD's direction.

The views are sweeping, and get ever better. Look up to see the distant goal; East Peak. At .3 mile, a connector path to Hoo-Koo-E-Koo FR branches right; some call it Easter Lily Trail. Stay left, up the steps.

In just under ½ mile, Temelpa crosses Hoo-Koo-E-Koo FR; an MMWD sign-post marks the junction. Left on Hoo-Koo-E-Koo leads to the top of the Double Bow Knot, right to Wheeler Trail. Cross the fire road and keep climbing … and climbing.

The next ⅓ mile is extremely steep and grueling. Boulders and encroaching sharp-pointed shrubs add to the challenge. Some underlying rocks are exposed, revealing sedimentary layers. But then, the reward: the large boulder on the left called Halfway Rock. (If you hit the Vic Haun Trail intersection, you've gone 25 yards past it.) The boulder itself, a block of erosion-resistant quartz tourmaline that fell from East Peak during a slide in the distant past, is wonderful enough, and the plaque affixed to it is among the mountain's jewels. It contains one of the most eloquent environmental statements ever expressed, the words of the Sioux chief Sitting Bull. (The quote is also found in *The Portable North American Indian Reader*, edited by Frederick W. Turner III [Viking Press, 1974].)

Behold my brothers, the spring has come; the earth has received the embraces of the sun and we shall soon see the result of all that love! Every seed is awakened and so has all animal life. It is through this mysterious power that we too have our being and we therefore yield to our neighbors, even our animal neighbors, the same right as ourselves, to inhabit this land. Yet hear me, people, we have now to deal with another race; small and feeble when our fathers first met them but now great and overbearing. Strangely enough they have a mind to till the soil and the love of possession is a disease to them. These people have made many rules that the rich may break but the poor may not. They take tithes from the poor and weak to support the rich who rule. They claim this mother of ours, the earth, for their own and fence their neighbors away; they deface her with their buildings and their refuse. That nation is like a spring freshet that overruns its banks and destroys all who are in its path.

Sitting Bull 1877

The original plaque, placed in the 1980s, was defaced in 1990. A good samaritan attempted to replace it (with MMWD permission) in 1993 and inadvertently shattered it. The replacement quickly fell off. Today's plaque, which one hopes will endure, was installed soon after.

Just up from Halfway Rock, at a newly signed intersection, is Vic Haun Trail. It descends, more gradually than Temelpa, to the Old Railroad Grade in the Double Bow Knot. To its right is the newly routed uphill continuation of Temelpa, on a section of the now-closed Telephone Trail. Sweeping views continue the rest of the way. At the next junction, in some 200 yards, Temelpa bends sharply right, away from the former Telephone Trail.

The rerouted Temelpa climbs switchbacks. A new bridge was built by the TCC in 2002. Temelpa crosses Devil's Slide, a massive rockfall that swept more than 1,000 vertical feet down the gully during the storm of January 1982. Late Tam geologist Salem Rice noted that the slide must have generated a tremendous roar, but apparently no one was nearby to hear it.

Continue ever up, enjoying the knockout views, from Mt. St. Helena to the north, across San Francisco, and beyond to the southeast. Old routes lace the hillside but Temelpa is clear to follow upward.

Temelpa Trail ends, signed, at the Verna Dunshee Trail loop roughly halfway around from the East Peak parking area. Forty yards to the right is the top of the '82 slide, shored by a wood structure labeled "the Great Wall of Mt. Tam."

Temelpa (variously spelled) is one name for the legendary lovelorn "Sleeping Maiden" who reposes on the mountain and gives the summit ridge its famous profile. While this legend, inspiration for many poems and stories, is not of Native American origin, it's a cherished one. The most famous recounting of the myth is Dan Totheroh's play, *Tamalpa*, which has been presented for a record eight seasons at Mountain Theater. Its closing line, recited as the maiden Tamalpa is borne to her final resting place, is, "Throw over her the purple cloak that she will always wear—a shroud of amethyst from tip of toe to crown of hair."

Temelpa Trail was formerly Summit Trail and one of Tamalpais's oldest, dating from around 1875. The name was changed in 1914. It has also been called Cushing's Trail, because it led up from the Cushing family's hotel in Blithedale Canyon. During a race in 1987, Tom Borschel ran from Lytton Square in downtown Mill Valley, elevation 64 feet, to the East Peak fire lookout, elevation 2,571 feet, via Summit Avenue and Temelpa Trail (using shortcuts now closed) in an astonishing 30 minutes, 32 seconds.

◼ Tenderfoot Trail

Cascade Drive to Edgewood Avenue, Mill Valley: 1.09 miles

TERRAIN: Deep woodland (City of Mill Valley)

ELEVATION: From 270 to 840 feet; steep

INTERSECTING TRAIL(S): Monte Vista FR (.1 mile), Cypress (.4 mile)

Note: Open to bicycles.

A pair of trails, Zig-Zag and Tenderfoot, rise toward Mountain Home from the west end of Mill Valley's Cascade Drive. They can be combined (Zig-Zag is extremely steep) for a loop, with rest and refreshments available halfway through at Mountain Home Inn.

Cascade Drive—flanking a creek and lined with redwoods and attractive homes—is a quintessential Mill Valley street. To reach Tenderfoot, follow it just over 1 mile from Old Mill Park and .2 mile past Cascade Falls. A sign beside the driveway of 477 Cascade reads "Tenderfoot Trails." The plural is no mistake; the hillside south of Cascade is laced with unmarked paths and intersections.

Start the climb by passing quietly to the left of the private residence. The first junction on Tenderfoot is in just 30 yards. Left (straight) is Monte Vista FR. Veer right. In another 50 yards, the broad Tenderfoot passes through a gate. A sign here instructs bicyclists—Tenderfoot is open to bikes, though is not a route for novices—to dismount when passing.

The second fork is at .2 mile. Spine-covered fruits fallen off chinquapin trees cover the ground here in early fall. The right path immediately enters private property; veer left. Fork three, by an old corrugated-iron switchback siding, is at .4 mile. Cypress Trail goes left, winding more than 1.5 miles to Cypress Avenue. Veer right.

At a brief clearing in Tenderfoot's woodland canopy, a striking vista of East Peak opens. Around 75 yards beyond is fork four. The upper, right option ends in 25 yards; veer left. The fifth and last fork, at .7 mile, is in deep woodland. Tenderfoot's sequence of turns is easy to remember—right, left, right, left, right.

Tenderfoot's remaining climb passes through a quiet redwood forest and bypasses a slide. A few yards later, the trail crosses a stream over a bridge of lashed redwood logs.

The topmost yards of Tenderfoot Trail were rerouted in 1990 to skirt the carport of a new home. The trail ends at Edgewood Avenue, beside a fire pump protected by fencing. Just to the left, beyond another home, is Pipeline Trail, leading toward the top of the Dipsea Steps. A ½ mile to the right on Edgewood is Mountain Home Inn, with Zig-Zag Trail just beyond.

There have been various proposals over the years to develop home sites along the historic Tenderfoot Trail. In 1980, concerned citizens mounted a major effort to keep it open. Evidence was cited that Tenderfoot had been used by Coast Miwoks, then by the earliest loggers. Additional adjoining private acreage was acquired in 1997–1998.

The name "Tenderfoot" may refer to the fact that the trail is more gently graded than the Dipsea steps, Zig-Zag Trail (which is twice as steep), the former (now overgrown) adjacent Mill Creek Fire Trail, or other old routes up out of Mill Valley.

▨ Warner Canyon (Falls) Trail

Elinor FR to Warner Falls: .47 mile

TERRAIN: Riparian; mostly redwood forest (MCOSD)

ELEVATION: Around 380 feet; almost level

INTERSECTING TRAIL(S): None; dead end

The lovely waterfall on Warner Creek can be accessed via this relatively little-traveled trail. The falls are known both as Warner, for the creek and canyon, and occasionally as Elinor, because access is by Elinor Avenue. The trail to the falls wasn't signed until 1994.

To reach the trailhead, follow Elinor FR .3 mile from its start at the upper end of Elinor Avenue. A bit over 100 yards beyond MCOSD-signed Tartan (Road) Trail, the fire road bends sharply left and uphill. In the middle of this bend, Warner Canyon Trail sets off level to the right.

The early section is wide. The trail was originally a road, but, like other old cuts in the area, narrowed as it became heavily overgrown with French broom. Indeed, parts of the later route became near impassable around 2000, and a sign encouraged hikers to pull the broom. Today, the broom is largely gone, but the plant is hardy.

Redwoods are abundant and maples and madrones are also common. So too is the shrub hazel, with leaves soft to the touch and edible nuts usually first grabbed by squirrels and birds. The trail rises almost imperceptibly.

In .1 mile, a giant laurel on the left has fallen and its cut branches lie below, but the tree lives on and thrives. Here, look right to see down to the floor of Warner Canyon.

The route narrows. At a prominent clearing, sun pours in and broom still flourishes. At the end of this open patch, a seep nourishes giant chain fern, the largest fern species in Marin. There is some poison oak.

The trail begins to noticeably rise as it meets Warner Creek. The falls and the end of the trail are just ahead. (The trail's apparent continuation above the falls quickly deteriorates.) The flow is lively after a winter rain but nonexistent by late spring. This is a quiet place, bordered by huge redwoods and colored in spring by abundant trillium.

Alexander Warner, a San Francisco physician, bought 170 acres in what was then called Juanita Canyon in 1885 for $6,000. For years, he brought his large family to summer there. The family sold the parcel (including 35 additional acres acquired in 1917) at the end of World War II. The lower portions were then developed. MCOSD began making acquisitions in Warner Canyon in the 1970s.

■ Wheeler Trail

Hoo-Koo-E-Koo FR to Eldridge Grade: .53 mile

Terrain: Light woods, rocky chaparral (MMWD)

Elevation: From 1,120 to 1,570 feet; very steep to extremely steep

Intersecting Trail(s): None

As a key link across the mountain's east face, Wheeler Trail is part of many circle routes around Tamalpais. It sets off uphill from Hoo-Koo-E-Koo FR at Slide Gulch (also called Devil's Slide), .2 mile north from the Temelpa Trail crossing. The gulch, a named feature on the mountain for more than 100 years, marks a long, prominent slide that runs southeast from below East Peak. At Wheeler's base are a dam and pipeline, remnants of the old Slide Gulch water intake.

Begin uphill from the Wheeler signpost. Bear sharply right a few feet up the trail (don't cross the creek). Wheeler rises very steeply, in parts extremely steeply, through a forest of thin redwoods. After ¼ mile, the trail emerges into chaparral, with manzanita the dominant shrub. The views—and effort—are breathtaking.

Keep climbing over the very rocky terrain. There are a few places to sit and enjoy the grandeur, gazing down at busy Marin below. At last, there is a welcome downhill. Fifty yards later, Wheeler ends at a signed, horseshoe curve in Eldridge Grade. Right leads down to the lakes, left, up to Northside Trail and East Peak.

The trail was largely built by Alfred Wheeler, an attorney who sailed to San Francisco from New York in 1849. In the 1850s, Wheeler prospered in San Francisco real estate. He loved to hike on Tam, and, seeing the need for a connection between the north and south sides of the mountain, decided to do the work himself.

The *San Francisco Chronicle* covered the September 1902 dedication ceremony, during which bronze tablets (now long gone) honoring Wheeler were placed at both ends of the trail. The account reads, in part:

For over two years, through summer's heat and winter's cold, this philanthropist, 80 years of age, toiled away with pick and shovel on the stubborn slopes of Tamalpais. He pursued his end with infinite patience, clearing a path over flinty rocks, hewing away the resisting chaparral, prying boulders out of the way, and all for a labor of love. . . . He is now only able to move about with the help of crutches, and will probably never see his trail again. . . . His thoughts dwell constantly on the heights of Tamalpais, and in his dreams he is still working away . . . on the winding path.

Wheeler died eleven months later. His *Chronicle* obituary said, "The [trail] work cost him his life."

▦ Zig-Zag Trail

Cascade Drive, Mill Valley, to Mountain Home: .5 mile

TERRAIN: Mostly redwood forest, some chaparral; unmaintained and marginal (City of Mill Valley and private, with easement)

ELEVATION: From 290 to 900 feet; extremely steep

INTERSECTING TRAIL(S): None

Zig-Zag Trail is part of the quickest route from Mill Valley to Mountain Home. Indeed, in the 1983 Dipsea Race, the late Mill Valley runner Ron Rahmer used it instead of the Dipsea Trail with astonishing success. (Rahmer's route was longer than the Dipsea Trail, but involved just one uphill, as opposed to the Dipsea's two. In any case, his new route was immediately banned.) Climbing at the rate of 1,220 feet per mile, Zig-Zag likely has the steepest average gradient (23 percent) of any route in this book—so steep that many might find descending it dangerous; it will be described uphill.

The trailhead is to the left of the driveway for the private residence of 550 Cascade Drive, where Cascade and Lovell Avenue meet. Please be courteous. An adjacent road leads to Cascade Dam, drained Cascade Reservoir, and now-abandoned Cascade Fire Trail. The reservoir, site of hippie-era carousing during the 1960s and '70s, was closed to the public after a drowning death, and old "closed" signs remain.

Zig-Zag starts by crossing a bridge, then goes uphill beside a fence surrounding a charming old covered reservoir that served as Mill Valley's early water source. It holds 68,000 gallons and is 9 feet deep.

Almost immediately, the extremely steep climbing begins. The switchbacks that gave the trail its name help a little, but do not let the few slightly easier stretches fool you: all are followed by more mountaineering. Much of the route goes through redwood forest—some mature, some with young, thin, trees.

The trail skirts several private parcels. Well up, Zig-Zag enters an open, rocky gully, which can be dangerously slippery to descend when wet. There are views above the chaparral shrubs to Mill Valley, "Little Tamalpais" (Corte Madera Ridge), and Tam's summit ridge. Huckleberry becomes abundant.

Zig-Zag re-enters woodland. There are a few paths left, including one to the newer home built between Zig-Zag and Mountain Home Inn. Though Zig-Zag once continued over the ridge down to Muir Woods, it now ends, unsigned (there was a trail sign here for decades), at the base of the dirt driveway into the Mountain Home overflow parking area. Fifty yards right is Gravity Car Grade. Mountain Home Inn and Panoramic Highway are just uphill to the left.

Zig-Zag Trail is shown but unnamed on the 1898 Sanborn map and named on the 1914 Tamalpais Fire Association map.

Second (middle) flight of the Dipsea steps, scheduled to be rebuilt.

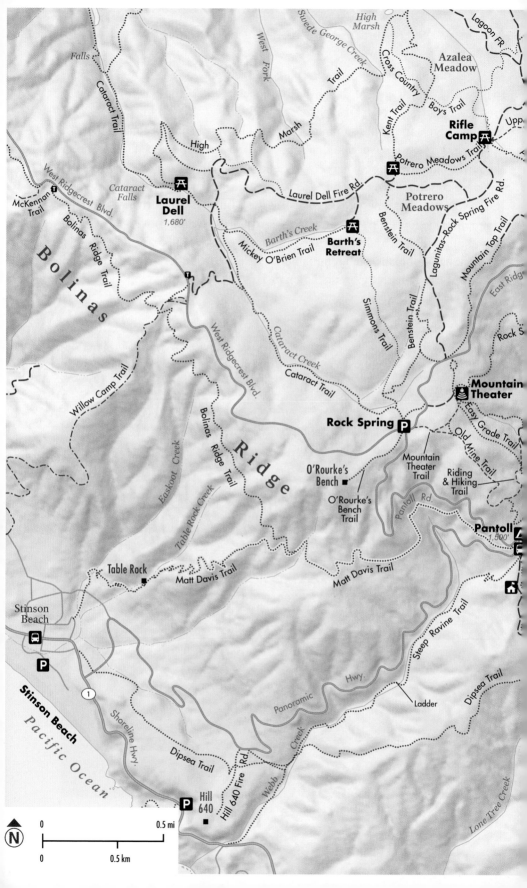

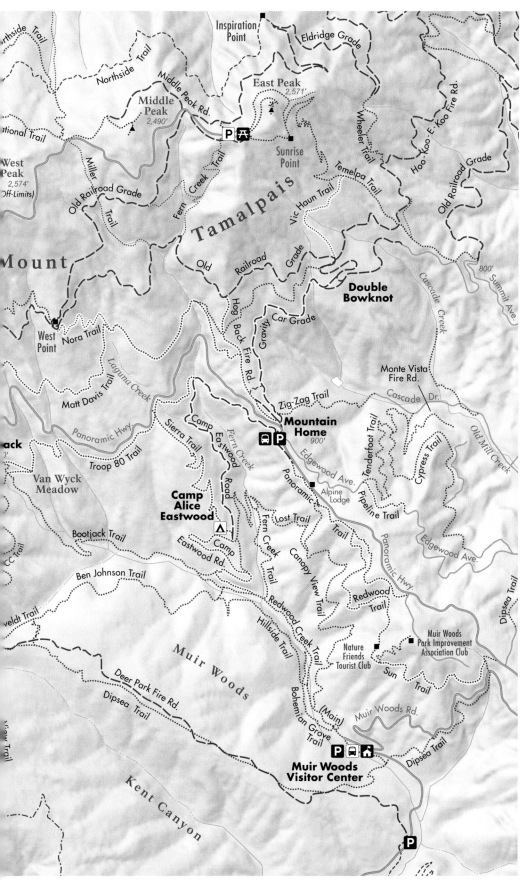

Sun Trail looking west to the Pacific

TRAILHEAD FIVE: MOUNTAIN HOME

Directions
Highway 101—Highway 1—Panoramic Highway near Mile Marker 2.69

Mountain Home has been a popular Tamalpais trailhead for more than a century. A dozen trails and fire roads converge there, fanning out to cover the mountain's south side. Many organized hikes start from this trailhead, and every Saturday morning for the past forty-five years, a group of runners sets off from it.

The parking lot, which is free, fills early on weekends. There is an overflow lot just north across Panoramic Highway, and one just south at the top of Camp Eastwood Road. The trailhead has a fountain built by the Tamalpa Runners in 1982, and two outhouses. A Marin Stagecoach Route 61 bus stops here several times a day (check the schedule online), which opens one-way-hike options.

The Alpine-themed Mountain Home Inn was built in 1912—the year MMWD was created, opening public hiking lands right to its edge—by a Swiss couple, Claus and Martha Meyer. There was a beer garden, restaurant, and guest rooms. The opening of Panoramic Highway in 1928 made the inn even more popular. Claus died in an automobile accident and Martha sold the inn in 1930. After several more ownership changes, and a few years of being closed altogether, the inn was completely remodeled and reopened in 1985. Today, it offers light refreshments and elegant dining, plus ten guest rooms.

Suggested Loops

1. Gravity Car Grade, 1.0 mile, to Old Railroad Grade—left, .9 mile, to Hogback FR—left, .7 mile, to start. **2.6 miles total**

2. Hogback FR, .3 mile, to Matt Davis Trail—left, .9 mile, to Nora Trail—right .5 mile, to West Point—right (downhill), 1.6 miles, on Old Railroad Grade to Hogback FR—right, .7 mile, to start. **4.0 miles total**

3. Hogback FR, .3 mile, to Matt Davis Trail—left, 2.3 miles, to Bootjack Picnic Area—left on Bootjack Trail, .4 mile, to Troop 80 Trail—left, 1.5 miles, to Camp Eastwood Road—left, .5 mile, to start. **5.0 miles total**

4. Camp Eastwood Road, 2.3 miles, to Redwood Creek Trail, Muir Woods—left, 1.0 miles, to Dipsea Trail—left, .8 mile, to Sun Trail—left, .7 mile, to Tourist Club—Redwood Trail, .5 mile, to Panoramic Trail—left, 1.0 mile, to start. **6.3 miles total**

5. Circumambulation (Circle) of Mt. Tamalpais: Gravity Car Grade, .9 mile, to Old Railroad Grade—left (uphill), .2 mile, to Hoo-Koo-E-Koo FR—right, .7 mile, to Wheeler Trail—left, .5 mile, to Eldridge Grade—left (uphill), .5 mile, to Northside Trail—right, 2.7 miles, to Rifle Camp—left on Rock Spring-Lagunitas FR, 1.2 miles, across Ridgecrest Boulevard to Mountain Theater—left on Rock Spring Trail, 1.7 miles, to West Point—Old Railroad Grade downhill, 1.5 miles, to Hogback FR—right, .7 mile, to start. **10.6 miles total**

◾ Camp Eastwood Road (Alice Eastwood Trail)

Panoramic Highway to Redwood Creek Trail, Muir Woods: 2.25 miles

TERRAIN: Mostly redwood forest; upper half paved; bicycles not permitted below Camp Eastwood (MTSP, MWNM)

ELEVATION: From 900 to 220 feet; gradual

INTERSECTING TRAIL(S): Trestle Trail (.1 mile), Troop 80 (.6 mile), Sierra (1.4 miles), Lower Fern Creek (1.4 miles), Plevin Cut (1.4, 1.9 miles), Bootjack Spur (2.1 miles)

This broad route through a beautiful canyon was originally graded to carry the track of the Mt. Tamalpais & Muir Roads Railway. Beginning in 1907, passengers could disembark at Mesa Station when traveling up or down on the main line between Mill Valley and East Peak and take the side trip toward Muir Woods. (The line never ran all the way to the valley floor of Muir Woods, only to the Muir Inn above.) The descent from Mesa Station was generally by gravity car, and the ascent, by steam-powered engine.

The upper part of the old Muir Woods line, in MMWD land above Panoramic

Highway, is called Gravity Car Grade in this book. Camp Eastwood (or Alice Eastwood) Road is the section below Panoramic Highway.

Camp Eastwood Road begins at a gate south of Panoramic Highway, at a small parking area just before Mountain Home Inn when coming from Mill Valley. The upper section of Eastwood is paved, and the asphalt may turn off some hikers. But this is a lovely route, and vehicles are rare.

Shrubs, punctuated increasingly over the years by Douglas-firs, dominate the opening section. Indeed, an impressive Douglas-fir with many low branches stands just 25 yards in on the left. Highway shoulder signs along the edge are recycled safety markers from other Marin roads.

In around ⅙ mile, the road passes below the Mountain Home trailhead parking lot; the outhouses are visible. The short connection to the parking lot is called Trestle Trail. At a scant .03 mile in length, Trestle (a trestle carried a water pipeline over the rail tracks here before Panoramic Highway was built) is the shortest named trail on Tam. Layered sandstone rocks prominently line the road cut.

Camp Eastwood Road makes a broad bend left as it crosses over Fern Creek, which can be a torrent in winter. Just on the other side of the creek, to the right, Troop 80 Trail sets off to Bootjack Trail.

Now, towering redwoods dominate. Indeed, the whole deep canyon at the left is called Redwood Canyon (Sequoia Canyon on old maps). Many giants still bear scars from long-ago fires.

The road next crosses over Laguna Creek. A water tank here serves Camp Eastwood. In another 100 yards, a huge Douglas-fir leans over the road, then rises perfectly straight. Look near here for tree poppies, a shrub with striking yellow flowers in spring.

After 1.4 miles, the road meets a broad paved clearing: Camp Alice Eastwood. There are fountains, tables, outhouses, and an amphitheater for campfire presentations. Two adjacent campgrounds can accommodate fifty and twenty-five campers. (Reservations are required and available through the California State Parks system.)

This was the site of the first Muir Inn, built in 1908 and original terminus of the gravity car line. The inn was destroyed by fire in 1913. A year later, the line was extended .6 mile down, near the canyon floor, and a second Muir Inn built at the terminus. During the 1930s, members of the Depression-era Civilian Conservation Corps (CCC) built their Camp Mt. Tamalpais here. The camp comprised about fourteen structures; the foundations of a few are still evident.

On May 1, 1949, the former CCC camp was renamed in honor of Alice Eastwood (1859–1953). It was her ninetieth birthday, and she came to the ceremony, despite heavy rain. Alice Eastwood is one of the most legendary of all

Mt. Tamalpais figures. She began hiking on the mountain in the early 1890s, often the only woman in an otherwise all-male group. She was curator of botany at the California Academy of Sciences from 1892 to 1949, and her passion was plants. Eastwood's specialty was the manzanita (genus *Arctostaphylos*), which are abundant on Mt. Tam. She is credited as the discoverer of a dozen of California's some sixty species. (A collection of her articles on Tam's flora was reissued by the Mount Tamalpais Interpretive Association.) Eastwood's home on Middle Ridge in Mill Valley was destroyed in the 1929 fire.

Several trails meet at the camp. To the left are the Plevin Cut and Fern Creek Trails. The former (too short to be separately described) slices around ⅓ mile off the descent of Camp Eastwood Road, while the latter is an alternate route to Muir Woods. To the right of Camp Eastwood Road is Sierra Trail, which rises to Troop 80 Trail.

Camp Eastwood Road, continuing to the right beyond a gate, is now unpaved (and called Alice Eastwood Trail on new signs). Some old maps call this section Stage Road; before the rail line was extended, the balance of the trip to Muir Woods was made by stagecoach.

The road passes through the rail bed's Plevin Cut. Then, a few yards later, it meets the bottom of Plevin Cut Trail. Look to the right for an overgrown old road. This is the lower section of the rail line that was extended down to the second Muir Inn in 1914.

Around ½ mile below the camp, the road makes a bend right at a clearing (which is disappearing as trees reclaim the site). This was the location of the second Muir Inn, which stood from 1914 until it was torn down in 1932. It had a view down to the canyon floor. Just a few yards below, at another bend and beside a redwood of enormous girth, is the signed top of Bootjack Spur. It drops .1 mile to Bootjack Trail.

Soon the asphalt-covered Redwood Creek (Main) Trail becomes visible. Camp Eastwood Road, now bordered by a wooden fence, meets it and ends. Just to the left is the lower end of Fern Creek Trail, a lovely loop companion. Beyond is the Muir Woods Visitor Center. Bridge 4 over Redwood Creek and the Ben Johnson and Bootjack Trails are to the right.

▨ Gravity Car Grade

Mountain Home to Old Railroad Grade at Double Bow Knot: .93 mile

TERRAIN: Former railroad cut; chaparral and lightly wooded (MMWD)

ELEVATION: From 900 to 1,100 feet; gradual

INTERSECTING TRAIL(S): Connector to Hogback FR (.1 mile)

The Mill Valley & Mount Tamalpais Scenic Railway, from downtown Mill Valley to near East Peak, was built in 1896. Its route is today's Old Railroad Grade. In 1907, a branch line, between Mesa Station in the grade's Double Bow Knot and the new Muir Inn, was added, and the railway was renamed Mt. Tamalpais & Muir Woods. The descent toward Muir Woods was usually by an engineless gravity car. The ride was both scenic and thrilling, with the posted top speed of 12 miles per hour often surpassed.

The railway's ridership declined in the face of new auto roads to the summit, the Depression, and the fire of July 1929. On October 31, 1929, the railway closed for the winter, never to reopen. Gravity Car Grade, now a dirt fire road with the tracks long gone, remains as a remnant of those special days.

Gravity Car Grade sets off from the end of the overflow parking lot just past the Mountain Home Inn (when coming from Mill Valley). This grade between the road and trailhead may seem puzzling, but there was actually no climb for the gravity cars. Instead, the tracks crossed directly through the Mine Ridge Cut, which was subsequently filled during construction of Panoramic Highway. The rest of the way is gently, almost imperceptibly, uphill.

As you enter the trail, a connector fire road rises to the left; it goes to the fire station on Throckmorton Ridge (Hogback FR). Introduced acacias, natives of Australia, mingle with redwoods. As the grade leaves the forest, views of southern Marin and San Francisco open. Shrubs line most of the way, though the grade passes through some half-dozen redwood groves at stream crossings.

Gravity Car Grade splits just before its end. In 100 yards, both forks connect to Old Railroad Grade, making its horseshoe turn through Double Bow Knot. Take the left fork to continue up the mountain, the right to descend to Mill Valley.

■ Hogback Fire Road

Mountain Home to Old Railroad Grade: .61 mile

TERRAIN: Chaparral; ridge top; (MMWD)

ELEVATION: 940 to 1,450 feet; very steep, slippery to descend

INTERSECTING TRAIL(S): Matt Davis (.3 mile), Hoo-Koo-E-Koo (.5 mile)

Note: Bicycles not permitted downhill

This very steep fire road is well used, as it is part of direct routes from the Mountain Home trailhead to popular destinations such as West Point, Bootjack, and Pantoll. One of the mountain's oldest routes, it was even more renowned when it was the principal hikers' access to East Peak from Mill Valley. However, its upper end, above Old Railroad Grade, has been closed for decades.

A paved road up to the Throckmorton Ridge Fire Station departs from Panoramic Highway 50 yards above Mountain Home Inn. Immediately right is the top of Zig-Zag Trail, the overflow parking lot, and Gravity Car Grade. Hogback FR climbs the ridge but many users stay on the slightly lower paved road. Traces of a former routing are visible just left of the road, including an old bench.

The dirt and paved options meet at the firehouse, built in 1959 and renovated in 2006. There is an information board and a water fountain at the barrier blocking uphill vehicular traffic.

Continue climbing. Just above the fire station on Hogback is the lowest point in elevation (around 1,060 feet) on Tamalpais, from which snowcapped peaks of the Sierra Nevada, 160 miles east, can be seen on clear winter days. Another treat is the abundant tree poppies (*Dendromecon rigida*). In late spring, their striking yellow flowers stand out amidst the manzanita.

A huge green water tank has replaced three smaller ones, and the old water spigot is also gone. Just above the tank is the start of Matt Davis Trail, heading left (west) to Bootjack.

The tough uphill continues. Hoo-Koo-E-Koo Trail crosses left and right. Left connects to Matt Davis in .2 mile, right goes to the Old Railroad Grade in the Double Bow Knot.

Hogback's climb ends at Old Railroad Grade, beside a prominent road cut. Left on the grade leads to West Point, right to Bow Knot. The long-closed continuation across the grade is still visible as a scar when looking at the mountain from Mill Valley.

"Hogback" refers to the ridge's shape in profile. Many people call the fire road "Throckmorton," the name of the ridge it climbs. San Francisco financier Samuel Throckmorton took over the huge Rancho Saucelito land grant, which covered much of southern Marin, from debt-ridden William Richardson in 1856.

He built a ranch home, called Homestead, in what is now Homestead Valley, near today's Montford Avenue/Linden Lane junction. Much of the estate was divided into dairy ranches that were rented to Portuguese settlers. Throckmorton died in 1883 at age seventy-five. His daughter, Susanna, ceded 3,790 acres, including the Mill Valley slope of Mt. Tamalpais, to the San Francisco Savings Union to settle debts against the Throckmorton estate. In 1890, what became central Mill Valley was auctioned off in lots. An alternate name is Mine Ridge, for a quicksilver (mercury) claim near the California Alpine Club just south of Mountain Home.

Though a fire road, the very steep Hogback is presently posted as closed to bicycles in the downhill direction. Old Railroad Grade, then Gravity Car Grade, is an alternate.

■ Matt Davis Trail

Hogback FR to Belvedere Avenue, Stinson Beach, plus spur to Buena Vista Avenue: 6.70 miles

TERRAIN: Mostly woodland; parts chaparral, grassland (MMWD, MTSP, GGNRA; segment part of Bay Area Ridge Trail)

ELEVATION: 1,100 to 1,500 to 60 feet; gradual, western part steep

INTERSECTING TRAIL(S): Hoo-Koo-E-Koo (.3 mile), Nora (1.0 mile), Bootjack (2.3 miles), Easy Grade (2.6 miles), Old Stage Road (2.6 miles), Coastal (4.3 miles)

Matt Davis Trail offers a wonderful east-west passage across the mountain. The trail traverses redwood-lined creeks, chaparral, magnificent open grassland, forests of towering Douglas-firs, and lush coastal flora on its way to Stinson Beach. Taking Matt Davis its full length—6.7 miles—and its return routes (all of which involve at least 1,500 feet of uphill) requires some planning. One option is a car shuttle. Another is to ride the West Marin Stagecoach Route 61 bus, which serves both ends (and intermediate points) of Matt Davis.

Though the west end of Matt Davis is accessible by car, most users join the trail at its east end, so we will, too. From Mountain Home, climb Hogback (Throckmorton) FR for .3 mile, past the fire station. The Matt Davis trailhead is to the left, just above the huge green water tank.

The trail begins up a few steps, then passes a water pipeline. Matt Davis is wide for a trail initially. This opening section was a later addition, built to provide MMWD with vehicular access to the water intake at Fern Creek. Tall chaparral shrubs alternate with redwood groves. The going is level to gently uphill. Panoramic Highway is occasionally visible (and audible).

In .3 mile, beside a splendid—and increasingly leaning—redwood with spiraled bark, Hoo-Koo-E-Koo Trail joins on the right. This is the start of the original Matt Davis Trail. Look above to see an old and no-longer-in-service outhouse.

The bridge ahead fords Fern Creek. Remnants of the old intake, a one-time water source, are visible.

The trail narrows, and you will pass stands of densely packed young redwoods. There are southern vistas in the clearings. A small meadow, known as Azalea Flat, lies a few yards to the left just before the noticeable uphill. Azaleas mark the overgrown entry.

In nearly a mile, at a bend just before a bridge over Laguna Creek, is the bottom end of Nora Trail, which goes uphill to West Point. Thirty yards before the junction is an old, non-working stone water fountain. Matt Davis levels and enters open terrain.

The trail cuts through chaparral. In 1984, a sizable area was the site of a controlled burn, and the landscape is now revegetated. Golden-fleece (*Ericameria arborescens*), which is quick to follow fire, stands out in bright green patches, and monkeyflowers add orange color.

The trail crosses Spike Buck Creek. As the terrain is now drier, redwoods do not line the creek here (although they are seen lower on the trail). Instead, hazels flank the bridge. The next bridge, also bordered by hazels, crosses a fork of Rattlesnake Creek. A rocky uphill leads to another bridge over a second Rattlesnake Creek fork. Azaleas are abundant.

Matt Davis then leaves MMWD and enters MTSP just outside Bootjack Camp. Bootjack was established as an overnight campground by the Tamalpais Conservation Club in the 1920s. It lost its isolation, but not its charm, when Panoramic Highway (which the TCC fought) was built right beside it in 1928. The Civilian Conservation Corps upgraded the camp in the 1930s, with classic fire pits and fountains. MTSP closed the campground in 1969 and the area became Bootjack Picnic Area. Then, in 2013, Bootjack was reopened for camping. At Bootjack, Matt Davis crosses Bootjack Trail, on its way from Muir Woods to Mountain Theater.

Matt Davis continues through the campground; follow the signs. After passing directly in front of the newer, upper bathrooms (presently closed), it cuts across a grassy slope between Panoramic Highway below and Old Stage Road above.

In .3 mile from Bootjack, Easy Grade Trail, going uphill to Mountain Theater, departs right. Climb a few steps to join and cross the paved Old Stage Road. It goes right to West Point, left down to Pantoll.

Pantoll Ranger Station is just to the left. The continuation of Matt Davis past Pantoll is a bit tricky. Follow the sign down the steps, then cross Southside Road (not Panoramic Highway) to another Matt Davis sign. There is a bench with a view. A path joins from the Pantoll parking lot, bringing the Bay Area Ridge Trail (for hikers) with it. Signs display a variety of distances: one on this path says it is 4.1 miles to Stinson Beach; where the path joins, the distance is given as 3.6 miles; at Stinson Beach (the west end of the trail), it's 3.3 miles back to Pantoll!

Matt Davis's remaining miles (whatever they may be—I measured 4.1) to Stinson Beach is sometimes called Matt Davis Extension, since it was built later. It is a pedestrian section of the Bay Area Ridge Trail. (In earlier editions of *Tamalpais Trails*, and on most maps, the next 1.5 miles of Matt Davis were also considered part of Coastal Trail.)

In the opening yards of the extension, the striking yellow flowers of the mariposa lily (*Calochortus clavatus*) stand out in late spring amidst the serpentine. Matt Davis quickly enters a cool, deep, Douglas-fir–dominated forest, where it remains for 1.2 miles. This nearly level stretch is one of the best places to see orchids in spring—calypso (*Calypso bulbosa*, invariably associated with Douglas-firs on Tam), spotted coralroot (*Corallorhiza maculata*), and others—but you'll have to look carefully. Several ravines carrying the upper forks of Webb Creek need to be forded. Look for a still-very-much-alive bay laurel extending horizontally from the left edge of the trail.

Matt Davis then emerges onto the open grasslands of Tam's west shoulder, one of the mountain's most dramatic changes of scenery. This is a spectacular area, with Tam's west wall towering behind and the Pacific below. A photograph from this vantage point graced the cover of Dorothy Whitnah's well-researched *An Outdoor Guide to the San Francisco Bay Area* (Wilderness Press, 1978). When the weather is mild, these gentle knolls are impossible-to-resist rest sites.

At a Bay Area Ridge Trail signpost, a path branches left to a cluster of trees atop "the Knolls," or "Big Knoll." This is Matt Davis's highest point, some 1,500 feet in elevation. You can usually first hear the ocean here, and the sound of the surf accompanies Matt Davis the rest of the way down.

The trail passes through two groves of bay laurels at stream gullies. At the end of the second, Matt Davis meets the Coastal Trail, now also known as Bolinas Ridge Trail, which continues right, all the way to Fairfax-Bolinas Road. Matt Davis drops left, through more grassland. There are great views to Bodega Head beyond Point Reyes on clear days.

Next is a long downhill through a bay laurel/Douglas-fir forest. Switchbacks from a 1980s reroute make the descent quite gradual, particularly in the upper reaches. (Avoid the shortcuts; there are scores of them, some remnants of the older route and others illegally cut.) Huckleberry is abundant, poison oak even more so.

The trail passes a sign, now leaning on the adjacent Douglas-fir, that notes

154

that the section just covered was built by the Youth Conservation Corps in 1978. The remaining descent, which was not reworked, is noticeably steeper, with many more wood and stone steps.

Matt Davis passes under a huge Douglas-fir. Though battered by lightning, it has sent several massive candelabra-like limbs skyward. Just beyond is the start of the wood railings that accompany the trail most of the rest of the way down. You will need to duck under several bay trees arcing over the trail.

The trail enters the canyon of Table Rock Creek. It then passes the edge of Table Rock, a splendid, level resting place with sensational views. (Another smaller, table-like rock, resting on other rocks and with the limbs of a bay tree resting in turn on it, sits at the intersection.) Table Rock can be clearly seen from the beach at Stinson. Be cautious of poison oak on the short approach. California buckeye is the common tree around the rock.

Matt Davis continues steeply down and passes the base of Table Rock. Near the rock during the month of February, you will be treated to the pink blossoms of flowering currant (*Ribes sanguineum*), which *Marin Flora* calls "among the choicest of our early spring flowering plants." Giant trillium is another early-spring regular here. The vegetation increasingly shows the ocean's influence, and there are more exotic shrubs, likely naturalized escapees from Stinson Beach gardens. (A sign here once read "Bischof Steps." Gary Bischof, now retired, was MTSP's chief trail-builder for many years.)

Matt Davis crosses a bridge to Table Rock Creek's right bank. Soon after, the trail briefly exits the woods onto a grassy hillside laced with morning glory. The trail returns to woodland, back to coastal scrub, then again into the forest.

Here, Matt Davis crosses Easkoot Creek via a bridge. At the next bend left is a magnificent old laurel with several downed, but living, trunks.

Matt Davis meets an unsigned fork. Right is a .1-mile spur to the junction of Belvedere, Buena Vista, and Laurel Avenues, an alternate trailhead and connection to Willow Camp Fire Road. Continue left, crossing another bridge, over the now-united Table Rock and Easkoot Creeks, beneath an alder tree.

Matt Davis rises a few yards to another fork. Left is a short path through grassland onto private property; veer right. The route drops as it crosses a final footbridge and ends on Stinson Beach's Belvedere Avenue. There are several signs, one warning about rattlesnakes, another about coyotes. Lower on the street are the Stinson Beach Community Church and Community Center. At Highway 1, you can reach the beach either by going left, then right on Arenal, or right to the heart of the town. Panoramic Highway and the western end of the Dipsea Trail are ¼ mile to the left.

Perhaps no one influenced Mt. Tamalpais's trails more than Matt Davis. Lincoln Fairley's book, *Mount Tamalpais, A History,* has a picture of Matt Davis and calls him a "champion trailbuilder." TCC labeled him "the dean of trail workers," no small accolade from that club. Davis, a one-time upholsterer, was for years TCC's paid trailsman. Davis built and lived in a couple of cabins in the Bootjack/Mountain Theater area from the 1920s to his death in 1938; he suffered a heart attack on the mountain and died on the Golden Gate Bridge while being transported to a hospital. Davis worked on the trail that bears his name in 1929; the extension was constructed in 1931. The long, superbly designed trail is a fitting monument.

▪ Nora Trail

Matt Davis Trail to West Point: .51 mile

TERRAIN: Mostly heavily wooded; lower part riparian (MMWD)

ELEVATION: From 1,360 to 1,780 feet; very steep

INTERSECTING TRAIL(S): None

Nora Trail is part of a well-traveled route between Mountain Home and West Point. Combined with Matt Davis Trail and Old Railroad Grade, it offers a popular loop option.

Follow Matt Davis Trail .9 mile from its eastern end to the bridge over Laguna Creek. There, Nora Trail rises to the right. Chain ferns and elk clover, a common Tam shrub with huge leaves that die back each year, line the creek bed. Nora crosses Laguna Creek over a bridge some 50 yards above. It then rises up the creek's right bank.

The trail veers west, away from the creek and out of the redwood forest. In clearings, San Francisco is visible. After crossing a second bridge, it winds into and out of tree cover. The going is very steep.

Nora crosses a small bridge, then another more sizable one. The opening around West Point becomes visible above. For many years, there was a fence near Nora's top to keep horses from entering.

Nora ends at the picnic tables at West Point. A few feet to the left is a bench dedicated to hiker Robert Schneider, "Who touched our lives as he passed this way." Farther left is a newer bench. Both overlook what is now a pleasing grassland, restored after encroaching non-native trees were cleared. Rock Spring Trail and Old Railroad Grade also meet at West Point.

Nora and Bob Stanton helped build the trail while caretakers of West Point Inn during World War I. They later operated a restaurant in San Francisco at the corner of Pine and Montgomery Streets. A card in the Mount Tamalpais History Project file offers the conjecture that Nora was a sister of Mickey O'Brien, who also has a trail named for him.

▪ Panoramic Trail

Junction of Panoramic Highway and Ridge Avenue to Camp Eastwood Road: .92 mile

TERRAIN: Hillside; disturbed vegetation (MTSP)

ELEVATION: Around 900 feet; almost level

INTERSECTING TRAIL(S): Redwood (.5 mile), Ocean View (.8 mile)

Panoramic Trail is well-used, thanks to its easy access at either end, both of which are served by the West Marin Stagecoach bus. The trail will be described from closer-in Ridge Avenue, although more users likely enter from Camp Eastwood Road by the Mountain Home parking area. Starting from Ridge Avenue provides Tam views; from Camp Eastwood Road, ocean views.

The Panoramic trailhead is at the northwest corner of Ridge Avenue and Panoramic Highway, at an MTSP signpost. Ridge Avenue leads to the Muir Woods Park Improvement Association clubhouse, and to a private (but open to hikers) paved road down to the Tourist Club.

The trail sets off parallel to the highway through a dense growth of blackberry bushes. The tasty berries ripen around July, and are invariably picked quickly. After passing the last private residence on the west side of the highway, the trail drops lower on the hillside, somewhat escaping traffic sounds.

The vegetation has changed dramatically since controlled burns began here in 1994. Most of the overcrowded broom is gone (although broom seeds are remarkably hardy and long-lived), along with other potential fire fuel. Green grasses now wave in early spring winds and native wildflowers, particularly morning glory, poppies, and blue eyed grass, are returning.

The Tourist Club can be glimpsed to the left. There are paths right, to the road, and left. The trail enters a redwood grove. A rusted automobile sits below, as it has for decades.

In ½ mile, beside introduced Monterey pines, is the upper end of Redwood Trail. It goes sharply left, down to the Tourist Club.

The trail passes a prominent rock. Just beyond, Panoramic meets the top of Canopy View Trail, which descends 1.5 miles to Muir Woods.

Directly across Panoramic Highway is Alpine Lodge, headquarters of the California Alpine Club, founded in 1913 and welcoming to new members. (The lodge's Henry Hertenstein Hall, added in 1953, may be rented for parties and other special occasions, and dormitory-style accommodations upstairs can also be booked.)

Panoramic Trail ends when it hits the top of paved Camp Eastwood Road at a gate. Mountain Home Inn is a few yards farther ahead across Panoramic Highway.

Panoramic Highway opened in 1928, the same year Tamalpais State Park was created. The two were, in fact, intimately tied. In the automobile-boom years of the early 1920s, Marin voters overwhelmingly approved a road-building bond measure that included a direct Mill Valley–Stinson Beach road. Advocates for a state park, whose proposed boundaries would be bisected by the road, feared the road would bring residential development, or at least raise the acquisition price of the privately owned land to prohibitive levels. After several years of fierce debate, the park was created and Panoramic Highway was built right through its center.

Ben Schmidt carved Panoramic Trail in 1969 so hikers could avoid walking on the road shoulder. Schmidt, dean of post–World War II trail-builders, was born near the trail. It originally extended south to the Dipsea Trail at Windy Gap, but private residences now block that segment.

Pipeline Trail

Between two sections of Edgewood Avenue, Mill Valley: .27 mile

TERRAIN: Redwood forest (City of Mill Valley)

ELEVATION: Around 820 feet; almost level

INTERSECTING TRAIL(S): None

Pipeline Trail was once "the most traveled and fondly remembered of all approaches to the mountain" (Fred Sandrock, *Mill Valley Historical Review,* Spring 1985). Hikers would come from San Francisco via ferry to Sausalito, take the Northwestern Pacific Railroad to Mill Valley, climb the Dipsea steps, then head deep onto the mountain on Pipeline.

The trail went to Mountain Home, crossed the Muir Woods railroad track via a bridge, then split into an Upper Pipeline to Bootjack Camp and a lower branch to Rattlesnake Camp. Pipeline was so popular that refreshment stands were set up beside it on weekends.

Today, Pipeline Trail, covered and carved up by Panoramic Highway and Edgewood Avenue and replaced by Matt Davis and Troop 80 Trails, remains a public access, closed-to-cars route for fewer than 500 yards. It now simply connects two segments of Edgewood Avenue.

To reach it, follow Edgewood Road south of the Mountain Home Inn guest parking lot. In about ½ mile, at a fenced-off yellow fire pump in front of a house beside the road, Tenderfoot Trail (unsigned) drops left. It goes down to Cascade Drive in Mill Valley. Continue straight on Edgewood, past the homes. When Edgewood ends at the second home's gate, veer right on the unsigned narrow path skirting the property. This is the surviving section of Pipeline.

The lovely trail winds along the hillside. Redwoods dominate in the deep, quiet canyon below. The old pipeline itself, badly battered, is still very evident in several places. A massive old stone pipe support—no one is moving this any time soon—is another relic. At a small bridge of lashed logs, look for the lovely, naturalized foxglove (*Digitalis purpurea*).

The trail ends when it widens and is again open to cars at 777 Edgewood Avenue. A most handsome sign marking Pipeline Trail has been added here. Edgewood continues to Sequoia Valley Road at the top of the Dipsea steps. It also passes the former Swiss Club Tell, a social club now converted into a residence; the old Belvedere Reservoir site, now a meadow off Sunnycrest Avenue; and, at Cypress Avene, a native plant garden.

Pipeline Trail, and the adjacent 8-inch riveted steel pipeline, was built in 1904. The pipeline brought water from intakes at Rattlesnake, Spike Buck, Laguna, and Fern Creeks to the Belvedere Reservoir, serving the then-developing communities of Tiburon and Belvedere. In 1967, the 3-acre open reservoir, plagued with leakage and a diminishing supply from the intakes, was replaced by a 5,000,000-gallon steel tank. The pipeline was completely abandoned soon after. Many other segments of the old pipeline remain, such as alongside Troop 80 Trail.

Helen Wild wrote a charming poem, *The Pipe Line Trail*, that was published in 1927 in TCC's *California Out-of-Doors* newsletter, during the time the trail was being carved up. The poem concludes: "Dear little brown trail among the green,/Your allurement your own destruction has been."

■ Redwood Trail

Panoramic Highway to the Tourist Club: .74 mile

TERRAIN: Largely open hillside, some woodland (MTSP)

ELEVATION: From 900 to 700 feet; gradual

INTERSECTING TRAIL(S): None

Redwood Trail is the principal route to the charming Tourist Club. To reach Redwood Trail, take Panoramic Trail from either Ridge Avenue or Camp Eastwood Road; Redwood Trail, signed, lies roughly halfway in between. (When coming from Camp Eastwood Road, Canopy/Ocean View Trail is passed first.)

Views out to the Pacific can be had at the start of the trail, which then passes under the first redwood, here isolated. The downhill briefly steepens. The trail enters a grove of bay trees. Poison oak may be abundant.

In .3 mile, the trail bends left at an old fence line. The area ahead was the site of a 1994 controlled burn, and some demarcation is still visible. A few yards into the open area, a bench dedicated to the memory of musician and philanthropist

Mimi Farina (sister of the singer Joan Baez), who lived nearby, commands a splendid vista. The Tourist Club is plainly visible, and you may occasionally hear German music on festival weekends.

The trail re-enters woodland. After a downhill through burn-rejuvenated grassland, the trail crosses a bridge beneath an impressive huge rock, then finally meets redwood forest. The next creek bed carries remains of an old water intake. Redwood Trail passes above the main Tourist Club lodge; steps on the right lead down to it. In the past, refreshments were sold here on weekends, but the clubhouse is presently closed to the public except on festival weekends in May, July, and September and other special occasions. Paths lead up left to private Tourist Club residences.

Redwood Trail continues a bit farther through club property, then ends at the base of a steep, paved road (closed to vehicles except on Tourist Club business), sometimes called Hazel Trail, which rises to Ridge Avenue. There is a classic Tourist Club sign at the intersection. Fifty yards uphill on the road is one end of Sun Trail, going to the Dipsea Trail.

Redwood Trail, in different routings, dates to 1900 or earlier. There once were plans to widen it and build homes along it. The trail has also been called Tourist Club Trail. The club, whose full name is *Touristen Verein-Die Naturfreunde* (Tourist Club-Nature Friends), was founded in 1882 and now has some 800 branches, mostly in Germany, Switzerland, and Austria. German-speaking hikers established the Tamalpais chapter in 1912. Visit the club's website to learn more.

▨ Sierra Trail

Panoramic Highway to Camp Alice Eastwood: 1.05 miles

TERRAIN: Mixed woodland and chaparral (MTSP)

ELEVATION: From 1,000 to 600 feet; gradual (mildly steep)

INTERSECTING TRAIL(S): Troop 80 (.1 mile)

Sierra Trail was once part of a broad firebreak called West Point Fire Trail; this old route was severed by Panoramic Highway. Today, Sierra Trail still plays a role in several loop options out of Mountain Home and Muir Woods.

The singed top of today's Sierra Trail is on the south side of Panoramic Highway, at a small parking area just before Mile Marker 3.66. West Point Trail was across the highway at the marker; the trail no longer exists. Sierra's trailhead sign used to say it was .7 mile to Camp Eastwood; trail work in 1980 has increased the distance to 1.1 miles.

Just 40 yards down, Sierra crosses Troop 80 Trail. Left leads to Mountain Home and right to Bootjack. Sierra goes straight ahead. This early section is fairly level, with a short uphill (the only one on the whole route). The trail runs atop an unnamed ridge, which is seen clearly from the Mountain Home parking lot.

Sierra Trail leaves the ridgeline and goes into deeper woods at the sign recognizing the rerouting by the Youth Conservation Corps in 1980. (There was an earlier re-routing in 1972.) Huckleberry is abundant, as are chinquapin trees. Native bunchgrasses remain green in summer and fall. When the trail emerges from the tree canopy into chaparral, which happens several times, southern views open.

Switchbacks wind the route downhill. The trail passes though stands of crowded, short, thin redwoods. Old-timers recall these groves as little-changed over the decades. It may be that the soil here is too hard for even the redwood's shallow roots to penetrate.

Well down, Sierra passes a stone octagon-shaped water tank foundation. There is a bench here, pointing the way to the "Picnicking and Camping Area."

Sierra Trail is fire road–width for the remaining descent. It meets the upper Camp B section of Camp Alice Eastwood, where there are bathrooms and fountains. Seventy yards below, Sierra ends at the main clearing (Camp A) of Camp Eastwood, where there are bathrooms, an amphitheater, and picnic tables. The first Muir Inn, original terminus of the gravity car rail line from Double Bow Knot, stood here from 1908 to 1913. Also meeting at the camp are Fern Canyon and Plevin Cut Trails (both going downhill), Camp Eastwood FR (uphill), and Alice Eastwood Trail (downhill).

John Muir co-founded the Sierra Club in 1892, naming it for his beloved mountain "range of light," and served as its first president. The club, which has been active on Tamalpais ever since, rebuilt this trail in 1946. Today, the Sierra Club offers more than 100 hikes annually on Tamalpais, all free, and has introduced countless thousands to the mountain.

▥ Sun Trail

Dipsea Trail to Redwood Trail at the Tourist Club: .69 mile

TERRAIN: Open, grassy hillside; some woodland (MTSP)

ELEVATION: 680 to 700 feet; almost level

INTERSECTING TRAIL(S): None

Sun Trail is an exemplar for those advocating removal of broom on Mt. Tamalpais. In the early 1990s, Sun Trail was choked by broom, which blocked views and restricted passage. With the broom subsequently cleared, sweeping vistas have been restored and native wildflowers are returning. Broom, however, is hardy, and its seeds are long-lived, so continuing work will be needed.

To reach Sun Trail, go .1 mile down the Dipsea Trail from Panoramic Highway opposite Bayview Drive. On the far side of a small bridge (placed in 1999), a path goes right. Then, in another 20 yards, signed Sun Trail veers right while the Dipsea descends left.

The views come immediately. They range from Tam's summit ridge on the north to the Marin Headlands on the south, with the Pacific in almost constant sight. Remarkably, the whole panorama is pristine open space, with virtually no homes visible.

Spring brings a riot of color to the green grass. There are the orange of poppies; yellows of buttercup, broom, and wyethia; blues and purples of blue eyed grass, lupine, and blue-dicks; pinks and reds from mallow, vetch, and paintbrush; and whites from the abundant morning glory and wild cucumber. The trail passes through a few bay laurel groves and the route remains level to gently rolling.

Sun Trail then descends into a grove of eucalyptus and Monterey pines. Just beyond, it ends at a broad dirt road (paved uphill). This road is known as Muir Woods Trail or Hazel Trail, and connects the Tourist Club with Ridge Avenue. Redwood Trail and the Tourist Club (see Redwood Trail descripton for more on the club) are just to the left.

Because there were so many dairies in the area, Sun Trail was long known as Cow Trail.

Troop 80 Trail

Camp Eastwood Road to Bootjack Trail, plus spur: 1.48 miles

TERRAIN: Light woodland (MMWD, MTSP)

ELEVATION: From 780 to 1,120 feet; gradual, eastern part steep

INTERSECTING TRAIL(S): Sierra (.4 mile), Troop 80 Spur (1.3 miles)

Troop 80 Trail, near the Mountain Home trailhead—shaded, fairly level, and with long views—is well traveled. Its drawback is its proximity to Panoramic Highway and the associated road noise.

To reach Troop 80, take the short path down from the north edge of the Mountain Home trailhead parking lot to Camp Eastwood Road. It is called Trestle Trail, named for the trestle that brought a water pipeline over the railroad cut here. Follow the paved road downhill a bit under ½ mile to Fern Creek, which flows below in a culvert. On the far bank, Troop 80 departs, signed, to the right.

The short opening stretch, rerouted in 1971, is Troop 80's steepest. Switchbacks quickly bring the trail up. After more climbing, the trail levels.

Troop 80, heavily forested in this eastern part, crosses Laguna Creek over a bridge. An old steel water pipeline embedded in the trail most of the way once brought water from several south side creeks (Rattlesnake, Spike Buck, Laguna, and Fern) to the Belvedere Reservoir in Mill Valley, then on to Belvedere (see Pipeline Trail description).

In under ½ mile, Troop 80 crosses Sierra Trail. Left leads down to Camp Eastwood, while Panoramic Highway is a few yards uphill. Shortly after is another stream crossing and redwood grove, a common mountain combination. Just ahead are an old wooden bench and a water trough in which hikers used to (but no longer!) dip their cups.

Continuing west, next up is a 60-foot-long curved bridge built by Matt Davis. East Bay views open. In the next deep redwood grove, an old horse trough sits beside the trail.

Troop 80 crosses Spike Buck Creek at 1.1 miles. To the left is the former Troop 80 routing, which a significant landslide turned into a dead end; its relatively new bridge (one of the sturdiest ever built on a Mt. Tam trail) became a "bridge to nowhere." The bridge is dedicated to William Dickerson, a popular Marin physician and longtime mountain runner, who died in the December 2004 Indian Ocean tsunami. Continue straight over the even newer bridge.

Next is Rattlesnake Creek, the westernmost of the creeks tapped as a water source and start for the pipeline. Again, the trail is in dense redwoods. A steep, heavily wooded canyon drops to the left.

At 1.4 miles, there is a clearing and a fork. Look behind you at the junction to spot steps down to Memorial Tree. Until it disappeared in 2003, a plaque on a boulder by the large Douglas-fir read *Dedicated May 2, 1920, by the Tamalpais Conservation Club in honor of the services rendered by its members during World War I.* (The plaque was not the original, as the conflict of 1914–1918 was called the Great War; "World War I" was not used until the next global conflict of 1939–1945.) Some 300 people attended the 1920 dedication service.

A sign points the way left to Van Wyck Meadow, or straight. The right option is now posted as Troop 80 Spur. It runs .1 mile to higher on Bootjack Trail than the main Troop 80, to the left.

Troop 80 Trail ends at delightful Van Wyck Meadow, a favorite resting spot. The boulder known as Council Rock stands in the middle. In the early twentieth century, this was site of Lower Rattlesnake Camp, and remnants of the camp survive. At Van Wyck Meadow, Bootjack Trail goes left downhill to Muir Woods, and right uphill to Troop 80 Spur, Alpine Trail, Panoramic Highway, and Bootjack Camp. Also here, TCC Trail departs to Stapelveldt Trail.

Troop 80 Trail was built in 1931, largely by Boy Scout Troop 80 from the Ingleside district of San Francisco. It basically replaced the once very popular Lower Pipeline Trail, which was disrupted when Panoramic Highway was constructed in 1928. A short-lived Mill Valley outdoors store called itself "Troop 80" for this Trail.

▦ Vic Haun (Old Plane) Trail

Junction of Old Railroad Grade and Hoo-Koo-E-Koo FR to Temelpa Trail: .51 mile

TERRAIN: Mostly chaparral, parts wooded (MMWD)

ELEVATION: From 1,220 to 1,580 feet; steep

INTERSECTING TRAIL(S): None

Vic Haun (also long known as Old Plane) Trail, though dating to the 1940s, has only recently been adopted and signed by MMWD. It offers great views, passes through some haunting woodland near an old plane crash site, and leads to one of the mountain's jewels, the Sitting Bull plaque.

Most visitors reach Vic Haun from lower on the Old Railroad Grade. The trail sets off uphill from the northeast corner of the grade's intersection with Hoo-Koo-E-Koo FR. The entire route is narrow, but the opening yards, through manzanita bushes, are the most overgrown. Vistas of San Francisco, Mt. Diablo, and the Golden Gate Bridge immediately open. In the first 100 yards is a curious intermingling of manzanitas, denizens of the dry chaparral, and slender red-woods, known for high moisture requirements. A bit above, chinquapin trees, which bear spine-covered nuts, border the trail as well. Look also for native bunchgrasses.

The stiff climb levels, then drops, to a forest of laurels. A rivulet is crossed. Just beyond, .3 mile from the start, is a second laurel grove. Look for a path to the right. (It is more noticeable when descending Vic Haun, when it can be mistakenly followed.)

This path leads down the bed of Cascade Creek. Take it to see remnants of the US Navy PBM-5 Mariner plane that went down here November 30, 1944, killing all eight crew members. The plane was flying from Alameda to the Hawaiian island of Oahu when it slammed into the fog-shrouded mountain. *It is unlawful to remove historic artifacts from Tam; this crash remains property of the United States Navy and is officially designated a gravesite.*

The continuation of the trail beyond the crash site was built a few years lat-er. There is a cooling redwood forest (note that all the redwoods grow below the trail, none above). A rock offers a resting site with a choice southern panorama.

The evergreens ahead are mostly introduced bishop and Monterey pines. This grove is quite prominent when viewed from the south.

Vic Haun ends when it hits Temelpa Trail. Left, Temelpa goes uphill to Verna Dunshee Trail, while right, it goes extremely steeply down to Hoo-Koo-E-Koo

FR. Tree poppies color the intersection bright yellow in late spring. Be sure to go the 25 yards downhill on Temelpa to the wonderful Sitting Bull plaque (see Temelpa Trail description) embedded in a boulder.

Old Erickson maps call the trail "Old Plane," since its lower half was cut in 1944 specifically to reach the wreck site; some old-timers call it "Airplane Trail." MMWD, Olmsted, and newer maps label it the Vic Haun Trail. Victor Emmanuel Haun was one of the founders of the California Alpine Club.

Trestle Trail, shortest named trail on Mt. Tamalpais, descends from Mountain Home toward Muir Woods.

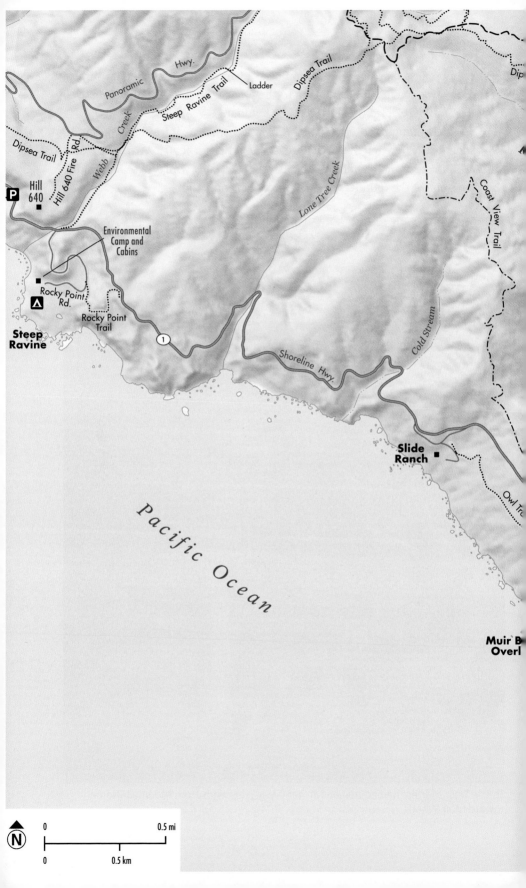

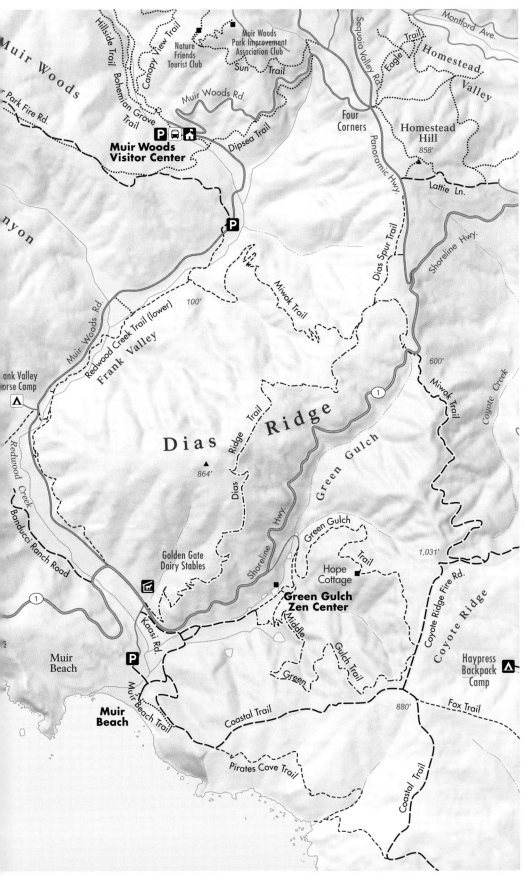

Along the Coastal Trail from Muir Beach south toward the Marin Headlands.

TRAILHEAD SIX: MUIR BEACH/HIGHWAY 1

Directions

Highway 1 exit off Highway 101—stay on Highway 1 through Tam Junction light—in 3 miles, veer left (still on Highway 1) to Muir Beach—at base of hill, left onto Pacific Way (at Pelican Inn) to Muir Beach parking lot.

In 1898, the Tamalpais Land & Water Co. put up for sale the dairy ranches on the southwestern slope of Mt. Tamalpais, all of which were part of the old Rancho Saucelito Mexican land grant. Constantino Bello, one of the Portuguese tenants, bought three of the ranches, totaling 491 acres (modern-day Muir Beach was part of that purchase).

Bello and his family operated Golden Gate Dairy, which continued in Portuguese hands into the 1950s. Richard and Evelyn Purvier opened a stable on the old dairy site in 1962, and boarding of horses continues to this day. A plan to build a resort on the dairy site ended when the National Park Service took over the area in 1974. Several dairy-era structures survive, including the creamery building (remodeled in 1972 into the community fire station) and the ranch house.

In 1919, Constantino's brother, Antonio, opened a tavern on what was then known as Bello Beach or Big Lagoon Beach, and a small resort sprang up around it. (During the Prohibition era, illicit smuggling of alcohol was common along the Marin coast.) Muir Beach Water Company was formed in 1928 to provide water for the new Bello Beach subdivision, and the row of pines still lining Pacific Way was planted as the entry. The name "Muir Beach" was formally adopted in 1940. During World War II, soldiers manned a military station, now the Muir Beach Overlook, watching for enemy ships.

In 1969, after a condemnation proceeding, the State of California bought 15.83 acres of beach, along with the run-down resort, for $247,000; an anonymous donor contributed half the purchase price. The buildings, then reputedly a haven for drug dealers, were promptly torn down. Muir Beach State Park lasted seven years; in 1976 the park was transferred to the new Golden Gate National Recreation Area. (Governor Jerry Brown signed the bill.) The popular Pelican Inn was built in 1979.

In 2014, GGNRA largely completed a multi-year project to restore the floodplain and improve the flow of Redwood Creek at its mouth to help improve the vastly reduced coho salmon run and habitat for the endangered red-legged frog. Among other changes, the beach parking lot was reconfigured and paved, an old Green Gulch levee was removed, and reconstructed Kaasi Road was opened to the public. In late 2014, all the young coho still in Redwood Creek—slightly more than 100—were removed to be raised in Sonoma County, with the goal of a healthier return.

The Muir Beach parking lot on Pacific Way off Highway 1, which is locked after sunset, is free. There is no other nearby public parking. The new Pacific Way/Kaasi Bridge by the lot's bathrooms connects the Mt. Tamalpais and Marin Headlands trail networks.

Three routes in this chapter—Owl, Rocky Point Road, and Rocky Point Trail—are reached farther north of Muir Beach, along Highway 1.

Suggested Loops

1. Cross bridge and left on Kaasi Road, .1 mile, to Coastal FR—up Coastal FR, 1.4 miles, to Coyote Ridge FR—Coyote Ridge FR, .2 mile, to Middle Green Gulch Trail—down, 2.1 miles, to Kaasi Road—left, .3 miles, to bridge and start. **4.1 miles total** *(4.3 miles if descent from Coyote Ridge FR via Green Gulch Trail)*

2. Cross bridge and left on Kaasi Road, .5 mile, to Dias Ridge Trail—up, 2.7 miles, to second Miwok Trail intersection—right on Miwok, 1.7 miles, to Coyote Ridge FR—right on Coyote Ridge FR, .8 mile, to Coastal FR—straight on Coastal, 1.4 miles, to Kaasi Road—left, .1 mile, to bridge and start. **7.2 miles total**

▮ Coastal Fire Road

Kaasi Road to Coyote Ridge FR: 1.40 miles
TERRAIN: Coastal scrub (GGNRA)
ELEVATION: 10 to 880 feet; very steep, parts extremely steep
INTERSECTING TRAIL(S): Muir Beach (.3 mile), Pirates Cove (.5 mile)
Note: Coastal FR continues an additional 1.5 miles south of the Coyote Ridge FR junction down to Tennessee Valley. That section is outside this book's geographic area of coverage.

From the reconfigured and resurfaced Muir Beach parking lot, cross the marsh over the new Kaasi Bridge. At the far end, Muir Beach Trail sets off right to the beach, then continues higher. Veer left. Another sign says it is 500 feet to the Coastal FR. At the next intersection, veer right and begin the fire road's tough uphill.

It's hard work but, in just 300 yards, ocean views open and increasingly expand, more than compensating for the effort. The vegetation is coastal scrub, dominated by baccharis.

In .3 mile, a sign marks the upper end of Muir Beach Trail. Downhill makes a short but somewhat hairy cliff-edge loop. Higher entries to paths right are posted as closed for habitat restoration.

At .5 mile, Pirates Cove Trail branches right (and is outside the scope of this book). Take the path right to the top of the hill for cliff-edge views.

The uphill again steepens, including one short section that is slippery to descend on a return. Tamalpa Ridge, embracing the three peaks of Mt. Tamalpais, becomes an impressive, and constant, sight to the left. You can also glimpse Hope Cottage, on Green Gulch FR, hidden behind a tree by a large boulder. To the right, a few young Douglas-firs are taking hold. Old fence posts are remnants of the area's century-long dairying days.

Coastal FR meets Coyote Ridge FR atop Coyote Ridge itself. Coastal FR continues right and down, to Fox Trail and Tennessee Valley (again, outside this book's area of coverage). Straight, in ⅙ mile, Coyote Ridge passes the top of Middle Green Gulch FR, quickly followed by the top of Green Gulch FR. Both offer appealing loops back to Muir Beach.

■ Coyote Ridge Fire Road

Miwok Trail to Coastal FR: .75 mile

TERRAIN: Coastal scrub (GGNRA)

ELEVATION: From 830 to 1,020 to 880 feet; rolling, parts steep

INTERSECTING TRAIL(S): Green Gulch (.6 mile), Middle Green Gulch (.6 mile)

Coyote Ridge defines the southernmost boundary of the Tamalpais Lands Collaborative and of the trails described in this book. Likewise, it is considered the northernmost part of the Marin Headlands. This fire road tops the ridge. High and treeless, it offers spectacular views its full length.

It is a tough climb to reach any part of Coyote Ridge. Most visitors access Coyote Ridge FR by ascending Miwok Trail from the Tennessee Valley trailhead parking lot. It's then 1.4 miles up, or 1.2 miles using the Miwok Cutoff. The Coyote Ridge junction is well signed.

The trail starts with a climb, initially steep. Views of the Pacific open within 100 feet. Coyote brush densely lines the road, and does so the rest of the way. The grade eases. Shortcut paths branch right.

Coyote Ridge FR reaches its crest in ¼ mile. Be sure to go the few yards right to the knoll at the ridge's highest point, where there are two survey markers. At 1,031 feet, there is only one hill higher (by just 10 feet) anywhere south to the Golden Gate. Take in the 360-degree views: Mt. Tamalpais's summit ridge, the East Bay, glimpses of the Golden Gate Bridge and the San Francisco skyline, Wolf Ridge, the Pacific out to the Farallon Islands, Muir Beach. (Or no views at all when the fog's in, a frequent situation.)

The fire road now trends down, but the views remain riveting. Old fence posts are reminders of more than 100 years of dairying. A somewhat surprising outcrop of boulders abuts the right edge.

At .6 mile are two close intersections on the right. The first is with Green Gulch Trail, which is actually a broad road. It descends past Hope Cottage to deep within the Green Gulch Zen Center. In another 200 feet is the top of Middle Green Gulch Trail. Bikes are allowed on it, but only in the uphill direction. It too drops to the Zen Center, near the gardens and Muir Beach.

Coyote Ridge FR ends ⅙ mile later at its junction with Coastal FR. Left is a drop to Fox Trail and on to Tennessee Valley. Right is the descent to Pirates Cove Trail and to Muir Beach.

Coyotes are making a comeback across Marin and sightings, even close ones, are no longer rare.

■ Dias Ridge Trail

Panoramic Highway to Highway 1: 3.03 miles

TERRAIN: Coastal scrub (MTSP, GGNRA; part of Bay Area Ridge Trail)

ELEVATION: From 620 to 780 to 15 feet; gradual to moderate

INTERSECTING TRAIL(S): Miwok (.2 to .3 mile)

Note: Open to bicycles and horses

Before Dias Ridge Trail was rebuilt (it formally reopened in May 2010), visitors followed an old ranch road west to near the ridge's crest, where they then had two choices, both bad. The option left exited onto Highway 1, where there was no road shoulder or connecting trail. The option straight deteriorated, then turned downright dangerous as it plunged to Frank Valley.

Now, well-graded switchbacks carry Dias Ridge Trail through its western half. Parts of the eastern half were also improved. The entire route of the former road is now Dias Ridge Trail, a multi-use route open to bicycles and horses.

Both ends of the trail are next to roads. The journey will be described from the entry closer to Mill Valley; going west provides ocean views. The signed trailhead is beside Panoramic Highway, near Mile Marker 0.18 (measured from the southern Panoramic Highway-Highway 1 junction). This is also ⅓ mile south from Four Corners—where Panoramic Highway, Sequoia Valley Road, and Muir Woods Road meet—and beside the new (2015) Mt. Tamalpais State Park boundary sign. There is off-road parking on the east side of the road.

Within yards, ocean views open out to the Farallon Islands on clear days. In 200 feet, Dias Ridge Trail meets Dias Spur Trail, which runs north ¼ mile, parallel to the highway, which it joins. Coyote brush lines both sides of the trail (and the whole area), and remains the dominant plant of the coastal scrub for the entire 3-mile route. The abundant white-threaded pappi, which carry its seeds for dispersal, give the plant the nickname "fuzzy wuzzy."

At ¼ mile, Miwok Trail enters on the left from Highway 1. Miwok carries Bay Area Ridge Trail hikers, equestrians, and mountain bikers from the south onto Dias Ridge. In another .1 mile, Miwok departs north. This continuing section, down to Redwood Creek Trail, is closed to bicycles.

Dias Ridge is among the foggier locales on Mt. Tamalpais, particularly in summer. But when it's fog-free, hikers and bikers savor the views. On the right is an iconic panorama of the entire south face of Mt. Tamalpais. To the left, beyond Green Gulch, is Coyote Ridge, where GGNRA trails and fire roads clearly beckon. Ahead, Pacific vistas steadily broaden. At .4 mile is a landmark rock outcropping, but beware of poison oak.

Two-thirds of a mile in, the trail encounters its first tree, a Douglas-fir, on the right. Highway 1, relatively close, becomes briefly visible. After passing a second Douglas-fir on the left, the trail descends. The third tree, an oak on the right, marks the 1-mile point. One hundred yards later, the trail enters a grove of bay laurels.

Dias Ridge Trail crests at 1.4 miles, with the 864-foot true top of Dias Ridge just to the right. A sign here marks the boundary between MTSP and GGNRA, which you now enter. Another sign says it is 1.5 miles ahead to the trailhead, 1.6 miles to Muir Beach. Yet another sign warns users to stay on the trail to protect the vegetation, which is being restored. The grove of trees that protects Hope Cottage, on Green Gulch Trail, is evident on the next hill south.

The remainder of Dias Ridge Trail is entirely new, and longer than the old route due to many switchbacks. California sagebrush becomes more common; crush the foliage to enjoy the fragrance. On the slope right, heather still colors the hillside of the now-gone Banducci Heather Farm. Nearer is the old Golden Gate Dairy, now a stable. Left are buildings of the Green Gulch Zen Center and its gardens.

A switchback right leads to a last straightaway parallel to Highway 1. The well-signed trailhead is between the landmark line of mailboxes for Muir Beach residents and the barn with the sign "Golden Gate Dairy." Pelican Inn, destination of many Dias Ridge travelers, is across the street. The inn, which dates from 1979, was built to resemble an older English pub. Meals and drinks are served, and there is overnight lodging. Also directly across Highway 1 is new Kaasi Road, the pedestrian, bike, and horse route to Muir Beach, and the auto road to the beach parking lot.

Around 1870, Samuel Throckmorton carved dairy ranches into the west slope of his originally 19,000-acre Rancho Saucelito. Most of the ranches—designated by the letters A through Z—were leased to dairymen from Portugal's Azores Islands, some of whom arrived via Hawaii. In 1898, the Tamalpais Land & Water Co., which foreclosed on Throckmorton's daughter, Susanna, put the ranches up for sale. William Kent bought several.

John Dias, one of Throckmorton's tenants, bought 420 acres (Ranch P and part of Ranch O) at $40 an acre in 1898. The Dias Ranch cow barns occupied land near the intersection of today's Panoramic and Shoreline Highways. In the pre-refrigeration era, milk was rushed to San Francisco via horse cart, rail, and ferry. John Dias died in 1917, one day after being kicked by a bull. Dias family members continued to work the ranch as the Sausalito Creamery, and cows grazed the slopes for decades.

Developers bought the Dias Ranch in the 1950s, and conservationists immediately began calling for its public acquisition. In 1960, the state purchased 376 acres and made it the southernmost part of Mt. Tamalpais State Park. Other Dias acreage was later absorbed into the Golden Gate National Recreation Area and, east of the ridge, into the Homestead Valley Land Trust. There was also some residential development.

Also in 1898, Constantino Bello (like Dias, from the Azores) bought three former Throckmorton ranches, totaling 491 acres. On Ranch M, he operated the Golden Gate Dairy, which continued in Portuguese hands until 1953. In 1962, Richard and Evelyn Pervier began leasing land for their Golden Gate Dairy Stables, and in 1968, William Caddell bought the parcel with plans to develop it as a resort. Ranch M—the cows gone—became part of GGNRA in 1974. Faced with GGNRA-mandated improvements to stem erosion and runoff into the coho salmon habitat of Redwood Creek, the Perviers withdrew in 1997. Only a dozen or so horses are still housed at the stables, now managed by Ocean Riders of Marin.

Dias Ridge itself is a spur off Tam's long Throckmorton Ridge, which descends all the way from East Peak.

▮ Dias Spur Trail

Panoramic Highway to Dias Ridge Trail: .25 mile

TERRAIN: Coastal scrub (GGNRA)

ELEVATION: Around 640 feet; almost level

INTERSECTING TRAIL(S): None

Just 200 feet into Dias Ridge Trail from Panoramic Highway, the signed Dias Ridge Spur Trail sets off right. It runs parallel to the highway for exactly ¼ mile.

The vegetation is entirely coastal scrub lined with coyote brush and the native blackberry. (Unfortunately, it is the non-native Himalayan blackberry that yields tasty, juicy berries in summer.) There are vistas of San Francisco Bay and the East Bay hills.

Dias Ridge Spur Trail meets Panoramic Highway near Mile Marker .53. A truck selling fresh fruits and vegetables is often parked nearby as well. Though it seems like there should be a connection on to Muir Woods, there isn't. The only continuing option is to cross Panoramic Highway into the trail network of the Homestead Valley Land Trust, such as onto Homestead Hill FR beyond the white gate opposite. Be forewarned that many lower Homestead Valley trails are overgrown, and poison oak is abundant. (See the Dias Ridge Trail description for background on the Dias name.)

Green Gulch Trail

Coyote Ridge FR to Green Gulch Farm Zen Center: 1.39 miles

TERRAIN: Coastal scrub, lower section wooded

ELEVATION: From 900 to 70 feet; very steep (GGNRA)

INTERSECTING TRAIL(S): None

Green Gulch and Middle Green Gulch Trails (described below), which are very close at both top and bottom, are natural loop partners. They traverse the same terrain, are never far apart, share the same vegetation and enjoy similar views. But there are differences. Green Gulch Trail is closed to bicycles (allowed uphill only on Middle Green Gulch), is steeper, and has a wooded section. But, most of all, Green Gulch Trail passes the jewel that is Hope Cottage.

The walk over Green Gulch Trail will be described downhill, as its base is presently a bit tricky to find. From the top of Middle Green Gulch Trail, go 50 yards left (east) on Coyote Ridge to the top of Green Gulch Trail. Savor the sweeping views, then begin the descent. There are still views on the way down, but only to the north. Coyote brush is by far the most common shrub.

A clump of trees and a rock outcropping are visible below, and you can discern a building within. That building is Hope Cottage, reached in exactly ½ mile. Five Monterey pines shelter it. The small cottage, utterly alone and with astounding views, is maintained by the Green Gulch Farm Zen Center and can be reserved for private retreats. A sign asks visitors to "please respect the privacy of those in retreat." George Wheelwright (see Middle Green Gulch Trail description) built the cottage as a refuge for his wife, Hope, when she was stricken with cancer.

In another ¼ mile, unexpected here, redwoods began lining the way, incongruous in the scrub. A derelict shack sits beside a spring. Encroaching vegetation, including poison hemlock, presses against the trail. A massive old Douglas-fir, its branches drooping and moss-covered, is at 1.1 miles.

Water tanks mark entry to the residential area of the Zen Center. So, too, does the first eucalyptus, and shortly thereafter, a cottage. Two hundred feet below is a junction, the first of the descent. The road left is a slight shortcut back to Muir Beach. Green Gulch Trail continues right another 250 feet down to a second junction and the main road through Green Gulch Farm Zen Center. There is a Green Gulch Trail sign here. Left is the main parking area (open to visitors), Guest House, Yurt Path, Welcome Center, children's playground, and vegetable gardens, then back to Middle Green Gulch Trail. At the base of Green Gulch Trail is the road to the main entrance, near Mile Marker 5.10 on Highway 1.

Green Gulch is named on nineteenth-century maps.

▩ Kaasi Road

Muir Beach Trail to Pacific Way: .51 mile

TERRAIN: Coastal scrub and marsh (GGNRA)

ELEVATION: 10 feet; level

INTERSECTING TRAIL(s): Coastal FR (.1 mile), Middle Green Gulch Trail (.3 mile)

In 2014, GGNRA completed a major restoration of the lowest reaches of Redwood Creek, where it empties into the Pacific at Muir Beach. The main goal was to help coho salmon reclaim their once-thriving run in the creek and, in the process, restore the health of the creek's delta marshland. Rebuilding Kaasi Road, which included removing an old Green Gulch levee, was part of the project.

Most visitors enter Kaasi Road (a name not used before the project) from the newly reconfigured Muir Beach parking lot. While "Kaasi" is a new name to Tamalpais maps, as the native Miwok word for "salmon," it has deep roots.

Cross the handsome new Pacific Way Bridge, considered part of Muir Beach Trail, over the marsh. Kaasi Road begins at the far end, to the left. A sign says it is 500 feet to Coastal FR, .3 mile to Middle Green Gulch Trail, and .5 mile to Dias Ridge Trail.

At the Coastal FR junction, a sign provides information about the Coast Miwoks, the first stewards of the land here (owning land was an alien notion to the native people). Coastal FR climbs very steeply to Coyote Ridge, where there are options on to Tennessee Valley. Four hundred feet farther, another interpretive sign tells of the return of red-legged frogs to a healthy marsh. Until recently, no frogs could be found here, but the pond is now choice habitat.

Ponds and wet terrain also suit newts, another local amphibian. Newts head, ever so slowly, to water to breed during the rainy season. They do this in suprising numbers (I once saw hundreds in December right after a heavy rain), so if you're there in wet weather, watch your step. Newts are best left alone; they're protected from predators by one of nature's deadliest toxins.

At the next junction, Middle Green Gulch Trail branches right into the Green Gulch Farm Zen Center before climbing to Coyote Ridge. Kaasi Road then crosses a new bridge, built as part of the restoration project. An old path into the Green Gulch farm plots is to the right. Kaasi Road bends left.

Native plants are being nurtured for replanting in a plot on the left. There is a remnant pond, where tules grow tall. Willows line Kaasi Road. The entire broad, marshy area was historically known as Big Lagoon.

Kaasi Road exits past a gate, formerly unsigned and rarely crossed, onto Pacific Way, the automobile route to the Muir Beach parking area. Directly opposite is the driveway to Pelican Inn. To the right, across Highway 1, is the base of Dias Ridge Trail.

Middle Green Gulch Trail

Kaasi Road to Coyote Ridge FR: 2.11 miles

TERRAIN: Coastal scrub (GGNRA)

ELEVATION: From 15 to 900 feet; gradual to steep

INTERSECTING TRAIL(S): None

Note: Middle Green Gulch Trail is open to bicycles in the uphill direction only.

To reach Middle Green Gulch Trail from the Muir Beach parking lot, cross the bridge and go left .3 mile. Monterey pines frame the start of the trail off Kaasi Road. Just in, you can see the marsh restoration work continuing after the old ranch dike was removed. Farther left is Highway 1, and higher still, a wind-sculpted tree, clinging to a rock, is silhouetted on Dias Ridge.

In .1 mile, the trail passes through a gate; be sure to close it behind you. In 100 feet, on the left, an interpretive sign discusses "Farming and the Cultural Landscape." In 1946, George Wheelwright and his wife, Hope (Richardson), bought 800 acres here, from the Redwood Creek floodplain at Muir Beach up to Coyote Ridge. Wheelwright, who had earned a fine arts degree from Harvard, returned there to study physics. While teaching physics at Harvard, he teamed with a brilliant student, Edwin Land, to found a company dealing with polarized light. The Polaroid Corporation was born, and Wheelwright's fortune was secured.

In 1956, Wheelwright introduced Hereford cattle to his ranch. In 1965, he became the first to sign up under the newly passed California Land Conservation (Williamson) Act, which offered tax incentives to owners of farmland near urban centers to keep the land in agriculture or as open space.

In 1970, Wheelwright donated 513 acres, including a mile of coastline, to the Nature Conservancy, which then passed it on to the newly formed Golden Gate National Recreation Area. He also sold 115 acres to the San Francisco Zen Center, apparently fearing that the National Park Service would tear down his beloved Hope Cottage (see Green Gulch Trail description) and other ranch buildings. Wheelwright lived many of his last years on the farm. He died in 2001, age ninety-seven.

The Zen Center continues to operate Green Gulch as both an organic farm and a Japanese-style Buddhist retreat called Green Dragon Temple, or *Soryu-ji*. (They have other retreats in San Francisco, as well as at Tassajara on the Big Sur coast.) The public is welcome to participate in the many programs. Vegetables grown here are served at San Francisco's Greens Restaurant, which the Zen Center opened in 1979. The farm is active, but passage is open to all.

This level stretch of trail is lined with willows. It passes straight through the vegetable gardens. At $^1/_3$ mile, a sign says that Middle Green Gulch Trail goes right, to Coyote Ridge, Tennessee Valley, and Rodeo Valley. Straight leads through the heart of the Zen Center and to the foot of Green Gulch Trail. The shop building here displays Buddhist sayings to ponder on the long walk ahead.

Follow the row of Monterey cypress to a second gate. Again, restore the latch. Immediately beyond, go left, though the route straight ahead appears wider (it is a dead end). The climbing begins here and continues all the way to the summit, somewhat eased by the many switchbacks.

In ½ mile, the first of several paths up from the Zen Center and Green Gulch Trail enters left. Middle Green Gulch Trail signs mark three such junctions. The first Douglas-fir is passed in an otherwise treeless coastal scrub. Later, several Monterey pines, with their long needles in bunches of three, can be seen. The species is not native to Marin but has become naturalized near planted groves, as at Green Gulch. Otherwise, low-growing shrubs such as coyote brush, blackberry, and lupine predominate. Polypody ferns (genus *Polypodium*) cling to rocks. Below to the right is a Zen Center pond.

At .9 mile, Middle Green Gulch crosses a spring. Look low here for water hemlock, the most toxic native plant in Marin. (There were reports, perhaps rumors, in the 1970s of a death on Mt. Tamalpais after someone ate water hemlock [genus *Cicuta*]; the plant resembles edible members of the parsley family to which it belongs.)

At 1.2 miles, the trail passes over wooden planks. A motion-activated camera has been used nearby to monitor wildlife. Many animals certainly do pass though here, as you can tell from abundant scat all along Middle Green Gulch.

A large old Douglas-fir stands on the left, after which trees become even more rare. Middle Green Gulch reaches the level of Hope Cottage, visible just across the way on Green Gulch Trail. The uphill eases, with the last stretch barely rising. Three hundred yards from the ridge, to the left, is a young, seemingly healthy Monterey cypress, just under 4 feet tall in early 2015. Perhaps it will grow, but conditions are difficult on these upper slopes, which are more exposed to wind.

Middle Green Gulch Trail ends at Coyote Ridge FR, on the crest of Coyote Ridge. Grand views south, east, and west suddenly open. It is ⅙ mile right to Coastal Trail for a loop option back to Muir Beach, or to Tennessee Valley. Just 50 yards left is Green Gulch Trail, another loop option, back to the Zen Center.

Miwok Trail

Coyote Ridge FR to Redwood Creek Trail: 3.73 miles*

TERRAIN: Upper parts coastal scrub, lower section oak-bay woodland (MTSP, GGNRA)

ELEVATION: From 910 to 110 feet; rolling, gradual

INTERSECTING TRAIL(S): Dias Ridge (2.0 to 2.1 miles)

*Miwok Trail runs an additional 6.6 miles south of Coyote Ridge, to Rodeo Lagoon at Rodeo Beach.

Note: Part of Bay Area Ridge Trail; horses permitted full length, bicycles permitted south of Dias Ridge Trail only.

Miwok is one of the longest trails in Marin County. It begins at the Bunker Road bridge over Rodeo Lagoon and ends at Muir Woods Road. Only the last, north-ernmost, 3.73-mile section between Coyote Ridge and Redwood Creek is within the Tamalpais Lands Collaborative map and thus described here.

Most visitors reach the Miwok-Coyote Ridge junction by ascending Miwok 1.5 miles from the Tennessee Valley parking lot. The area is signed but can be tricky when fog obscures familiar views.

There is a short climb at the start; the next 1.5 miles to Highway 1 are al-most all gently downhill. Coyote brush lines both sides of the broad route, and there are views of Mt. Tamalpais and across Mill Valley to San Francisco Bay and the Marin Headlands.

In less than 100 yards is the first of three shortcut paths left connecting to Coyote Ridge FR. At .6 mile, a few struggling Douglas-firs grow in a bend to the right. At .9 mile, an old white gate is a landmark amidst the otherwise continu-ous coastal scrub. Just past, the descent steepens a bit.

Miwok drops into a wooded area and views are left behind (they will re-turn). Much of the vegetation here is non-native, including eucalyptus trees and rows of the shrub cotoneaster, which has red berries and is native to China.

Miwok Trail meets Highway 1 at a well-signed parking pullout. Panoramic Highway is .2 mile up the road, Muir Beach at the base of the road left. Follow the path straight to cross Highway 1. Miwok resumes on the north side, where there are a few additional parking spots.

It is a gradual climb through the often-windswept scrub. The National Park Service is clearing cape ivy (*Delairea odorata*) here; it is also known as German ivy. The GGNRA website description of the project describes it as "the California coast's biggest and baddest weed. If the National Park Service had its way, we would be circulating a mug shot of this bright green vine. It is such a pain that it is the first wildland weed that the California Department of Agriculture has decided to develop a biocontrol for."

Within 250 yards, views of San Francisco Bay reopen. In another 100 yards, East Peak, then Middle Peak, then West Peak come into view. Wyethia's huge yellow flowers are conspicuous in early summer.

In ⅓ mile from Highway 1, Miwok Trail meets Dias Ridge Trail on the crest of the ridge. Right leads to Panoramic Highway. To continue on Miwok, go left. In .1 mile, Miwok leaves the ridge, dropping to the right (north). This section of Miwok is also part of the Bay Area Ridge Trail and is used by equestrians.

The descent is gradual, but work when you're coming up late in a long loop. In 100 yards is an old stone foundation from dairy ranching days. The vegetation is lush. Buttercups, poppies, yarrow, irises, blue eyed grass, and cucumber are some of the more colorful flowers. Blackberries, strawberries, gooseberries, and snowberries ripen in late summer. Spittlebugs, ensconced in their protective foam, are found on many of the plants.

Two hundred yards down is the first tree, a young Douglas-fir. Just below is an oak, with hazel growing alongside. The trail crosses over a few muddy seeps.

At .9 mile below Dias Ridge, Miwok Trail passes a horse hitching post and a bench. The trail then descends into enchanted woodland of old oaks, bay laurels, and ferns. In June, the display of columbine here surpasses perhaps that to be seen anywhere on the mountain. Unfortunately, also abundant is poison oak. Be cautious.

There is a brief return to grassland. Then, by a rock outcropping, Miwok literally passes atop a magnificent oak with a gnarled, twisting trunk. It next crosses a creek over a bridge. A sign notes that the section of Miwok just passed was rebuilt by the Youth Conservation Corps in 1981. The trail again hits grassland.

Miwok ends 50 yards later at its junction with Redwood Creek Trail in Frank Valley. Although a path (Redwood Creek Spur Trail) on the opposite bank leads to Muir Woods Road by Mile Marker 2.56, there is no dry crossing of Redwood Creek on foot here much of the year. The nearest bridge is .3 mile to the right, also the direction for continuing on the Bay Area Ridge Trail. Left leads to Muir Beach.

The Miwoks were the sole residents of Mt. Tamalpais for thousands of years. The Spanish dubbed a Miwok leader "Marino," or Chief Marin, and the name passed on to the county when California became a state in 1850. "Tamalpais" itself is of Miwok origin. (See the history chapter for more.)

◼ Muir Beach Trail

Muir Beach parking lot to Coastal FR: .39 mile

TERRAIN: Coastal scrub (GGNRA)

ELEVATION: From 280 to 10 feet; extremely steep

INTERSECTING TRAIL(S): None

This trail has two distinct halves. The first is the flat opening section, crossed by everyone going to Muir Beach. The second is narrow, rutted, extremely steep, and—with its severe drop-offs—among the most marginal sections described in this book. (It is signed and named by GGNRA, and is even part of the suggested hike on the information panel in the parking lot. The Parks Conservancy website says, "Avoid the Muir Beach Trail if you're scared of heights.") But there are rewards, as upper Muir Beach Trail offers jaw-dropping views of the ocean surf immediately below.

For most visitors, Muir Beach Trail is most safely taken uphill, so that is how it will be described. A short, all-ocean side loop is possible by then descending Coastal FR, or longer loops by climbing Coastal to Coyote Ridge and descending Middle Green Gulch or Green Gulch Trails.

Muir Beach Trail begins at the near end of the new bridge from the Muir Beach parking lot over the marsh. Lovely art panels show some of the plants and animals that may be seen. Willows and alders line the far end of the bridge, as they do so many Marin coastal stream and wetlands.

Across the bridge, veer right. Left is Kaasi Road, leading to Coastal, Middle Green Gulch, and Dias Ridge Trails. In 75 yards is the main entry to Muir Beach, over mats atop the sand. Almost all trail users depart here. Continue left, where there are steps down to the beach.

Opposite, more than 100 steps carry Muir Beach Trail steeply uphill. The ocean breaks against the rocks directly beyond the edge. I've seen Pacific bottlenose dolphins, a species only observed in the Bay Area since 2010, cavorting in the main cove at right. Fog is common, but the surf is always loud. A couple of wide areas offer cliffside rest stops.

Fifty feet above the final overlook, which is the broadest, Muir Beach Trail ends when it meets Coastal FR. It is $\frac{1}{3}$ mile down to Kaasi Road and .2 mile up to Pirates Cove Trail.

■ Owl Trail

Muir Beach Overlook to Slide Ranch: 1.09 miles

TERRAIN: Coastal scrub (GGNRA)

ELEVATION: From 440 to 190 feet; gradual

INTERSECTING TRAIL(S): None

This little-known and little-visited trail may have the most spectacular ocean vistas of any route described in this book. Now that it has been signed by GGNRA, surely more will come to enjoy Owl Trail.

Muir Beach Overlook, between Mile Markers 6.96 and 7.00, is a must-stop for travelers on Highway 1 (and not just for the restrooms!). Picnic tables offer stunning ocean views and steps lead down to even more dramatic vistas. During World War II, the US government took over the site and installed three underground manned fire-control stations. Soldiers waited patiently to communicate enemy ship locations to troops manning gun batteries closer to the Golden Gate Bridge. Fortunately, no guns were ever fired from those batteries.

The overlook access to Owl Trail sets off from the first picnic table (when driving in) and is not presently signed. At right just in is a glimpse of a home on Seascape Drive, but visitors are invariably looking left, at the ocean. You can hear the roar of waves breaking on the rocky shore.

In 200 yards, the trail meets Highway 1 at a turnout. There is an Owl Trail sign here, noting that Slide Ranch Educational Farm is .9 mile away.

The vegetation is coastal scrub, mostly baccharis, with sage, blackberry, mustard, and lupine, plus poison oak, which is also common. The very few trees are all non-native. The trail trends down, with several sets of steps.

At .6 mile, a sign warns hikers to stay off a path left, then another just beyond warns not to go up right. Directly below is the first of two yurts, part of Slide Ranch.

The trail then meets a line of introduced eucalyptus, Monterey pine, and Monterey cypress trees. One of the latter has a particularly massive trunk. It was in these trees that a great horned owl lived and gave the trail its name. Surely others followed.

Bend left at the fenced pasture. There is a short, steep section down to the goat enclosure. Owl Trail meets the main dirt road through Slide Ranch. The trail may be said to continue an additional 100 yards up the slope to the visitor parking area, where there is another Owl Trail sign.

Steeply sloped Slide Ranch was Ranch U in Samuel Throckmorton's division of his Rancho Saucelito. Miguel Roberto was the original purchaser, acquiring the land when the leased ranches were put up for sale in 1898. In 1967, a Los Angeles developer purchased the ranch and its buildings, which by then were in disrepair and reputedly a haven for drug dealers. Plans for an ocean front hotel were presented. Mill Valley residents Doug Ferguson and Huey Johnson, western director of the Nature Conservancy, spearheaded an effort to save the property. In 1969, the conservancy, with Ferguson as lead financial contributor, purchased 134 acres. Susan Washington-Smyth and husband Ed Washington, who had ties to the Grateful Dead band, then turned Slide Ranch into a teaching farm. It opened to the public in 1970 and has been delighting and educating schoolchildren and others—some 8,000 each year—ever since.

In 1974, the National Park Service purchased Slide Ranch from the Nature Conservancy and added it to the surrounding Golden Gate National Recreation Area.

Rocky Point Road

Highway 1 to Rocky Point: .94 mile

TERRAIN: Coastal scrub; upper part asphalt (MTSP)

ELEVATION: From 380 to 50 feet; gradual

INTERSECTING TRAIL(S): Rocky Point Trail (.4 mile)

This road leads down from Highway 1 to Steep Ravine (or Rocky Point) Environmental cabins and campground. A gate blocks cars—only overnight guests have the lock's combination—so the route, though largely paved, is included in this book. With perfect footing and a gentle grade, Rocky Point Road is ideal for enjoying the fabulous ocean views.

The trailhead is by Highway 1 Mile Marker 11.04. There is parking for a few cars. (Do not confuse the turnout with a bigger one just to the north, for Red Rock Beach.) Opposite, Steep Ravine Trail begins its long and lovely climb to Pantoll. In July and August, the top of Rocky Point Road is covered with the purple-red flowers of *Clarkia amoena*, commonly known as "farewell-to-spring" or "summer's darling." Webb Creek, which carves Steep Ravine, flows under Highway 1 through a pipe and continues down to the beach.

The descent to the cabins is glorious, with ocean views and the sound of the surf all the way. A sign warns of a newt crossing, and there is a newt informational sign by the bathroom below.

At .4 mile, signed Rocky Point Trail sets off left, by a fence line. It also connects to Highway 1. The vibrant reds of California fuchsia brighten the road edge from late August into fall.

In another 200 yards, at a gate, a dirt fire road comes in on the left. It arcs around to again meet the paved road, making a loop of this lower half of Rocky Point Road.

The pavement meets the Steep Ravine cabins. Perched just above the breaking surf, they are among Tam's man-made treasures. The cabins were on land owned by William Kent. In 1960, his estate donated 240 acres here to MTSP. The cabins themselves remained under private control (to the dismay of many) until the state renovated them and opened them to the public on a reservation basis. Call the California State Parks reservation service well in advance; the cabins book very quickly. In fact, they are the most popular overnight sites in all the state park system. But be prepared for a rustic experience, as none of the cabins has water, electricity, or bathrooms, and mice are regular visitors.

The ten cabins (there were once twelve) are numbered and carry names reflecting local history and features. They are: William Kent (1, wheelchair-accessible), Dipsea (2), Thaddeus Welch (3), Rocky Point (4), Willow Camp (5), Webb Creek (6), Hot Springs (7), San Andreas (8), Farallon (9), and Whale Watchers (10).

A path leads down to the mouth of Webb Creek, site of a once-popular hot spring. The spring, buried by falling boulders during reconstruction work on Highway 1 in 1960, is now accessible only in fall, at low minus tides. Then, it is possible to dig in the sand to reach the spring's warm water. Another path, lined with poison oak, skirts the edge of the Rocky Point cliffs. One of the offshore rocks is topped with an old concrete-and-metal foundation.

Continue on the dirt loop to the six campsites, with equally special settings. They are: Abalone (1), Cormorant (2), Starfish (3), Pelican (4), Kelp (5), and Hot N Tot (6, for the Hottentot fig, a naturalized succulent abundant here). There is a pond just before the uphill begins.

On the climb back, Rocky Point Trail offers a loop option that involves a ½-mile walk along the edge of narrow Highway 1.

▓ Rocky Point Trail

Highway 1 to Steep Ravine Road: .36 mile

TERRAIN: Coastal scrub (MTSP)

ELEVATION: From 420 to 220 feet; steep

INTERSECTING TRAIL(s): None

Rocky Point Trail offers a route down to the Steep Ravine cabins and campground; the other access is paved Rocky Point Road (previously described).

The trail descends from a turnout, with very limited parking, off Highway 1 just south of Mile Marker 10.67. An easy-to-miss signpost now marks the entry. Directly across the highway was the base of the historic Lone Tree FR. In 2005, MTSP bulldozed and obliterated the eroded route to allow it to return to nature.

In recent years, Rocky Point was narrow and lined with poison oak. The trail has since been cleared, and while poison oak is still there, it's now avoidable.

Veer right at the start. In 100 feet, Rocky Point Trail crosses a gully over a bridge. In 400 feet, a path branches right. In another 100 yards, the trail passes a large, resistant chert boulder. Chert on Tam is often characterized by the evenly spaced layering that this boulder displays perfectly.

But it is the ocean view that is the trail's main appeal. Below is a wild, stunning stretch of Pacific coastline.

Aromatic California sagebrush outnumbers even baccharis, usually the predominant shrub in coastal scrub. A few short Douglas-firs have taken root, the largest beside a rivulet. The sunny slope yields bounteous wildflowers in spring.

The trail ends at paved Rocky Point Road, which continues down to MTSP's ten Steep Ravine cabins, six campsites, and the rugged shore of Rocky Point. The paved road can be taken uphill for a loop but the ½-mile walk on Highway 1's edge back to the trailhead may not be appealing.

KIRKE WRENCH

Muir Beach Overlook

A huge rock marks the upper end of Canopy View Trail where it meets Panoramic Trail.

TRAILHEAD SEVEN: MUIR WOODS NATIONAL MONUMENT

Directions

Highway 101—Highway 1—Panoramic Highway to "Four Corners" intersection—left down Muir Woods Road to parking areas.

Almost all of Mt. Tamalpais's virgin redwood and Douglas-fir forests were logged in the years soon after the 1849 California Gold Rush. The stand in Redwood (sometimes called Sequoia) Canyon escaped because of its relative inaccessibility and lack of a harbor at Muir Beach. Many of the trees were nearly 1,000 years old and some rose more than 250 feet. After the laying of a rail line into downtown Mill Valley in 1889 and the grading of a crude wagon road from Mill Valley into the canyon in 1892, the redwoods became a tourist attraction.

To preserve the virgin forest for future generations, William and Elizabeth Kent purchased 611 acres—the canyon and adjacent hillside—in 1905 for $45,000. Kent's holding was almost immediately jeopardized when, in 1907, plans were advanced to condemn the canyon for a reservoir, with the trees to be logged prior to flooding. Later that year, the Kents donated 295 acres, the heart of the canyon, to the American people under the 1906 Antiquities Act, which gave the president broad authority to protect national treasures.

187

Muir Woods was the sixth monument designated (and the first donated by an individual), coming into the federal fold two days before the Grand Canyon. The Kents insisted that the park be named for John Muir, dean of the nation's environmental movement. Muir said, "This is the best tree lover's monument that could be found in all the forests of the world."

Automobiles first entered Muir Woods in 1908—there were once plans for a gasoline station just outside the main entrance—but were banned from the grove proper in 1924. Kent's private access road was widened in 1926 and tolls collected at the two entry points, Four Corners and Frank Valley Road. In 1939, the road passed to the county. A stone portal at the former Four Corners toll site remains. The monument now attracts more than 1,000,000 visitors annually from all over the world.

The monument is open daily from 8 AM to sunset. After decades of free entry, an admission fee was instituted in 1997. This fee, collected at the main entrance, has since been raised several times, to $10 on January 1, 2016, with children 15 and under still free. (See the monument's website for updates.) From 2011 through 2015, after the California State Parks system experienced a major financial crisis, the National Park Service dedicated part of the entry fee to help maintain Mt. Tamalpais State Park.

The visitor center, which opened in 1989, was built in the style of the 1930s Works Progress Administration buildings. It is open 9 AM to 6 PM, and is a must-stop for learning more about the monument and Mt. Tamalpais. Just inside the entrance are a gift shop and cafeteria, both run by a concessionaire, and the monument's administrative offices. There are restrooms in the parking lot and adjacent to the cafeteria, and a water fountain at the Redwood Creek-Fern Creek trail junction. Picnicking is not permitted inside the monument.

In the fall of 2015, long-debated plans to ease traffic congestion on the roads into Muir Woods were approved, among them, parking restrictions along Frank Valley Road (which is often lined with parked cars for up to a mile west of the monument's entrance) and a visitor fee-reservation system. Since 2003, a federally funded shuttle has carried visitors between the Manzanita parking lot (under Highway 101 at the southern approach to Mill Valley) and the monument; the shuttle, currently operated by Marin Transit, runs only on weekends and holidays, and its winter schedule is limited.

On Muir Woods Road, between the monument and Muir Beach, are access points to Deer Park FR (at Mile Marker 2.09), lower Redwood Creek Trail (several, starting from opposite Deer Park FR), and Heather Cutoff Trail (Mile Marker 3.21). All three are in MTSP, but are included within this trailhead.

Suggested Loops

1. Redwood Creek Trail, .9 mile, to Bridge 4 and Hillside Trail—left, .7 mile, to Bridge 2—right .3 mile, on Main Trail, to start. **1.9 miles total**

2. Redwood Creek Trail, .2 mile, to Canopy View Trail—right, 1.3 miles, to Lost Trail—left, .6 mile, to Fern Canyon (Creek) Trail—left, .4 mile, to Main Trail—left, .6 mile, to start. **3.1 miles total**

3. Dipsea Trail west from overflow parking lot (or Deer Park FR when the Redwood Creek bridge is out), 1.6 miles, to Ben Johnson Trail—right, 1.3 miles, to Redwood Creek Trail—right, 1.0 mile, to start. **3.9 miles total** (or 4.9 miles for Deer Park FR start)

4. Redwood Creek Trail, .9 mile, to Bootjack Trail—right (straight), 1.5 miles, to Van Wyck Meadow—right, .9 mile, on Troop 80 Spur and Trail to Sierra Trail—right, 1.0 mile, to Camp Eastwood—right, .9 mile, on Camp Eastwood Road (downhill) to Redwood Creek Trail—left, .7 mile, to start. **5.9 miles total**

5. Redwood Creek Trail, .9 mile, to Bridge 4 and Ben Johnson Trail—left, 1.3 miles, to Dipsea Trail—right, .3 mile, to TCC Trail—right, 1.8 miles, to Van Wyck Meadow—right on Bootjack Trail, 1.5 miles, to Redwood Creek Trail—straight, .9 mile, to start. **6.7 miles total**

6. Muir Woods (Frank Valley) Road at Santos Meadow, Mile Marker 3.21 (elevation 100 feet) to Heather Cutoff Trail, 1.5 miles, to top—right on Coastal FR, 2.1 miles, up to Deer Park FR—right on Deer Park FR, 2.4 miles, down to Muir Woods Road—cross road and right on lower Redwood Creek Trail, 1.2 miles, to connector across Redwood Creek (no bridge) and start (Muir Woods Road can be joined earlier when water is high). **7.2 miles total**

◼ Ben Johnson Trail

Redwood Trail to Dipsea Trail: 1.27 miles

TERRAIN: Redwood forest (MWNM)

ELEVATION: From 240 to 860 feet; very steep

INTERSECTING TRAIL(S): Hillside (.1 mile), Stapelveldt (1.0 mile), Deer Park FR (1.2 miles)

Ben Johnson Trail passes through one of the quietest, deepest, wettest forests on Mt. Tamalpais, and is well used in walks out of Muir Woods.

To reach the Ben Johnson trailhead, take the asphalt-covered Redwood Creek (Main) Trail to its end at Bridge 4 (the fourth bridge over Redwood Creek from the entrance arch). Bootjack Trail continues straight while Ben Johnson rises to the left, across the bridge. A signpost points the way toward the Dipsea

Trail, Pantoll, and Stinson Beach. Just on the other side of the bridge, to the left, is Hillside Trail, which connects back to Bridge 2. Ben Johnson veers right, uphill.

The climb is a long one, but the route is well graded and the coolness of the woods brings relief. Steps carry the trail up over the steepest early part. Runners find Ben Johnson—covered in soft redwood duff and without excessive roots and rocks—one of the better downhill trails.

Ben Johnson crosses several streambeds, two of them over bridges each fashioned from a single redwood. The redwoods and Douglas-firs are enormous; several of the former, opened by fire, can be entered. Huckleberry is abundant.

A welcome seat is embedded in the hillside. Just beyond, a small clearing in the tree canopy permits glimpses of Throckmorton Ridge. Higher, a downed redwood took out another bench and forces a slight detour.

After a mile of climbing, Ben Johnson Trail meets a signed three-way junction. A pause at the bench here in the deep woods is obligatory. Straight ahead is the start of Stapelveldt Trail, rising to Pantoll. Ben Johnson continues left, following the sign to the Dipsea Trail. Newer switchbacks, bordered by fences, carry it uphill another well-wooded ¼ mile.

Ben Johnson crests a ridge, then crosses Deer Park FR in the magical area known as Deer Park. To the left (east) is a magnificent stand of virgin redwoods. Just to the right is the fire road's junction with the Dipsea Trail. Ben Johnson Trail goes another 20 yards straight ahead to end at the Dipsea.

Ben Johnson was once superintendent of Samuel Throckmorton's southern Marin dairy ranches. He apparently also worked at the San Francisco Mint. He then moved to a cabin just downstream from the present Bridge 4 on the floor of Redwood Canyon. There is an 1892 reference to Redwood Creek referred to as "Johnson's Creek." Johnson built the trail that carries his name around 1900, when he became gamekeeper for the Tamalpais Sportsman's Club. The trail provided hunters with access to the club's lands higher on Tam. (After the mountain's bears, elk, and mountain lions had been hunted out of existence here by the 1880s, deer and quail remained as quarry.) Johnson died of tuberculosis in 1904 at age fifty-one. The trail has been known as Dead Horse Trail and Sequoia Trail.

Bohemian Grove Trail

Redwood Creek (Main) Trail, between Bridges 1 and 3: .41 mile

TERRAIN: Redwood forest (MWNM)

ELEVATION: From 220 to 230 feet; flat

INTERSECTING TRAIL(S): Hillside (.27 mile)

Bohemian Grove Trail is the new name for the section of trail that borders the right bank (when facing downstream) of Redwood Creek between Bridges 1 and 3. The even more heavily traveled section along the opposite bank, from Bridges 1 to 4, is now known as Redwood Creek Trail.

Within yards on passing through the historic entrance arch, visitors to Muir Woods National Monument face a choice. They can head right to the cafeteria, gift shop, and restrooms; they can go straight on the "main" trail; or they can cross Redwood Creek over Bridge 1 (the current bridge dates from 1993) onto Bohemian Grove Trail. Most venturing into the woods walk a loop combining Bohemian Grove and Redwood Creek Trails.

In early winter, look into the creek for steelhead and coho salmon migrating upstream. The once-healthy runs have been vastly reduced in recent decades, but recent improvements where the salmon enter Redwood Creek at Muir Beach are cause for optimism.

Just past the bridge, sharp-eyed visitors looking right may spot the plaque reading *1803 EMERSON 1903* affixed to a redwood adjacent to the Pinchot Tree (which is well marked on the Redwood Creek Trail) about 10 feet above the ground. It was placed in 1903, five years before Muir Woods was proclaimed a national monument, to mark the 100th anniversary of the birth of New England writer, philosopher, and nature lover Ralph Waldo Emerson. Jack London was among those attending the ceremony. It may be the oldest surviving plaque on Mt. Tamalpais.

The redwoods are, of course, the stars of the trail, and they don't disappoint. Several colorful, well-written information signs add to a deeper understanding of redwood forest ecology.

At .2 mile, there is a sign beside the fallen Solstice Tree (currently dated at 536 years), so named because it fell on the winter solstice, December 21, 2010. Adjacent is a plaque to the now-towering Bicentennial Tree, which only dates from 1776.

You then enter the signed Bohemian Grove of redwoods. In 1892, members of San Francisco's all-male Bohemian Club, founded 20 years earlier, held their first "Jinks" encampment here. A rough road was carved to the remote, still privately owned woods for the occasion. Club members erected a giant Buddha, shown on the interpretive panel. The canyon in summer turned out to be too cold, and the club purchased a large redwood grove in Sonoma County; the Jinks, now attracting many of the nation's most prominent figures (still men-only), are held annually to this day. In Bohemian Grove is Muir Woods' tallest tree, a redwood measured at 252 feet.

At ¼ mile, Bridge 2 crosses the creek under an arching bay tree branch. To the left, Hillside Trail begins its journey, a bit above the valley floor, to Bridge 4, providing another loop option. Some 15 yards before the bridge, look right for a redwood with a particularly large burl about 20 feet up. Burls, which can weigh up to 50 tons each, are swollen masses of undeveloped buds, an alternative, asexual method of reproduction. Why some redwoods grow burls and others don't is still not fully understood.

Bohemian Grove meanders another ⅛ mile to Bridge 3, which must be crossed to continue. Left leads to (in order), Fern Creek Trail; Camp Eastwood Road; and Bootjack, Ben Johnson, and Hillside Trails.

■ Bootjack Trail

Muir Woods Trail to Mountain Theater, plus spur: 2.77 miles

TERRAIN: Lower part riparian redwood and Douglas-fir forest; upper part tan-bark oak woodland with some grassland (MWNM, MTSP, MMWD)

ELEVATION: From 240 to 1,980 feet; very steep

INTERSECTING TRAIL(S): Troop 80 Spur (1.5 miles), TCC (1.5 miles), Troop 80 (1.6 miles), Alpine (1.9 miles), Matt Davis (2.0 miles), Old Stage Road (2.2 miles)

No Mt. Tam trail (and only three fire roads—Willow Camp, and Eldridge and Old Railroad Grades) has a greater differential between its start and end elevations than Bootjack. Covering its full length is no easy task. But the journey is worthwhile, for Bootjack Trail passes through some of the mountain's loveliest and most diverse areas and connects treasures such as Muir Woods, Van Wyck Meadow, Bootjack Camp itself, and Mountain Theater.

Bootjack Trail starts at the far end of the asphalt-covered Redwood Creek (Main) Trail, at Bridge 4. Here, too, left across the bridge, Ben Johnson Trail begins its climb. Bootjack immediately leaves Muir Woods National Monument and enters Mount Tamalpais State Park.

Early going, along the left bank of Redwood Creek, is fairly level. Giant redwoods, rivals to those passed on the approach walk, tower above. Beside one is a plaque, dating from the late 1920s, to *The memory of Andrew Jay Cross, Pioneer in Optometry, 1855–1925*. Cross was president of the American Optical Association in 1900–1901, and his 1911 book, *Dynamic Skiametry in Theory and Practice*, is still in print. The broad area here was once a picnic site maintained by Muir Woods; a later, more precise survey moved the boundary southeast.

In .1 mile, Bootjack Spur departs to the right. It climbs .1 mile to meet Camp Eastwood FR beside a particularly huge redwood. That junction was the site of the second Muir Inn (1914–1932), and travelers continued down to the canyon floor over this spur.

The next trail intersection comes at 1.4 miles, making this one of the longest such stretches on the mountain. Bootjack passes through wondrous terrain, deep in forest, beside vigorous and waterfall-laden Redwood Creek. The crowds of Muir Woods seem miles away. Here, Bootjack rivals the Cataract and Steep Ravine Trails as Tam's best waterfall walk after a heavy rain.

The trail crosses eight main bridges (with handrails) up to Van Wyck Meadow. Azaleas are abundant. Around $1/3$ mile in, the trail has been rerouted to the right; keep off the blocked path. Steps lead down to a pool in Redwood Creek.

After its gentle start, Bootjack begins to climb in earnest. There is an old, 30-foot-long wooden railing on the right. In fall and winter here and just below, you may be lucky enough to see hibernating ladybugs (*Hippodamia convergens*, also called ladybird beetles or convergent lady beetles). Carried by the wind, swarms find their way to the exact same site year after year. At peak times, they cover rocks, bridges, live and dead branches and trunks, and ferns.

Above, Bootjack Trail crosses Redwood Creek for the first time, to its right bank. The relatively long bridge (the fourth on the ascent) was rebuilt after a 2012 slide, and the whole middle section of Bootjack Trail was closed for nearly two years. (It reopened January 2014.) It replaced a bridge built in 1983 after another storm washout. A respite is all but mandatory. Azalea, elk clover (with its enormous leaves), goldcup oak, redwood, hazel, and poison oak border the bridge. Maples add color.

Beyond this bridge, Bootjack climbs out of the canyon onto an enchanting ridge. Just west is Rattlesnake Creek, which meets Spike Buck Creek (and, higher, Bootjack Creek) to form Redwood Creek. Native grasses grow amidst the rocks and woodland, and water rushes left and right. Paths lead to choice resting spots.

Bootjack Trail then trends right, back to Spike Buck Creek. It crosses to Spike Buck's left bank, which it then follows closely uphill. Just past the bridge, hundreds of stone and wood steps carry Bootjack Trail steeply higher. Some of the steps are recycled old trail signs, such as "No Dogs, 8 PM–7 AM" and "Groups Only." A fallen Douglas-fir, dated when cut for passage (2/1/94), will be a landmark for years. Higher, look in summer for Indian pink (*Silene laciniata* ssp. *californica*). Its bright red petals, deeply cleft, would stand out any time; they are particularly striking among the year's last woodland wildflowers.

A tough haul of 150 wood-and-stone steps in two sections leads to the delightful grassy clearing of Van Wyck Meadow. In the middle of the meadow is a large sandstone boulder, Council Rock. Behind is the charming sign: Van Wyck Meadow, Pop. 3 Steller's Jays. (Steller's jays [*Cyanocitta stelleri*] are ubiquitous in Tamalpais's forests.)

In February 1989, MTSP placed a plaque on the old stone fireplace left, under a goldcup oak, thanking the Tamalpais Conservation Club, "Guardian of the Mountain," for decades of support; the plaque was later stolen. Note the water pipes from the days when this meadow was the site of Lower Rattlesnake Camp, later called Van Wyck Camp, one of the most popular of the mountain's old gathering spots. In August, the clearing is covered with hundreds of rosinweed (*Calycadenia multiglandulosa*) plants, most about a foot tall and with sticky, fragrant stems.

Sidney M. Van Wyck, Jr. (1869–1931), a graduate of the University of California, Berkeley; lawyer; and TCC president, played a leading role in the creation of Mt. Tamalpais State Park. Donating his services, he worked to sway public opinion and secure the necessary state legislation, and was in court during the condemnation proceedings in 1927–1928 to acquire the land of James Newlands and William Magee. They had refused to sell their 500-plus-acre parcel between Mountain Home and Bootjack to the state, hoping instead to develop it. The land, when finally purchased for the $52,000 price set by the court, formed the heart of the new park.

Troop 80 Trail departs to the right. It goes to Camp Eastwood Road, near Mountain Home. At the meadow's left, TCC Trail begins its 1.4-mile trip to Stapeldt Trail.

Bootjack continues left through a patch of false lupine. It immediately resumes climbing, passing a huge, smooth-faced boulder. At this point, the trail is back in the trees, largely tanbark oak and redwood. The next intersection is with the west end of Troop 80 Spur Trail, which goes right .2 mile to meet Troop 80 at the Memorial Tree.

Just beyond is an old fountain. This was the site of Upper Rattlesnake Camp, another one-time popular hiker's haunt.

Alpine Trail comes in from the left and rises to Pantoll. A bench at this junction was made from a classic old Rattlesnake Camp sign. Thirty yards higher, look right at a massive redwood. Is it one tree, split when young by lightning, or two trees growing remarkably close?

The sound of cars on Panoramic Highway becomes evident. After crossing a couple of bridges, Bootjack Trail meets the highway at a West Marin Stagecoach stop. Cross the road into the parking lot and go right, up steps past a fountain and bathrooms, into the restored Bootjack Camp. Originally built by the Tamalpais Conservation Club around 1920, Bootjack was an isolated campground until Panoramic Highway was built next to it in 1928. The new state park maintained twenty-nine campsites here until all were closed in 1969, when the site became Bootjack Picnic Area. Then, through a cooperative effort between MTSP, MMWD, and TCC, fifteen walk-in campsites were restored. A dedication ceremony marking the reopening was held May 3, 2014.

Wind your way through Bootjack to pick up the trail at its intersection with Matt Davis Trail. Matt Davis goes left to Pantoll and right toward Mountain Home while Bootjack continues straight up.

The trail passes below an MTSP residence. It was originally built by the Tamalpais Conservation Club in 1925 as its "Trailsman's Cabin." (Some timbers came from William Kent's even older hunting cabin above the Dipsea Trail to the west.) MTSP enlarged it in 1955. Master trail-builder Matt Davis was a resident in the 1920s and '30s.

Bootjack meets an asphalt road. To the far right is the entry to the residence. Above is Old Stage Road, heading to West Point (right) and Pantoll (left). A few yards to the left, opposite a fountain and chlorinator building, is the foot of Riding & Hiking Trail.

Bootjack continues steeply uphill. Above a rocky stretch, the trail hits a grassy hillside. This clearing is prominent from many vantage points south of the mountain. In the 1880s, it struck someone as having the shape of a bootjack, a device used to help remove boots, particularly riding boots, and the name has stuck. In late spring, the clearing is ablaze with yellow from poppies and mariposa lilies. The view from a bench with the word "Ranger" carved into it is blocked by a Douglas-fir.

Switchbacks, one with a small sign dubbing it "the Gucci," carry the trail ever upward, although not so steeply as in years past. A sign credits the former Youth Conservation Corps with doing the rerouting in 1980. The next bench was made out of the "Station" section of the same sign as the previous bench.

Bootjack Trail ends at a junction with Easy Grade Trail just below the Mountain Theater stage. Easy Grade descends to Old Stage Road near Pantoll. To the left are the theater's dressing rooms. Sing a song, recite lines from a play, or just sit and enjoy this special site.

Bootjack Trail appeared on the 1898 Sanborn map, and ran farther through what is now the heart of Muir Woods National Monument.

Canopy (Ocean) View Trail

Muir Woods to Panoramic Highway: 1.52 miles

TERRAIN: Deeply wooded; heavily used (MWNM, MTSP)

ELEVATION: 220 to 900 feet; steep

INTERSECTING TRAIL(S): Lost (1.3 miles)

As the first trail up out of Redwood Canyon when entering Muir Woods from the main entrance, Canopy View (formerly Ocean View, a name still much used) is well trod, at least in the early going. Many, not prepared for more than 700 feet of uphill, turn back. Others depart to complete lovely loops with Lost and Fern Canyon Trails, or with Camp Eastwood Road. Be forewarned that there are no ocean views until near the trail's top, which is the reason that Canopy View is now the official name.

The trailhead is .1 mile in from the visitor center, opposite the Pinchot Tree. Canopy View begins its long uphill on steps. Towering redwoods line the trail along with trillium, fairy-bells, and sword ferns. In .1 mile, a huge Douglas-fir straddles the trail's left margin. Above, Douglas-firs begin to replace redwoods, particularly where sunlight penetrates over the ridges.

At .4 mile, the trail levels somewhat as it leaves Muir Woods National Monument and moves into Mt. Tamalpais State Park. A welcome bench appears just after passing a water pipeline embedded in the trail. The bench looks out over a cluster of redwoods called the David Sarlin Grove. The grove was dedicated in 1998 through the Save the Redwoods League. (There is also a David Sarlin Grove in Portola Redwoods State Park.) In .1 mile, an oak forms an arch over the trail.

Soon after crossing a creek, Canopy View steepens. California nutmeg trees, with needles similar to those of the Douglas-fir but longer and sharper, grow to 60 feet beside the trail. Howell noted them in his *Marin Flora* more than sixty-five years ago.

At .8 mile, in a clearing known as Fir Tree Point, the trail opens. Look here for aromatic pitcher sages (*Lepechinia calycina*). They are woody shrubs, 1 to 4 feet tall, with two-lipped white flowers in spring. Rub the opposing leaves to capture the strong fragrance. There is another stand of redwoods, thinner and more crowded than those below because the trees are now at the margin of their habitat. An old bench where Lost Trail departs down to the left is well used. Lost Trail offers a loop option.

The trail now leaves the deep woodland. Ahead is more open, broom-covered grassland and, finally, views. First, there is a vista of Tam's summit ridge. Then, a few yards later, look back to finally see (as promised) the ocean. The trail passes beneath a huge rock, a choice resting site.

Canopy View ends when it meets Panoramic Trail. To the left is Camp Eastwood Road, which returns over a more gradual grade to Muir Woods. Farther left is Mountain Home Inn. To the right, toward Ridge Avenue, is another loop option back, via Redwood Trail to the Tourist Club, then the Sun and Dipsea Trails. A few yards up is Panoramic Highway. Alpine Lodge, headquarters of the California Alpine Club, is directly across the road.

■ Deer Park (Dipsea) Fire Road

Muir Woods Road to Coast View Trail: 3.03 miles

TERRAIN: Upper part redwood forest, middle part grassland, lower part lightly wooded (MTSP, MWNM; part of Bay Area Ridge Trail)

ELEVATION: From 150 to 1,500 feet; steep, parts very steep

INTERSECTING TRAIL(S): Dipsea (several times between .9 mile and 2.5 miles), Ben Johnson (1.9 miles)

Note: There is a completely separate Deer Park FR out of the Deer Park trailhead in Fairfax. This route is called Deer Park (Dipsea) FR, as it is such an integral part of the Dipsea Trail and Dipsea Race. Indeed, the Dipsea Trail and Deer Park FR are contiguous over four stretches and intersect several other times. During the five or so months each year when the plank carrying the Dipsea Trail over Redwood Creek is removed, runners and hikers are directed onto Deer Park FR. "Dipsea FR" is an alternate name.

Deer Park (Dipsea) FR sets off from Muir Woods Road at a gate between Mile Markers 2.09 and 2.10. This is ½ mile west from the Dipsea Trail crossing of Redwood Creek. There is parking directly across Muir Woods Road, although spots even this far from the monument's entry arch fill on busy days. The east end of (Lower) Redwood Creek Trail is also across the road.

The uphill is immediately very steep. Shrubs, including abundant native blackberries (not nearly as tasty as the introduced species), line the left. To the right is deep woodland.

After .5 mile of stiff climbing, the fire road meets the Dipsea Trail, entering from the right. A sign marks the junction. This is the upper end of the winter bridge detour.

The uphill eases a bit. This next 1-mile-long section, in which the Deer Park FR and Dipsea Trail intertwine, is known as the Hogback, for its appearance in profile. Pictures from the 1920s, when the land here was fenced and grazed, show only grassland. Now, coyote brush is a common shrub and Douglas-firs have gained more than a foothold.

The Dipsea Trail combines with the fire road. They rise together, then the trail continues straight and the fire road veers right. (Many Dipsea racers remain on the fire road, marginally longer but with more room to pass.) There are sweeping views toward the Pacific and of the Tam summit ridge.

Again the Dipsea Trail briefly joins the fire road, this time to depart to the right. (Each intersection is signed.) The two meet again, with the trail now exiting to the left.

Deer Park FR then enters Muir Woods National Monument; the MTSP boundary sign is beside a huge fallen tanbark oak. This is one of the special parts of Tam: an unexpected stand of giant, virgin redwoods and Douglas-firs high on its slope. Their relative inaccessibility, then William Kent's protection, spared these giants from logging. This cool, haunting, magical area is little traveled, as most visitors follow the Dipsea Trail. It was once known as Kent's Deer Park, hence the fire road name. George Lucas filmed part of his fantasy movie *Willow* here, and there is evidence of a 1997 fire.

At a signpost, Ben Johnson Trail crosses. Right leads to Stapelveldt Trail, then on down to Muir Woods for a loop option. Left connects within a few yards to the Dipsea Trail. The Dipsea Trail itself joins, and the two then run uphill together for 100 yards until the trail departs right, up the hill known as Cardiac.

The fire road continues rising through deep woodland to the westernmost tip of Muir Woods National Monument. Huge redwoods and Douglas-firs tower above. One of the latter, on the left, is particularly enormous, with a huge girth supporting three tall trunks.

Deer Park FR exits the woodland into grassland. Ocean views, sometimes to the Farallon Islands, dramatically open. For decades, the fire road's upper end was here, at its junction with the former Coastal FR, and it was Coastal that continued up to Pantoll. But in 2004, Coastal FR was replaced by the new Coast View Trail. Now, new (2014) MTSP signs designate Deer Park FR as connecting to Pantoll. (This makes both ends of the fire road accessible by car.)

Bend right and up to continue. In 500 feet, Deer Park FR crosses the Dipsea Trail for a last time. This is the highest point (1,360 feet) of the entire Dipsea Trail, a summit well known to all racers as "Cardiac." The knoll right is a popular resting site. The water fountain here was dedicated June 7, 2013. Eve Pell, who won the Dipsea in 1989, spearheaded fundraising for the fountain to honor her late husband, Sam Hirabayashi. At the time of his death, Hirabayashi held all but one of the single-age Dipsea records for runners 74 through 83. The fountain uses a design by William Penn Mott, Jr.; similar Mott-designed stone fountains were built in the 1930s by the Civilian Conservation Corps at Bootjack, Pantoll, Mountain Theater, and elsewhere on Tamalpais. Mott went on become head of the California State Park system (their training center is now named for him), then director of the National Park Service (1985–1989).

In another 125 yards, Deer Park FR crosses (Lower) Old Mine Trail. To the right, Old Mine goes to Pantoll. Fifty yards left, it goes to a bench with a stunning view. The bench is dedicated "Dear Veterans, Welcome Home," and is wheelchair accessible over the reworked Old Mine Trail.

Deer Park FR then enters dense woodland. Douglas-firs now cover Lone Tree Hill to the left; indeed, there was once only one tree on it, a redwood. You can see traces of an old road when the hill was being readied for sale and subdivision, a fate averted when MTSP purchased 30 acres in April 1960.

Deer Park FR runs parallel and just above Old Mine Trail to a gate marking the MTSP maintenance area. The final ¼ mile, past the yard and several state park residences and offices, is paved. Deer Park FR ends when it meets the top of Steep Ravine Trail at Pantoll.

The route has also been known as Old Mine Truck Road because it went on to an old mine below Pantoll. It appeared as a trail on the 1898 Sanborn map, then was widened in the 1930s. "Deer parks," fenced hunting preserves, date back to Anglo-Saxon times in England.

Heather Cutoff Trail

Redwood Creek Trail to Coast View Trail: 1.46 miles

TERRAIN: Coastal brush and grassland; horses permitted (MTSP)

ELEVATION: From 75 to 440 feet; gradual

INTERSECTING TRAIL(S): None

This unusual trail was built with twenty-one gently graded switchbacks to make ascents and descents easier for horses. Heather Cutoff also plays a role for those on foot as part of loops on the southwest flank of Mt. Tamalpais.

The trail technically begins from Lower Redwood Creek Trail, at an MTSP signpost. Because the 200 yards to Muir Woods Road involves crossing Redwood Creek without a bridge, most hikers join Heather Cutoff Trail from the entrance gate to Frank Valley Horse Camp (by Mile Marker 3.21). The camp, directly ahead, opened in 1991 to accommodate equestrian groups. Heather Cutoff goes diagonally left from the gate, across Santos Meadow, to another MTSP signpost. Here the climbing begins.

The many switchbacks provide extra time to enjoy the expanding views. The first vista is of the western end of Frank Valley. What was once the Banducci family's flower farm can still be discerned in the valley, but the area is returning to a natural state. Coyote brush is the most abundant plant along the trail, but blackberry, thimbleberry, twinberry, monkeyflower, sage, strawberry, Indian warrior, and, alas, poison oak are also common. Chain ferns thrive in a muddy seep, ⅓ mile up.

The trail ever rises. You can easily see how far you've climbed, and what remains. Well up, you can finally see over Dias Ridge to the Pacific.

Heather Cutoff crests (and ends) at its junction with the broad Coast View Trail. Indeed, spectacular ocean views open. Expect blustery winds as well. Coast View goes left .2 mile to a dead end at Highway 1. Right on Coast View, the first intersection is 2.1 miles uphill, with Deer Park FR.

Also just to the left is the MTSP/GGNRA boundary, and the old heather farm. Founded by Amadeo Banducci, Sr., in the 1920s, it was an important Bay Area wholesale flower supplier for decades. Heather, in its many varieties, was a key crop. The farm remained in the Banducci family until 1980, when, after a court battle, GGNRA condemned it and took over the land. The Banduccis continued their operation through a lease. In 1994, GGNRA cut off the main water source, wells near Redwood Creek, in an effort to shore up a diminishing salmon run, and the flower farm ceased operation, although Banducci family members continued to live on the property.

Heather is a non-native shrub in the same family (Ericaceae) abundantly represented on Tamalpais by madrone, manzanita, and huckleberry. Its pink-purple flowers can appear in December, and heather colors the hillside through the year. Plaques affixed to railroad ties in some of the switchbacks credit the rebuilding of the trail—called by its earlier name of Perkins Trail—to the Marin Conservation Corps (now known as Conservation Corps North Bay) in 1983. Erosion problems closed the former routing.

▥ Hillside Trail

Redwood Creek (Main) Trail, from Bridge 2 to Bridge 4: .70 mile

TERRAIN: Redwood forest; heavily used (MWNM)

ELEVATION: From 230 to 360 to 240 feet; gradual

INTERSECTING TRAIL(S): None

Since Hillside Trail is part of the easiest loop option in Muir Woods, it is well traveled. The signed entrance is off Redwood Creek (Main) Trail at Bridge 2, ¼ mile from the monument's entrance archway. The trail immediately climbs a few steps, frightening off some visitors, but the route is then quite easy. Indeed, work done on the trail in 2012, shoring up its erosion-prone slope, has left it even smoother, more level, and broader than before.

Hillside Trail gently rises above the creek floor. More Douglas-firs begin appearing amidst the redwoods. The Main Trail remains visible below.

The only major trail landmark is a sweeping bend around a canyon. A particularly large Douglas-fir is in the middle, where there is (or has been; the trail continues to be reworked) a bench and footbridge. At this bend, I've seen trillium growing directly out of a redwood, several feet above any soil.

Beyond, Hillside begins dropping and ends at its junction with Ben Johnson Trail, which is starting its climb left to the Dipsea Trail. A few steps lead down to Bridge 4 over Redwood Creek. Cross and go right to complete a loop. Left is the start of Bootjack Trail, which rises to Mountain Theater.

Hillside Trail, which appears on maps from the 1920s, was restored in the mid-'30s and renamed Hillside Nature Trail. There were signs for a self-guided nature tour along it until 1964. It was closed for nearly five years in the early 2000s for another major restoration, and again in late 2014.

▥ Lost Trail

Fern Canyon Trail to Canopy View Trail: .52 mile

TERRAIN: Deeply wooded, lower half redwoods, upper half Douglas-firs (MTSP)

ELEVATION: From 310 to 750 feet; very steep

INTERSECTING TRAIL(S): None

Lost Trail, when combined with Canopy View and Fern Canyon Trails, offers Muir Woods visitors a lovely loop walk. (Lost Trail itself is, however, just outside the monument, in Mt. Tamalpais State Park.)

To reach Lost Trail, take Lower Fern Creek Trail up from the monument's canyon floor. In .4 mile, Lost Trail leaves Fern Creek Trail to the right at a marked intersection. The junction is near Fern Creek Trail's first crossing of Fern Creek itself. (The historic long bridge here was destroyed by a falling redwood in the winter of 2002–2003; rebuilding took years.)

Lost Trail opens with steps—more than 250 in total—and remains very steep, with few respites throughout. This helps keep it relatively little traveled, quiet and peaceful. A bridge is crossed at .2 mile, and steps take the trail up the rest of the way.

At .3 mile, a giant Douglas-fir borders the right edge and Douglas-firs replace redwoods as the dominant tree. A bit above, a multi-trunked coast live oak beside the trail stands out.

As the stiff climb continues, the forest canopy opens slightly. Two steep canyons are crossed. Lost Trail actually drops a few feet to end at its junction with Canopy View (also known as Ocean View) Trail, amidst a redwood grove. Canopy View goes left (uphill) to Panoramic Trail and Panoramic Highway by Mountain Home (a quicker access to Lost Trail), and right (downhill) back to Muir Woods.

The trail dates to around 1914. It was partly buried by a landslide in the 1930s and "lost" for some 30 years—it didn't even appear on post–World War II Freese maps. The trail was finally recleared and given the name "Lost." Then, for years, the upper trail sign was lost as well. It is well signed today, beside a welcome bench.

■ Lower Fern Creek Trail

Muir Woods Trail to Camp Alice Eastwood: 1.03 miles

Terrain: Redwood forest; riparian (MWNM, MTSP)

Elevation: 230 to 580 feet; lower part almost level, upper part steep

Intersecting Trail(s): Lost (.4 mile), Plevin Cut (1.0 mile)

This is a lovely trail, as enchanting as the one along Redwood Creek through the heart of Muir Woods, but without the crowds. Visitors to the monument should well consider traversing it, or at least the almost-level section to the third bridge over Fern Creek.

The trailhead is ¼ mile past Cathedral Grove and Bridge 3 when coming from the main Muir Woods entrance. It is here that Fern Creek itself, one of the longest and liveliest streams on Tamalpais, ends at its junction with Redwood Creek.

At the start, a plaque informs visitors that *Ferns Return to Fern Creek*. The wood fencing and plantings are part of an MWNM effort to restore the creek's habitat. Within less than 100 yards of the trailhead is the fallen Kent Tree. A massive Douglas-fir, at 280 feet, it was once the tallest tree in Marin County. It measured 26 feet, 8 inches in circumference. (Marin's tallest tree is now a redwood in Roy's Redwoods, off Nicasio Road. The monument's tallest is a redwood in Bohemian Grove.)

The tree was a favorite of William Kent, who donated the land that became Muir Woods. During a storm in 1982, the top 40 feet fell. In early January 2003, a crack was observed in the tree. Then, on March 18, 2003, the entire 700-year-old giant crashed to the earth. It took all or part of several redwoods with it, including one pinned directly underneath. As fallen trees are part of forest ecology, Kent Tree will be left where it fell; the trail has been rerouted a few yards above and around. Visitors should enjoy observing changes here within this new opening of the forest canopy.

Beside the fallen tree is a historic plaque, affixed to a boulder. It reads: *William Kent, Who Gave These Woods and Other Natural Beauty Sites to Perpetuate Them for People Who Love the Out-of-Doors, 1864–1928 TCC.*

The 3-ton boulder was brought to Muir Inn by railroad car, then farther down the canyon by wagon. Just before its placement, the boulder slipped into Fern Creek and had to be rolled back by hikers. The dedication ceremony was held in May 1929, a year after Kent's death (March 13, 1928). There is now also a newer sign explaining the tree's fall, with a portrait of Kent.

The trail heads into the canyon of Fern Creek, seemingly a world apart from the sometimes bustle of Muir Woods. It leaves Muir Woods National Monument in .1 mile, entering Mt. Tamalpais State Park. Bridges cross first to the creek's right bank, then back to the left. A more noticeable uphill begins.

The trail crosses a feeder stream, then meets Lost Trail, which rises very steeply right to Canopy View Trail. Fern Creek Trail used to cross Fern Creek for a third and last time here over a wonderful, down-sloping bridge. At 103 feet, it was perhaps the longest trail bridge on Tam. The bridge was crushed in August 2002 by a falling redwood as massive as the one on which it was originally supported. The state park, lacking funds to design and replace the bridge, posted Fern Creek Trail as closed for years. The replacement bridge now has problems of its own, with the far end impassable after heavy rains.

Across the creek, the trail climbs steeply out of Fern Creek Canyon. Still, there remain many giant redwoods to enjoy, including several fire-scarred monarchs joined at the base to form double or triple trees. Traces of the asphalt that once covered the trail are still visible.

Near its top, Fern Creek Trail meets signed Plevin Cut Trail, a shortcut if returning to Muir Woods via Camp Eastwood Road. Look to the right here to see the concrete foundations from the first Muir Inn, built in 1908 and destroyed by fire in 1913.

Fern Creek Trail ends at the paved open clearing of Camp Alice Eastwood, near the outhouses. The area was the original lower terminus of the Mountain Railway's Muir Woods branch line, site of the first Muir Inn, then a CCC tent camp during the 1930s. Now it is a popular group camp. The other trails meeting here are, clockwise: Alice Eastwood Trail downhill (a loop option), Sierra, and Camp Eastwood Road uphill.

The trail appears on the 1898 Sanborn map. It was considered as the western half of Zig-Zag Trail until construction of Panoramic Highway in the 1920s severed Zig-Zag. New maps refer to it as Lower Fern Creek Trail, the "lower" added to distinguish it from the separate "Upper" Fern Creek Trail much higher. Fern Canyon Trail was another long-time name.

Redwood Creek Trail (Main)

Muir Woods entrance to junction of Ben Johnson and Bootjack Trails: .88 mile

TERRAIN: Redwood forest; riparian; asphalt and boardwalk surface; heavily used (MWNM)

ELEVATION: 220 to 240 feet; almost level

INTERSECTING TRAIL(S): Bohemian (.1 mile, .4 mile), Canopy View (.2 mile), Hillside (.3 mile), Lower Fern Creek (.6 mile), Camp Eastwood Road (.7 mile)

Note: In 2014, the main trail through Muir Woods National Monument was officially signed and designated as Redwood Creek Trail, even though there already is another trail of that name downstream, in Mt. Tamalpais State Park. To avoid confusion here, the Redwood Creek Trail through the heart of the monument is also designated as "Main," a name commonly used before the change, and "Upper." The downstream Redwood Creek Trail (described immediately following) is designated as "Lower."

By any name, this is much the most heavily used trail on Mt. Tamalpais. More than a million visitors a year, from scores of countries and speaking dozens of languages, follow it at least part way from the monument entrance. Along the trail tower many of the county's tallest and oldest trees. Coho and steelhead salmon still swim up Redwood Creek to their spawning grounds. Come to the monument early (it opens at 8 AM daily) or in winter to enjoy the area in relative solitude, or take pleasure in sharing this very special place with others. Adjoining trails, which head high on the mountain, are rarely crowded. The trail is completely accessible to those who use wheelchairs.

Redwood Creek (Main) Trail begins under the restored entrance arch. The prominent first redwood on the right stands 190 feet tall and is estimated to be 500 to 800 years in age. Just beyond, a path on the right leads to a gift shop and the cafeteria run by a concessionaire, plus restrooms and park offices. In a few more yards is Bridge 1, rebuilt in late 1993 across Redwood Creek. Traces of no fewer than sixteen now-gone bridges across Redwood Creek in Muir Woods have been uncovered.

Redwoods are, of course, the stars of this trail. These long-lived monarchs have thick bark, up to 12 inches, which keeps out insects and fungi. The bark also helps make redwoods exceptionally fire-resistant; many healthy redwoods show evidence of the last great fire that swept through the area in 1845. In winter, the trees' male cones release clouds of pollen, imparting a golden cast to the area.

A crosscut section of redwood, its rings marked with historical events, is a popular stop. Just beyond, Canopy View Trail departs uphill to the right. Opposite is a wood-floored area where ranger tours begin. A plaque placed by the Sierra Club in 1910 marks the Pinchot Tree. Gifford Pinchot was the first head of the US Forest Service. Ironically, Pinchot, called *Friend of the Forest, Preserver of the Common-Wealth* on the Sierra Club plaque, became the club's, and John Muir's, bitter enemy not long after the plaque was installed. He supported the damming of Yosemite's Hetch Hetchy Valley, a project Muir fervently opposed. Just behind (and to the right of) the Pinchot Tree is a double-trunked giant, the Emerson Tree. (See the Bohemian Trail description for its story.)

Across Bridge 2 is one end of Hillside Trail. It runs just above the canyon to Bridge 4, and offers a popular loop option. A nature trail starts here as well.

The bridges are good places to look for coho (*Oncorhynchus kisutch*) and steelhead (*O. mykiss*) salmon returning to spawn in the creek of their birth after one to three years in the ocean. They appear in Redwood Creek when winter storms breach the sandbar that blocks the creek's mouth at Muir Beach. Females deposit thousands of eggs in shallow depressions, and males fight to cover them. Adult coho salmon then die, but some steelhead survive to go back to the ocean. On average, only six of 100,000 eggs complete the full life cycle. The coho run has been declining to extinction-like levels here as it has along the entire central California coast. In the summer of 2014, all remaining coho were removed from Redwood Creek and taken to a hatchery in Sonoma County, with the plan of returning them to a healthier future. The CCC built the rock revetment along the creek bank here.

By Bridge 3 (.4 mile) is Cathedral Grove. Quiet, or silence, is requested when passing through. Here in 1971, a 225-foot redwood fell, taking a second redwood down with it. People walking near its shallow roots had compacted the soil and it could no longer hold sufficient moisture. The incident led to the construction of the wood barriers that now line the whole trail.

The trail forks around Cathedral Grove, which contains some of the monument's largest trees. Azaleas grow beside the creek. On the right fork, a plaque and sign mark where delegates from around the world, meeting in San Francisco to frame the United Nations charter, gathered on May 19, 1945, to honor President Franklin D. Roosevelt, who had died the previous month.

At .7 mile, Lower Fern Creek Trail departs right. In the late 1800s, the old road through Frank Valley forked here, one branch following Fern Creek to East Peak, the other following Redwood and Bootjack Creeks to West Peak. One hundred yards up Fern Canyon is the famous Kent Tree, now fallen but still well worth a visit. Fern Canyon Trail also offers excellent loop options, with Lost and Canopy View Trails or with Camp Eastwood FR. About 50 yards past the junction, on the right, long stood an albino redwood tree, its pale foliage standing out in the sea of green. Unable to photosynthesize, the albino relied on nourishment from roots of an adjacent redwood.

In 50 more yards, on the left, a turnout marks the site of a cabin that stood from around 1885 to 1928. Ben Johnson lived there in the 1890s when he was gamekeeper for the Tamalpais Sportsman's Club, whose members hunted deer in the area. Just beyond, Camp Eastwood FR begins its climb to Mountain Home.

Redwood Creek (Main) Trail ends at Bridge 4 by the monument's boundary. The trail straight ahead is Bootjack, which rises all the way to Mountain Theater. Ben Johnson Trail sets off left on its way to the Dipsea Trail. A few yards up on Ben Johnson, just over the bridge, is the far end of Hillside Trail.

Early on, the canyon and creek were known as "Sequoia." The scientific name for what is now called sequoia, the world's most massive tree found in only a few groves in the Sierra foothills, is *Sequoiadendron giganteum*. The coast redwood is *Sequoia sempervirens*.

Old maps, such as Erickson, labeled this trail as part of Bootjack Trail.

▨ Redwood Creek Trail (Lower)

Muir Woods Road opposite Deer Park (Dipsea) FR to Highway 1, plus spur: 2.04 miles

TERRAIN: Riparian; light woods and grassland, often muddy; part of Bay Area Ridge Trail (MTSP)

ELEVATION: From 110 to 20 feet; almost level

INTERSECTING TRAIL(S): Miwok (.3 mile), Heather Cutoff (1.2 miles)

Note: See Redwood Creek Trail (Main) immediately preceding.

Lower Redwood Creek Trail plays a role in many long-distance hikes as it provides a level link between the trail networks of Mt. Tamalpais and the Marin Headlands. One drawback is that most of the trail is within a few yards of Muir Woods Road. On the other hand, it's also within a few yards of charming Redwood Creek.

Both ends of Redwood Creek Trail are easily accessible; I'll describe it east–west, from the Muir Woods National Monument side. The trailhead is directly across Muir Woods Road from Deer Park FR, between road Mile Markers 2.09 and 2.10, ½ mile west of the Muir Woods overflow parking lot and just west of the Muir Woods/Mt. Tamalpais State Park boundary. On busy days, Muir Woods visitors park this far from the main entrance. (Parking along the road will be restricted under an NPS plan now moving forward.) At the trailhead on the south side of the road is an MTSP sign as well as one for the Bay Area Ridge Trail, of which Redwood Creek Trail is a part for its opening .3 mile (hikers and horses only).

The abundant lacy-leaved plant on the left in the opening yards (and much of the rest of the way) is poison hemlock. Its scientific name is *Conium maculatum*; "maculatum" means "spotted," referring to the blotched stems. The poison Socrates drank was prepared from the root of this type of hemlock, an Old World native introduced to California.

In .1 mile, the trail crosses Redwood Creek. The long-time bridge here was destroyed by a falling red alder in the winter of 1993–1994, then replaced several months later. Fifty feet past, on the right, is a huge redwood, possibly the largest in the canyon outside of Muir Woods National Monument.

The trail now winds along Redwood Creek's left bank, through what is known as Frank Valley, but just who "Frank" was remains an unsolved mystery. (At press time, there is hint of a breakthrough.) Redwood Creek, which cuts through the heart of Muir Woods, is one of the strongest flowing undammed creeks in Marin. It still supports a salmon run, albeit at a fraction of former levels. It is hoped that work completed in 2014 to open the mouth of the creek specifically to help the salmon will reverse the trend.

At .3 mile is the junction with the north end of Miwok Trail. Miwok, one of the longest trails in Marin, rises left to Dias Ridge Trail, which offers a loop option. It takes with it the hiking and equestrian section of the Bay Area Ridge Trail.

The next stretch, through a grassy meadow, is likely to be muddy in winter. At .6 mile, a signpost marks an entry, "Redwood Creek Spur," from Muir Woods Road (at Mile Marker 2.56), but there is no bridge over the creek. Kent Canyon, which formerly (but no longer) had a route up it, is on the other side of Muir Woods Road, behind a pair of MTSP residences.

One hundred yards beyond, the trail meets what is left of an old building, one of several remnants of the area's dairy days. There are still pipes and a rusted tank inside. Azores Islands native Joe De Ponte acquired two dairy ranches in the 1930s and operated them until 1962, when he sold his 286 acres to Mt. Tamalpais State Park. On July 9, the day he was preparing to move out and relocate to Petaluma, De Ponte suffered a massive heart attack and died on Tamalpais.

Just ahead is a spot that may require a leap after heavy rain. A few yards farther is a massive tree that still has not been definitively categorized. It came from an early 20th century Frank Valley nursery specializing in exotic trees.

In another 100 yards, the trail crosses Redwood Creek over a hikers' bridge (horses ford on the right). There are vestiges of a dam in the creek here. Just beyond, the trail skirts to within 25 yards of Muir Woods Road (at Mile Marker 2.81) and a signpost marks the connecting path.

Blackberry is abundant over the next stretch. At 1.1 miles, another marked path connects right with Muir Woods Road (Mile Marker 3.10). Duck under the branches of a willow tree. A few yards past, the trail crosses Redwood Creek for the last time on a long (and a bit shaky) pedestrian-only bridge. An alder tree stands at the start.

At 1.2 miles, a signpost marks the Heather Cutoff Trail. Heather crosses Redwood Creek (without a bridge), then Muir Woods Road by the Frank Valley Horse Camp gate, before rising to Coast View Trail. If the water is high, you can still make the connection to Heather Cutoff by continuing .1 mile farther, to a path that connects to the road and walking back on the pavement.

The trail enters a wooded area. In late winter, you may be lucky enough to spot giant wakerobin (*Trillium chloropetalum*) in bloom here. It has three deep-maroon petals clustered above three stalkless large leaves. It is the rarer of the two trillium species found in Marin County. Not rare, however, is the poison oak you'll also find here.

The trail emerges from the woodland. Redwood Creek itself crosses to the opposite (north) side of Muir Woods Road, where it remains. Just beyond is a fork. A sign points to the upper left fork as the continuation of Redwood Creek Trail to Muir Beach. The lower right option connects to Muir Woods Road (at Mile Marker 3.43).

The road remains in view. Look across, past a sand volleyball court(!), to buildings of the now-gone Heather, or Banducci, Flower Farm, begun by Amadeo Banducci when he purchased the old Ranch S around 1930. (For more on the Banducci Flower Farm, see the Heather Cutoff Trail description.)

There is a small bridge over a rivulet. The trail passes near a grove of eucalyptus trees, and skirts an area where several giants have been felled. There is a final bridge crossing.

The purple flowers of periwinkle, a non-native garden plant, alongside the trail indicate that homes are nearby. Sure enough, a few switchbacks bring Redwood Creek Trail down to the edge of the town of Muir Beach at the signed western trailhead. Fifty yards ahead is Shoreline Highway (Highway 1). To the right, the highway crosses Big Lagoon Bridge. (An early name for Redwood Creek was Big Lagoon Creek.) To the left, less than ¼ mile away at the old Golden Gate Dairy barn, is the base of the reconstructed Dias Ridge Trail. Across from it is Pacific Way, the auto entry to the Muir Beach parking lot, and Pelican Inn. Opposite the inn's driveway is new Kaasi Road, another way to reach Muir Beach, Green Gulch Farm, and Marin Headlands trails.

Just before the Fern Creek Trail starts its long climb out of Muir Woods, it crosses one of the longest bridges on Mt. Tam.

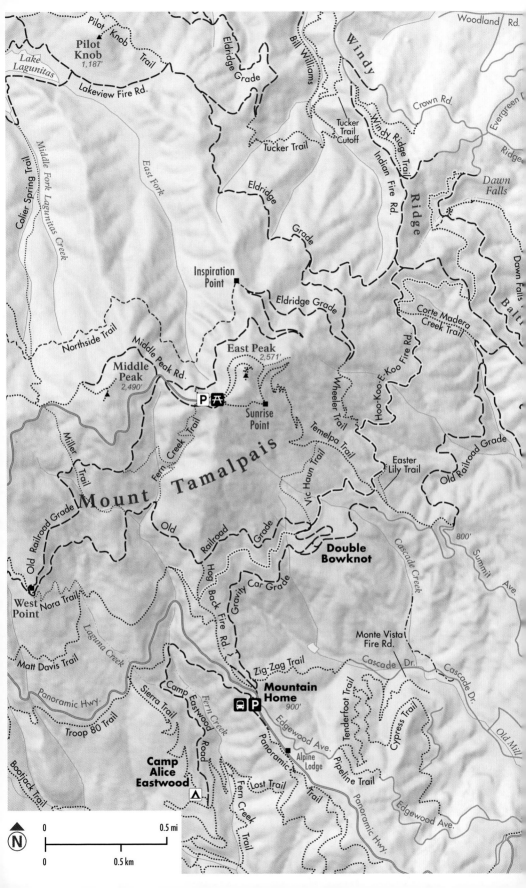

Pastoral woodland remains close to what was once Marin's main highway.

TRAILHEAD EIGHT: OLD STATE HIGHWAY

1. Directions to Kent Woodlands trailheads, Kentfield

Highway 101—west on Sir Francis Drake Blvd. (exit)—left on College Ave., Kentfield—right on Woodland Road—left on Evergreen Drive—left on Crown Road to end.

    OR: Woodland Road—right on Crown Road to Harry Allen Trailhead.

    OR: Left off Evergreen onto Ridgecrest Road to end.

    OR: Straight on Evergreen Drive to end.

    OR: Right off Woodland Road onto Goodhill Road, then left on (northern) Crown Road to end.

2. Directions to Baltimore Canyon, Larkspur

Highway 101—west on Tamalpais Drive (exit), Corte Madera, to Redwood Ave. —right on Corte Madera Ave. (which becomes Magnolia Ave.)—left on Madrone Ave. to end (Water Way). *OR* left on Piedmont Road.

3. Directions to Escalon Drive, Mill Valley

Highway 101—East Blithedale Ave. (exit), Mill Valley—right on Camino Alto— left on Overhill Road (Northridge subdivision)—right on Escalon Drive.

The twisting road that served as the state highway in Marin until the Redwood Highway (Highway 101) opened in the 1920s now has four different names as it crosses the eastern edge of Tamalpais. In Mill Valley, it is called Camino Alto. Going north, the name changes to Corte Madera Avenue at the hill's crest. Past Redwood Avenue, it is then Magnolia Avenue into Larkspur. The Kentfield section, to Sir Francis Drake Boulevard, is now College Avenue.

There are many trailheads along the old highway corridor, generally onto Marin County Parks preserves, so without bathrooms, fountains, or parking lots. Kent Woodlands, an elegant residential area the Kent family began subdividing in 1936, has several trailheads. The most popular is at the southern end of Crown Road. Others are off northern Crown Road, the upper end of Ridgecrest Road (for King Mountain trails), and the top of Evergreen Drive.

King Mountain can also be accessed in Larkspur from the top of Skylark Drive (off Magnolia) and from Cedar Avenue, near downtown. Both have scant parking. Just south of downtown Larkspur is shaded, creekside Baltimore Canyon (also called Larkspur and Madrone Canyon), another favorite starting point.

In Corte Madera, there are three fire road access points (again with very limited parking) off steep Summit Drive. Continuing south, there are three public open-space entries directly adjacent to the road near the Corte Madera/Mill Valley border. Two are just before the road's crest, and one just after on the Mill Valley side. Lower in Mill Valley is a popular access at the north end of Escalon Drive.

Suggested Loops, Old State Highway Corridor

1. Ridgecrest Road (Kent Woodlands) trailhead (elevation 600 feet)—King Mountain Loop Trail (either direction). **2.0 miles total**

2. Baltimore Canyon trailhead (elevation 160 feet)—Dawn Falls Trail, .1 mile to Barbara Spring Trail—uphill, .3 mile, to Southern Marin Line FR—right, 1.3 miles, to Dawn Falls Trail—right, 1.2 miles, to start. **2.9 miles total**

3. Phoenix Road (Kent Woodlands) trailhead (elevation 580 feet)—Windy Ridge Trail, .5 mile, to Indian FR—straight on Indian FR, 1.0 mile, to Eldridge Grade—right, 1.5 mile, down to Tucker Trail—right, 1.0 mile, to Tucker Cutoff—right, .3 mile, to Crown Road (north)—right .1 mile, to start. **4.4 miles total**

4. Southern Marin Line FR trailhead (elevation 510 feet)—Southern Marin Line FR, 2.8 miles, to Huckleberry Trail—right, .6 mile, to Corte Madera Ridge FR—right, .5 mile, to Blithedale Ridge FR—right, .8 mile, to Hoo-Koo-E-Koo Trail—right, .9 mile, to Southern Marin Line FR—left, .1 mile, to start. **5.7 miles total**

■ Barbara Spring Trail

Dawn Falls Trail to Southern Marin Line FR: .34 mile

TERRAIN: Riparian; deep woodland (MCP)

ELEVATION: From 170 to 490 feet; extremely steep and rugged

INTERSECTING TRAIL(S): None

Although near a trailhead, Barbara Spring Trail's steepness keeps it little-used. But, combined with Dawn Falls Trail and Southern Marin Line FR, it offers a pleasing 3-mile loop close to downtown Larkspur. Be cautioned that Barbara Spring Trail, not originally carved for hiking, is rougher than most other Tamalpais trails, and quite steep.

Barbara Spring Trail rises from an MCOSD signpost 100 feet upstream from the bridge over Larkspur Creek, off the far west end of Madrone Avenue (where there is a small parking area). Enter between two redwoods. The trail's start is the steepest section on the route, but there's more ahead.

The trail climbs beside a deep creek canyon; the water and woods muffle any urban noise. Downed madrones may require scrambling. Madrones colonize many Tam hillsides that have been cleared after logging or a fire. Later, redwoods and Douglas-firs rise above them, blocking the sunlight and killing them.

The middle section of Barbara Spring is in light-dappled woodland, and not overly steep. But just after passing a junction of rivulets (follow the left fork), the uphill is again extremely steep. You'll have to step high to get over some roots.

The trail ends when it meets level Southern Marin Line FR at a marked intersection. It is 1.2 miles left to the fire road's Larkspur end, .3 mile right to H-Line FR, and 1.3 miles right to Dawn Falls Trail.

The "Barbara" of the trail's name is unknown. One account says Larkspur firemen wore it in during fitness training runs. From the late 1960s, a group known as the Larkspur Canyon Gang rode fat-tire, single-speed, modified Schwinn "clunker" bicycles over Barbara Spring, some of the earliest mountain biking anywhere. The route has also been called "S" Trail, for its shape. The trailhead sign says Barbara "Springs," but I'll stick to the singular.

Camino Alto (Del Casa/Marlin) Fire Road

Camino Alto to Marlin Drive: 1.19 miles

Terrain: Grassland, light woods (MCP)

Elevation: From 350 to 490 to 200 feet; parts very steep

Intersecting Trail(s): Escalon-Lower Summit FR (.6 mile)

This may be considered as three distinct routes, not surprisingly named Camino Alto, Del Casa, and Marlin FRs. They are combined as one here because they flow into one another without much to separate them. Users are almost entirely nearby residents walking dogs, jogging, or strolling, enjoying the easy access and great views.

The fire road begins at an MCP gate signed "Camino Alto" just below the summit of the auto road Camino Alto, to the left (west) when coming from Mill Valley. One hundred feet lower on Camino Alto, on the east side, is a gate and entry into the Bob Middagh Trail and the Alto Bowl Preserve. There are a handful of spots on the east side of the road. At the entry, a post gives the name, "Camino Alto FR," latitude (N37 degrees, 54.955 minutes) and longitude (W122 degrees, 31.567 minutes).

The route opens with a steep climb to a fenced water tank. Immediately there are vistas of the San Francisco skyline. Most of the trees are oaks. By mid-winter, many of them have a yellowish tinge from male flowers hanging in tassels. Unless recently cleared, broom, both French and Scotch, may also line the fire road.

The fire road crests, and there is suddenly a stunning shot of Mt. Tamalpais. A path departs here, staying above the fire road, which now drops. At .6 mile it meets a four-way junction dubbed the "Escalon Octopus" by MCP rangers. Escalon FR goes left to Escalon Drive in Mill Valley (where most Camino Alto FR travelers enter) and right to a bigger junction known simply as the "Octopus." Here, the signpost reads N37 degrees, 54.703 minutes and W122 degrees, 31.754 minutes. Go straight.

Camino Alto FR rises again. A few yards up, a path goes right, down into deeply wooded MCP lands above the Mill Valley Municipal Golf Course. The fire road crests again beside a row of private homes. The far house, where the fire road bends right, burned in 1993 when an MCOSD worker accidentally started a grass fire while welding a gate. It was owned and occupied at the time by singer Grace Slick of Jefferson Airplane fame.

More views of Mt. Tamalpais tower over the nearer ridge, dubbed Little Tamalpais. The fire road then drops very steeply. Lupine, clover, and yarrow are among native wildflowers holding out against the otherwise pervasive broom.

The fire road meets a gate, marked with an MCOSD "Camino Alto" sign, at the top of Mill Valley's Del Casa Drive (opposite 270). Del Casa is an alternate access to the fire road. Camino Alto FR continues beyond another MCOSD-signed gate just a few yards to the left. This lower section was added in 1989.

The downhill is steeper still. Oaks line the right edge, grasses the left side. Camino Alto FR ends at a gate beside a private residence at 150 Marlin Drive. Downtown Mill Valley is ½ mile due east.

Camino Alto means "high road" in Spanish, an apt name for this historic route that was long the main north–south highway in southern Marin. Redwood Highway (Highway 101), built in the 1920s, and later, the opening of the Richardson Bridge in 1931, greatly diminished Camino Alto's role.

▦ Citron (Cedar) Fire Road

Cedar Avenue, Larkspur, to King Mountain Loop Trail: .69 mile

TERRAIN: Grassland, some woodland (MCP)

ELEVATION: From 200 to 575 feet; steep

INTERSECTING TRAIL(S): None

This fire road was only formally opened to the public in 1993, when it was added to the Marin County Open Space District. The trailhead, marked by an MCOSD "King Mountain Open Space Preserve" sign beside an oak tree, is at a rocky, unpaved turnaround just above the residential section of Larkspur's Cedar Avenue.

From Magnolia Avenue, go west on Ward Street, right on Hawthorne Avenue, then left on Willow Avenue to reach an easier trailhead, a 150-yard lane, signed "Fire Road, Do Not Block," midway on the first block of Willow Avenue. There is no provision for parking by the fire road gate and very few legal spots (delineated by white markings) on Willow or Cedar Avenues. "Citron" refers to a "paper" (as in, never developed) street of that name on early subdivision maps.

Few Tamalpais trails are being transformed as rapidly as Citron. A few years ago, the route was completely lined with the aggressive, flammable, non-native invaders French broom, acacia, and eucalyptus. In 2013, Marin County Parks launched an ambitious four-year King Mountain Fire Fuel Reduction program over 20.5 acres. The non-natives were to be tackled with cutting, followed by grazing Boer goats, then applications of herbicide. The change is already dramatic and it will be interesting to follow nature's course.

The first tree just up on the left is a majestic old valley oak; restoration of the oak woodland is one of the project's aims. The fire road climbs both gently and moderately steeply. In spring, poppies, blue eyed grass, and white patches of morning glory stand out amidst the grasses. Views continue to expand.

At a bend right, a path departs left into the woods and descends to Olive Avenue. Then, another fire road veers right along the knoll. It quickly meets the private property of the historic Escalle estate, which extends down to Magnolia Avenue. The fire road can be quite muddy in winter.

Citron's first (slight) downhill ends near a fence. Beyond, left and down on the asphalt, is a water tank. Right and down is an alternate entrance to the fire road from Skylark Apartments, atop Larkspur's Skylark Drive. (That entrance, at the southwest corner of the complex, has forbidding "Do Not Enter" lettering on the pavement, but there is a public easement. Veer right twice when descending, left twice when coming up from Skylark.)

Citron FR continues left and up. There is a vista of Tam's East Peak. Citron FR ends 250 yards above the Skylark fence at King Mountain Loop Trail, destination of most travelers. Take it right or left for a 2-mile loop.

Although several Marin streets carry the name "cedar," and many cedar trees have been planted as ornamentals, true cedars (genus *Cedrus*) are not native to North America.

◼ Corte Madera Ridge Fire Road

Corte Madera Avenue, Corte Madera, to Blithedale Ridge FR: 1.69 miles

TERRAIN: Chaparral and light woodland (MCOSD)

ELEVATION: From 300 to 850 feet; rolling, parts very steep

INTERSECTING TRAIL(S): Harvey Warne (.1 mile), Escalon-Lower Summit FR (.1 mile), Huckleberry (1.6 miles), Glen FR (1.6 miles)

Departing as it does directly from a main road, Corte Madera Ridge FR is one of Tam's more easily reached routes. It also offers splendid views, of Mt. Tam when ascending, of San Francisco when dropping. It is, however, quite steep, and has a .2-mile discontinuity over a street.

The fire road begins from an MCOSD-signed gate to the right when going up Corte Madera Avenue from Corte Madera, opposite Chapman Avenue and a few yards before the Mill Valley town limits sign. There is very limited nearby off-road parking.

The initial uphill is through dense woods. A path left rises to Camino Alto FR.

In .1 mile, the fire road meets a major, still unsigned junction dubbed "the Octopus" by MCP rangers. An MMWD pump house is the main landmark. There are eight options (hence the name). Far left, two paths head into the wooded ridge. The fire road left is Escalon-Lower Summit to Escalon Drive in Mill Valley. A paved driveway, added in 1990, goes down to Sarah Drive in Mill Valley and up (private) to a home higher on the ridge. Straight across, Corte Madera FR continues climbing. Escalon-Lower Summit FR to the right leads to Summit Drive in Corte Madera. On the far right, signed, is Harvey Warne Trail (.18 mile, so not separately described). It leads back to Corte Madera Avenue just north of this fire road's base.

Continue the very steep climb. Until a major fire management clearing effort here during the winter of 1996–1997, both sides of the fire road were completely lined with broom. Now, the ridge's native oak woodland is revealed.

The fire road passes within yards of a home. In 1991, the City of Mill Valley filed an eminent domain lawsuit to acquire the 53-acre Mycix property, slated for development. After several years of back and forth, an agreement was reached out of court in 1995 (and finally settled in 1997). Forty-two acres were acquired as open space. The $500,000 price was paid in equal thirds by the City of Mill Valley, the Marin County Open Space District (helped with a gift from the Tamalpais Conservation Club), and neighboring homeowners. Five residential lots were carved from 7.4 acres, and the adjacent homes built. Another 3.8 acres was designated as private open space for the homeowners.

The route dips. The uphill resumes. In .7 mile, the fire road meets a gate at Corte Madera's narrow Summit Drive. There are two options up: .2 mile on the asphalt or an overgrown path to the left, behind a separate gate. This is the highest part of Christmas Tree Hill, so named because, in a tradition dating back to the 1930s, residents collectively display lights in the shape of a Christmas tree as seen from the east. The star at the very top of the tree is placed on top of one of the homes passed.

The path and road meet atop Summit Drive near the gate and the MCOSD sign that marks the continuation of Corte Madera Ridge FR. There are only a couple of parking places here, with no parking after sunset. The road to the left of the gate leads to a private residence.

The fire road circles high above Warner Canyon. The actual ridgetop of what is called Little Tamalpais is a few yards up on the right; a path traverses it. A fire road that old maps showed branching left is now overgrown.

There are several Mt. Tam vista points. Look back to get equally dramatic San Francisco skyline views. In .6 mile from the Summit Drive gate, the fire road meets a four-way intersection. Huckleberry Trail drops right to Southern Marin Line FR. To the left, Glen FR descends Warner Canyon to Mill Valley.

Corte Madera Ridge FR rises to command a glorious view north and south, drops, then rises again. It ends at its junction, called Judy's Corner by some equestrians, with Blithedale Ridge FR. The top of 937-foot Blithedale Knoll is just above. This is another stunning view site. Blithedale Ridge FR goes left to Mill Valley and right to Indian FR.

The previously described 8,000-acre Corte Madera del Presidio rancho covered much of the southeast of the mountain. Granted to John Reed by the Mexican government in 1834, the land, on which redwoods once ran down to the bay margin, was logged early, then more heavily in Gold Rush days. Note that there is a completely separate Corte Madera Creek Trail running between Hoo-Koo-E-Koo FR and Old Railroad Grade.

▪ Dawn Falls Trail

Piedmont Trail to Hoo-Koo-E-Koo Trail: 1.84 miles

TERRAIN: Deep woodland; riparian (MCOSD)

ELEVATION: 140 to 640 feet; eastern half almost level, western half very steep

INTERSECTING TRAIL(s): Barbara Spring (.6 mile), Ladybug (1.1 miles), Southern Marin Line FR (1.6 miles)

Dawn Falls is one of the more accessible of the mountain's larger waterfalls, just 1.5 miles west of central Larkspur. This redwood-lined trail through Baltimore Canyon is well used all year; in winter, for viewing the falls, in summer as a cool escape.

Presently, the only public access to the trail's eastern end is via the recently upgraded Piedmont Trail. In 2007, a half-acre of private property was acquired—Marin Conservation and MCOSD led the effort to raise its $450,000 purchase price—to possibly add a second access. Behind the fence east at the start is the home where rock icon Janis Joplin lived at the time of her death (in Los Angeles) in 1970.

From the property line fence at the base of Piedmont Trail, broad Dawn Falls Trail—this section was called Baltimore Canyon FR on old maps—sets off west, upstream on Larkspur Creek's right bank. (Right and left are always determined by facing downstream.) The back yards of houses along Madrone Avenue are across the creek, which varies from a torrent in winter to dry in early fall. On the left, there is still evidence of the massive 1982 slide. The upper end of the slide is shored up along Southern Marin Line FR, well above.

A bridge, built by the Boy Scouts, marks the short connection to Water Way, which has a few parking spots and is a popular entry to Dawn Falls Trail's eastern half.

In another 100 feet is an old fence. It was erected in 1971 to block a group of "hippies" from their encampment on what is now Ladybug Trail. (The book *Larkspur, Past and Present* tells how the former landowner, Adolph Tiscornia, and a hired hand once patrolled here with shotguns.) A public outcry ensued and the fence was breached. The incident was one of several that helped sway voters the following year to create the Marin County Open Space District, and many of the new district's earliest purchases were near here.

Just beyond, the trail goes over a short hill. In the creek are remnants of a dam that once stored drinking water for Larkspur. After a drowning in the

1920s, the dam, no longer in use, was dynamited. The route narrows to trail width; the broader road was maintained as vehicular access to the dam.

The trail skirts the edge of lively Larkspur Creek. After a sizable rain, the creek overruns sections of the trail, requiring some scrambling along the bank. (A boardwalk added in 2014 helps.) Redwoods line the way. Left are several old blue-basalt rock quarry sites. Some of the basalt went into downtown Larkspur's historic Blue Rock Inn.

In the meadow on the right was a one-time wintering ground for ladybugs; I've seen them completely cover the vegetation here. The ladybugs rode thermal winds here from the Sacramento Valley in fall, then back in spring. But, perhaps due to trail work (or the invasive broom), they stopped coming.

Just beyond, a new (2014) bridge takes the trail across the creek; it formerly remained entirely on the right bank. But the diversion is short, for, in 100 feet, there's a second bridge (built in 2006). Here, Dawn Falls Trail recrosses the creek and, to the right, Ladybug Trail sets off up to King Mountain Loop Trail.

The trail ambles through the lovely woodland. Another 2014 bridge makes for easier passage. Then, switchbacks, cut in the mid-1980s carry the trail upward. Dawn Falls comes into view. Two forks of Larkspur Creek converge and promptly plummet 25 feet. Come after a mid-winter rain and you'll be rewarded with a torrent; in the summer, the falls are barely a trickle. There are rocks on which to sit and enjoy this special place.

More switchbacks and steps lead up to Southern Marin Line FR at a signed junction. It is .3 mile right to Kentfield's Crown Road, actually a closer trailhead to Dawn Falls.

Cross the fire road to continue. This upper part of Dawn Falls Trail, though old, was improved and signed only in 1988. It rises very steeply up the red-wood-lined creek canyon. Dawn Falls Trail ends at its junction with Hoo-Koo-E-Koo Trail. To the right is a downhill back to Southern Marin Line FR, to the left, a climb to Blithedale Ridge.

In 1849, a syndicate of Maryland fortune seekers calling themselves the Baltimore & Frederick Mining and Trading Co. shipped a saw mill around Cape Horn. (Other members of the group took the shorter route across the Isthmus of Panama, which proved miserable, and several died.) The partners installed the mill at the mouth of this heavily wooded canyon, at what is now West Baltimore Avenue just off Magnolia. The company began logging the canyon's giant redwoods, some said to be nearly 300 feet high, and one reputed to be the tallest tree then ever found. The lumber was carted by oxen to an estuary of Corte Madera Creek, floated to the docks at Ross Landing (by today's College Avenue–Sir Francis Drake intersection), then shipped to San Francisco. The firm, its workers afflicted by gold fever, sold the mill after just five months. All of

Baltimore Canyon's old growth redwoods (with possibly a few exceptions above the canyon floor) were cut in the next few years. Today's route along the creek follows the original logging road.

Since Dawn Falls faces southeast, the "Dawn" perhaps refers to the wooded area's early morning light. Larkspur Creek was also earlier known as Arroyo Holon.

◼ Escalon-Lower Summit Fire Road

Escalon Drive, Mill Valley, to Summit Drive, Corte Madera: 1.26 miles

TERRAIN: Southern half grassland, northern half woodland; heavily used (MCOSD)

ELEVATION: Around 400 feet; almost level

INTERSECTING TRAIL(S): Camino Alto/Del Casa FR (.1 mile), Corte Madera Ridge FR (.7 mile), Harvey Warne (.7 mile)

A level fire road runs between Mill Valley's Escalon Drive and Summit Drive in Corte Madera. It tops the southernmost section of the long Southern Marin Line, through which water from the Bon Tempe Treatment Plant is piped all the way to the Alto Tank, off Escalon Drive. Only the 2.8-mile section between Kent Woodlands and Larkspur is considered the Southern Marin Line FR.

There is then a discontinuity in the fire road south; this southern section is called Escalon FR, or Escalon-Lower Summit FR (Some maps divide the route at the "Octopus" junction, using "Escalon" and "Lower Summit" for the two halves. I'll continue to combine them since they were built as, and truly are, one route.) There is adequate street parking only on the Mill Valley end, in the Northridge subdivision—there are often dozens of cars here, as the fire road is very popular with dog walkers—so that is our starting point.

At the gate, a signpost gives the coordinates: latitude North 37 degrees, 54.605 minutes, longitude West 122 degrees, 31.784 minutes. Compare them to those posted at the first junction north. Almost immediately, there are lovely views of the San Francisco skyline. Broom, which thrives along disturbed Tam road cuts, is abundant or occasional, depending on how recently it was cleared.

In .1 mile, the fire road crosses Camino Alto FR. This four-way junction, only recently signed, is called "Escalon Octopus" by rangers. The fire road left leads up and over to Del Casa Drive in Mill Valley and right to Camino Alto. Note the first of many indications of the pipeline.

The next virtually flat stretch is lightly wooded. Most of the trees are oaks, with several madrones. There is then an unexpected redwood grove. Just past are many blue MMWD posts, bearing letters of the water lines they mark. There are striking views of Mt. Tamalpais.

The fire road then meets the Octopus junction. Corte Madera Ridge FR crosses left (up to higher on Corte Madera's Summit Drive, then to Blithedale Ridge) and right (down to Camino Alto). The paved option down left is marked with a blue MCOSD sign indicating that there is a public easement down to Mill Valley's Sarah Drive. Escalon-Lower Summit FR continues directly across, passing the water pump building. Harvey Warne Trail descends .18 mile to Camino Alto. Two paths complete the eight "octopus" options here. (See Corte Madera Ridge FR for the story of how the land here was saved, at least partially, from development.)

The last ½ mile, in which the slight uphill is noticeable, is well-wooded. Madrone, laurel, redwood, and shrub hazel are most common. Several paths veer off right to cross the woodland between the fire road and Camino Alto. There is also a path up left to Corte Madera Ridge FR.

The fire road ends at a gate with an MCOSD "Northridge, Blithedale Summit" sign between private residences at 151 and 155 Summit Drive in Corte Madera, on what is called Christmas Tree Hill (see Corte Madera Ridge FR description for an explanation of that name). Parking is extremely limited on this northern end; use only designated spaces outlined in white. This access point is called Lower Summit by rangers because there are two MCOSD entry gates higher (Middle Summit and Upper Summit).

From the gate, you can go uphill a few yards on Summit to steps labeled Spring Trail, part of the long Hill Path, and follow them down to the junction of Tamalpais Avenue and Camino Alto in central Corte Madera. Higher on Summit are loop options with Corte Madera Ridge FR.

In 1912, one of the battles of the Mexican Revolution was fought in a city named Escalón. The name has come to signify "stepping stone."

Hoo-Koo-E-Koo Trail & Fire Road

Southern Marin Line FR to Matt Davis Trail, plus spur: 4.04 miles

TERRAIN: Part woodland, part chaparral (MCOSD, MMWD)

ELEVATION: From 510 to 1,200 feet; gradual, short parts steep

INTERSECTING TRAIL(S): Dawn Falls (.5 mile), Blithedale Ridge FR (.9 mile), Corte Madera Creek (1.5 miles), Wheeler (2.3 miles), connector to Temelpa (2.5 miles), Temelpa (2.7 miles), Old Railroad Grade (3.1 to 3.2 miles), Vic Haun (3.1 miles), Hogback FR (3.9 miles)

Hoo-Koo-E-Koo (most people emphasize the second syllable, some the third) is among the more colorful of the mountain's trail names. Coast Miwok researcher Betty Goerke refers to a group of native people around Nicasio as "Hukuiko." Dan Totheroh called the local native people "Hookkoeko" in his play *Tamalpa*, performed as the "Mountain Play" a record seven times beginning in 1921. Harry Allen, president of the Tamalpais Conservation Club when the trail was started in 1915, applied the name after Miwok middens (shell mounds) were found near the route. It was also designated as Kentfield–Ocean Trail since, combined with Matt Davis Trail, it could be taken to the Pacific.

In the 1950s, Hoo-Koo-E-Koo's lower, easternmost section was covered during development of Kent Woodlands, and the middle segment, half its length, was widened to a fire road. The trail and fire road designations are used as appropriate.

Hoo-Koo-E-Koo Trail presently begins 100 yards in from the Kentfield end of Southern Marin Line FR. It rises to the right, at an MCOSD sign, at the fire road's first bend. Hoo-Koo-E-Koo Trail immediately enters woodland, and climbs. The opening yards are the steepest (and least distinct) of the entire 4-mile distance. In .1 mile, a path, actually an old segment of the trail, enters on the right; veer left.

The trail runs parallel to and above Southern Marin Line FR, which is occasionally visible. Wildflowers are abundant by February. The trail crosses a rivulet over a small stone bridge, added in 2004. A steep path drops left. Fifty yards beyond, signed Dawn Falls Trail descends to the fire road and on to Dawn Falls and Baltimore Canyon.

The trail rises into open chaparral, and offers views over Baltimore, or Madrone, Canyon. It then meets and crosses Blithedale Ridge FR. The fragrance of ceanothus pervades this intersection in spring.

Directly across the ridge top, the trail begins circling above Blithedale Canyon. Around ¼ mile past the Blithedale crossing, on the right, is Echo Rock, an outcropping of greenstone basalt. Basalt is formed in ocean floor fissures; the greenish tinge comes from the mineral chlorite. Echo Rock is well named: turn toward it and shout and your companions will hear the echo. In certain conditions, you can hear every word of conversations nearly a mile away in the canyon.

Hoo-Koo-E-Koo then enters a dense stand of young redwoods. Just ahead, at Corte Madera Creek, there is a signed intersection. Corte Madera Creek Trail drops steeply left toward Old Railroad Grade. An old, pre-slide Hoo-Koo-E-Koo Trail routing continues straight and quickly ends. Clamber right up a few root-covered yards to Hoo-Koo-E-Koo FR.

The fire road right (called a spur of Hoo-Koo-E-Koo here) runs 400 steep uphill yards to a junction with Blithedale Ridge FR, just below Knob Hill and Indian FR. It offers a loop option back to Crown Road. Knob Hill is of historical significance, as the boundaries of four 1830s Mexican land grants, covering virtually all of Tamalpais, met at its summit.

Continuing left, Hoo-Koo-E-Koo FR crosses the creek, which flows even in mid-summer. A horse trough is a newer addition.

The climb is noticeable, but gradual. At stream crossings, open areas with long views alternate with groves of redwoods. The demarcation in vegetation is abrupt; redwood forest left of the fire road, chaparral to the right.

In one of the deeper redwood groves, signed Wheeler Trail sets off right, beginning a very steep climb to Eldridge Grade. A concrete platform, part of the old Slide Gulch water intake, is in the creek bed to the right.

In .2 mile, a connector (known as Easter Lily Trail) to Temelpa Trail descends left. A small tanbark oak guards its entrance, which now has a generic MMWD sign. In another ⅛ mile, Hoo-Koo-E-Koo FR crosses the infamously steep Temelpa itself. Left leads down to Fern Canyon Road (the paved section of Old Railroad Grade) in Mill Valley and right all the way up to Verna Dunshee Trail below the East Peak summit.

Hoo-Koo-E-Koo turns from the eastern to the southern flank of the mountain, and broad new vistas open. At a creek crossing lined with redwoods, two generically signed paths drop left on opposite banks. The second is the old, now unofficial Murray Trail. Both descend .2 mile to Old Railroad Grade a few yards in from Fern Canyon Road.

Fifteen yards later, Hoo-Koo-E-Koo meets the grade itself near the top of the Double Bow Knot. The grade goes uphill to the right, on its steady climb up Tamalpais. Signed Vic Haun (or Old Plane) Trail also rises from this junction. Hoo-Koo-E-Koo continues left, combined with the grade.

Within less than .1 mile of downhill, Hoo-Koo-E-Koo branches to the right, once again as a trail. At this same junction, a former connector path rises to higher on Old Railroad Grade.

This lovely stretch of Hoo-Koo-E-Koo runs in and out of redwood groves and has sweeping southern panoramas. After .6 mile at trail-width, Hoo-Koo-E-Koo crosses Hogback FR. To the left is Mountain Home Inn, which had been visible earlier, and up to the right is Old Railroad Grade.

At this point, Hoo-Koo-E-Koo has less than .2 mile remaining. Near its end, it crosses a stream over a bridge and passes a magnificent redwood with spiraled bark. This spiraling is also occasionally found in sequoias, cousins of the redwoods. Remains of two old outhouses are just above here.

Hoo-Koo-E-Koo ends at its junction with Matt Davis Trail, beside Fern Creek. Matt Davis then fulfills the promise of a trip to the ocean , while left is a return to Hogback FR above Mountain Home.

Huckleberry Trail

Southern Marin Line FR (Larkspur end) to Corte Madera Ridge FR: .61 mile

TERRAIN: Half chaparral, half lightly wooded (MCOSD)

ELEVATION: From 480 to 860 feet; very steep

INTERSECTING TRAIL(S): None

Huckleberry Trail rises from the Larkspur end of Southern Marin Line FR. The trail's start, marked by an MCOSD signpost, is 10 yards before the second gate when approaching from Sunrise Lane in Larkspur, 10 yards past the fire road gate when coming from Kentfield's Crown Road. Sunrise Lane is reached from Magnolia Avenue via Wiltshire and Marina Vista Avenues, and has almost no parking.

Though most of Huckleberry's stiffest uphill is in the early going—the opening yards are extremely steep—this is a tough climb all the way. Not surprisingly, huckleberry bushes line the trail. Chinquapin is the common short tree.

About 250 yards up, at woodland's edge by a stand of tanbark oaks, are a handful of tall western rhododendron bushes on both sides of the trail. Their magnificent rose-colored flowers, arguably the showiest on Tam, are usually in peak blossom around the first of May. Rhododendrons are in the same genus as the more locally abundant western azaleas (and in same family, Ericaceae, as huckleberry) but keep their leathery leaves all year. Rhododendrons are more often associated with coastal woodlands to the north; this is one of only about five places where they grow naturally in Marin. (Ben Schmidt, who helped build the trail in the 1950s, preferred his original name of Rhododendron Trail.)

The trail passes a few groves of thin redwoods and narrows to squeeze through. In its upper reaches, Huckleberry Trail is more open, passing through chaparral, with broad views. Manzanita and huckleberry are the common shrubs.

One last redwood grove and Huckleberry meets Corte Madera Ridge FR at a four-way intersection. Left on Corte Madera Ridge goes to Summit Drive in Corte Madera, and right to Blithedale Ridge FR. Be sure to climb a few yards to the right for an exceptional Tam view. Glen FR goes straight ahead; it branches into two forks that descend both sides of Warner Canyon.

Huckleberry is abundant along many of Tam's trails. The 3- to 8-foot shrub has toothed leaves and white-to-pink bell-shaped flowers in clusters. In late summer and fall, the small berries make delicious eating; they're sweetest when black.

▓ Indian Fire Road

Phoenix Road, Kentfield, to Eldridge Grade: 1.33 miles

Terrain: Ridge top; chaparral bordered by light woodland (MMWD)

Elevation: From 560 to 1,400 feet; lower half very steep to extremely steep, upper half gradual

Intersecting Trail(s): Evergreen FR (.4 mile), Windy Ridge (.4 mile), Blithedale Ridge FR (.8 mile)

Indian FR starts almost 400 feet higher than nearby Phoenix Lake trailheads, offering quicker access to the upper mountain. It traverses an exposed ridge above the deep canyon of Bill Williams Gulch, with views almost the whole way. But sections are as steep as any fire road on the mountain and, to make the going even tougher, some of the elevation gains are lost in four separate dips, requiring additional climbing.

Indian FR's lower section has long been paved over as Phoenix Road, which branches from the northern section of Kent Woodlands' Crown Road. The start is at an MMWD-signed gate, on the right when going uphill on Phoenix Road. A few yards past, at the end of Phoenix Road, is another gate behind which Harry Allen Trail drops and Windy Ridge Trail rises. The latter, shaded and more gradual, rejoins Indian FR for a short loop option.

Indian FR is immediately very steep; there's more of the same ahead. The stiff uphills are followed by short level or downhill stretches, earning this segment the designation of "the roller coaster." (Another "roller coaster" on Tam is Blithedale Ridge FR.) The first crest comes in 200 yards, where there is a classic Mt. Tamalpais summit scene. A 250,000-gallon water tank is on the left. Sharp-pointed chaparral pea lines the left edge. Ceanothus shrubs provide blue color and a pleasing fragrance in early spring.

In .4 mile, there is a four-way junction, presently unsigned. Far left, Windy Ridge Trail returns to the start. Left, Evergreen FR—just under ¼ mile, so not separately described—descends extremely steeply to Evergreen Drive and then Crown Road (which, taken left to Harry Allen Trail, also offers a loop). Go straight, up.

A tough up, down, then up again—descending going the other way can be quite slippery—leads to another fire road on the left. This is the northern end of Blithedale Ridge FR, 100 yards above its junction with Hoo-Koo-E-Koo FR. Continue uphill. A classic old sign points the way to Larkspur's Baltimore Park, once the nearest railroad station, and to Mill Valley.

About 150 yards higher, just before a bend right, was the former Indian Fire Trail. One of the oldest trails on the mountain (referred to in an 1876 article), it offered a precipitous trip to the summit. The CCC widened it to a 100-foot firebreak in the 1930s. It is now closed, blocked at its several crossings of Eldridge Grade above to limit erosion and to allow vegetation to cover its still visible slash.

Indian FR enters some shade, and the uphill finally eases. Look right, over Bill Williams Gulch, to see the part of Indian FR you've already climbed. There's a brief downhill.

The fire road continues climbing into redwoods. An old water tank stands at a crossing of a fork of Bill Williams Creek. Another 100 yards of uphill brings Indian FR to its end at Eldridge Grade. Left, it is 2.4 miles up to the East Peak parking area; right leads down to the lakes.

"Indians" began populating Marin's shores perhaps as long as 8,000 years ago. But within just a few years of permanent European settlement in Marin, which began with the establishment of Mission San Rafael Arcángel in 1817, these Coast Miwoks were virtually extirpated by European diseases, to which they had no natural immunity. A Marin population of some 3,000 in 1800 was reduced by 90 percent by 1840.

King Mountain Loop Trail

Around King Mountain: 1.95 miles

TERRAIN: Mostly oak-madrone woodland; some redwood forest (MCOSD, private easement)

ELEVATION: Around 600 feet; mostly gradual and level, parts steep

INTERSECTING TRAIL(S): Citron FR (.6 mile), Wilson Way (1.4 miles), Ladybug (1.5 miles)

In 1994, a delightful new loop trail on the hitherto private upper reaches of King Mountain was opened to the public. Marin County Open Space District workers, led by then Senior Ranger John Aranson, who had hiked the area as a boy, cleared old routes, cut new ones, opened some fences, and added trail signs. The county acquired 131 acres outright and 129 acres of easement in a deal with the Tiscornia Estate, long-time owners of King Mountain. In exchange, the county approved plans for four estate-sized homes (later consolidated by a single buyer) atop the mountain's summit. (Kathleen Lipinski's painting of a pristine King Mountain looking toward Tam graced the cover of the fourth edition of *Tamalpais Trails*.)

King Mountain Loop Trail can be accessed from four trailheads: Wilson Way, Cedar Avenue, and Skylark Drive, all in Larkspur, and Ridgecrest Road in Kent Woodlands. Wilson Way (from Madrone Avenue via Redwood Avenue and Oak Road) is a long, narrow, and twisting street with limited parking. Cedar Avenue requires a .7-mile uphill trek on Citron FR. The Skylark Drive entry, beside a huge apartment complex, has virtually no public parking. So the Ridgecrest Road trailhead is used here.

The entry from Ridgecrest Road will likely change somewhat when construction atop King Mountain is completed. Presently, a dirt road sets off behind a gate by the last house on Ridgecrest. Follow it 100 yards to King Mountain Loop Trail, which goes left and right behind MCOSD "Public Trail" signs. Straight ahead is a gate and private property. Many visitors note that the loop somehow feels net downhill (obviously impossible) when followed in the clockwise (left) direction, so we'll head that way. Go either way and you'll start down and finish up.

Dozens of steps open the route as it descends steeply. This is an entirely new (1995–1996) section, replacing an old route called Pipeline. The loop trail meets an old fence at a bend right over the last of the steps.

A bridge brings the trail over a creek, with a log bench on the far side. The route is now deep within a redwood forest, though a huge Douglas-fir borders the left edge 100 yards from the bridge. There is quiet in this woodland, although it is less than 1 mile from Magnolia Avenue.

About ¼ mile past the bridge, the trail passes under a nutmeg tree, with its long, sharp needles. A pair of massive redwoods, both with their tops now gone, may have been spared during the logging that otherwise denuded the hillside. It is interesting to note the progression of trees as the trail circles south. First, redwoods are dense on the wettest, shadiest north slope. Then, nutmegs, unusual this low on Tamalpais, grow in abundance. They're followed by bay laurels, many arcing in fantastic shapes. Finally, madrones prevail near the first intersection.

At .6 mile, the trail crosses Citron (Cedar) FR. Left goes to the Skylark Apartments and on down to Larkspur's Cedar Avenue. Right is a dead end at the private property line. The trail continues directly across, immediately passing a massive old coast live oak named the Grandfather/Grandmother Tree. (Efforts are continuing to keep the ailing tree alive. Its natural immune system has been strengthened, its trunk treated with a lime wash, competing undergrowth cleared, and the soil nourished.)

Fifty yards beyond, the trail meets an open area with views extending to Mount Diablo and the San Francisco skyline. This pattern of light woodland and open areas is repeated the rest of the way.

The trail runs fairly level through a typical Tam broad-leaved forest of coast live oaks, madrones, tanbark oaks, and buckeyes. Broom, however, has crowded out many of the native wildflowers; efforts to control the broom, which is a fire hazard, continue. There are views across Baltimore Canyon of the heavily wooded north wall of Corte Madera Ridge, also known as "Little Tamalpais."

228

At 1.4 miles, after a short downhill, the trail meets a signed junction. Left is a 100-yard connector, called Wilson Way Trail on the sign, to a water tank and the top of Wilson Way. Continue straight across and bend right.

This next section is part of the 1994 rebuild. In 200 yards there is another fork, also marked by an MCOSD signpost. Left and down is Ladybug Trail to Baltimore Canyon. Take it at least a few yards to a clearing with a knockout view of Mt. Tamalpais.

Soon, homes high in Kent Woodlands are glimpsed, then the palm trees that rise above the approach path. There is a final short, very steep pitch.

Patrick King and partner William Murray bought 1,234 acres of lower Ross Valley from the cash-starved Ross family in the late 1860s. The two then divided the parcel. Murray got the northern part, which included today's Kent Woodlands. King took the southern half, including today's downtown Larkspur and the hill that came to be known as King Mountain. There is an adjacent lower hill known as Little King.

Ladybug Trail

King Mountain Loop Trail to Baltimore Canyon: .47 mile

TERRAIN: Broad-leaved woodland (MCOSD)

ELEVATION: From 575 to 180 feet; steep, parts very steep

INTERSECTING TRAIL(S): None

Ladybug Trail was an informal path upgraded by MCOSD when King Mountain was opened to the public. It sets off downhill from the King Mountain Loop Trail, .1 mile left from the Wilson Way (Larkspur) access. An MCOSD sign marks the junction.

A few yards down, the forest canopy briefly clears. Enjoy one of the best of all vistas of Mt. Tamalpais.

One-quarter mile down is a level area covered by madrones. There are still traces of a 1960s "hippie" communal encampment here. Residents trekked in on the path that preceded today's Ladybug Trail and drew water from the creek below. Continuing down, the trail's formerly steepest and most slippery sections are now gentle switchbacks.

The trail ends when it crosses Larkspur Creek at a new (2006) bridge to Dawn Falls Trail. Before the bridge was built and Ladybug was rerouted to meet it, the trail met Larkspur Creek just downstream at a clearing in the dense woodland. This clearing had long been a wintering home to tens of thousands of ladybugs (also known as ladybird beetles). The ladybugs rode wind currents here from the Central Valley in fall, then rode them back again in spring; *Hippodomia convergens* is the most common, and familiar, of some 125 California ladybug species. But the clearing was disturbed and the ladybugs have not returned. It is hoped that they will.

MCOSD field personnel originally called the route Contractors' Trail, for want of any better designation. I coined the more appealing "Ladybug" Trail name, and MCOSD officially adopted it.

▩ Piedmont Trail

Piedmont Road, Larkspur, to Dawn Falls Trail: .35 mile

TERRAIN: Deep woodland (MCOSD)

ELEVATION: From 210 to 140 feet; gradual

INTERSECTING TRAIL(S): None

Piedmont Trail is relatively new, replacing a rough path that crossed private property and connected Piedmont Road to Dawn Falls Trail. In 2007, MCOSD acquired a half-acre of that property to ensure through access. The district improved the trail just prior to its opening to the public. Note that there is no parking at the Piedmont trailhead, and very little lower on Piedmont Road.

To reach the trailhead, follow Piedmont Road off Magnolia Avenue. After it becomes one-way uphill, there is a bend right (Coleman Avenue). Park in a designated white-marked space either before or after this bend and begin by walking up the remaining stub of Piedmont Road. Beyond a couple of houses, Piedmont Road is unpaved. You will then see one more lone house and beyond it, an MCOSD signpost, "Welcome to Baltimore Canyon Open Space Preserve," the start of Piedmont Trail.

Immediately, you are in enchanted woodland, yet so near Magnolia Avenue. Laurels dominate in the early going; just past the first bend, the one on the left is among the tallest in Marin. A few feet beyond, also left, is a vine maple. A new bridge was added in 2015. Increasingly, redwoods line the way. They help make this a pleasant hike on even the hottest summer days.

Beyond a second bend is another, older MCOSD signpost, identical to the one at the trailhead. The trail opens fairly level. A new (2015) bridge crosses a rivulet. Beyond, steps carry the trail downhill. Madrone Avenue homes bordering Larkspur Creek come into view. The trail skirts the edge of private property, the last house on West Baltimore Avenue. It was once owned, and lived in, by singer Janis Joplin (see Dawn Falls Trail description).

Piedmont Trail drops a final few steep yards to the east end of Dawn Falls Trail. Dawn Falls follows the creek left to the falls and, beyond, to Southern Marin Line FR.

Southern Marin Line Fire Road

Crown Road, Kent Woodlands, to Sunrise Lane, Larkspur: 2.78 miles

TERRAIN: Moderately wooded hillside; heavily used (MCOSD)

ELEVATION: Around 500 feet; level

INTERSECTING TRAIL(S): Hoo-Koo-E-Koo (.1 mile), Dawn Falls (.3 mile), H-Line FR (1.2 miles), Barbara Spring (1.6 miles)

Because Southern Marin is the longest truly level fire road on Tam and is easily accessible, it is popular among all user groups: hikers, dog-walkers, runners, and bikers. Most people call the route Crown Road because it is a continuation of that Kent Woodlands street and the principal access. (There is virtually no parking at the Larkspur end, and additional "no parking" signs were added to the Kent Woodlands side in 1989.)

Southern Marin Line FR is proper, however. It was graded in 1951 as part of MMWD's Southern Marin Line project. A 24-inch water pipeline runs under (and, at one point, beside) the fire road, bringing water from what was then the new Bon Tempe treatment plant to southern Marin.

The fire road begins beyond the gate, where there is an information panel. Mt. Tamalpais towers above, an impressive sight. To the east is King Mountain, Corte Madera Ridge, and, on clear days, Mount Diablo.

In 100 yards, Hoo-Koo-E-Koo Trail rises on the right. It climbs to Blithedale Ridge FR, then on to Matt Davis Trail. Loops can be made by taking Hoo-Koo-E-Koo and returning to Southern Marin Line by Dawn Falls Trail, H-Line FR, or Huckleberry Trail.

In .3 mile, Dawn Falls Trail crosses. It is a short descent left to the falls. A loop can be made by continuing down Dawn Falls Trail and returning to Southern Marin Line on the very steep Barbara Spring Trail. To the right, Dawn Falls Trail rises to Hoo-Koo-E-Koo. A few yards beyond the Dawn Falls junction is a small suspension bridge nicknamed "the Little Golden Gate." It carries the southern Marin water pipeline over a bend, then back under the fire road.

A few vista spots open, but the route is now mostly wooded. Baltimore Canyon stretches well below. Depending on whether there has been a recent clearing effort, French broom may be abundant or scarce. The resilient shrub invariably returns.

At 1.25 miles, at a pump station, H-Line FR sets off uphill to the right. Branches of the pipeline diverge here from within the fenced enclosure to southern Marin water tanks. A water fountain, including one for the many dogs that enjoy this trail, is a welcome and relatively new addition.

In another ⅓ mile, an MCOSD signpost on the left marks the top of Barbara Spring Trail, which descends to Baltimore Canyon. Beyond, a pair of fences block off a slide area. Continue winding around the many bends. The terrain again opens. Look back for more Tam shots.

Southern Marin Line FR ends at a gate. A few yards beyond on the right is Huckleberry Trail, which goes uphill to Corte Madera Ridge FR. The street ahead is Sunrise Lane, which drops, beyond a second gate, to Marina Vista Avenue in Larkspur. An old sign at this end, "#10 Fire Road," which pointed to a private residence, led many users to mistakenly call Southern Marin Line, "Fire Road 10." The pipeline continues to the Alto water tanks in Mill Valley.

▓ Tucker Cutoff Trail

Northern Crown Road, Kent Woodlands, to Tucker Trail: .26 mile

TERRAIN: Light woodland (MMWD)

ELEVATION: From 530 to 420 feet; steep

INTERSECTING TRAIL(S): None

Tucker Cutoff offers the shortest route to Tucker Trail, and that accounts for virtually all its use. The cutoff descends, unsigned, from directly opposite the Crown Road/Phoenix Road street sign high in Kent Woodlands. Go past the railing. Trail work has eased the formerly precipitous opening yards. Rub the California sagebrush leaves here to enjoy its delightful fragrance. Star lily is reliably in profusion in January. As *Marin Flora* says, "Its creamy-white star-like flowers are always beautiful."

By .1 mile, the trail enters a light tree canopy. You can glimpse Bald Hill to the right. The woodland deepens. Be sure to look up left to see the hundreds of thin redwoods on the hillside.

The cutoff ends at a crest of Tucker Trail. The Bill Williams Trail junction is 50 yards to the left. Harry Allen Trail, which offers a loop option back to Crown Road, is .7 mile to the right.

The cutoff, which has long appeared on maps, was more heavily used in the days when the Northwestern Pacific Railroad dropped hikers off at stations along Tam's east edge. Local passenger service ended in 1941.

▣ Windy Ridge Trail

Phoenix Road, Kentfield, to junction of Indian/Evergreen FRs: .45 mile

TERRAIN: Woodland (MCOSD)

ELEVATION: From 580 to 800 feet; moderately steep

INTERSECTING TRAIL(S): None

Note: Open to bicycles

Several roads and trails branch off from the northern section of Crown Road high in Kent Woodlands. Proceeding up Crown from Goodhill Road, the first is Harry Allen Trail, which drops to Phoenix Lake. Just ahead, Crown Road branches left, unpaved, for ¼ mile, and Phoenix Road begins. Opposite the junction, Tucker Cutoff Trail drops right behind the steel barrier. Next, Indian FR sets off uphill to the right. At the upper end of Phoenix Road, behind a wood barrier with an MCOSD "Northridge/Baltimore Canyon" sign, Harry Allen Trail continues to the left, dropping to reconnect with the southern half of Crown Road. And, directly ahead, Windy Ridge Trail begins its climb.

Windy Ridge (originally, Kent FR) was narrowed by broom, which threatened to block it altogether. Now, the cleared route is designated as Windy Ridge Trail and is comfortably broad; it remains open for bicycle use. The climb continues through a forest of redwoods, young and at the edge of their prime habitat. Tanbark oaks and madrones are common as well.

The trail crests at an unsigned four-way junction in a dip in Indian FR, which runs atop Windy Ridge itself. Right, Indian FR goes right back to Phoenix Road for a short loop. (Windy Ridge Trail is a shaded alternative to the exposed, steeper Indian FR.) Left is a stiff climb to Eldridge Grade. Sharply left, Evergreen FR plunges .2 mile (so is not separately described) to Evergreen Drive high in Kent Woodlands, with Crown Road the next cross street below. (The middle section of Evergreen FR is extremely steep and slippery.)

The old Kent FR originally connected to the Kentfield stop on the Northwestern Pacific Railroad line. The fire road's entire course was through Kent property, although through passage by hikers was generally permitted. The family developed Kent Woodlands after World War II. The original Kent family home (now owned by others) still stands at the base of Evergreen Drive, across Woodland Avenue. In 1985, MCOSD purchased 30 acres of Windy Ridge, which had been zoned for six homes, from the Kent family for $350,000. A special deed condition reads: "To preserve a family tradition, one day each year, each of the former owners and their spouses shall be granted the right to cut a limited quantity of greens for their own private, non-commercial use as Christmas decoration."

Campground behind Pantoll Ranger Station

TRAILHEAD NINE: PANTOLL & BOOTJACK

Directions
Highway 101—Highway 1—Panoramic Highway

Pantoll (or Pan Toll) is the junction on *Pan*oramic Highway where a *toll* house once stood. Earlier, the area was known as Summit Meadow. Alpine, Easy Grade, Matt Davis, Old Mine, Stapelveldt, and Steep Ravine Trails, plus Deer Park and Old Stage Roads all converge here.

Pantoll is headquarters for Mount Tamalpais State Park, but, due to budget cutbacks, the ranger station is not always open. There are bathrooms and fountains, and a large map (with several now-closed trails) placed in 1988 by "Friends of Coco Bellis," a Mill Valley resident who died in a car accident that year. Friends of Mt. Tam installed a bicycle repair station in 2014. Down the asphalt road are ranger residences and the maintenance yard. There are also sixteen campsites (see the Recreation chapter for more information).

The West Marin Stagecoach Route 61 bus, which runs between Marin City and Bolinas, stops at Pantoll and opens many one-way hiking and biking options. (Check the website for schedule and current fares.)

At Pantoll, Southside (or Pantoll) Road rises to Ridgecrest Boulevard at Rock Spring, with knockout views along the way. A gate bars access at night, during high fire danger days, and during rare snowfalls. There are no officially designated trails along the road but, opposite the largest parking area 1 mile up, a couple of paths set off west. New maps call the road's bend here "Hogue Point," in honor of late MTSP ranger Randy Hogue.

Around ¼ mile east of Pantoll on Panoramic Highway (just below Mile Marker 5.13) is Bootjack Camp, another popular trailhead. The Tamalpais Conservation Club developed Bootjack as a campground shortly after its founding in 1912. MTSP took it over in 1928, the same year Panoramic Highway opened and ended the area's remoteness. Camping ceased at Bootjack in 1969, but was resumed in 2013 when fifteen sites were restored. The Matt Davis Trail connects Pantoll and Bootjack.

In 1991, a parking fee was instituted at both the Bootjack and Pantoll lots. Annual parking passes can be purchased online at the California State Parks website and at the ranger station. There are a handful of free spaces at the base of Southside Road.

Suggested Loops from Pantoll Ranger Station (elevation 1,500 feet)

1. Alpine Trail, .4 mile, to Bootjack Trail—left, .8 mile, across Panoramic Highway, through Bootjack Camp, to Mountain Theater—Easy Grade Trail, .7 mile, to Old Stage Road—right, .1 mile, to start. **2.0 miles total**

2. Stapelveldt Trail, 1.0 mile, to Ben Johnson Trail—right, .2 mile, to Deer Park FR—right, 1.0 mile, to start. **2.2 miles total**

3. Steep Ravine Trail, 1.6 miles, to Dipsea Trail—left, 1.4 miles, to Deer Park FR—left, .2 mile, to Old Mine Trail—right, .3 mile, to start. **3.5 miles total**

4. Old Stage Road, .1 mile, to (Upper) Old Mine Trail—left, 1.0 mile, to Mountain Theater Trail—right, .2 mile, through Mountain Theater to Rock Spring Trail—right, 1.4 miles, to West Point—right, 1.8 miles, on Old Stage Road to start. **4.5 miles total**

5. Matt Davis Trail west, 1.6 miles, to Bolinas Ridge/Coastal Trail—right (straight), 1.4 miles, to Willow Camp FR—right, .1 mile, across Ridgecrest Blvd. to Laurel Dell FR—straight, .5 mile, to Laurel Dell—right on Cataract Trail, 1.2 miles, to Rock Spring and across Ridgecrest Blvd.—left, .1 mile, on Mountain Theater Trail to Old Mine Trail—right, 1.0 mile, to Old Stage Road—right, .1 mile, to start. **6.0 miles total**

Alpine Trail

Pantoll to Bootjack Trail: .35 mile

TERRAIN: Redwood forest (MTSP)

ELEVATION: From 1,500 to 1,280 feet; steep

INTERSECTING TRAIL(S): None

Alpine Trail is short and, in its upper half, very close to Panoramic Highway. Still, it plays a role in many hikes from Pantoll. The signed trail begins at the West Marin Stagecoach bus stop by Pantoll Ranger Station. Also beginning here, on the right, is Stapelveldt Trail.

Alpine immediately enters a redwood forest, and begins a steep, steady descent. Panoramic Highway is just across the gully. The trail crosses a small bridge. Huge redwoods tower above; one is particularly massive. Lower, the highway noise is muted.

Alpine ends when it meets Bootjack Trail by an old bench. Left on Bootjack leads up to Panoramic Highway and Bootjack. Right goes downhill to Troop 80 Trail and Van Wyck Meadow, with options on to Muir Woods or Mountain Home.

The trail was one of the first projects of the California Alpine Club, and has been called Alpine Club Trail. The club, formed in 1913 and active on Tamalpais and in the Sierra, has its headquarters at Alpine Lodge, 730 Panoramic Highway, just below Mountain Home. The name "Alpine," synonymous with mountains, appears elsewhere on Tamalpais. Alpine Dam, which created Alpine Lake, was built at the old Alpine Bridge over Lagunitas Creek.

Coast View Trail

Deer Park (Dipsea) FR to Highway 1 at Mile Marker 7.35: 2.68 miles

TERRAIN: Mostly grassland and coastal scrub, plus wooded section (MTSP, GGNRA)

ELEVATION: 1,360 to 460 feet; gradual

INTERSECTING TRAIL(S): Heather Cutoff (2.3 miles)

Note: Open to bicycles

In 2004, some 14,000 feet of Coastal FR below the Dipsea Trail crossing was rerouted, narrowed, and made more gradual (the steepest grades were eased from 30 percent to a maximum of 12 percent). The resulting multi-use (open to bicycles) trail was renamed Coast View Trail.

The project was controversial. The Tamalpais Conservation Club sued to halt it, fearing a trail open to bikes would end up being used exclusively by cyclists, would negatively affect the historic Dipsea Trail, and would set a dangerous precedent. A compromise was reached, and the new route was reworked to a width of 5 to 6 feet, instead of the originally proposed 4 feet. In any case, Coast View Trail lives up to its name.

To reach the top of Coast View, take either lower Old Mine Trail or Deer Park FR (required for bicycles) out of Pantoll. When the two routes rejoin, drop 125 yards on the fire road to the Dipsea Trail crossing, then another 500 feet. Here, Coast View sets off straight ahead (there are presently two options that soon merge), while Deer Park FR goes left, taking the Bay Area Ridge Trail with it down to Frank Valley. The next trail intersection is more than 2 miles away.

The opening 100 yards of Coast View are a bit uneven, with a gully down the center. The route improves, but rocky sections mix with smoother ones throughout. Long-time visitors marvel at how the terrain here has changed. What was once all grassland when cows grazed these slopes is now covered with coyote brush. Grassland and coastal scrub intermingle the entire descent.

The first trees, a paired oak and Douglas-fir, are at .4 mile, where Coast View briefly skirts the edge of a woodland. There is the shortest of rises on the otherwise downward course. At .8 mile, Coast View bends left to open a dramatic view of the three peaks of Tamalpais.

Past a moss-covered oak, Coast View enters a forest bypassed in the old Coastal FR. Huckleberry and blackberry shrubs line the edge as Coast View cuts through rows of twisting bay laurel trees. A grand old Douglas-fir stands on the right before Coast View exits back into the open, exactly 1 mile into the route.

This is a special area, with no other nearby trails in the entire vast southwest quadrant of Mt. Tamalpais. Cold Stream Canyon, utterly pristine, is to the right. A few dead trees make a haunting silhouette on its ridge. To the left is Kent Canyon, also trailless.

In 1959, landowner Tony Brazil and friend Roane Sias planted thousands of Monterey pines high in Kent Canyon on a section of Brazil's 2,150-acre ranch. They planned on selling 3- to 6-foot Christmas trees to finance their children's college educations. The site was called the Brazil-Sias Christmas Tree Farm. MTSP bought the entire 2,150-acre Brazil Ranch in 1968 before any trees were ever sold. Sias, a World War II pilot who twice escaped from German prisoner of war camps, died in 2014.

In 1979, Hillsborough resident Albert Shansky donated funds for construction of Camp Shansky (or Shansky Backpack Camp) amidst the old tree farm. It was named for his late son, Lee, who had been an avid hiker on Tam. There were four campsites for hikers, including one called "the honeymoon suite." In February 1989, a windstorm destroyed the camp and grove. Scores of trees were toppled, and others were cut down soon after. The camp never reopened. A few years later, remnants of the camp, and the grove, were removed.

Coast View has its one real uphill. Then, at 1.4 miles, 250 yards beyond the crest, is a completely unexpected, and perfectly located, picnic table. You can choose your view: Mt. Tamalpais or the Pacific Ocean. Just past is a view down left to Frank Valley, cut by Redwood Creek. The expanse of Santos Meadow is clear. A sharp bend left opens views back to Lone Tree Hill, the route's start.

Encroaching shrubs narrow Coast View. One is gumweed (*Grindelia hirsutula*), still in bloom in mid-summer and recognizable by the creamy, sticky fluid atop it. Slide Ranch, with its fenced pastures and yurts, comes into view. The trail makes a hairpin turn left around a lichen-covered boulder.

At 2.3 miles, Coast View meets an old gate and post. The fence line marks the boundary of Mt. Tamalpais State Park and entry into Golden Gate National Recreation Area. Heather Cutoff Trail, closed to bikes, drops left to Muir Woods.

Take the left option to continue on Coast View. The final .4 mile is a broad road parallel to Highway 1. Here, Coast View runs atop the former Banducci Brothers flower farm (also known as Heather Farm), which supplied Bay Area wholesalers with heather and other flowers beginning in the 1920s. The property became part of GGNRA in 1980, although the farm continued in operation. But in 1994, the Banduccis lost their right to pump irrigation water from wells near Redwood Creek—it was considered harmful to the creek's threatened salmon run—and flower farming ceased. GGNRA is replanting the area, but you'll pass a stand of the long-gone farm's heather bushes. The tiny pink-purple flowers bloom by January.

The row of eucalyptus trees marking the route's signed exit onto Highway 1, at Mile Marker 7.35, is now gone. A parking area, popular with tourists stopping to take photographs, is across the road. Unfortunately, there is presently no trail connection. Owl Trail is directly below but can only be reached by going right on Highway 1 to Slide Ranch or left to the Muir Beach Overlook.

Easy Grade Trail

Matt Davis Trail to Mountain Theater, plus spur: .60 mile

Terrain: Tanbark oak woodland (MTSP)

Elevation: From 1,540 to 1,980 feet; steep

Intersecting Trail(s): Old Stage Road (.1 mile), Easy Grade Spur (.2 mile), Riding & Hiking (.2 mile)

Easy Grade Trail is a well-used route between Pantoll/Bootjack and the Mountain Theater. The trail starts from Matt Davis Trail, though it is likely more commonly joined at its first intersection, just 20 yards higher, directly across Old Stage Road.

It continues uphill into a tanbark oak/Douglas-fir forest. In a bit over .1 mile of climbing, a brief opening on the right offers a view of Mountain Home and, well beyond, Mt. Diablo.

Twenty-five yards after Easy Grade crosses a rivulet, there is a fence line and a T intersection. This is the first of three intersections within 100 yards, making this a rather tricky area to navigate, even with new signs at each junction. At this first one, Easy Grade Spur comes in on the right from Old Stage Road and the united Easy Grade Trail rises to the left.

Just beyond is another three-way intersection. Veer right along the fence; left is a short connector to Riding & Hiking Trail. At the end of the fence, Riding & Hiking Trail crosses at a four-way intersection. To the left it goes to (Upper) Old Mine Trail, to the right down to Old Stage Road. Continue straight and uphill.

Easy Grade re-enters deep woodland. There is a particularly impressive old oak on the right. A pipeline is embedded in the trail's left margin. There is another opening, with a great shot of Tam's summit peaks.

Easy Grade ends when it meets the top of Bootjack Trail at Mountain Theater. Woodpeckers love the trees here. To the left is the old building with the actors' dressing rooms. Follow the asphalt path to the Mountain Theater stage. Look there for the plaque dedicated to the memory of longtime play director Dan Totheroh: *My Feet Will Mark the Trail of Stars.*

The Civilian Conservation Corps built Easy Grade in the 1930s as a new route to Mountain Theater. It was less steep, an "easier grade," than the original Bootjack Trail. But since Bootjack was rerouted in 1980, with more switchbacks, the two routes now differ little in grade.

▥ Hill 640 Fire Road

Panoramic Highway to Hill 640: .30 mile

Terrain: Grassland (GGNRA)

Elevation: Around 640 feet; rolling

Intersecting Trail(s): Dipsea (.1 mile)

This fire road was carved during construction of a World War II military installation on the coastal bluff. Enter through the "Fire Lane" gate opposite Mile Marker 7.86 on Panoramic Highway. (Another gate, behind which a short fire road drops to the Dipsea Trail, is 75 yards uphill.)

Hill 640 FR sets off southwest. There are immediately glorious views of Stinson Beach, Bolinas, and the Pacific. In 100 yards, the fire road crosses the Dipsea Trail. (Few Dipsea racers know the spot, as most use shortcuts on and off Panoramic Highway instead.) Stinson Beach is 1 mile to the right via the Dipsea Trail, Mill Valley is 6 miles left. Clinging to a rock on the left are an isolated

Douglas-fir and many poppies.

The fire road gently rises, then descends. A broad path forks uphill to the right, leading past a few planted Monterey pines to the top of the knoll and some bunker remnants. Hill 640 FR meets a lone eucalyptus. Beyond, the route simply peters out at the edge of the steep drop to Highway 1. Steep Ravine cabins are visible well below.

A path to the right leads to a descending row of abandoned concrete bunkers that once served as base-end stations for the US Coast Artillery. Triangulation measurements were taken from here and other similar coastal stations, such as those by Muir Beach Overlook, in order to locate enemy ships and calculate firing distances. The data was then to be relayed to Marin Headlands gun batteries overlooking the Golden Gate.

Since the hill at the fire road's end is 640 feet in elevation, the US Geological Survey map calls it Hill 640. It has also been labeled White Gate Ranch Trail, reflecting the historic ranch of that name that once existed here.

Old Stage Road

Pantoll to West Point: 1.83 miles

TERRAIN: Lower part paved, woodland; upper part chaparral (MTSP, MMWD)

ELEVATION: From 1,500 to 1,785 feet; gradual

INTERSECTING TRAIL(s): Matt Davis (.1 mile), Old Mine (.1 mile), Easy Grade (.1 mile), Easy Grade Spur (.3 mile), Riding & Hiking (.4 mile), Bootjack (.4 mile)

Old Stage Road was originally graded in 1902 as a wagon road to connect the Mill Valley & Mt. Tamalpais Scenic Railway at West Point with the coastal towns of Stinson Beach (then called Willow Camp), Bolinas, and Olema. A daily morning stagecoach departed from the West Point Inn and returned, with six horses pulling uphill, in the afternoon. A plan to extend the railway to Stinson—William Kent owned the entire right-of-way—never came to fruition, as the automobile was already making its mark.

Much of the original stage road below Pantoll is now covered by Panoramic Highway. One surviving segment, between Pantoll and Bootjack Trail, is paved. But the uppermost 1.4 miles remain a dirt road from which old stage days can still be imagined.

Two paved roads rise across Panoramic Highway from Pantoll Ranger Station. The one on the left is Pantoll, or Southside, Road, open to cars heading higher on the mountain. On the right, behind a gate, is Old Stage Road. A sign marks it as part of the Bay Area Ridge Trail.

Old Stage is gently graded throughout. There are several trail intersections in the opening .1 mile. The first, in 50 yards, is with Matt Davis going west to

Stinson Beach. Ten yards later, Matt Davis departs on the right, going east toward Bootjack. In another 60 yards, Old Mine Trail heads up left to Rock Spring. Twenty yards farther, Easy Grade Trail goes left up to Mountain Theater and right a few yards down to Matt Davis Trail.

The next intersection is $\frac{1}{6}$ mile later, when Easy Grade Spur rises left to Easy Grade Trail. Trees line the road, but occasional breaks offer views. Highway reflector signs, recycled from other county roads, dot Old Stage's margin.

In just under ½ mile, on the right, are a water chlorination building, drinking fountain, and bench. Opposite, Riding & Hiking Trail rises to Easy Grade and then Old Mine Trail. A few yards beyond, an asphalt road veers right; it leads to an MTSP residence. Bootjack Trail crosses that road and continues left up to Mountain Theater. Soon after, Old Stage Road becomes dirt-surfaced.

Open chaparral replaces the forest canopy, and the views are superb the rest of the trip. A gate marks the boundary between MTSP, which you are leaving, and MMWD lands. The uphill is gentle, more noticeable when you look back or ahead. There are no intersecting trails for 1.3 miles.

Old Stage Road crosses over the upper reaches of several important Tam creeks, in order, Bootjack (near Bootjack Trail), two forks of Rattlesnake, and Spike Buck. Old stonework, chain ferns, and azaleas mark each crossing. Sticky monkeyflower, manzanita, chamise, toyon, and chaparral pea are commonly seen growing amidst the serpentine. A stand of Sargent cypress trees is prominent. So too are a couple of massive serpentine rock walls left, perhaps the largest on Tamalpais.

West Point Inn is visible well before it is reached. Here, stage passengers could connect with the railway, dine, or spend the night. The inn still offers overnight lodging (by advance reservation only) and light refreshments. There are restrooms, picnic tables, and benches. The area, now with a grassy "lawn" to the south, looks different since encroaching trees were cleared. Routes meeting here, in order clockwise, are: Rock Spring to Mountain Theater, Old Railroad Grade uphill, the grade downhill, and Nora to Matt Davis.

▉ Riding & Hiking Trail

Old Stage Road to Old Mine Trail: .40 mile

TERRAIN: Mostly woodland, parts grassland; horses permitted (MTSP; equestrian section of Bay Area Ridge Trail)

ELEVATION: From 1,580 to 1,700 feet; gradual

INTERSECTING TRAIL(S): Easy Grade (.2 mile)

In 1945, the California state legislature authorized establishment of an equestrian route that would wind through thirty-six counties between Mexico and the Oregon border. This Riding & Hiking Trail was to pass across Mt. Tamalpais. After some debate, a decision was made to use existing Tam trails and fire roads rather than build new ones.

This trail was an exception, built specifically to accommodate equestrians as well as hikers. Redwood signposts, painted yellow on top, marked the incomplete project. (Very few are left on Tamalpais.) In 1989, Riding & Hiking Trail became an equestrian section of the new Bay Area Ridge Trail.

Riding & Hiking Trail sets off from the upper end of the paved section of Old Stage Road, 100 feet west of the Bootjack Trail crossing. The trailhead is opposite a chlorinator building, where there is a water fountain and a bench.

The trail begins in a peaceful woodland of laurel, tanbark oak, and Douglas-fir. The uphill is gradual.

In around ⅙ mile, just past a huge oak, the trail enters a grass clearing. There is a four-way junction where Easy Grade Trail crosses left down to Old Stage Road and right up to Mountain Theater. Riding & Hiking Trail continues straight. In 50 yards, over a slight rise, is another junction. The path to the left is a short connector back to Easy Grade. New signs, with arrows, help guide visitors to their destinations in what remains a bit of a tricky area.

Riding & Hiking continues gently up. One of the historic yellow-topped signposts long stood at the edge of the next grassland. There are splendid views back to Tam's three summits and Mt. Diablo and ahead to the Pacific.

The trail returns to tanbark oak woodland. There are level sections, even dips. Riding & Hiking Trail ends when it meets Old Mine Trail. Horse riders can then continue on Old Mine (uphill only) to Rock Spring.

Stapelveldt Trail

Pantoll to Ben Johnson Trail: 1.02 miles

Terrain: Deep woods; lower half riparian (MTSP)

Elevation: From 1,500 to 920 feet; steep

Intersecting Trail(s): TCC (twice at .4 miles)

Visitors to Pantoll seeking the joys of a redwood-lined, creekside trail usually opt for justly famous Steep Ravine. But Stapelveldt Trail, with Ben Johnson Trail a direct route to Muir Woods, serves nicely as well.

Stapelveldt Trail sets off from behind the West Marin Stagecoach stop at Pantoll. Alpine Trail also begins here; it veers left while Stapelveldt goes right.

The early yards through the Pantoll campground were once confusing, as campers had worn many paths, but new signs and trail work now make the route clearer. There is a trail sign at a crest above Campsite 15.

Stapelveldt leaves the camp's ridge line and begins its steady, all-downhill journey. In .3 mile, three small bridges are crossed in quick succession. Honey-suckle and huckleberry border the first. At the next two, look for rose shrubs.

Just beyond, Stapelveldt meets TCC Trail at a bridge. A bench has been fash-ioned from an old trail sign. Old maps show a Camp Stapelveldt here. Left, TCC goes 1.4 miles to Bootjack Trail at Van Wyck Meadow. TCC and Stapelveldt de-scend together for 20 yards to a second three-way junction, where TCC departs right to the Dipsea Trail.

Stapelveldt then descends the deepening canyon. Switchbacks, shored by railroad ties, were built by the Youth Conservation Corps in 1978. (The added turns also make the route from the TCC junction to Ben Johnson a bit longer than signs indicate.) The unnamed creek left heads to Redwood Creek, then on to Muir Woods. Three feeder rivulets are crossed on bridges.

Ever-more-massive redwoods, some branchless to 100 feet up, line the way. One fire-scarred giant has a cavity large enough to enter. The trail squeezes be-tween another towering pair of trees. Low-growing oxalis, or redwood sorrel (*Oxalis oregana*), borders the trail beginning in late winter.

Stapelveldt drops steeply before its end. The trail terminates at its junction with Ben Johnson Trail, which goes straight ahead down to Muir Woods, and right up to Deer Park FR and Dipsea Trail. There is a bench to rest on at this lovely, quiet spot.

In 1989, Fred Sandrock of the Mt. Tamalpais History Project published evi-dence that the trail was named for Wilhelm (William) Stapelfeldt. Stapelfeldt, born in Germany in 1839, came to San Francisco, where he worked as a grocer. He was apparently a hiking partner of legendary Tamalpais figures such as Emil Barth, Edward Ziesche, and Alice Eastwood, and did much trail work. He died in 1912. The trail has known some half-dozen different spellings.

◼ Steep Ravine Trail

Pantoll to Highway 1: 2.12 miles

Terrain: Riparian; redwood forest (MTSP)

Elevation: From 1,500 to 430 feet; very steep

Intersecting Trail(s): Dipsea (1.6 miles, 1.7 miles)

Steep Ravine is always named among the most beautiful trails on Mt. Tamalpais and in all the Bay Area. Few who traverse it come away unmoved. There are so many treasures to be found along its way that I am loath to single out just these few.

The trail begins a few yards below Pantoll Ranger Station, to the right off the road leading to the maintenance area. The upper part has been rerouted, with switchbacks added to lessen its steepness and to help prevent erosion.

The route starts, and remains, fairly near Panoramic Highway. But a bit lower, Webb Creek, which is adjacent the rest of the way, muffles road noise (and drowns it completely in winter).

In .3 mile, at the base of the switchbacks, is a bench, particularly welcome to those ascending. At this bend are the canyon's uppermost redwoods. One in particular is enormous, among the most impressive on Tamalpais outside of Muir Woods. Redwoods remain companions on the remainder of the route down.

The trail crosses a few rivulets, feeders to Webb Creek. Then, in .5 mile, the trail meets Webb Creek, which began above Panoramic Highway, where it makes the first of its eight bridged creek crossings—here, to the right bank. Just beyond, the trail squeezes between two towering redwoods, joined at their shallow roots.

If your attention can be diverted from the creek, the redwoods, and the carpets of sword ferns covering the hillsides, you'll find many other floral treasures. An abundant and showy favorite is trillium, or wake-robin. Look for its characteristic three broad leaves and, atop a slender stalk, the three-petaled flower. The color varies, white fading to pink.

Red elderberry (*Sambucus racemosa*) is abundant along the creek. The shrub, which rises to 10 feet, has a characteristic five-section compound leaf. In spring, its clusters of creamy white flowers form pyramids. In fall, they bear red berries. (The US Department of Agriculture warns against eating red elderberries, and *Marin Flora* cautions against ingesting blue elderberry, *S. nigra*, also found on Tamalpais.)

At the second Webb Creek bridge (rivulets are forded by smaller bridges), look for clintonia, in the lily family. It has large glossy leaves, deep rose flowers, and blue berries in early summer.

Just beyond is the famous Steep Ravine ladder. It takes the trail down a precipitous rock face beside a waterfall. Proceed cautiously. (In the early 1970s, legendary Tam trail runner Byron Lowry, on his first trip down Steep Ravine Trail, came upon this unexpected sheer drop at breakneck speed. Unable to stop, he proceeded and somehow emerged unscathed.)

Below the ladder, at 900 feet elevation, a stand of redwoods has been designated as Jim Wright Grove. Wright was president of Tamalpais Conservation Club in 1926–1927, the most critical year in the club's battle to create Mt. Tamalpais State Park. He died in 1937.

The trail continues ever down, with the grade usually gentle enough to permit gazing at the sylvan wonders. Just before Bridge 3, a "doorway" has been cut in a downed redwood. It will continue to be a feature of the trail for many years. This bridge was wrecked in a storm in December 2014, closing the trail for more than a month until it could be replaced. Past the bridge is another waterfall. The bright red berries (poisonous!) of baneberry (*Actaea rubra*) brighten the green foliage here in summer.

Just after Bridge 4 is a slight rise in the trail, then a steep drop over steps to Bridge 5. Two more bridges follow close together. Beyond the last, a downed redwood serves many as a well-sculpted bench. An old pipeline lies in the creekbed.

Steep Ravine Trail then meets Dipsea Trail, which descended the other side of the same canyon (a section of the Dipsea Trail known to racers as "Steep Ravine"). Dipsea crosses Webb Creek here, but do not go over the bridge unless you are taking Dipsea back to Pantoll, a classic loop.

Dipsea and Steep Ravine Trails run together beside the reservoir, once part of the Stinson Beach water supply. At the base of the uphill (known as "Insult" in the Dipsea Race), a path branches left to Webb Creek. Continue uphill a few yards. Beside a power pole, Steep Ravine Trail veers left at a marked intersection.

This lower stretch of Steep Ravine (sometimes called Webb Creek Trail) is less visited. Many find it as appealing as the more famous upper section. It is lush, and may well have a greater variety of native plant species than any comparably sized stretch of trail in the Bay Area.

After a slight rise, the trail meets a clearing. A broad path branches right, soon to reconnect with Dipsea. Steep Ravine continues, also broad. Incredible as it may now seem, this was the original routing of California's Highway 1, before the road was rebuilt closer to the coast.

A sharp left leads the trail away from the former roadbed and under an impressive old spreading buckeye. Also passed here is a massive redwood, the last on the trail. Delicate blue forget-me-nots, originally garden escapees but now established in Tam's redwood forests, dot its base. A bridge provides the last crossing of Webb Creek.

Thaddeus Welch, whose landscapes of Tamalpais are considered among the finest ever painted, lived in this tranquil area from 1900 to 1905. He and his artist wife Ludmilla built a cabin in a level clearing on the creek's right bank. Only the sharpest-eyed observers will find any traces of the Welches' stay, which include some introduced German ivy. It was Welch who coined the name Steep Ravine.

Soon after the bridge is a bench, recycled from an old trail sign. There aren't many more tranquil settings on the mountain. The flora here is verdant all year. In late summer and fall, berries abound. They include (with botanical name when not previously cited): elderberry, baneberry, oso berry (*Oemleria cerasiformis*), twinberry (*Lonicera involucrata*), strawberry, California blackberry, thimbleberry (*R. parviflorus*) and salmonberry (*R. spectabilis*).

The last .1 mile of the trail was rerouted in 1992, both to keep it beside Webb Creek and to bring it out directly across from Rocky Point Road (eliminating a previous short but dangerous walk on Highway 1). The final yards now face a large yellow sign warning drivers on Highway 1 to slow to 20 MPH. The spell is broken.

Steep Ravine Trail exits beside a parking area at Mile Marker 11.04. Down the gated road are the Steep Ravine cabins, an environmental campground, and the mouth of Webb Creek.

William Kent purchased the Steep Ravine area in 1904 with the intention of extending the Mt. Tamalpais Railway to Stinson Beach, where he also owned land. On March 12, 1928, the day before his death, he deeded Steep Ravine to the State of California for inclusion in the brand-new Tamalpais State Park. One of the Steep Ravine cabins is named for him, another for Welch. (The cabins were built and owned by the Kent family.) The present Steep Ravine Trail was constructed by the CCC in 1935–1936 over an earlier path.

■ TCC Trail

Bootjack Trail at Van Wyck Meadow to Dipsea Trail: 1.8 miles

TERRAIN: Douglas fir forest (MTSP, MWNM)

ELEVATION: 1,040 to 1,280 feet; gradual

INTERSECTING TRAIL(S): Stapelveldt (1.4 miles)

Constructed by the Tamalpais Conservation Club, this is one of the better-designed of the mountain's trails. It crosses some eleven deeply wooded canyons, yet runs fairly level with a barely noticeable rise for its whole 1.8-mile length.

TCC Trail sets off from Van Wyck Meadow to the right of an old stone fireplace when descending Bootjack Trail from Panoramic Highway. The rock structure, in which pipes are still evident, was part of Lower Rattlesnake Camp, a favorite haunt of Tam hikers in its 1920s heyday. On the fireplace beneath a goldcup oak, a plaque dedicated to the Tamalpais Conservation Club, for which the trail is named, was placed in 1999. It is now missing.

The trail immediately enters deep woodland, where it remains the whole length. In 20 yards, the first creek is crossed on a bridge. Affixed to a laurel 25 yards beyond is one of the old trail signs the TCC placed throughout the mountain; it is now illegible. Douglas firs, many of them huge "wolf-trees," their bases circled by sizable branches, are dominant. Redwoods line all of the creek canyons. Somewhat similar in foliage to both are a few California nutmegs. At the second creek is a restored old sign bench, pointing the way to the Ben Johnson, Stapelveldt, and Dipsea Trails.

The trail winds around canyon after canyon, some with bridges over the creeks, some with only rivulets to step over. Huckleberries line the route in profusion. The fairly steady elevation gain is barely noticeable (unless you're tired!).

In 1.4 miles, TCC Trail crosses a bridge and meets Stapelveldt Trail. A sign-post and another sign bench mark the junction. Straight ahead, Stapelveldt rises to Pantoll. To the left, TCC and Stapelveldt run together for 20 yards to a second junction. Stapelveldt departs downhill to the left, to Ben Johnson Trail; veer right.

Another bridge is crossed. The building crew left a sign—similar are found on many of the more recent MTSP bridges and switchbacks—naming the workers and date of construction (1/12/83).

TCC Trail enters Muir Woods National Monument, then quickly ends when it hits the Dipsea Trail. Just uphill to the right is the crest of Cardiac Hill, a stunning view site. Downhill leads to Deer Park FR and Ben Johnson Trail.

The Tamalpais Conservation Club was formed by a band of hikers in 1912 for "preservation of the scenic beauties and fauna of Mt. Tamalpais and its spurs and slopes." The club's first major activity was a trail cleanup day, and they have since done more trailbuilding and maintenance than any other volunteer group. TCC was a leader in the fight to create Mt. Tamalpais State Park, and remains vigilant in living up to its motto, "Guardian of the Mountain."

This trail, built during WWI by TCC trail crews, was originally named Houghton Trail for Samuel Monroe Houghton, a TCC founder and its president from 1913 to 1914, the year he died. The trail is also sometimes shown as T.C.C.

KIRKE WRENCH

Bootjack Trail

Steep Revine Trail just west of the Pantoll Ranger Station

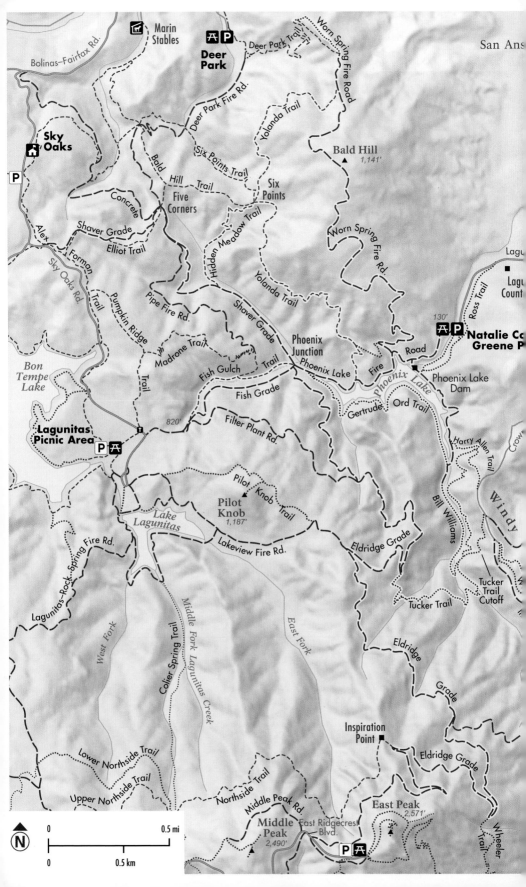

Worn Springs Fire Road

TRAILHEAD TEN: PHOENIX LAKE

Directions
Highway 101—Sir Francis Drake Boulevard (exit) west 3 miles into Ross, then left on Lagunitas Road to end

---

Phoenix Lake, convenient to all in the populous Ross Valley, has long been a well-used entry to Mt. Tamalpais. Indeed, it was becoming so popular in the 1980s that the Town of Ross restricted parking on nearby streets. Now, the twenty-four spots in the trailhead lot often fill and drivers line up to wait for an opening; a sign reminds not to idle engines. The lot is free (MMWD, which shares jurisdiction of the lot with Ross, abandoned its short-lived fee program). The next closest parking, on weekdays only, is the dirt margin of Lagunitas Road beside the Lagunitas Country Club. Many visitors park near Ross Common, where there is an up to three-hour time limit (check signs), and literally "go the extra mile."

Entry to the parking area and lake is through Natalie Coffin Greene Park, a gift to the public by the Greene family of Ross; Natalie Coffin Greene (1885–1966) was active in civic affairs. Beyond the park's stone portals is Dibblee Road, named for another pioneer Ross family. It was paved in 2003 despite some protests; the speed limit is 5 MPH. Beginning in the 1870s, horse-drawn carriages brought tourists over Lagunitas Road to Lake Lagunitas. The entry gate is closed every night as well as on high-fire-danger days.

From the parking area, a fire road rises ¼ mile to Phoenix Dam, which was built in 1905 to create the reservoir of Phoenix Lake. Another pedestrian entry to Phoenix Lake is via Ross Trail, which sets off from just before the stone portals. There is also a path to the dam from the charming picnic area adjacent to the parking spaces.

There are portable toilets in the parking lot and at Phoenix Dam. Water fountains are in the picnic area and 50 yards north from the dam. It is 3.6 miles around Phoenix Lake from the junction of Glenwood Avenue and Lagunitas Road, and 2.33 miles, eschewing shortcuts, around the lake itself. Phoenix Junction, from which Eldridge, Fish, and Shaver Grades rise, is .6 mile from the dam, counterclockwise.

Suggested Loops from Phoenix Dam (elevation 180 feet)

1. Around Phoenix Lake. **2.3 miles total**

2. Phoenix Lake FR counterclockwise, .6 mile, to Phoenix Junction—right on Shaver Grade, .4 mile, to Hidden Meadow Trail—right, .7 mile, to Six Points Junction—right, 1.3 miles on Yolanda Trail to Phoenix Lake FR—left .4 mile, to start. **3.4 miles total**

3. Phoenix Lake FR clockwise, .5 mile, to Bill Williams Trail—left, .6 mile, to Tucker Trail—right, 1.1 miles, to Eldridge Grade—right, 1.6 miles, to Phoenix Junction—left, .6 mile, on Phoenix FR to start. **4.4 miles total**

4. Phoenix Lake FR counterclockwise, .4 mile, to Yolanda Trail—right, 2.2 miles, to Worn Spring FR—right, 2.2 miles, to Phoenix Lake FR—left, .1 mile, to start. **4.9 miles total**

5. Phoenix Lake FR counterclockwise, .1 mile, to Worn Spring FR—right, 2.5 miles, to Deer Park Trail—left, .8 mile, to Deer Park FR—left, 1.1 miles to Shaver Grade—left, 1.2 miles, to Phoenix Junction—Phoenix Lake FR left, .6 mile (or right, 1.7 miles), to start. **6.3/7.4 miles total**

Bill Williams Trail

Southern tip of Phoenix Lake to Tucker Trail: .64 mile

TERRAIN: Redwood forest; riparian (MMWD)

ELEVATION: From 200 to 380 feet; gradual

INTERSECTING TRAIL(S): None

Bill Williams Trail starts from the southern tip of Phoenix Lake, where the fire road and trail sections of the loop route around the lake meet, ½ mile from the dam (clockwise).

Bill Williams leaves the lake's shore at fire-road width. It climbs gently into the deep woodland of Bill Williams Gulch. Maples and redwoods predominate. In around 200 yards is a wide area, used as an MMWD vehicular turnaround. A sign points the way toward Tucker Trail.

The trail, now narrow, dips and crosses a pipeline that carries water from the Bon Tempe Treatment Plant. A pump above, off Eldridge Grade, drives the water up and out of the gulch to Kent Woodlands.

Bill Williams Trail follows a narrow ledge above Bill Williams Creek, one of the sources of Phoenix Lake. This lovely, fern-covered area remains cool on the hottest of summer days, and the creek roars in winter.

In ½ mile, the trail crosses the creek on a bridge. There are remnants of the old stone Bill Williams Gulch Dam. A wood plaque affixed to the base of a redwood beside the bridge dates the dam to 1886. It served as an early water source for central Marin until the larger dam downstream created Phoenix Lake in 1905. The remnant dam creates a small waterfall in winter.

A few yards upstream of the dam, the trail crosses back over to the creek's left bank. There is no bridge, so fording may be a problem in winter. Follow the creek's edge. A short, steep uphill leads to a crest and a fork. Descend and cross, in rapid succession, two bridges over forks of Bill Williams Creek. The first was built by Eagle Scouts of Marin's Troop 101.

The trail then rises very steeply up some seventy-five steps to end at its signed junction with Tucker Trail. Left on Tucker leads to the Tucker Cutoff, then Harry Allen Trail. Right on Tucker is a climb to Eldridge Grade.

Bill Williams lived in a cabin in the first gulch upstream from the dam in the 1860s. His background is little known; some thought he was a Confederate Army deserter. Alice Eastwood referred to him as "an old wood-chopper." Legend persisted that he buried his treasure somewhere in the gulch and a story is told that the men building Phoenix Dam spent more time looking for Bill Williams' gold than working. There was another fruitless treasure hunt when Phoenix Lake was drained in the mid-1980s. A different Bill Williams Trail ran atop Bolinas Ridge before construction of Ridgecrest Boulevard.

◾ Eldridge Grade

Phoenix Junction to Ridgecrest Boulevard: 5.46 miles

TERRAIN: Lower part forested, upper part mostly chaparral (MMWD)

ELEVATION: From 200 to 2,250 feet; gradual

INTERSECTING TRAIL(S): Filter Plant Road (.8 mile), Tucker (1.6 miles), Lakeview FR (2.0 miles), Indian FR (3.1 miles), Wheeler (3.7 miles), Northside (4.3 miles)

Eldridge Grade opened on December 13, 1884, the first road to the summit ridge of Mt. Tamalpais. Construction took only five months and cost $8,000, with most of the work done by Chinese laborers. Long-time Tam explorer Brad Rippe has located one of the old work camps high off Eldridge. The grade was built for horse-drawn wagons, with wide turnouts and a slope rarely exceeding 1 foot in 14 (7 percent). Six-horse, ten-passenger Tally-Ho wagons set off over it from the luxurious Rafael Hotel in San Rafael for regular excursions.

The road was the vision of John Oscar Eldridge, who raised the funds and gained the necessary easements. Eldridge came to California from New York by sea in 1849 at the age of twenty-one. Instead of rushing to the gold fields, he stayed in San Francisco and became a successful auctioneer. Later, he brought street lighting to San Rafael as a co-founder of the San Rafael Gas Company. His daughter married Sidney Cushing, who went on to lead the building of the rail line up Mt. Tamalpais in 1896. (Mountain Theater is named for Sidney Cushing.) Eldridge died just two months after the road opened, and it was named for him.

In the early 1900s, when horse-drawn carriages became obsolete, Eldridge Grade fell into disrepair, and plans were advanced to pave it for auto use. MMWD voted against the idea. Along with the Old Railroad Grade (which was also saved from a paving proposal), Eldridge Grade remains one of the most-used summit routes for hikers and bikers.

Eldridge is one of three fire roads that rise from Phoenix Junction at the northwest tip of Phoenix Lake. With your back to the lake, Eldridge is to the left, Fish Grade is in the middle, and Shaver Grade is on the right. Eldridge begins under a dense canopy of trees, mostly bay but with redwoods plentiful. In the 1980s, there were major slide problems in the first ½ mile, at times narrowing the grade to a slim trail. Just past the first big bend, a short dip—Eldridge is otherwise uniformly uphill—is a remnant of MMWD repair work. Skunks are denizens of culverts in the canyon crossings.

In .8 mile, Filter Plant Road, which connects to Fish Grade, comes in from the right. A water fountain was added at the intersection in 1992. At the next fork, go right, or take the more gently sloped option left, which loops around an MMWD pump building.

As Eldridge rises, the terrain becomes ever drier. Madrones and tanbark oaks are more prevalent, with redwoods only at stream crossings. Tucker Trail, which offers a lovely, steep route back toward Phoenix Lake, joins at a wide, right-hand bend in the grade. At the next bend, a sign on a trough identifies Bear Wallow Spring; there were once both black and grizzly bears on Tam. (Grizzlies were extirpated from the mountain around 1849, black bears by the 1880s.) Views continue to open, particularly to the east.

Lakeview FR, from Lake Lagunitas, joins the grade on the right. An old trail sign marks the intersection. Just above, chinquapin, a small tree in the oak family, is common. By late summer, its spiny, bur-like fruit capsules line the edge of the grade here. Eldridge's surface becomes increasingly rocky. The next fire road to enter is Indian, on the left. It descends to Kent Woodlands.

Continue right. Views to the south of San Francisco and the San Mateo coastline expand. To the east it is possible, on sparkling winter days, to see the snow-capped Sierra.

At a wide horseshoe curve, Wheeler Trail enters on the left. Descending to Hoo-Koo-E-Koo FR, it is part of many Tamalpais circumambulation routes. The next big bend to the left is known as Sawtooth Point. Soon after, at a wide curve left, an old sign points to the broad start of Northside Trail, which runs all the way to Rifle Camp. Just inside is the scenic rock plateau of Inspiration Point.

The next big bend, to the right, is below the rock formation known as North Knee. Eldridge passes above the deep canyon formed by the East Fork of Lagunitas Creek, which is beginning its long cross-Marin journey to Tomales Bay.

Eldridge Grade ends at paved Ridgecrest Road. It originally went farther, to West Peak, but construction of Ridgecrest in the mid-1920s covered the old route, shortening its total length nearly 2 miles. East Peak is to the left. Middle Peak FR and Old Railroad Grade are a few yards downhill.

▦ Fish Grade

Phoenix Junction to Sky Oaks Road: .76 mile

TERRAIN: Redwood forest; riparian; upper part paved (MMWD)

ELEVATION: 200 to 720 feet; very steep

INTERSECTING TRAIL(S): Fish Gulch (.6 mile)

The steepness of Fish Grade is legendary and intimidates some visitors. Yet many hike, run, and bike up it regularly as the most direct route between Phoenix Lake and the "upper lakes" of Lagunitas, Bon Tempe, and Alpine. Lined by redwoods, it is shady and attractive.

Fish Grade is the middle of the three fire roads—Eldridge and Shaver grades are the others—that rise from Phoenix Junction. Narrower Fish Gulch Trail, on the opposite bank from Fish Grade, also sets off uphill here.

There is no getting lost on Fish Grade; just keep climbing up, up, up through the cool, quiet forest. The canyon below is Fish Gulch. The creek through it is not officially named, but Fish Creek seems obvious.

Fish Gulch Trail rejoins Fish Grade. Combined, they immediately meet paved Filter Plant Road, which sets off left to the MMWD filter plant and then Eldridge Grade. A few yards below the junction is the best view of the pipeline that carries water from Bon Tempe Lake to the filter plant.

There is another 225 yards of stiff uphill on asphalt (considered part of Fish Grade here, not Filter Plant Road). The array of valves to the right is the Bon Tempe Headworks, which regulate water flow.

The grade ends at a movable barrier on Sky Oaks Road that blocks private vehicles. Just right on the road, Pumpkin Ridge Trail sets off uphill. Bon Tempe Lake is across. Left leads to the Lake Lagunitas parking area.

A Mr. Fish had a camp in the present Lake Lagunitas area in the 1860s. The original grade was built around 1873, when the dam that created the lake was completed. That first grade is now Fish Gulch Trail. The current Fish Grade was carved in 1903 to bring water pipelines down from the planned Tamalpais Dam, which was never completed.

▓ Fish Gulch Trail

Phoenix Junction to Fish Grade: .57 mile

TERRAIN: Heavily wooded; riparian (MMWD)

ELEVATION: From 200 to 600 feet; very steep

INTERSECTING TRAIL(S): Concrete Pipeline FR (.4 mile)

Fish Gulch Trail is the only trail out of Phoenix Junction; the other four spokes are all fire-road width. It sets off uphill, unsigned, between Fish and Shaver Grades.

The climb, which goes through oak-madrone woodland, is very steep. A water pipeline is visible beside the trail. The trail—originally broader—was cleared in the early 1870s to bring a water line down from the new Lake Lagunitas. The trail is actually the original Fish Grade (the present Fish Grade was built in 1903), and is sometimes called Old Fish Grade.

Fish Gulch Trail meets the narrow, southern end of Concrete Pipeline FR, which connects to Five Corners and on to Fairfax-Bolinas Road. The remaining ascent is the steepest yet. The fire road (Fish Grade) across redwood-lined Fish Gulch gets steadily closer. In winter, water rushes through the creek below. There's a last incline past an MMWD building known as a baffle chamber.

Fish Gulch Trail veers left to rejoin Fish Grade. A path goes straight ahead to the Bon Tempe Headworks. A few yards uphill on Fish Grade is paved Filter Plant Road, which goes left to the filter plant and Eldridge Grade. Fish Grade continues steeply up $\frac{1}{8}$ mile to Sky Oaks Road.

In the 1860s, a Mr. Fish lived and worked at the site of the present Lake Lagunitas, and the area was called Fish's Camp.

■ Harry Allen Trail

Phoenix Lake to Crown Road, Kent Woodlands: 1.15 miles*

TERRAIN: Heavily wooded; .24 mile paved (MMWD, MCOSD)

ELEVATION: From 200 to 580 to 480 feet; steep

INTERSECTING TRAIL(S): Tucker (.3 mile), Tucker Cutoff (.6 mile), Indian FR (.7 mile), Kent FR (.7 mile)

*Includes .24 mile of paved Phoenix Road, which now divides Harry Allen Trail.

Harris (Harry) Stearns Allen, president of the Tamalpais Conservation Club (1916–1917), spent his Sundays building this trail over a three-year period in the early 1920s. It connected his home at 55 Olive Avenue (which still stands, though completely altered) in Larkspur's Baltimore Canyon to Phoenix Lake. The development of Kent Woodlands following World War II covered much of the old route, and diminished its importance.

Today, the trail is in two parts, severed by paved Phoenix Road atop Windy Ridge. The lesser-known eastern half was recleared and signed in 1987. Although both ends of that segment are accessible by car and offer adequate parking, most users join the Harry Allen Trail at Phoenix Lake, so we will, too.

Take Phoenix Lake FR clockwise .4 mile from the dam to the marked Harry Allen Trail intersection. The steep initial grade lessens when the trail enters the forest. Look in winter and spring for delicate maidenhair fern, with its green, fan-shaped fronds branching off slender black stalks. The spores are found under the reflexed outer margins of the fronds. *Adiantum*, the fern's genus name, comes from the Greek word for "unwettable," because the fronds shed water.

Just beyond a creek crossing, the trail meets the lower end of Tucker Trail. Many visitors leave Harry Allen here, taking Tucker either up to Eldridge Grade or, with Bill Williams Trail, back to Phoenix. Harry Allen continues up left.

Several paths cross, remnants of a more extensive trail system dating from the days when hikers approached the mountain from Northwestern Pacific Railroad stops to the east. Passenger train service ended in 1941.

The trail climbs out of its forest canopy and passes the introduced garden shrub called Pride of Madeira (*Echium candicans*), a sure sign that homes are near, which indeed they are. The trail unceremoniously runs into a gap in a rusted guardrail opposite 123 Crown Road. A pair of Marin Municipal Water

District signs marks the junction.

To pick up the second half of Harry Allen Trail, go right on the pavement along the spine of Windy Ridge. In .1 mile, a fire road goes left, an unpaved segment of Crown Road. Tucker Cutoff Trail, to Tucker Trail, drops right. Continue up Phoenix Road. In another .1 mile, an MMWD gate to the right marks the start of Indian FR. A few yards beyond, at the end of the pavement, is a wood barrier with an MCOSD sign. Beyond it is Windy Ridge Trail. Immediately on the left behind the gate, signed "Trail to Crown Road," is the continuation of Harry Allen Trail.

Squeeze between two redwoods. Narrow and, in places, eroding, Harry Allen Trail descends through a redwood forest. Huckleberry is abundant in the several clearings. In .1 mile, the trail goes over the roots of a stately madrone on the left edge that is losing its sunlight to the faster-growing redwoods, and is, therefore, dying.

Paved Crown Road becomes visible. At a final bend left, paths set off right and up. The final 75 yards of Harry Allen are steep and root-covered. The trail ends near 320 Crown Road. The entry is marked with an MCOSD "Welcome to Baltimore Canyon Open Space Preserve" sign. Crown Road goes right, past Idlewood Road and Evergreen Drive, to the Southern Marin Line (Crown) FR trailhead and left back to Phoenix Road.

Harry Allen was born in 1870 in Carson City, Nevada. His family relocated to Petaluma when he was four. He graduated from the University of California, Berkeley, in 1892 and began a career in journalism. Allen bought his Larkspur property in 1897; he first built a log cabin on it, then, in 1929, the larger house. He died in 1947.

▨ Hidden Meadow Trail

Shaver Grade to Six Points: .82 mile

TERRAIN: Grassy hillside; lower part riparian; horses permitted (MMWD)

ELEVATION: 270 to 550 feet; gradual, upper half very steep

INTERSECTING TRAIL(S): None

Hidden Meadow Trail is barely more than 1 mile from the popular Phoenix Lake and Deer Park Trailheads, yet it offers peace and an unspoiled quality reminiscent of early California. From Phoenix Junction, follow Shaver Grade ½ mile up Phoenix Creek, passing a now-closed former entry to Hidden Meadow Trail. The present trailhead is signed, to the right, and just before Shaver begins rising steeply.

Hidden Meadow Trail borders Phoenix Creek, soon crossing it over a bridge to enter magical Hidden Meadow itself. The meadow's grassy knolls are indeed hidden from the rest of the world. The first tree, left, is a buckeye. Next, right, is a coast live oak, followed with buckeyes left and right. Beyond is a stately valley oak, often bearing many galls, each housing a new generation of wasps.

Hidden Meadow was formerly known as Marshall Gulch for the Marshall family who operated a dairy here around the turn of the century. Cattle grazed the area until 1916. A Mt. Tamalpais History Project walk in 1988 turned up an old milk bottle from the ranch. (Note that it is unlawful to remove historic artifacts from the mountain without a permit.)

The trail begins climbing the southwest face of Bald Hill. Across a rivulet is the first of many railroad-tie switchbacks built by the Marin Conservation Corps in 1997 to stem erosion. They eased the steepness and made the route longer.

The trail leaves the oak woodland for the grassy hillside and snakes its way higher. The lovely pastoral setting, and often hot climbing, calls for a leisurely pace.

Hidden Meadow Trail ends at Six Points Junction. The four (not five) other spokes are, from left to right: Bald Hill Trail to Five Corners, Six Points Trail to Deer Park, Yolanda Trail to Worn Spring FR, and Yolanda back to Phoenix.

Hidden Meadow Trail was apparently built, or significantly upgraded, in the 1930s.

Phoenix Lake Fire Road & Gertrude Ord Trail

Loop around Phoenix Lake: 2.33 miles

TERRAIN: Riparian; oak-buckeye woodland; half trail, half fire road; horses and bicycles permitted on fire road only; heavily used (MMWD)

ELEVATION: Around 175 feet; level to slightly rolling

INTERSECTING TRAIL(S), clockwise from dam: Ross (at dam), Harry Allen (.4 mile), Bill Williams (.5 mile), Eldridge Grade (1.7 miles), Fish Grade (1.7 miles), Fish Gulch (1.7 miles), Shaver Grade (1.7 miles), Yolanda (1.9 miles), Worn Spring FR (2.2 miles)

The loop around Phoenix Lake is one of the most beloved routes on Mt. Tamalpais. Its popularity arises from its easy accessibility, level terrain, and the beautiful setting. The full circuit comprises two distinct parts of almost identical distance: a fire road (open to horses and bicycles) that goes left and right from the dam, and a trail along the lake's south and west shore.

Phoenix Lake was formed when Marin County Water Company, a predecessor to MMWD, constructed a dam in Phoenix Gulch in 1905. Phoenix, with a capacity of 178 million gallons, is now the second smallest of the MMWD reservoirs. It is also lowest in elevation. Indeed, because it is some 300 vertical feet below the Bon Tempe Filter Plant through which drinking water must pass, the lake is not regularly part of the county supply. Its water can, however, be used in an emergency; a pump was installed in the center of the lake when a drought threatened in 1989 and was used in the dry winter of 2013–2014. Phoenix Lake was most recently drained in 1984, when the current concrete spillway replaced an old wooden one.

Most visitors to Phoenix Lake come from Ross, reaching the dam by climbing either Ross Trail or the ¼-mile-long connector fire road from the parking area. We'll follow the loop clockwise from where this fire road meets the dam. This offers views of Tam's summit; going the other way affords vistas of Bald Hill.

Start by crossing the dam. Some visitors go no farther than the four benches here. The first is dedicated to Gertrude Moore Ord Pollock; the Ord name is tied to Phoenix Lake. The fourth and last is dedicated to my friend, the late James M. Tasley (1931–2004). When his son Craig died, Jim financed lights atop East Peak during the Christmas season as a memorial, and the tradition continues. Ross Trail enters on the dam's far side, the junction marked with a signpost pointing the way to Ross and to Tucker Trail.

Continuing on the fire road, you'll notice several paths to the lake's shore. Fishing has long been popular.

In a bit under ½ mile, Harry Allen Trail rises on the left. It connects to Tucker Trail and continues up to Kent Woodlands. The fire road then drops to the lake's southern tip, which is often dry before the first winter rains. Straight ahead, into the redwoods, is Bill Williams Trail, which starts at fire-road width. It too leads to Tucker Trail.

To continue the loop around the lake, go right, up the steps. This next 1.2-mile trail section is officially designated by MMWD as the (Gertrude) Ord Trail, although few visitors call it that. Gertrude Ord was a popular equestrienne and her husband, Eric, was a president of the Tamalpais Trail Riders. Horses are no longer allowed on the Ord portion.

The trail rolls gently along the lake's quieter southwest shore, though it would still be rare not to meet at least several other walkers and runners. Two-thirds of the way in, at a cove, the trail goes left. Steps lead the way up; a plaque on the top step honors the Eagle Scout builder, John Kniesche. There is then a drop to a bridge and completion of the cove circuit. Particularly in summer, many users bypass this cove and cut directly across the dry or shallow streambed.

After a second bridge, also the work of Eagle Scouts, forks branch left and right. Both lead back to the fire road; the right fork is a 100-yard shortcut. When back on the fire road, go right to complete the loop. To the left, at the northwest tip of the lake, is Phoenix Junction, from which Eldridge, Fish, Old Fish, and Shaver Grades rise.

The circuit continues on what was once a county road connecting San Rafael to Bolinas. It passes several buildings (some used as MMWD residences and all off-limits) of the former Porteous Ranch. Prominent is the handsome Phoenix Log Cabin. Built in 1896 in the Queen Anne style by Porteous Ranch coachman and foreman Martin Grant, the cabin was restored by MMWD (for district use only) in 1989. Look closely to enjoy the many charming touches, such as the exterior window frames. In the next bend just past, Yolanda Trail sets off uphill across the south slope of Bald Hill.

The loop's last junction is with broad Worn Spring FR, which climbs to the top of Bald Hill. A few yards beyond is a water fountain and a trough for horses. Just ahead is a private MMWD ranger's residence. A memorial plaque honors Clayton Stocking, an MMWD employee who lived there for 42 years (see the Stocking Trail description). An informational panel on the water supply was added here in 2014. Back at the dam, there is an outhouse.

The distance around Phoenix Lake, avoiding the few shortcuts, is 2.33 miles. The late Tam historian Fred Sandrock says the name "Phoenix" is a corruption of the William Phenix family name; they were emigrants from Great Britain who settled in what is now the lake bed sometime around 1850.

Ross Trail

Lagunitas Road, Ross, to Phoenix Dam: .66 mile

TERRAIN: Wooded hillside; parts rocky (Town of Ross, MMWD)

ELEVATION: From 80 to 200 feet; gradual, rolling

INTERSECTING TRAIL(S): None

Ross Trail is an attractive alternate to the open-to-autos road to Phoenix Lake. To enter, walk among the redwoods along the south side of Lagunitas Road past the Lagunitas Country Club, which extends the right to pass and maintains a water fountain here for "thirsty joggers." Veer left, away from the road. Measurement begins where the trail passes between a pair of posts and begins to rise. The stone entrance pillars of Natalie Coffin Greene Park are below right.

The woods here are lush with vegetation. Spring wildflowers reliably begin blooming by mid-January. Leading the way, and abundant along the trail, are milk maids and fetid adder's tongue. The latter, in the lily family, has a pair of broad, brown-spotted leaves and three-petaled, purple-striped, "ill scented" flowers. Botanist John Bigelow first described it for science from a sample collected in 1854 on Mt. Tamalpais. Blossoming later is the fragrant mint yerba buena (*Satureja douglasii*).

Ross Trail drops to near the Phoenix Lake parking lot; paths connect to it. Ross (or Windy) Hill, 763 feet high, looms above to the left. A major slide here in

1986 cut Ross Trail. A wood bridge crosses the heart of the slide.

The trail, boggy and rocky in places, runs above the park's picnic area and Ross Creek. An MMWD sign welcomes you to the watershed. Polypody ferns grow out of a rock in the middle of the trail. A fallen bay tree, its branches lying on the ground, still sends live stalks upward. As you approach Phoenix Lake you might, in winter, hear the sound of water roaring down the dam's spillway. Just before the trail's end, steps bring a path up from Ross Creek.

The trail ends at Phoenix Lake FR on the southeast edge of Phoenix Dam. An MMWD sign, "Ross," is at the intersection. An arrow also points the way left to Tucker Trail.

Scotsman James Ross was a '49er who, in 1857, bought a largely intact 8,000-acre land grant covering what came to be known as Ross Valley. He died at age fifty in 1862. The North Pacific Coast Railroad station of Sunnyside—today's Ross Post Office, restored to a railroad motif in 2000—was renamed Ross in 1882. The Town of Ross was incorporated in 1908.

▥ Shaver Grade

Phoenix Junction to Sky Oaks Road: 1.69 miles

TERRAIN: Wooded, parts deeply; lower part riparian; heavily used (MMWD)

ELEVATION: From 180 to 775 feet; steep

INTERSECTING TRAIL(S): Hidden Meadow (.5 mile), Concrete Pipeline FR (1.0 to 1.1 miles), Elliott (1.1 miles, 1.4 miles, 1.5 miles), Deer Park FR (1.1 miles), connector fire road to Bald Hill Trail (1.1 miles), Alex Forman (at top)

Shaver Grade is quite popular with travelers on the north side of Mt. Tamalpais. It is less steep than Fish Grade in going between Phoenix Lake and the upper lakes, and is a direct connection between Phoenix and the important Five Corners junction. Though Shaver's upper end is accessible by car, most users join the grade from Phoenix Lake.

Shaver Grade has a rich history. Isaac Shaver (1828–1886) came overland to California from New York in 1852. In 1864, he built a sawmill near the present Alpine Dam and graded a road to haul the wood to his lumber mill at Ross Landing (near the junction of today's College Avenue and Sir Francis Drake Boulevard). From there, shallow-draft schooners went out Corte Madera Creek. The Tamalpais section of that route was the original Shaver Grade and the now-gone Logging Trail. The mill closed in 1873. The present Shaver Grade was a section of the old county road from San Rafael to Bolinas.

Shaver was credited with building many of downtown San Rafael's earliest homes, and he owned seventy of them by 1880. Ever enterprising, he paid $50 for the redwood timbers of the original (1817) San Rafael Mission when it was razed in 1870. He was president of San Rafael's first library, and a street near today's library bears his name. Shaver reportedly drowned himself after being falsely accused of wrongdoing in a land transaction. His widow, Harriet, lived until 1941.

Shaver Grade is the fire road on the right at Phoenix Junction when your back is to Phoenix Lake; it begins only slightly uphill. The woodland beside Phoenix Creek has a timeless, pastoral feel. Hidden Meadow Trail, to nearby Hidden Meadow, branches right at a signpost. Then the uphill begins in earnest.

Arc around the big bend and gain views of Bald Hill. The grade, in an area recently shored up, then meets Concrete Pipeline FR. Left leads to Madrone Trail and Lake Lagunitas. Shaver and Concrete Pipeline run together uphill, above a tunnel for the water pipeline, for 200 yards to the key junction of Five Corners. Clockwise, the five other spokes (yes, there are six), are: Elliott Trail, Shaver Grade continuing uphill, Concrete Pipeline FR, Deer Park FR, and a connector fire road up to Bald Hill Trail.

Madrones line the way above Five Corners. Shaver again meets Elliott Trail, crossing left and right. There's a brief downhill. At a saddle, Elliott Trail meets Shaver again. A final climb leads to the Alex Forman Trail, just below paved Sky Oaks Road. Across Sky Oaks Road are both a path (labeled Dam Trail) and the auto access (also part of the old county road) to the Bon Tempe Dam parking area and Alpine Lake.

Tucker Trail

Harry Allen Trail to Eldridge Grade: 1.65 miles

TERRAIN: Deep forest; riparian (MMWD)

ELEVATION: From 300 to 800 feet; steep, upper section very steep, ends gradual

INTERSECTING TRAIL(S): Tucker Cutoff (.7 mile), Bill Williams (.7 mile)

Heavily wooded Tucker (or Camp Tucker) Trail is one of the loveliest on the mountain. In summer, it offers a cool respite from the heat and in winter, rushing creeks and waterfalls add to its attractions. The trail's proximity to Phoenix Lake enhances its popularity. The upper half is, however, steep, and after winter rains, requires some agility crossing streams.

Tucker Trail branches to the right off Harry Allen Trail at a signed intersection .2 mile up from Phoenix Lake. California buckeyes line Tucker's early yards before the trail heads into deeper woods. Bill Williams Creek can be heard, and glimpsed, rushing below.

After winding .7 mile through the forest, Tucker meets unsigned Tucker Cutoff Trail on the left. The cutoff rises ¼ mile to Windy Ridge, and is actually a much shorter access to Tucker Trail. Tucker then drops 50 yards to meet Bill

Williams Trail at a signed junction; continue left on Tucker to Eldridge Grade. Bill Williams descends via steps to the bridge below and returns to Phoenix Lake.

Veer left to the head of the canyon for the first of the trail's crossings of the three main forks of Bill Williams Creek, here, the easternmost. A bridge now replaces the former leap. The trail becomes steeper, rising to a ridge above the canyon of the creek's middle fork. At 1.1 miles is the second stream crossing, without a bridge (you're likely to wet your feet in peak rainy conditions). Continue climbing through this peaceful, isolated forest. The third and last crossing is of the creek's west fork. A sturdy, handsome bridge was added here in 2012. There's another stiff uphill to a trail sign at 1.5 miles.

This level spot is old Camp Tucker. Here, a Mr. Tucker, who logged the area in the late 1800s, apparently built and lived in a cabin. Later, the clearing housed picnic tables. During and just after heavy rain, look straight and up to see an impressive waterfall. It is, however, quite ephemeral.

Tucker's last .2 mile is fairly level. The trail finally leaves the forest canopy for its first broad views of Indian FR and beyond.

Tucker ends at a wide bend in Eldridge Grade just below Bear Wallow Spring. Phoenix Lake is 1.6 miles downhill on the grade and Lakeview FR is .4 mile uphill.

Tucker Trail appeared on the 1898 Sanborn map of Tamalpais.

◼ Worn Spring Fire Road

Phoenix Lake to top of Deer Park Trail: 2.51 miles

Terrain: Grassland; some light woodland (MMWD, private/traditional use)

Elevation: From 200 to 1,100 to 510 feet; very steep

Intersecting Trail(s): Spur of Yolanda (.1 mile), Yolanda (2.1 miles), connectors to Redwood Road and Oak Avenue (2.1 miles), Buckeye (2.2 miles, 2.5 miles), Deer Park (2.5 miles)

Note: A section of Worn Spring FR crosses private property.

Bald Hill occupies a special place for residents of Ross Valley. Baldy, as it is affectionately called, is visible from just about everywhere in the valley, and its pristine upper slopes are integral to the quality of life for the area's residents. Up close, Baldy is even lovelier, a quintessential California hill, green in winter and spring, golden in summer and fall. Worn Spring FR traverses the entire west side of Baldy. It offers a splendid trip any time of the year.

Worn Spring is the first fire road rising above Phoenix Lake when going counterclockwise from the dam, past the water fountain. The climb is unrelentingly steep all the way to the top. At the first bend to the right, in less than 100 yards, a steep spur of Yolanda Trail branches left. Soon after, views open. The whole journey is a visual treat.

In less than .4 mile, the fire road passes the covered Ross Reservoir, which dates to the 1920s and has a capacity of 1,000,000 gallons. You can often smell the chlorine added to the water. (MMWD plans to remove the aging reservoir and replace it with two new storage tanks.) Worn Spring's continuation, widened to a fire road after World War II, is to the left. Just above is a gate.

The fire road climbs even more steeply. A grove of trees, watered by Worn Spring, appears, and to the right are vistas of Baldy's treeless, upper, grassy slopes.

In .5 mile, the fire road drops slightly, the only downhill, and crosses over Worn Spring for a second time. Worn Spring, emerging from Bald Hill here in this grove of madrones, oaks, and laurels, was tapped as a water source from 1881 until the completion of Alpine Dam in 1919. It was pressed into service again during the drought of 1976–1977. A trough to the left is carved "Worn Springs." This grove offers the last shade of the climb.

The fire road rises above the tree line and the scenery is superb. You could be in the Marin of 150 years ago. (A photograph taken here by Jim Vitek showing East Peak behind trees burnt in a fire was on the cover of the first three editions of my *Tamalpais Trails* book.) Above are signs of a 1993 fire.

Where the fire road bends right, halfway up to the summit, a knoll to the left offers a stunning shot of Tamalpais. (Friends have dubbed the chert outcrop here "Barry's Bench," for they know how much I love this area.) Views to the East Bay, then of the San Francisco skyline, then of the greenbelt to the northwest open higher.

Near the summit, the fire road passes an MMWD boundary sign and enters private property. Few visitors realize that Baldy's summit is privately owned, since access has long been permitted. Most visitors continue on Worn Spring FR, so the description will continue as well. However, access cannot be guaranteed. A 1992 ballot measure to form a joint tax assessment district in San Anselmo, Ross, and Fairfax to acquire this uppermost 60-acre parcel narrowly missed achieving the necessary two-thirds majority.

The summit, 1.7 miles from the start, is reached via a broad 50-yard connector to the right. A US Geological Survey post is buried near the peak. As splendid as the views have been, those from the very top are more spectacular, as the north opens up as well. It might be windy but, in any case, enjoy the 360-degree panorama. You've earned it!

Return to Worn Spring FR and go right. Across is a second summit of Baldy. In .1 mile, there is a fork. The unnamed fire road down to the right, though long open, is not separately described as it is part of the same private parcel. It runs .8 mile to the top of Upper Road West in Ross.

Veer left to stay on Worn Spring. You are descending the north side of Bald Hill, and this stretch was once known as Bald Hill Fire Trail and Corral Trail. A ½ mile down from the summit is a fence line of a residence, the highest on Bald Hill.

Just beyond, the fire road drops to a saddle. To the left is one end of Yolanda Trail. To the right, behind a gate, is a short, broad connector on private property to Oak Avenue in San Anselmo. After a somewhat acrimonious legal fight in 1993–1994 (more than 100 hikers were sued by the new property owner), the public's right to an easement across this connector was secured. A few feet beyond, also to the right, an extremely steep and slippery path descends ¼ mile through MCP and private land to San Anselmo's Redwood Road.

The boundary between MMWD and private lands runs down the center of the fire road. There is a short uphill, then a short downhill through oak woodland. At the bottom of this saddle, Buckeye Trail goes left to bypass the next climb. The path right, and its several offshoots, all enter private property.

Worn Spring crests its final hill, then descends. There are fine views to the northeast. The fire road forks. Right leads to Sky Ranch, a former equestrian facility long owned by Robert Cary (who once also owned the summit of Bald Hill). After Cary died in 2013, the 17-acre property was listed for sale for $1.7 million and there were concerns it would be developed. In 2015, through a joint effort by the Marin Open Space Trust (MOST), the San Anselmo Open Space Committee, the Coastal Conservancy, and others, the property was purchased and added to MCP's Bald Hill Preserve. The gated access road from the top of Fairfax's Crest Road is now part of the preserve, but, at .24 miles, not separately described.

The steep downhill drops past the other end of Buckeye Trail, then the signed top of Deer Park Trail, which connects to Deer Park. A path on the right enters the forest but leaves MMWD jurisdiction and crosses private land as it descends into Fairfax. Not far beyond, Worn Spring FR comes to an abrupt, indistinct, and unmarked end. The precipitous, eroded, narrow path straight ahead plummets directly down to the Deer Park parking lot.

In 1857, James and Anne Ross (and two partners whom the couple soon bought out) purchased most of today's Ross Valley from bankrupt Benjamin Buckelew. A daughter, also named Anne, married San Franciscan George Worn. James Ross's will called for a large cash dowry for daughter Anne and her sister Rebecca (Makin), and most of the land had to be sold to pay it. Worn later recovered parts of the acreage. The Worns operated a dairy ranch, called Sunnyside, on the slopes of Bald Hill, with a ranch house on the present site of the San Francisco Theological Seminary.

Though I am reluctant to admit to favorites, going down Worn Spring FR from the top of Bald Hill to Phoenix Lake is certainly near the top of my list.

■ Yolanda Trail

Phoenix Lake to Worn Spring FR, plus spur: 2.23 miles

TERRAIN: Woodland, middle part grassy hillside with steep dropoff; horses permitted, except on spur (MMWD)

ELEVATION: 180 to 650 feet; gradual, southern part steep

INTERSECTING TRAIL(S): Hidden Meadow (1.3 miles), Bald Hill (1.3 miles), Six Points (1.3 miles)

Yolanda is among the most beautiful, and best loved, trails on Tam. Most of the year, it captures the early morning sun; in summer, the last light as well. The trail makes a semicircle around the western side of Bald Hill, with Mt. Tamalpais's summit almost constantly in view. The trail is also among Marin's richest in wildflowers. After a riot of color in spring, pink willow herbs bloom after mid-summer and California fuchsias add red through November. Yolanda's proximity to the Phoenix Lake and Deer Park trailheads further contributes to its popularity.

The trail rises from Phoenix Lake at a marked signpost just before the restored old log home when going counterclockwise around the lake. An alternate-entry spur, closer to the dam but markedly steeper, is just up Worn Spring FR from Phoenix. The latest MMWD trails plan calls for upgrading this spur.

Yolanda starts uphill through oak-madrone woodland. There is an MMWD residence and a corral in the fenced, off-limits enclosure just below, part of the old Hippolyte Dairy Ranch. The Porteous family bought 1,100 acres here in 1883, and renamed the property Porteous Ranch.

The spur from Worn Spring enters from the right, along the ridgeline, by a "No Horses" sign. In spring, this part of the trail is lined with irises. After a good climb, the bulk of the trail's total rise, you leave the trees for another special part of Yolanda.

The trail, carved onto the steep southwest slope of Bald Hill by the CCC in the 1930s, offers stunning Mt. Tam vistas—and an equally stunning drop down the hillside if you're inattentive!

Though but a mile as the crow flies from the heavily populated Ross Valley, Yolanda appears tranquil and timeless. Fifty yards into the open area, the trail passes entrances on the right to now-gone Burnt Trail. Yolanda winds its way, gently rising and dropping, around Bald Hill. There is more woodland nearing Six Points.

At five-spoked Six Points Junction, Yolanda bends to the right. This last section of Yolanda (sometimes called Yolanda North, as opposed to Yolanda South just covered) is along Baldy's north face. Except for one open stretch, it is well wooded, unlike Baldy's sun-baked south face, which does not favor trees.

The gently rising trail is every bit as peaceful as before. At a lovely Mt. Tam view knoll, a path veers left. Soon, another path goes up right. Occasionally visible down in the valley on the left is the old Deer Park School. There are muddy patches in winter, some bearing hoof marks.

Yolanda re-emerges into the open at its terminus, Worn Spring FR. Both left on the fire road, toward Deer Park, and right, to the top of Baldy, border private property. The fire road straight ahead goes to San Anselmo's Oak Avenue over a public easement granted to MCOSD.

Just left of the Oak Avenue FR here, a slippery, precipitous path drops through deep woodland (and partly on private property) to a high point on San Anselmo's Redwood Road. Its lower section is land acquired in the mid-1990s by the Town of San Anselmo and MCOSD, which manages the parcel.

The origin of the name Yolanda, attached in 1905 to the first railroad stop west of San Anselmo (the trail originally connected to the station), has eluded researchers. "Yolanda" is the Spanish name for the violet flower (*iolanthe* in the original Greek). Yolanda is also the name of a San Anselmo street near the old station.

RYAN WHITE

Yolanda Trail

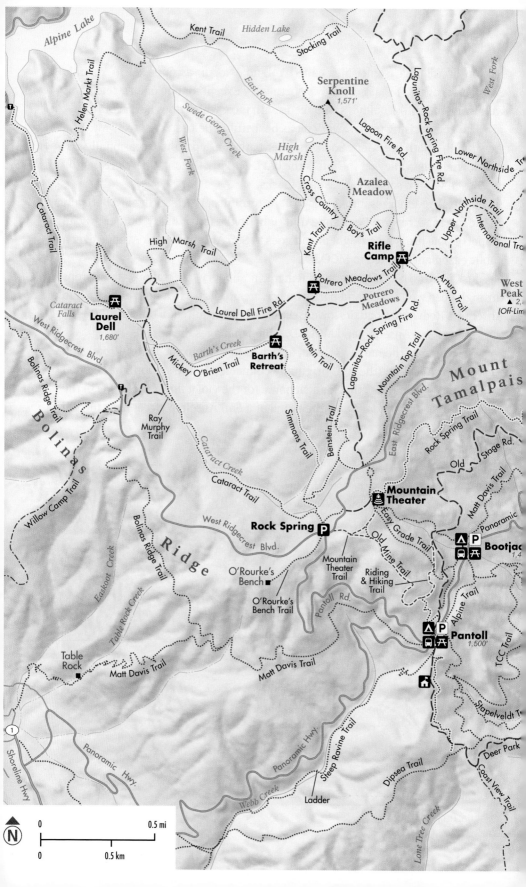

View from Old Mine Trail

TRAILHEAD ELEVEN: ROCK SPRING

Directions

Highway 101—Highway 1—Panoramic Highway—Southside (Pantoll) Road to junction with Ridgecrest Boulevard

---

When a group of hikers saw hunters with a deer carcass at Rock Spring, they were galvanized to form the Tamalpais Conservation Club (TCC) in 1912. A year later, the club held its first annual picnic/hike there. In 1917, TCC helped establish the Mt. Tamalpais Game Refuge to ban hunting on the mountain. TCC also played the lead role in the creation of Mt. Tamalpais State Park in 1928. Rock Spring remains popular for its stunning views, access to trails high on the mountain, and free parking. (The lot was paved in 1997 in preparation for a planned fee-parking program that was never implemented.)

The trailhead is at the junction of Ridgecrest Boulevard and Southside (Pantoll) Road. Gates at Pantoll and on Ridgecrest just in from Fairfax-Bolinas Road bar automobile access to Rock Spring between sunset and 9 AM. On high fire-alert days, or during rare snowfalls, vehicular access to Rock Spring may also be blocked. On Sundays from mid-May through June, Rock Spring is jammed with Mountain Play patrons. There is an outhouse by the parking area, along with picnic tables and an interpretive display board. There is, however, no water fountain; the nearest can be found at Mountain Theater. Rock Spring itself flows into a stone enclosure just down Cataract Trail.

Across Ridgecrest Boulevard from the parking lot, paths climb both view knolls flanking Southside Road. The one right (southwest) is separately described as O'Rourke's Bench Trail. Embedded atop the other knoll is Forbes Bench, honoring John Franklin Forbes. He and other hikers of the Cross Country Boys Club used to gather there, and Alice Eastwood read Sherlock Holmes installments in *Collier's Magazine*. The bench was placed by Forbes' son, John Douglas Forbes, in 1981.

Many call the area Rock Springs, but purists correctly point out that there is only one spring.

Suggested Loops from Rock Spring (elevation 1,940 feet)

1. Mountain Theater Trail (across road), .1 mile, to Old Mine Trail—right, 1.0 mile, to Old Stage Road—left and immediate left up Easy Grade, .6 mile, to Mountain Theater—left on connector, .3 mile, to start. **2.0 miles total**

2. Cataract Trail, 1.1 miles, to Mickey O'Brien Trail—right, .7 mile, to Barth's Retreat—connector fire road, .2 mile, to Laurel Dell FR—right, .2 mile, to Benstein Trail—right, 1.2 miles, to Cataract Trail—left, .1 mile, to start. **3.5 miles total**

3. Rock Spring Trail, .1 mile, to Ridgecrest Blvd.—left, .1 mile, to Rock Spring-Lagunitas FR—left, .8 mile, to Potrero Meadow—left, 1.6 miles, on Laurel Dell FR to Cataract Trail—left, 1.2 miles, to start. **3.8 miles total**

4. Cataract Trail, 1.5 miles, to High Marsh Trail—right, 2.2 miles, to Kent Trail—right up, 1.0 mile, to Potrero Camp—connector up, .1 mile, to Laurel Dell FR—across to Benstein Trail, 1.2 miles, to Simmons Trail—left up, .1 mile, to start. **6.1 miles total**

◼ Benstein Trail

Simmons Trail to Laurel Dell FR, plus spur: 1.16 miles

Terrain: Deep woodland (MMWD)

Elevation: 1,920 to 2,250 to 1,980 feet; steep

Intersecting Trail(s): Rock Spring-Lagunitas FR (.6 to .7 mile)

Benstein Trail is the most direct route from Rock Spring to Potrero Meadow. Its start was rerouted in the mid-1980s to stem erosion damage to the meadow at Rock Spring. To reach it, follow Cataract Trail 100 yards downhill from Rock Spring and veer right at the MMWD signpost, "To Benstein." In .1 mile, Benstein splits off to the right from Simmons Trail at another signpost.

Benstein climbs, with occasional help from stone and wood steps, at the edge of a Douglas-fir forest. Steve Petterle, then with MCOSD, dubbed the area right "Serpentine Swale." Beyond, the main entrance to Mountain Theater is visible. In .3 mile, at a signpost, a .1-mile spur (sometimes called Benstein Extension) to Ridgecrest Boulevard branches right. In early summer, the dried grassland here is dotted bright yellow with showy flowers of mariposa lily and blue with brodiaea.

At .4 mile, Benstein crosses Ziesche Creek. A .2-mile connector, sometimes called Ziesche Trail for Edward Ziesche, who had a cabin in the area, drops left through the woodland to Simmons Trail. Indeed, there may be more faint paths in the Benstein-Simmons region than any comparably sized area on Tam.

A bit more uphill brings Benstein across a Ziesche Creek feeder. Veer right and go up through the serpentine rock outcrop, where the trail is briefly indistinct. At .6 mile, Benstein meets and joins Rock Spring-Lagunitas FR along Tam's summit ridge. Go left, toward Rifle Camp. In 100 yards, Benstein departs from the fire road to the left at a signpost. (Yes, this can be a bit tricky.)

The trail heads into deep woodland. This is one of the best places on Tamalpais to spot the celebrated calypso orchid (*Calypso bulbosa*). The orchids grow here only beneath Douglas-firs. Look in early spring and you may be lucky enough to see hundreds. (Of course, never pick wildflowers on the mountain.)

Benstein descends, at times steeply. A giant Douglas-fir, with low branches, stands isolated in a forest clearing. One hundred yards below, a seven-trunked tanbark oak borders the trail's left edge.

Benstein enters an open serpentine outcrop. Mt. St. Helena, and even higher peaks farther north in Mendocino County, can be seen on clear days. The nearby trees, many dead or dying, are Sargent cypress. A path, which the Mt. Tamalpais History Project named for the group's founder, Lincoln Fairley, used to go left to Barth's Retreat; MMWD has done restoration work here and the area is now strictly off-limits. Benstein becomes rock-strewn, and slippery when wet.

Benstein drops to its end at Laurel Dell FR. A path has been worn in across to Potrero Picnic Area (formerly Potrero Camp). To the right is the main Potrero Meadow, and to the left is Barth's Retreat.

Henry Benstein was an inveterate mountain hiker and a regular at Potrero Camp. In 1921, he recruited his youngest son, Albert, to help build this trail as a shortcut between Rock Spring and Potrero. Originally called Potrero Camp Trail, it was renamed in Benstein's honor after he died in 1938. A miscarved trail sign, reading "Bernstein," helped trigger a lively debate over just whom the trail was named for. In 1992, I received a letter from Henry's daughter, Diane, settling the issue in favor of "Benstein."

■ Cataract Trail

Rock Spring to Alpine Lake: 2.89 miles

TERRAIN: Heavily wooded; riparian; parts rocky (MMWD)

ELEVATION: From 1,970 to 650 feet; very steep, parts extremely steep

INTERSECTING TRAIL(S): Simmons (.1 mile), Ray Murphy (1.0 mile), Mickey O'Brien (1.2 miles), Laurel Dell FR (1.2 to 1.3 miles), High Marsh (1.5 miles), Helen Markt (2.3 miles)

Cataract Trail is always listed near the top of favorite Tamalpais trails. It is lovely at any time of year but really comes into its own in winter, particularly during and after a storm. Cataract Creek, which the trail parallels, is then a torrent, cascading down waterfall after waterfall amidst deep woods. Since Cataract Trail is accessible on both ends by road, and because it is so steep and has only very strenuous loop possibilities, many use a car shuttle to cover its full length. The trail also has many (often-slippery) rock steps, and some find it safer and more enjoyable to walk uphill.

Marin Conservation Corps, in conjunction with MMWD, did significant work on Cataract Trail in 1999–2001 to make it safer and less prone to erosion. Among improvements were more than 80 new stone and wood steps, new railings at scenic lookout points, and two new bridges low on the trail. There are plans to do further work and make Cataract Trail, which is a bit dangerous for such a popular route, safer.

The trail starts directly from the gate at the Rock Spring parking lot. Below the rocks to the right is the source of Rock Spring. Cataract Creek begins its flow to Alpine Lake from the area farther to the right, called Serpentine Swale. In about 100 yards, the combined Simmons and Benstein Trails branch right. Just beyond, Rock Spring is fed, untreated, into a stone pool (right) from the storage tank (left). This pool is now choked with watercress and rushes.

A fence and sign mark the first of two Cataract Trail reroutings built by MMWD and MCC in 1991. The trail enters riparian forest, where it remains the rest of the way. At the first bridge, two Cataract feeders merge. Stay on the right bank. There is another bridge, crossing Ziesche Creek at its merger with Cataract Creek.

The trail used to follow the creek's right bank, passing through a meadow. To protect this meadow, a bridge at .4 mile takes the trail over Cataract Creek at the start of the second rerouting. A huge ancient laurel stands next to the bridge. This new section, through a forest of Douglas-firs, is a delightful addition. Azaleas dot the creek bank and maples add color in fall.

The trail briefly passes an open area that is dotted with wildflowers from February through July. Late blooming, and showiest of all, is the leopard lily

(*Lilium pardalinum*), with its large orange flowers. A path left snakes up to Ridgecrest Boulevard.

At .8 mile, another new bridge brings Cataract Trail over Cataract Creek, back to the right bank and its original routing. The trail now remains on the creek's right bank for another 1.5 miles. About ¼ mile beyond, where a faint path goes left, look carefully in the creek bed to spot an old airplane engine. On October 4, 1945, two Corsair planes flying out of Alameda on a training exercise collided at 10,000 feet. Falling debris ignited a 400-acre fire on the Simmons Trail. Both pilots parachuted out; one landed at Stinson Beach, while the second, badly injured, was found by a TCC trail worker near the Matt Davis Trail. The other engine is above Mickey O'Brien Trail.

Less than 50 yards below, the Ray Murphy Bridge and Ray Murphy Trail depart left over Cataract Creek. The 200-foot trail (not separately described) connects with Laurel Dell FR; the 1983 bridge was named for Murphy, a former MMWD chief ranger, after he died. (The airplane engine was plainly visible 20 yards upstream from this bridge until a massive Douglas-fir toppled in 1997 and blocked the view.) There is no other bridge over Cataract Creek for 1.3 miles.

The trail emerges briefly from the forest in the wonderful meadow known as Laurel Dell. At the start of the clearing, to the right, is Mickey O'Brien Trail, heading to Barth's Retreat. Formerly, Cataract Trail cut left to join Laurel Dell FR here, but that involved a creek and wet meadow crossing that was sometimes impassable after winter rains. Now Cataract Trail is routed right, onto a bridge over Barth's Creek and a new ⅛-mile section of trail.

The new section of Cataract skirts the edge of Douglas-fir woodland and meets Laurel Dell FR just past the old bathroom. This meadow once was graced with a beloved mountain dogwood tree (*Cornus nuttallii*). In his 1949 *Marin Flora*, John Thomas Howell wrote, "This, one of western America's most beautiful flowering trees, is at present known in Marin County from only a single individual on Mount Tamalpais near Laurel Dell."

Cross Laurel Dell FR to enter the dell's shaded picnic area and to continue down Cataract Trail. Laurel Dell has been a favorite hikers' resting spot for over a century (although the water fountain here has been removed).

Just below Laurel Dell, Cataract Trail encounters the first of several impressive waterfalls that accompany it the rest of the way down. Cataract meets the west end of High Marsh Trail, which winds to Kent Trail. The junction is signed and has a bench.

The trail and adjacent creek begin plunging more steeply; caution is in order, particularly when the rock steps are wet and slippery. A steel railing offers some protection when passing beside another of the falls. Look near the railing in May for the lovely blue-and-white flowers known as Chinese houses (*Collinsia heterophylla*). The redwoods and Douglas-firs beside the creek are tall, among the most impressive on the mountain. Far from any road, this is a magical stretch.

At 2.3 miles, another waterfall feeds a most appealing pool, originally blocked off to create a water source. Here, Cataract meets the signed west end of Helen Markt Trail. Helen Markt rolls nearly 2 miles without an intersection to Kent Trail. The short stretch to the next bridge is extremely steep. Countless photos have been taken from this narrow, angled bridge, with its great views down and up.

The trail continues plunging; be ever cautious. The stone steps can be particularly dangerous. (A hiker fell into the creek here during the winter of 1991–1992.) Two turnouts offer special views of the cascades.

As the trail nears the shore of Alpine Lake, two newer bridges cross previously tricky fords. The last bridge replaces one that washed out during a storm in February 2014 (stranding hikers and necessitating intervention by Marin Search and Rescue).

The trail and Cataract Creek meet Alpine Lake. This is a favorite spot for fishermen. The creek's journey is over, but the trail, now level, continues another ⅓ mile. By early February, Cataract is lined with countless fetid adder's tongue; its three-parted flower is a distinctive purplish/brown. Trillium (in late winter) and clintonia (in early summer) are two showier lily family members also common here. This broader stretch was once part of the old San Rafael-Bolinas stagecoach road.

Cataract Trail ends at Fairfax-Bolinas Road at a big bend near Mile Marker 8.09. (Many visitors start here; the few parking spots fill after winter storms.) In 2014, MMWD installed an information board and signs warning hikers that they faced a long and tough walk. Alpine Dam is a couple of hundred yards to the right.

Cataract Trail appeared on the 1898 Sanborn map. The CCC rebuilt it in the 1930s.

The northwest end of Cataract Trail is at Alpine Lake and Fairfax-Bolinas Road.

▓ Mountain Theater Trail

Rock Spring to Mountain Theater: .25 mile

TERRAIN: Grassland; horses permitted to Old Mine Trail (MTSP; part of Bay Area Ridge Trail)

ELEVATION: From 1,980 to 2,020 feet; gradual

INTERSECTING TRAIL(S): Old Mine (.1 mile)

Mountain Theater Trail starts across Ridgecrest Boulevard from the eastern side of the Rock Spring parking area, behind a white gate. There are both MTSP and Bay Area Ridge Trail signs. A second path here climbs the knoll to Forbes Bench.

The broad trail rises up the grassy hillside. In 150 yards, at a spectacular view site, Old Mine Trail branches off right. Mountain Theater Trail skirts a hill, with more excellent vistas. A path branches left to Old Mine.

The trail enters Madrone Grove (also called Sherwood Forest), a picnic area just below the amphitheater itself. "Tanbark Grove" would also be apt, as there are magnificent old tanbark oaks here as well. Beyond is Mountain Theater.

The first Mountain Play, *Abraham and Isaac*, drew 1,200 spectators in 1913. William Kent then donated the theater site to the Mountain Play Association in 1915 as a memorial to his friend and business partner Sidney Cushing. (Its modern proper name is Sidney B. Cushing Memorial Amphitheatre.) Cushing was the prime mover behind the Mt. Tamalpais Railway; he committed suicide in 1909 after suffering a stroke.

The present stone-seat amphitheater was constructed by the Civilian Conservation Corps in the 1930s based on a design by Emerson Knight. As a condition of the CCC's work, the 7-acre site was deeded to the state park. The stone blocks, weighing up to two tons, were quarried elsewhere on Tam, brought by truck, then placed in position using a cable-and-winch system. There are forty rows of seats, each 1,000 feet long. They are often filled to capacity during Mountain Play weekends in May and June.

Music Stand (Camp) Trail

Laurel Dell Fire Road to Music Camp: .28 mile

TERRAIN: Wooded; riparian (MMWD)

ELEVATION: From 2,000 to 1,820 feet; very steep, very poor condition

INTERSECTING TRAIL(S): None

Note: The trail is in very poor condition and is not indicated on the map; it is included here only because old-timers would question its omission.

In the 1950s, mountain veteran Ben Schmidt placed a music stand and some seats for his musician friends in one of the remotest parts of Tam. In the decades that followed, only hard-core Tam hikers knew the exact location of the "Music Camp," and finding it was a badge of accomplishment. Visitors left coins, Buddhist prayer flags, wind chimes, and other tokens. In 1997, MMWD, acceding to many requests, finally signed the trailhead, although the route was well below their usual standards. In 2010, MMWD removed the signpost and cleared the camp of most knick-knacks left by hikers over the years.

Music Stand Trail sets off north of Laurel Dell FR, directly opposite the broad connector to Barth's Retreat and the Simmons and Mickey O'Brien Trails. It descends over serpentine rocks and through chamise. A creek bed, which doubles as the upper end of the trail, comes into view. In a few yards, the trail branches left of the creek bed and is then clearer to follow.

The downhill, through forest, is steep. The trail follows the uppermost reaches of the West Fork of Swede George Creek, crosses to the right bank of the creek, then back to the left bank. Thirty yards from this recrossing, and ¼ mile from the start, veer left at a Douglas-fir with two trunks fused at their base. Many miss this turn (and Music Camp).

In 50 yards, in a sylvan setting, is the remnant old Music Camp, which may or may not be graced with a rusted music stand or two; diehards have been restocking the site since MMWD cleared it, and who knows what you'll find. But you may still sing or play music here; this is, after all, Music Camp.

Ben Schmidt, one of my mentors on the first edition of *Tamalpais Trails*, likely knew more about the mountain's hidden trails than any other Tamalpais veteran, and was also one of the most important trail builders. Raised on Tam in a cabin near the Tourist Club, Schmidt counted music as one of his passions—mountaineering and maps were also on the list. Olmsted named this trail for him. The trail has also been called "Frank Meraglia," for another mountain veteran who died in the mid-1970s. Music Camp Trail is yet another name.

Old Mine (Upper and Lower) Trail

Mountain Theater Trail to Coast View Trail: 1.49 miles (including a .2 mile discontinuity)

Terrain: Upper part grassland, lower part tanbark oak woodland; horses permitted above Riding & Hiking Trail (MTSP; part of Bay Area Ridge Trail)

Elevation: From 2,000 to 1,460 feet; upper half steep, lower half wheelchair-accessible

Intersecting Trail(s): Riding & Hiking (.6 mile), Old Stage Road (1.0 mile)

Note: Old Mine Trail is now divided into two halves: Upper, above Panoramic Highway, and Lower, below. They are separated by .2 mile through the Pantoll area. I'll describe them together, as a single Old Mine Trail

Old Mine Trail is one of Tam's lovelier routes, with spectacular vistas and colorful floral displays. From the Rock Spring parking area, cross Ridgecrest Boulevard, veer left, and follow Mountain Theater Trail uphill. In about 100 yards, there is a signed junction. Mountain Theater Trail continues left to the theater and Old Mine Trail branches right. To the right of the intersection, amid a grove of trees near the hilltop, is Forbes Bench.

This upper section of Old Mine, to Riding & Hiking Trail, is a hiker-equestrian segment of the Bay Area Ridge Trail. The views out over the grassland are among the finest anywhere on Tam. A path departs left toward the theater.

Old Mine crosses a serpentine outcropping. The first path to the top of the hill is currently closed for erosion control; users have worn in another just beyond. Make the short ascent for even more stunning views. On luminous winter days, the snow-capped Sierra are visible, along with Mt. Diablo, the San Francisco skyline, both towers of the Golden Gate Bridge, and the Pacific. The hill is popular as a wedding site and as a place to fly kites.

Old Mine begins dropping steeply. In April, lupines by the thousands color the grassy slopes blue; it's among the most striking floral color displays on Tam.

The trail runs beside, and then through, a woodland. Tanbark oaks are abundant. At .4 mile, a massive Douglas-fir with huge lower limbs grows along the trail's left margin. Pantoll, the trail's destination, briefly comes into view.

After some switchbacks, Old Mine meets Riding & Hiking Trail, which goes left to Easy Grade Trail and Old Stage Road. Veer right, back into the forest. Old Mine swings left and meets asphalt-covered Old Stage Road at a signed junction.

The original Old Mine Trail is now severed by Old Stage Road and Panoramic Highway. To pick up the "Lower" half of the trail, go right to Pantoll and cross Panoramic. Follow the paved maintenance road downhill from the ranger station.

Lower Old Mine Trail resumes 40 yards past the Steep Ravine Trail turnoff.

This section has been leveled and widened to provide wheelchair access to a bench at a lovely view site at its end. In compliance with the Americans with Disabilities Act, the trailhead sign gives gradient and terrain information as well as distance (.56 mile). Old Mine is also a pedestrian segment of the Bay Area Ridge Trail.

One-quarter mile into the Douglas-fir forest, signed on the right, is the old mine that gave the trail its name. The mine site was rediscovered in 1952 by MTSP ranger Jim Whitehead. The sign copies the original May 1863 filing of the "Denos Claim." Louis Denos was a pioneer Marin settler. During this time, there was a modest gold rush on Tam; more than a dozen claims were filed, but none were profitable. (Some Tam quartz outcroppings include traces of gold.)

Old Mine continues parallel to and just below Deer Park FR, the biking route from Pantoll to Coast View Trail. Old Mine then meets Deer Park FR and continues another 50 yards across it to the bench. There are sweeping Pacific, San Francisco, and East Bay views. The bench was dedicated on Veteran's Day 2010, and a sign on it starts, "Dear Veterans, Welcome Home." Deer Park FR down is the southern continuation of the Bay Area Ridge Trail.

O'Rourke's Bench Trail

Rock Spring to O'Rourke's Bench: .41 mile

TERRAIN: Grassland (MTSP)

ELEVATION: From 1,980 to 2,070 feet; gradual

INTERSECTING TRAIL(S): None

This trail leads to the stunning view knoll of O'Rourke's Bench. It sets off directly across the road from the Rock Spring parking area, up the grassy slope to the southwest. The two entries only have "No Bikes/No Parking/No Dogs" signs. A small Douglas-fir at the start is decorated during the Christmas season.

O'Rourke's Bench Trail climbs 100 yards to the top of the knoll, where there is a wind gauge. This area was added to Mt. Tamalpais State Park in 1953. The Kent family, which owned the 265-acre parcel, donated half the purchase price. A bequest from John Miller (for whom Miller Trail is named) provided additional funds.

The views are spectacular. The trail meets a serpentine outcropping, barren of plants save for an occasional poppy. Though the path left looks better, go directly over the rocks. It is evident that plants find serpentine a tough environment. Keep ever uphill.

The trail passes a laurel shielded from prevailing west winds by a huge boulder. Just beyond, it cuts through a small grove dominated by three trees: a tanbark oak, a goldcup oak, and a massive Douglas-fir with holes made by woodpeckers and filled with acorns.

The trail veers left up into an isolated stand of laurels; other paths lace the hillside. Enter to savor one of the mountain's treasures, O'Rourke's Bench. Carved from the rocks, it commands a panoramic view, even of the Sierra when standing on the bench on clear winter days. The plaque on the bench reads:

"Give Me These Hills and the Friends I Love, I Ask No Other Heaven." To Our Dad O'Rourke, in Joyous Celebration of His 76th Birthday, Feb. 25th. 1927. From the Friends to Whom He Showed This Heaven.

You'll surely want to stay a while, even if the area's notorious wind and fog are swirling. Many visitors leave flowers.

Richard Festus "Dad" O'Rourke was an impeccably dressed mountain veteran who led his wife and four daughters, and legions of others, on hikes over Tamalpais. He is credited with being a catalyst for the founding of both the Tamalpais Conservation Club and the Mountain Play Association—both of which he served as president—and was custodian (superintendent) of Muir Woods National Monument in 1921–1922. Much beloved, he was honored by this bench at his favorite resting place, which he called "Edge of the World." In Lincoln Fairley's book, *Mount Tamalpais, A History*, there is a splendid picture of O'Rourke and his wife sitting on the bench on the day of its dedication.

▉ Potrero Trail

Potrero Picnic Area to Rifle Camp: .33 mile

TERRAIN: Meadow and riparian woodland (MMWD)

ELEVATION: Around 2,000 feet; almost level

INTERSECTING TRAIL(S): None

This trail, which long had no official name, connects the two Potrero Meadows (lower and upper). It sets off east from Potrero Picnic Area (or Potrero Camp), just below Laurel Dell FR, opposite the north end of Benstein Trail. A few yards in on Potrero Trail, just over the plank bridge, is the top of Kent Trail, which descends 4 miles to near Bon Tempe Dam.

Potrero Trail passes between meadow and riparian woodland, each of which is charming. The creek, an upper branch of Swede George, remains to the left; the trail skirts its left bank.

A couple of wooded stretches yield to Upper Potrero Meadow, one of Tam's crown jewels (and inspiration for my Potrero Meadow Publishing Company). This broad expanse of grass is lovely any time of day, any time of year. Savor the short walk across its northern edge. The early yards may be somewhat boggy;

other routes across even wetter parts of the meadow are now closed. Near the end, on the left, is the site of a once well-tended garden. The military housing that stood atop the ridge south for fifty years is now gone.

Potrero Trail ends at its intersection with Rock Spring-Lagunitas FR. Rifle Camp another favored picnic site, is a few yards ahead.

▥ Rock Spring Trail

Rock Spring to Old Railroad Grade at West Point: 1.70 miles

TERRAIN: Mostly wooded, sections open, short part asphalt (MTSP, MMWD)

ELEVATION: 1,970 to 1,780 feet; gradual

INTERSECTING TRAIL(S): None

This historic trail is well graded and well wooded, and has breathtaking views. It is also popular because it connects three of the mountain's special places: Rock Spring, Mountain Theater, and West Point.

Rock Spring Trail sets off from the Rock Spring parking lot, to the right (east) at the Cataract Trail sign. The trail passes below the shaded tables. In early spring, look under the Douglas-fir trees for purple-pink calypso orchids, always a challenge and treat to find. Beneath the rocks here is the source of Rock Spring; work was done in 1933 to keep it flowing all year. In 1972, the spring's outlet was relocated to its present site, just down Cataract Trail.

In .1 mile, the trail hits Ridgecrest Boulevard directly across from the main entrance to the Sidney B. Cushing Memorial Theater (Mountain Theater). Cross the pavement and enter the theater; it is open year-round. The next section is an asphalt path. In 40 yards, at a fork, is a plaque. Placed in 1986, it honors the Civilian Conservation Corps for constructing the amphitheater fifty years earlier. Hauling, shaping, and placing the thousands of serpentine rocks (some weighing more than 2 tons) to make seats was an extraordinary undertaking.

Veer left. This approach to the upper seats of the theater, which is taken by thousands on Sunday play dates during May and June, seems oddly quiet the rest of the year.

You will pass a second plaque dated 1983. It honors three men: William Kent, who donated the theater site; Sidney Cushing, the driving force behind the Mt. Tamalpais Railway; and Alfred Pinther, who served as president of the Mountain Play Association, California Alpine Club, and Tamalpais Conservation Club.

A few yards beyond, a trail sign points the way, right, to the upper ends of the Bootjack and Easy Grade Trails. Rock Spring Trail goes straight ahead, across the top row of the amphitheater. Sit and enjoy views out to the East Bay.

The trail continues on the other (northeast) side of the theater, past a pair of drinking fountains. It immediately encounters, on the left, Pohli Rock, which commands a stunning view site. Salem Rice, the leading authority on Mt. Tamalpais's geology, dates the rock's greenstone to a sea floor lava flow some 400 million years ago.

To many who love Tamalpais, Pohli Rock is holy ground. It has long been intimately connected to the Mountain Play, for which it has been used as a prop in several productions; people also watched the play from atop it.

Most significant are the two plaques affixed to it. One reads: *I Lingered on the Hill Where We Had Played, Garnett Holme, 1873–1929.* Holme, a drama instructor at the University of California, Berkeley, was one of the prime movers behind the creation of the Mountain Play, and served as its first director. He died in 1929, after a fall on the mountain. His ashes are embedded in the rock.

The other reads: *To Austin Ramon Pohli, a Lover of This Mountain, Who Died May 20, 1913, Aged 20 Years, This Rock Is Dedicated.* Pohli was the son of Emil and Kate Pohli. Mrs. Pohli was one of the founders of the Mill Valley Outdoor Art Club and chairwoman, in 1904, of a committee fighting to save Muir Woods (then called Sequoia Canyon). Ramon Pohli was a University of California student when he met Holme, who appointed him the Mountain Play's first business manager. Pohli fell to his death while climbing near Snow Creek Falls in Yosemite just twenty days after the triumphal opening of the very first Mountain Play, the success for which he was given large credit. Pohli's ashes were scattered on the mountain. The rock was formally dedicated to him on May 17, 1914.

Just beyond, at a boundary post, the trail leaves MTSP and enters MMWD (the water district donated the acreage of Pohli Rock to the state park). A few yards past, a path, once known as Telephone Trail 2, heads off left. One hundred yards later, by a classic old MMWD sign, another path rises left. Continue through the light woodland. The downgrade is barely noticeable. A double bridge fords a rivulet, then another bridge crosses the headwaters of Rattlesnake Creek.

At .9 mile, the trail passes across a band of treeless serpentine. On the far side, look on the right for Colier Rock, a serpentine boulder commanding a great vista. It bears a patina-covered bronze plaque: *To John M. Colier, a Lover of Nature.* This is the Colier of Colier Spring and Colier Trail, and this was his favorite view spot.

A second, even more prominent, open serpentine stretch is crossed. No vegetation grows here, so the gray-green area stands out from afar. Two bridges built by Tamalpais Conservation Club in 1999 cross rivulets.

At 1.3 miles, an old signpost once marked the lower end of Eastwood Trail, which was closed by MMWD in 1993 to control erosion. In 1923, Alice Eastwood, who hiked and botanized on these slopes for decades, wrote, "The Eastwood Trail is so named because I recognized it as a short cut to the Potrero

[Meadow] from West Point and open most of the way though very steep. It was cleared by John Colier." She is honored on Tamalpais by Camp Alice Eastwood Campground.

Continue straight. You will begin to have glimpses of West Point Inn. The trail crosses Spike Buck Creek. Rock Spring Trail passes the remnant of an old stile that once kept horses off the route. In another 100 yards, the trail ends at Old Railroad Grade, here circling around West Point Inn. Nora Trail is to the right.

Rock Spring Trail was shown on the 1898 Sanborn map as West Point Trail. Since West Point was a name added to Tamalpais in 1896 during construction of the Mountain Railway, the trail seems to date to 1896–1898.

KIRKE WRENCH

The West Point Inn, at the westernmost bend of Old Railroad Grade.

■ Simmons Trail

Cataract Trail to Barth's Retreat: .95 mile

Terrain: Mixed forest and open serpentine; parts rocky (MMWD)

Elevation: 1,960 to 2,210 to 1,960 feet; very steep

Intersecting Trail(s): Benstein (.1 mile)

Simmons Trail plays a part in many loop trips from Rock Spring. It is also the direct route to two of the mountain's gems, Barth's Retreat and Music Camp. The trail offers splendid vistas as it passes over the haunting western edge of Tam's summit ridge.

To reach Simmons, follow Cataract Trail 100 yards down from the Rock Spring parking area to a signpost. Simmons, combined with Benstein Trail, branches to the right.

Simmons crosses Cataract Creek, here only a trickle. In 100 yards, Benstein departs to the right on its way to Potrero Camp. Since that is near the other end of Simmons Trail, Benstein is a natural loop partner.

Simmons veers left to follow the left bank of Ziesche Creek. Pioneer Tam hiker Edward Ziesche built a cabin here in the 1880s. The site of the cabin, which was razed around 1935, was rediscovered in 1988 by the late Phil Frank, creator of the cartoon "Farley" and an avid Tam explorer. The area is crisscrossed with faint, old paths, including an earlier routing of Simmons.

The trail crosses the creek over a bridge. Amidst a stand of introduced redwoods was the one-time Camp Norway. Two forks present themselves and soon unite. Just up the main fork, left, affixed to a dead Douglas-fir, there used to be a replica of an old Barth's Retreat sign (the original is in the Lucretia Little History Room of the Mill Valley Public Library).

The trail begins to climb, initially ascending through a forest. Ceanothus is abundant. Simmons then enters an open serpentine area. The trail is lined with chaparral shrubs. The uphill is steep and rocky, but the views ahead reward the effort.

Before the crest and the first Sargent cypress, old paths cross. The one right was once known as Perkins Pass Trail. Left, experienced hikers can meander through the serpentine maze to a pair of manmade stone structures: the Throne and (lower) the Fort.

Simmons Trail levels at its crest of just over 2,200 feet. This starkly lovely area is the western edge of the Mt. Tamalpais summit ridge. Sargent cypress are the only trees found on the serpentine substrate. John Thomas Howell's description of Sargent cypress in his *Marin Flora* may well have been inspired here: "These gray-green trees blend with the gray-green rock of the serpentine barrens to form a picturesque and memorable part of the Mount Tamalpais scene."

Look carefully at the trees and, on many, you'll see mistletoe (*Phoradendron densum*) growing off the branch tips. Mistletoe is a parasitic plant that robs the trees of nutrients; *phoradendron* comes from the Greek word for "tree-thief." This mistletoe species is also poisonous to humans.

A bonsai-looking manzanita sits in the middle of the trail, surrounded by rocks. The trail passes briefly through another forest, then opens in an area known as Buck Meadows. There is a welcome hitching post/bench from which a view of Point Reyes is framed.

Simmons continues its descent through a predominantly Douglas-fir forest. A path forks right at the trail's final bend. Left is an ancient outhouse.

Simmons ends at Barth's Retreat, where there are picnic tables and a water spigot (untreated, so now signed as non-potable). Mickey O'Brien Trail sets off from here to Laurel Dell. A bridge, dedicated to the memory of Harold Allen Atkinson (1903–1983), crosses Barth's Creek. Atkinson was an active member of the Tamalpais Conservation Club for decades; his name appears on an April 21, 1912, trail cleanup assignment list.

Barth's Retreat has been a popular picnic site for more than a century. Emil Barth, a versatile musician and music teacher, was associated with the mountain from 1886, when he arrived from Germany. He built a cabin here and named it Casa Escondida; he lived in it, part-time, until his death in 1926. His obituary in the January 1927 TCC newsletter, *California Out of Doors*, said: "No one knew the trails and unfrequented paths as he did, no one loved them more, and few have done as much as he to find beauty spots and build trails to reach them." Barth's wife donated his extensive music collection to the San Francisco Public Library in 1937.

A broad connector to Laurel Dell FR rises from Barth's Retreat. Halfway up, on the left, is a plaque to long-time MMWD patrolman Joseph Zapella: *Friend of the Hikers*. Across Laurel Dell FR from the connector's junction is the unmarked upper end of Music Stand Trail.

Simmons Trail dates from around World War I. The late Fred Sandrock of the Mt. Tamalpais History Project speculated that it may be named for Spanish-American War veteran Colonel Charles A. Simmons, who made a film promoting the virtues of California and was an early donor to the Tamalpais Conservation Club. Simmons also organized a series of "Hospitality Hikes," some of which were on Tam. He died at fifty-seven in 1931.

Bon Tempe Dam, built in 1948, created Bon Tempe Lake.

TRAILHEAD TWELVE: SKY OAKS ROAD

Directions
Highway 101—Sir Francis Drake Blvd. (exit) west, Greenbrae, to San Anselmo—
left on Center Blvd., which becomes Broadway in Fairfax—left on Bolinas Road,
1.4 miles, to Lake Lagunitas sign

Sky Oaks Road runs 1.9 miles from Fairfax-Bolinas Road to the Lake Lagunitas
parking area. It provides daytime vehicular access to three lakes—Lagunitas,
Bon Tempe, and Alpine—and a vast network of trails. A number of trails and
fire roads directly meet Sky Oaks Road between the gate by the MMWD ranger
station (.3 mile up) and the Lake Lagunitas lot: Taylor, Alex Forman, Bullfrog,
Shaver Grade, Bon Tempe Dam Trail, Bon Tempe Trail, Pumpkin Ridge, and Fish
Grade. At Redwood Cove, 1 mile from the ranger station, a ramp provides access
to Bon Tempe for wheelchair-using fishermen.

The parking area for Bon Tempe Dam and Alpine Lake is reached by the
only right turn off Sky Oaks Road, .4 mile from the upper gate. This unpaved
road, a segment of the San Rafael-Bolinas County Road, dates to the stagecoach
era of the 1870s. A path labeled Bon Tempe Dam Trail on a post at Sky Oaks
Road parallels the road on the left; it's preferable to walk when cars are kicking
up dust. There are new information panels by the outhouse, but no fountain.

The Lake Lagunitas parking lot, once known as Lagunitas Junction, is at the end of Sky Oaks Road. Adjacent are outhouses, water fountains, and creekside picnic areas with tables and grills. Facing the lake, there are four ways to access it. On the far left is a fire road signed as Lakeview, which goes up, then down to the lake (passing the driveway for the lake keeper's house). To its right, another fire road, perhaps the most-used entry, goes straight to the dam. From the picnic area, a path adjacent to the spillway meets the dam. And from the bridge over the creek, Rock Spring-Lagunitas FR rises to the lake and Bon Tempe Trail goes right.

A parking fee is charged for automobiles on Sky Oaks Road; annual passes are sold at MMWD headquarters and at the watershed/ranger office. Applications can also be downloaded online. The gate by the MMWD ranger station/office is closed nightly, as early as 5 PM in December and as late as 9 PM in June. Do not get locked in!

In 1924, the University of California contracted with Frank Howard Allen to build a summer training camp in the meadow, Sky Oaks, for engineering students. Some 300 students attended each year. During the 1930s, the Depression-era CCC had one of its two Mt. Tamalpais camps here; the other was at what is now Camp Alice Eastwood. On December 9, 1941, two days after the Japanese attack on Pearl Harbor, National Guard troops moved in, and Sky Oaks was used for military training during World War II. After the war, the university did not renew its lease. The Sky Oaks Girl Scout Camp was the next tenant, before relocating to nearby Camp Arequipa.

The entry area just past the ranger station was renovated in 2014. A road median was created, two toll machines were installed, and the parking spaces reconfigured. A shade structure—a replica of the East Peak fire lookout—was added, along with a toilet, water fountain, horse trough, and information signs.

Suggested Loops: Lake Lagunitas Parking Area (elevation 730 feet)

1. Loop of Lake Lagunitas. **1.8 miles total**

2. Loop of Bon Tempe Lake. **3.9 miles total**

3. Sky Oaks Road, .2 mile, to Fish Grade—right, .2 mile to Filter Plant Road—right, 1.0 mile to Eldridge Grade—right, 1.2 miles, to Lakeview FR—right, .8 mile, to Lake Lagunitas FR—right, .6 mile (or left, 1.2 miles), to start. **4.0 miles/4.6 miles total**

4. Bon Tempe (Shadyside) Trail, 3 miles, to Lower Berry Trail—up left, .5 mile, to Rock Spring-Lagunitas FR—up right, .5 mile, to Rocky Ridge FR—right, 1.8 miles, to Bon Tempe Dam—right on Bon Tempe (Shadyside) 1.4 miles, to start. **4.9 miles total**

5. To Lake Lagunitas FR, .1 mile—right (counterclockwise), .6 mile, to Colier Trail—up right, 1.1 miles, to Northside Trail—left, 1.6 miles, to Eldridge Grade—left down, 2.3 miles, to Lakeview FR—left, .3 mile, to Pilot Knob Trail—right, .8 mile, to connector to parking lot—right, .2 mile, to start. **7.0 miles total**

Suggested Loop: Bon Tempe Dam Parking Area (elevation 670 feet)

Cross dam, .4 mile, to Rocky Ridge FR—left up, .6 mile, to Stocking Trail—right, .6 mile, to Kent Trail—right down, 2.3 miles, to Alpine Pump FR—right, .8 mile, to dam and start. **4.7 miles total**

Suggested Loop: Sky Oaks Entry Parking Area (elevation 700 feet)

Bullfrog FR, .9 mile, to Bon Tempe Road—left up road or Dam Trail, .5 mile, to Sky Oaks Road—cross road and left, .5 mile, on Alex Forman Trail, to start. **1.9 miles total**

Alex Forman Trail

Sky Oaks Ranger Station to Lake Lagunitas parking lot: 1.78 miles

Terrain: Mostly grassland, parts wooded (MMWD)

Elevation: Around 700 to 750 feet; almost level, rolling

Intersecting Trail(s): Shaver Grade (.5 mile), Elliott (.6 mile), Pumpkin Ridge (.8 mile), Bon Tempe (1.4 miles)

Alex Forman Trail, formerly known as Sky Oaks Trail and Sky Oaks-Lagunitas Trail, is an alternative to paved Sky Oaks Road for hikers and equestrians. Horses were regularly posted as off-limits in wet winters but have been allowed since drainage improvements were made in 2002.

The trail begins at the MMWD ranger station employee parking area. Note the basketball backboard made from an old trail sign. Opposite, Taylor Trail sets off downhill to Concrete Pipeline.

Alex Forman Trail runs behind the buildings; look left and down to see a cage used to temporarily house stray dogs. It approaches Sky Oaks Road, where most visitors join, opposite the new parking area. A stone bench, facing east, is dedicated to Forman, who died in 2009: *From His Sierra Club Friends*. An inscription written by Lauren Vannet opens, "May you walk this trail with open eyes and hearts." This grassy hillside, rich with wildflowers (and poison oak!), is among the earliest places to see shooting stars. Poppies, Chinese houses, blue-and-white brodiaeas, larkspurs, creamcups, and farewell to spring are just some of the more colorful blossoms that follow.

The trail enters shade alongside a creek bed. In ½ mile, it crosses the top of Shaver Grade a few feet below the paved road. Just after is the top of Elliott Trail, which drops to lower on Shaver Grade. Continue straight.

Alex Forman Trail then meets Pumpkin Ridge Trail, an alternate route to Lake Lagunitas, along the ridge. Less than 50 yards ahead, it comes to the edge of Sky Oaks Road, where there is an alternate entry up left to Pumpkin Ridge Trail and a few parking spaces.

In this next open area are vistas of Mt. Tamalpais. A hiker/equestrian crossing, marked by white road bumps, leads to Bon Tempe (Sunnyside) Trail. Continue through baccharis shrubs and grassland.

Alex Forman Trail passes a wheelchair-accessible outhouse beneath the huge redwoods of Redwood Cove. Massive stumps suggest even larger trees in the past. The trail continues up, into woodland, as it rounds the cove. The terrain opens again.

The trail drops to and crosses Sky Oaks Road, again marked by white road bumps. A few yards past the small parking area, Bon Tempe Trail comes in from the right. The next .4 mile to the Lake Lagunitas parking area is now signed as Alex Forman Trail but is also considered part of the Bon Tempe loop, and described there.

Alex Forman, a native of New York City, won election to the MMWD Board of Directors in 2000, 2004, and 2008. Earlier, he held leadership positions with the Sierra Club. He succumbed to cancer in 2009 at age sixty-two, and Sky Oaks Trail was renamed in his honor that November.

Alpine Pump Fire Road

Bon Tempe Dam to Kent Trail: .5 mile

TERRAIN: Riparian; lightly wooded (MMWD)

ELEVATION: From 720 to 650 feet; gradual

INTERSECTING TRAIL(S): Rocky Ridge FR (.1 mile)

This fire road is the main access to Kent Trail and, therefore, to many of the treasures of Mt. Tam's north side. It sets off from Bon Tempe Dam on the opposite side from the spillway and parking area. Here also is one end of the Shadyside half of Bon Tempe Trail.

In 20 yards, Rocky Ridge FR departs to the left, beginning a long, stiff uphill. Alpine Pump FR descends toward Alpine Lake. In 1903, work started here on Tamalpais Dam but the project stalled. After MMWD was created, Alpine Dam was built instead. The foundations of Tamalpais Dam are still visible here across Alpine Lake when the water level is low.

The fire road continues to drop and meets Alpine Lake by a pump house, which dates to 1956. From here, water is pumped up to Bon Tempe Lake, then on through the treatment plant to southern Marin consumers. To the left is the signed start of Kent Trail, which winds its way to Potrero Picnic Area. A line of orange-red markers stretches across Alpine's surface to the pump. The fire road was built to provide access to the pump house, so is also called Pumphouse FR.

Note that the separate fire road descending from Alpine Dam is sometimes called "Alpine-Kent Pump."

Bon Tempe (Shadyside and Sunnyside) Trail

Around Bon Tempe Lake: 3.19 to 4.12 miles

TERRAIN: Half woodland, half grassland; riparian; .1 mile paved; horses permitted except at Pine Point (MMWD)

ELEVATION: Around 730 feet; almost level

INTERSECTING TRAIL(S), Clockwise from Bon Tempe Dam: Alex Forman (1.8 to 2.2 miles), Rock Spring-Lagunitas FR (2.5 miles), Lower Berry (2.8 miles), Alpine Pump FR (3.8 miles)

Circling Bon Tempe Lake is one of the most popular walks and runs on Mt. Tamalpais. The reason is simple: it's easy to reach, almost level, and absolutely beautiful. But determining the distance, or even just the circuit, is tricky.

First, the distance question. The shortest trail loop around the lake is 3.19 miles. That omits two of the lake's charming peninsulas, Pine Point and another, which is unnamed, just east of the dam. The Pine Point circuit adds .77 mile. The stretch near the dam adds .16 mile. So the full loop, hugging the edge of the lake, is 4.12 miles.

Now, just which is the Bon Tempe Trail? The Pease map and the newest MMWD signs divide the circle route into four trails: Sunnyside, Pine Point, Shadyside, and Alex Forman. But most visitors regard the loop as one trail. So that will be the approach here: Bon Tempe Trail is the full circuit at lake's edge. It will be described clockwise from the Bon Tempe Dam parking area.

Follow the steep dirt road up from the parking area—an upper parking lot was closed in 1991—past the outhouse and information signs. At the first junction, a new wood signpost points left for Sunnyside Trail, right for Shadyside Trail. This is the start of the loop. Veer left.

The broad road—it was most recently widened in 1997—climbs through oak woodland, then crests in open grassland. Just ahead is the first of the two choices on how to do the loop. Left, marked with a generic MMWD sign, is the .16-mile shortcut path up and over the small hill. It yields perhaps the choicest view spot on the entire loop. Or, go right on the broader route at lake's edge. You will pass an MMWD building and oaks perfect to sit under and read. The two options join as a narrow trail. This section of Bon Tempe has few trees, so catches the sun, hence the name "Sunnyside."

The next inlet is Hamburger Cove, a popular fishing spot. The area has a pastoral quality and is particularly appealing in the soft light of morning and dusk. But it can also be quite hot here in summer, and muddy in winter.

The trail circles a secluded inlet aptly called Hidden Cove. Fishermen sit on the lake's edge, waiting for a bite.

About 1 mile in, after passing through light woodland, Bon Tempe Trail is routed onto Sky Oaks Road. Go right. Across the pavement is an entry to Alex Forman Trail. Rounding the bend on the pavement, the route passes the splendid redwood tree that gives Redwood Cove its name. The outhouse and fishing ramp are wheelchair-accessible. About 75 yards beyond, a set of steps, built in 2104 to replace a formerly steep drop, brings the trail back to the lakeshore. Opposite, across the road here, new steps also connect to Alex Forman Trail.

Cross a footbridge and, 40 feet later, you will encounter a key intersection, presently unsigned. Go right to circle the Pine Point peninsula, and add .77 mile to the route. There used to be a maze of paths through Pine Point but in 2014,

MMWD restricted visitors to one designated route at lake's edge. In the 1930s, non-native pines were planted on the peninsula to provide shade. Many of the trees have died and many others have been cut. This stretch, favored by fishermen, is charming, has lovely views, and is well worth the detour.

For the shortest loop option, go left. After a short rise to a small parking area, a sign notes that the continuing route right to the Lake Lagunitas parking lot is the Alex Forman (formerly Sky Oaks) Trail. Thus, the next .4 mile is part of both Alex Forman and Bon Tempe Trails. The area immediately ahead is well wooded, but many of the trees appear stressed, and many lie fallen.

The next junction, again a few yards past a footbridge, is with a broad maintenance road (called Bon Tempe Channel) that comes in from the right. This is the exit for the Pine Point peninsula option. The maintenance road continues left to Sky Oaks Road. Veer left and go around the array of valves (the Bon Tempe Headworks) at the southernmost tip of the lake. These valves regulate the flow of water from Bon Tempe to the nearby treatment plant.

The trail meets the edge of the Lake Lagunitas parking lot. Nearby are water fountains, a lovely picnic area, and outhouses. Cross the bridge over Lagunitas Creek. The "Shadyside" of Bon Tempe Trail, 1.4 miles from here to Bon Tempe Dam, continues around the lake to the right, up a short rise.

After hugging the shore at the lake's southeast corner, Shadyside emerges into an open area as it circles a cove. The trail then re-enters forest, where it remains. On the near side of the first of Shadyside's three bridges is the foot of Lower Berry Trail, cut in 2001. It rises to the Rock Spring-Lagunitas FR. On the other side of the bridge, a sign notes that what was once lower Stocking Trail is "closed due to hazardous conditions."

The next mile is very gently rolling and peaceful, with views out over the lake. Huge Douglas-firs and redwoods tower above the trail. Many tanbark oaks here have succumbed to Sudden Oak Death Syndrome.

About ½ mile past the third bridge, the trail descends a few steps onto Bon Tempe Dam. Alpine Pump FR, on the left, leads to the base of both Rocky Ridge FR and Kent Trail.

Cross the dam to complete the loop. To the left is the eastern tip of long, thin Alpine Lake. To the right is one of the lovelier sights in the Bay Area: Mt. Tamalpais reflected in the waters of Bon Tempe Lake. At the far end is a hanging sign from construction of the dam in 1948.

Bon Tempe is an Americanized version of the Swiss-Italian surname Bautunpi. Brothers Giuseppi and Pasquale Bautunpi leased 1,180 acres here in 1868 and ran a dairy ranch. By 1874, they had 88 cows and produced 115 pounds of butter a day. The main ranch buildings, below Bon Tempe Dam, were removed in 1918 just before Alpine Lake was filled.

Bon Tempe Lake was formed by the third major dam on Lagunitas Creek, after Lagunitas and Alpine. (Five years later, Peters Dam, creating Kent Lake, became the fourth and last.) It has a capacity of 1.3 billion gallons, ten times larger than Lake Lagunitas upstream but significantly smaller than Alpine and Kent downstream. The loop trail was built largely by the Tamalpais Trail Riders just after the lake was filled.

▪ Bullfrog Fire Road

Sky Oaks Road to eastern tip of Alpine Lake: .92 mile

TERRAIN: Half grassy meadow, half riparian (MMWD)

ELEVATION: Around 680 feet; almost level

INTERSECTING TRAIL(S): Meadow Club Road (.2 mile)

Bullfrog FR is a level, off-road alternative to Sky Oaks Road in traveling between the ranger station and Alpine and Bon Tempe Lakes. Both ends of Bullfrog are reachable by car. The route will be described from the new parking lot near Sky Oaks Ranger Station, where the current signs call it "Sky Oaks Meadow Trail."

The opening half of Bullfrog had long been a barely passable, muddy bog in winter. To keep visitors dry, and to protect the flora and fauna that depend on water flow within the meadow, the Marin Conservation Corps, working for MMWD, undertook a major trail-rerouting project in 2003. Some 3,700 linear feet of the 60-year-old fire road were abandoned, 1,200 feet of new trail built, and a 180-foot boardwalk added over the wettest section.

Enter the broad, tree-bordered, arrow-straight road. Branching immediately left is the old, boggy Bullfrog route, now closed. (The new opening stretch is still often wet.) Dips have been added to improve drainage, but they require a leap after heavy rains. This meadow is rich with animal life; deer and turkeys are common, and coyotes are not unusual.

In .2 mile, just before a short rise to a fence, Bullfrog veers left. The route straight ahead is Meadow Club Road; it borders, then leads to, the private Meadow Club Golf Course.

Cross the boardwalk—frogs are all but guaranteed here—and bend right. Blue eyed grass (*Sisyrinchium bellum*) and buttercups (*Ranunculus californicus*) color the meadow in spring. Bullfrog parallels its old routing, then rejoins it.

Bullfrog swings due south and a short rise brings the fire road to an old quarry. Stone from here was taken to build Bon Tempe Dam. MMWD currently uses it as a storage area but has plans to fill and revegetate the site. Just past and across from the old quarry is the best—but still not always dry—crossing of Bon Tempe Creek. Left across the creek is Azalea Hill Trail, Alpine Lake fishing spots, and now-closed Liberty Gulch Trail.

Bullfrog continues level. This is a delightful, shaded stretch, ideal for a short nature walk. (We took our young daughters here many times.) The pond on the left is another haven for frogs, and turtles can often be spotted in the channel on the right.

Bullfrog ends at a gate adjacent to a parking lot. The eastern tip of Alpine Lake is to the right. The dirt road beyond, open to autos, is part of the historic San Rafael-Bolinas County Road, built in 1877–1878. Bon Tempe Dam is just above.

Bullfrogs, now widespread, were introduced to California in the early 1900s. They are the largest of the western frogs, up to 8 inches, with booming calls. Other native Tam frog/toad species include the western toad, the red-legged and yellow-legged frog (both endangered), and the 2-inch Pacific tree frog.

▧ Colier Trail

Lake Lagunitas to International Trail: 1.50 miles

TERRAIN: Riparian; deep woodland; parts rocky (MMWD)

ELEVATION: 790 to 2,280 feet; extremely steep

INTERSECTING TRAIL(S): Northside (1.1 miles), Lower Northside (1.1 miles)

Colier (or Colier Spring) Trail follows the Middle Fork of Lagunitas Creek up from Lake Lagunitas to Colier Spring, and continues to the saddle between West and Middle Peaks. For riparian woodland beauty, it rivals the more famous Cataract Trail, but is even steeper. Indeed, its middle part is as steep as any trail on the mountain. Those prepared to tackle it will be both challenged and rewarded.

The trail begins at a signpost beside the middle of the three bridges when circling Lake Lagunitas in either direction from the dam. Colier starts rather level beside the right bank of the Middle Fork of Lagunitas Creek, which here flows unfettered for the last time until Samuel P. Taylor State Park. Below, the creek is dammed to form Lake Lagunitas, Bon Tempe, Alpine, and Kent Lakes.

Colier crosses the creek three times in the first .3 mile. None of the crossings are marked or have bridges, so expect to rock hop after a winter rain.

The trail then becomes extremely steep, and the climb is unrelenting the rest of the way. Colier rises on the divide between two branches of the Middle Fork, then follows the western branch. Because the trail is infrequently cleared and used, it is often interrupted with fallen limbs. There is also some scrambling over rocks. The trail was rerouted in the mid-1960s, which accounts for several faint alternate routes. The steepness forces rest stops, and everyone needs them. Ramrod-straight redwoods mix with madrones and tanbark oaks. Enjoy the serenity of one of the most peaceful parts of the Bay Area.

At 1.1 miles, the trail meets Colier Spring at a five-way intersection. The spring, once known as Butterfly Spring, has long been a favorite resting spot among veteran Mt. Tam visitors. A rough-hewn bench beside a huckleberry bush offers a welcome place to sit after the tough climb. Huge redwoods, in one of the highest-in-elevation groves on Tam, tower above the site. Cool spring water poured from the pipe until the powerful winter storm of 1982 apparently shifted the stream's flow.

Northside Trail comes in from the left. It leaves to the right, split as Northside (or Upper Northside) and Lower Northside. The later-built continuation of Colier Trail continues uphill. An historic sign pointing to the five options disappeared in the early 1990s.

The trail is now above the headwaters of the Middle Fork. A shortcut path branches right; continue uphill to the left. An old TCC marker pointing the way to West Point was long fastened to a California nutmeg tree, but is now gone.

Colier ends at International Trail. Go left 100 yards to the top of International on Ridgecrest Boulevard to enjoy one of the best views on Mt. Tamalpais. Or, if you don't want the solitude broken, take International right and downhill back to Upper Northside.

The late Louise Teather, in her book *Place Names of Marin*, describes the man behind the trail and spring's name: "John Munro Colier (or Collier) was a Scot, described as a lovable and wealthy eccentric who sometimes pretended to be a tramp and went about asking for handouts. He hiked Mt. Tamalpais and worked on the trails for many years, and when he died in 1916, a marker was placed [at his favorite view site on Rock Spring Trail] in his memory." Colier was a vice-president of the Cross Country Club and a charter member of TCC. Harold Atkinson, in his unpublished "History of the Tamalpais Conservation Club," said, "[Colier] was the original conservationist. . . . He knew every shady nook and spot, every water course, every pool on Tamalpais." Besides this trail, Colier is credited with building Alice Eastwood Trail (now closed). Colier, a bachelor, left a sizable bequest to Children's Hospital in San Francisco.

▨ Concrete Pipeline Fire Road

Junction of Fairfax-Bolinas and Sky Oaks Roads to Fish Gulch Trail: 2.78 miles

TERRAIN: Redwood forest and light woodland (MMWD)

ELEVATION: Around 500 feet; almost level, one hill

INTERSECTING TRAIL(S): Taylor (.6 mile), Canyon (.7 mile), Deer Park FR (1.3 miles), broad connector to Bald Hill Trail (1.3 miles), Shaver Grade (1.3 to 1.4 miles), Elliott (1.3 miles), Madrone (2.5 miles)

Save for one hill midway and the immediate opening yards, Concrete Pipeline is level its entire length. The flat route is even longer when you include the 1.33-mile section just across the Fairfax-Bolinas Road. That northern section, also known as Pine Mountain Tunnel Road, is not described here as it is just outside this book's boundary and crosses private property (though is open to visitors). Concrete Pipeline is also popular because there is free parking at its trailhead, although the number of spaces was reduced after Fairfax-Bolinas Road was widened and repaved in 1994.

The fire road sets off from a gate opposite 700 Bolinas Road, a few yards below the base of Sky Oaks Road and the "Lake Lagunitas" sign. MMWD buildings here are part of the Jory Gatehouse, which was associated with the former Jory Ranch. Just in, road noise fades and the redwood-lined route becomes lovely and peaceful.

Concrete Pipeline does indeed follow a water pipeline (originally of concrete) that is just under the fire road's surface; sections are visible at bends in the road. The pipeline is graded downhill at a uniform 1 per 1,000 feet.

The first large redwood grove is unofficially named for Ron Symons, a Drake High School cross-country runner (and friend) who fell to his death in an accident in the Marin Headlands. Drake's home cross-country course is entirely on Concrete Pipeline.

The first intersection on the right is Taylor Trail, which goes up to Sky Oaks Road. Just beyond, Canyon Trail drops to the left. There's then a short dip and rise around a sweeping bend. Snowberries abound here in winter, and the area is particularly rich in spring wildflowers. Ahead, newer wood edging left marks the 1-mile point.

The fire road rises as it approaches the key junction of Five Corners. The pipeline itself goes under Five Corners through what is called the Porteous Tunnel; this area was once part of the Porteous Ranch. At Five Corners, Shaver Grade and Concrete Pipeline briefly combine as they descend to the right. At the next junction, .1 mile below, Shaver Grade splits off downhill to the left. Veer right.

It is then almost 1 level mile (actually, about 60 yards short) on Concrete Pipeline to the Madrone Trail intersection, which makes the route popular with runners. A sign here informs bicyclists that there is no outlet at the far end of the fire road.

At the next broad bend left over the creek, now-gone Logging Trail once crossed. The next stretch is lined with redwoods. It's a favorite haunt of deer, and I've seen bobcats here as well. Hound's tongue, common on the left margin, heralds spring with blossoms in January and, in some years, December.

The fire road passes two MMWD buildings, the historic Phoenix Gate House and pump station. Between them, Madrone Trail rises uphill on the right, to

Pumpkin Ridge Trail.

Bikes are not permitted beyond this point, as Concrete Pipeline drops and narrows to trail width. Pipeline ends at its unsigned junction with Fish Gulch Trail, which comes in from the left. The uphill continuation straight ahead, part of the original Fish Grade, is considered in this book within Fish Gulch Trail.

Concrete Pipeline FR was built in 1918 for the Alpine Dam project to bring its namesake concrete water pipeline from Alpine Lake through the Pine Mountain Tunnel to the main distribution network. (The pipeline emerges from the tunnel at the far end of the fire road section directly across Fairfax-Bolinas Road.) A second, parallel steel pipeline was added in 1926. In 2003, work began on a major pipeline upgrade, part of a voter-approved Fire Flow Master Plan, and the fire road was closed for nearly a year during construction.

■ Cross Country Boys Trail

Rock Spring-Lagunitas FR to High Marsh Trail at High Marsh: 1.01 miles

TERRAIN: Heavily wooded, part chaparral (MMWD)

ELEVATION: From 1,760 to 1,520 feet; upper part gradual, lower half very (section extremely) steep

INTERSECTING TRAIL(S): Lagoon FR (.1 mile), Azalea Meadow (.3 mile), Kent (.6 mile)

It is certainly a trek to reach Cross Country Boys Trail, this section's most distant from a road. And it was once hard to follow when you finally arrived. But in 2010, MMWD reworked lower Cross Country and added signposts at each intersection.

From the Lake Lagunitas parking lot, climb Rock Spring-Lagunitas FR for 1.8 miles. The Cross Country Boys junction is signed, to the right, and Lower Northside Trail is left. You can also reach Cross Country Boys by walking 1.6 miles down Rock Spring-Lagunitas FR from Ridgecrest Boulevard.

There are many dying shrubs and trees in the downhill opening section. Cross Country Boys goes over a footbridge with a plaque for its builder, Steven Wight of Marin's Eagle Scout Troop 101. In .1 mile, the trail crosses Lagoon FR.

Cross Country Boys heads into deep forest with towering Douglas-firs. The descent is steeper. The trail veers sharply right; in another 50 yards, a second small bridge appears and immediately after, a third, this one with hand railings.

Here Cross Country Boys meets Azalea Meadow. In May and June, fragrance from the blossoming azaleas pervades the meadow and attracts pollinating bees by the thousands. Pause to enjoy one of Tam's jewels.

The trail skirts the south side of Azalea Meadow and crosses a fourth bridge. A short rise brings the trail to its junction with Azalea Meadow Trail, which goes up left to Rifle Camp. Azalea Meadow's former continuation right, down to Willow Meadow, is clear but is not a designated trail. Cross Country Boys continues straight.

Enjoy the peaceful forest. At .6 mile, Cross Country Boys meets Kent Trail at a four-way junction by the edge of chaparral. This is the site of the old Cross Country Boys Club Camp; the trail was built to reach it. Kent goes left up to Potrero Camp and right down to High Marsh Trail.

The much steeper and more rugged continuation of Cross Country Boys Trail to High Marsh is a later addition. It plunges down into manzanita-dominated chaparral, with long vistas above and between the shrubs. Rattlesnakes have been known to nest just below the Kent junction. Be careful not to brush the sharp-pointed chaparral pea.

You will pass a splendid, isolated, twelve-trunked oak. From the tree, you can see northwest to Tomales Bay and beyond to the Point Reyes peninsula. Just below, Cross Country Boys goes through a corridor of tall manzanitas. Chinquapin trees, then madrones, become more common. A section is extremely steep, but quiet is assured.

Cross Country Boys Trail ends at High Marsh Trail—in winter, you'll first pass a small pond just above—directly across from High Marsh. The marsh is gradually receding; old-timers note how much smaller it is now than it was just a few decades ago, and it dries in summer. Still, it remains a mountain treasure. High Marsh Trail goes left to Cataract Trail, and right 200 yards to Kent Trail.

The Cross Country Boys Club was formed in 1891 as an offshoot for "fast hiking men" of the Sightseers Club, itself founded three years earlier. (Fred Sandrock cited the Tamalpais Club, founded in 1881, as the oldest hiking group on the mountain.) Only a handful of women, Alice Eastwood among them, were admitted as associate members. In *Mount Tamalpais, A History*, Lincoln Fairley reprints a delightful 1905 account of a sub-group of the club called the Hill Tribe: "[They] prowled these hills year after year . . . over the endless trails, light of pack and light of heart . . . Their sole object seemed to be the hills, and for wide views from them, and the silent places."

■ Filter Plant Road

Fish Grade to Eldridge Grade: 1.0 mile

TERRAIN: Wooded, mostly with redwoods; western half paved (MMWD)

ELEVATION: From 620 to 520 feet; western part level, eastern part gradual

INTERSECTING TRAIL(S): None

Though paved more than half of its exactly 1-mile length, Filter Plant Road is still popular, as it opens several loop options in the lakes area. To reach its western end, follow Sky Oaks Road 1.5 miles from the ranger station to the final bend right before the Lake Lagunitas parking lot. On the left side of the bend, behind a gate constructed in 1997, is the paved upper portion of Fish Grade. There are parking spaces across the road. Follow Fish Grade down ⅙ mile (a stretch that can just as easily be considered part of Filter Plant Road). Asphalt-topped Filter Plant Road splits off to the right while Fish Grade continues downhill.

The paved portion of Filter Plant Road is level. Redwoods line the way. It's rare to be on a paved road so peaceful and lovely, but be aware that vehicles do occasionally pass.

In .6 mile, the route meets the filter plant, formally the Bon Tempe Water Treatment Plant. The structures, built in 1959, are painted green to minimize their visual impact. Much of southern Marin's drinking water, some 20 million gallons a day from Bon Tempe Lake, flows through the plant. Chemicals, particularly aluminum sulfate, are introduced here to gather foreign matter into "floc" particles. The water is slowly mixed, building up the size of the floc particles until they settle out. The water is then passed through filter beds of graduated gravel, sand, and anthracite coal to remove further impurities. Lime, to reduce corrosion, and chlorine, to kill bacteria, are also added. (The district's other treatment plant, built in 1962 and somewhat larger, is in the San Geronimo Valley.)

Veer left, then right around the huge tank to continue. A wastewater recovery pond is to the left. There is a rare perspective down to Phoenix Lake. A steep service road heads uphill as the pavement gives way to dirt.

A pleasant, gradual, tree-lined descent brings Filter Plant Road to its end at Eldridge Grade. To the right, the grade rises to the top of Tam, to the left it drops to Phoenix Junction. In 1992, a water fountain, one of the very few on Tamalpais away from a parking area, was installed at this intersection.

Some maps and water district personnel call this road the Southern Marin Line, of which it is indeed a part. But since there is a sizable gap in Southern Marin Line across Bill Williams Gulch to the east, I reserve that designation only for the section between Kentfield's Crown Road and Larkspur's Sunrise Lane. Filter Plant Road is a common name among many long-time users.

■ Kent Trail

From Alpine Lake to Potrero Camp: 3.85 miles

TERRAIN: Varied; deep woodland, chaparral, riparian (MMWD)

ELEVATION: From 650 to 1,980 feet; steep, parts very steep

INTERSECTING TRAIL(S): Helen Markt (1.5 miles), Stocking (2.3 miles), connector to Serpentine Point (2.7 miles), High Marsh (2.9 miles), Cross Country Boys (3.5 miles), Potrero (3.9 miles)

Few Tam trails provide a better wilderness experience than Kent Trail. Throughout its length, from its early segment beside Alpine Lake to its middle section amidst one of the mountain's deepest forests, through its upper reaches with sweeping northern vistas, Kent Trail offers solitude, variety, and beauty.

Kent Trail begins from the shore of Alpine Lake, at the base of the fire road down from Bon Tempe Dam. The trail sets off just to the left of the pump station. An MMWD sign indicates that it is 4.2 miles to Potrero Meadow. A line of buoyant orange/red balls stretches across Alpine Lake here, marking the pipeline to a mid-lake pump.

Within 50 yards, the first of several narrow paths, some former logging skid rows, comes in from the left. An old pipeline, abandoned in 1956, runs along the route for some 2 miles.

The trail arcs around Alpine Lake coves. At the first, and later at others, are masses of azaleas, in flower in May and June. Huge Douglas-firs line the shore. The site of Kent Cabin, which was used by the Kent family for fishing retreats, is now under Alpine Lake. When the water level drops sufficiently in summer, Cheda Island emerges. It is named for Virgilio Cheda, an MMWD board director at the time of the building of Alpine Dam. The island was more prominent before Alpine Dam was raised in 1940, which deepened the lake.

The rolling trail crosses several streams, some requiring a bit of rock hopping to cross in winter. The biggest crossing is of Van Wyck Creek, at 1.1 miles. A bridge was finally added here in 1994.

Kent then encounters a short, steep uphill. Huckleberry is abundant over the next mile. The trunk of a huge Douglas-fir bends toward the trail, then straightens upward. Just beyond, on the right, is an even more impressive Douglas-fir, one of the most massive on Tam. Its lowest branch alone is bigger than many sizable trees. Older trees still carry blackened scars from the big 1945 fire that swept the north side of Tam. Ahead, the trail has been rerouted up and over a slide. A bridge here is dedicated to Jerald P. Hymanson, the former owner of Fairfax Hardware, who died in 2011 at age eighty-five.

Less than .2 mile later, look for the Helen Markt Trail post. Straight ahead, Helen Markt winds 1.75 miles to Cataract Trail. Kent Trail bends left to begin a long climb to Potrero Meadow.

The lowest part of the climb has been repaired and widened, but the pipeline embedded in the trail is still clearly visible. Huckleberry lines and narrows the way; their small, edible, tasty black berries ripen in August.

After .3 mile of uphill, you begin to hear the waters of the East Fork of Swede George Creek. The old pipeline is carried around a bend by a trestle. On the opposite bank, an immense landslide from 1982 still leaves an unusual scene of massive disturbance. It was here that a concrete rubble diversion dam was built on the East Fork and the 6-inch steel pipeline was run toward new Lake Lagunitas in 1888. Swede George Creek water was an important part of Marin's supply, particularly before Alpine Dam was completed in 1919. Swede George was a local woodcutter who died in 1875.

Just higher on Kent Trail, also on the right, is the standing water of Foul Pool. Then the trail enters a magnificent redwood grove, one of the loveliest and quietest spots on Tam. Younger redwoods circle the fallen "mother" trees from which they sprouted. Spend some time here and let the solitude work its wonders.

After about a mile of uphill from Alpine Lake, Kent Trail meets Stocking Trail at an intersection that was formerly tricky but is now well signed. Kent veers off right uphill and Stocking goes east (left) to Hidden Lake, which is less than 100 yards away, and on to Rocky Ridge FR.

The climbing gets even steeper, but later, wood steps help reduce the strain. In .4 mile from Stocking, just after leaving the tree canopy, a path branches left but quickly deadends. An important fork comes 100 yards later, at the rock crest. To the left is a short connector to the vista point of Serpentine Point (or Knoll) and to routes back to Bon Tempe and Lagunitas Lakes. Kent veers right. After a descent, Kent crosses the former Willow Meadow Trail. To the left is enchanting Willow Meadow itself.

Fifteen yards later, Kent Trail crosses the East Fork of Swede George Creek, which flows all year here, over a bridge. One hundred yards on is a formerly four-way intersection. MMWD added a signpost here in 1993, and newer ones since, but the area is still dubbed "the Bermuda Triangle," an acknowledgment of all the hikers who have gotten lost around here. To the left is the now-closed lower section of Azalea Meadow Trail. Kent continues straight, to Potrero Meadow. To the right is High Marsh Trail, with High Marsh itself .1 mile away.

After another .6 mile of steep uphill, Kent crosses Cross Country Boys Trail, within the forest canopy but with chaparral just yards away. Cross Country Boys goes left to Azalea Meadow and Rock Spring-Lagunitas FR and drops right to High Marsh.

Kent enters the chaparral. There are views north and west, including of

Tomales Bay, the Pacific, and the Point Reyes peninsula. After some stone steps, Kent Trail crests at just over 2,000 feet in elevation. The trail drops a bit as it returns to woodland.

Shortly thereafter, Kent ends at Potrero Camp (now Potrero Meadow Picnic Area), at the edge of lower Potrero Meadow. Tables, an old outhouse, a line of azaleas, the meadow, and choice of sun or shade make this a favorite picnic spot. The larger upper Potrero Meadow is .3 mile to the left via Potrero Trail. Just to the right, over the small bridge, a path known to some as Swede George Trail descends into the woods. A 100-yard connector fire road and path rise to Laurel Dell FR by Benstein Trail.

No family name is more closely associated with Mt. Tamalpais than Kent. See the chapter headed "The People of Mt. Tam" for a summary of contributions of William Kent and the Kent family.

The often-realigned Kent Trail appeared on the 1898 Sanborn map.

▥ Lagoon Fire Road

Rock Spring-Lagunitas FR to Serpentine Knoll: .64 mile

TERRAIN: Mostly chaparral (MMWD)

ELEVATION: From 1,860 to 1,560 feet; steep

INTERSECTING TRAIL(S): Cross Country Boys (.1 mile), connector to Kent Trail (.6 mile).

Note: MMWD's 2004 Road and Trail Management Plan recommends closure of this fire road; the erosive gully down its center is causing it to deteriorate and it is being narrowed by encroaching vegetation.

Lagoon FR was carved by the CCC in the 1930s as one of several broad fire-protection breaks running down Tamalpais. It ended up playing a key role as a supply route in the battle against the huge fire of 1945.

Because Lagoon FR's upper end is easier to locate than its lower end, and is barely farther from a trailhead, the route will be described downhill. In ascending Rock Spring-Lagunitas FR from Lake Lagunitas, Lagoon is the second of two fire roads that drop right (Rocky Ridge FR is the first). Lagoon's upper end, 1.9 miles and nearly 1,300 feet in elevation above the lake, is well signed. (When this book went to press, a sign still directed hikers "To Upper Berry Trail, 100 yards," although Upper Berry is now closed.) A second sign just below notes that the road is not a through route for cyclists.

Lagoon descends through woodland. In wet winters, you may hear the East Fork of Swede George Creek roaring below left. At 100 yards down is the now invisible Upper Berry Trail crossing. In another 60 yards, Cross Country Boys Trail goes left and right.

The fire road leaves the woods for views above the chaparral, although these vistas are disappearing as the trees grow. Its surface is distinctive: iron-rich red clays mingle with blue-green serpentine. The prominent large outcropping of Serpentine Knoll (or Point), the fire road's destination, is visible. In the 1980s, several pig traps were placed beside Lagoon to combat the feral pig population; the eradication program was successful and the traps are now gone.

Lagoon narrows, then widens, a pattern repeated on the descent. It leaves the forest canopy and moves into the serpentine. Uphill, about 100 yards later, is a signpost, "Serpentine Knoll." Views are outstanding from this landmark. At the crest, a short but important signed connector to Kent Trail departs left. The continuation over the knoll onto the former Lagoon Extension Trail to Rocky Ridge FR is no longer maintained.

There is some debate over which "lagoon" the fire road's name refers to. Some think it is Hidden Lake, as there once were plans to extend the fire road there. Others feel it refers to the seasonally wet area by the fire road just south of Cross Country Boys Trail.

■ Lake Lagunitas (Loop) Fire Road

Around Lake Lagunitas: 1.58 miles

TERRAIN: Riparian, tanbark oak-madrone woodland; heavily used (MMWD)

ELEVATION: Around 800 feet; almost level

INTERSECTING TRAIL(S), clockwise from east end of dam: Connector road to parking area (.1 mile), Lakeview FR (.5 mile), Colier (1.0 mile), Rock Spring-Lagunitas FR (1.4 miles)

Note: While there are historical reasons to view the loop around Lake Lagunitas as three separate roads—Lakeview, South Shore, and Rock Spring-Lagunitas—these three blend seamlessly together, and most users feel they are on a single route.

Circling Lake Lagunitas is one of the most delightful short walks the mountain has to offer, and is a favorite among families with young children. There are four approaches from the parking lot. Perhaps the most used borders the left (east) edge of the picnic area, so that will be the starting point for the loop.

Climb the 150-yard broad connector road. It passes an old building now used as the MMWD sign shop just before meeting Lagunitas Dam. This is a lovely spot, with Mt. Tamalpais both towering above the lake and reflected in the water. In 2014, an informational panel, "Your Drinking Water," was installed here.

Go left up the stone steps. Just above is the private residence of MMWD's lake keeper. In 1877, the first telephone line in Marin County was laid to the then-new lake keeper's residence. (The original house burned to the ground in

1925.) To the right is a path down to one of several benches dotting the lake's shore. In .1 mile, a broad connector (MMWD considers it to be part of Lakeview Road) comes in on the left. It rises to the start of Pilot Knob Trail, then drops back to the parking area.

The circuit passes paths right to peninsulas that offer some of the choicest, most idyllic benches and grassy resting sites in all the Bay Area. Beyond, the grassy face of Pilot Knob rises above.

At .5 mile is a fork. Lakeview FR goes straight to Eldridge Grade and Lake Lagunitas FR veers right to begin the section known as South Shore Road. The route crosses the East Fork of Lagunitas Creek over a bridge. The three forks of Lagunitas Creek, each crossed on the loop, were impounded to create Lake Lagunitas.

There is a picturesque view across the lake. The loop's halfway mark comes at the end of the straightaway, where the fire road bends left.

Just before the next bridge, over the Middle Fork, signed Colier Trail sets off on an extremely steep climb to Colier Spring and Ridgecrest Boulevard.

After the third bridge (across West Fork), the fire road passes a pump station sitting on a pier over the lake. From here, water was pumped all the way up to the former military base atop West Peak. Shortly past, Rock Spring-Lagunitas FR departs sharply left on its long uphill to Potrero Meadow and Ridgecrest Boulevard.

After a couple of bends, there is another fork. Rock Spring-Lagunitas FR continues straight down to the parking lot and the loop goes right over Lagunitas Dam. A plaque on the near end acknowledges the role of the San Francisco Foundation, which then administered the multi-billion dollar bequest of the late Beryl Buck to the citizens of Marin County, in financing restoration work after the storm of January 1982. Check the log booms here for turtles sunning themselves. (MMWD has been actively removing non-native turtle species, many dumped by people.)

After heavy winter rains, the spillway may roar with overflow water rushing down to Bon Tempe Lake. Complete the loop—it is 1.58 miles (I measured it with a wheel, twice!)—by crossing the dam.

Lake Lagunitas (*lagunitas* is Spanish for "little lakes") is the oldest and highest in elevation of the five man-made reservoirs on the north side of Mt. Tamalpais. It is in one of the wettest areas of Marin; more than 90 inches of rain fell in the 1982–1983 and 1997–1998 seasons. The dam creating the lake was completed in 1873, constructed largely by Chinese laborers working for William Tell Coleman's fledgling Marin County Water Company. Water initially went to Coleman's subdivision (today's Dominican area) in San Rafael and to San Quentin prison. The road around the lake followed two years later.

In 1988, a program was begun to make the lake, long a fishing oasis—Coleman released 20,000 trout into it as early as 1875, and remnants of a 1930s hatchery are evident below the spillway—self-sustaining for trout.

■ Lakeview Fire Road

Lake Lagunitas FR to Eldridge Grade: .78 mile

TERRAIN: Lightly wooded (MMWD)

ELEVATION: From 800 to 980 feet; lower part almost level, upper part steep

INTERSECTING TRAIL(S): Pilot Knob (.5 mile)

Lakeview Fire Road is well used as a connection between Lake Lagunitas and Eldridge Grade. It may properly be regarded as starting at the Lake Lagunitas parking lot—as the MMWD sign indicates—rising and dropping to the lake's east shore. Here, Lakeview will be considered as starting from its junction with Lake Lagunitas Loop FR ½ mile from the dam when traveling clockwise. Lakeview continues straight while Lake Lagunitas FR loops right.

The almost-treeless southern face of 1,187-foot Pilot Knob towers above on the left. (In 2014, MMWD barred all off-trail travel on this face of Pilot Knob.) A meadow opens on the right. Lakeview then enters an open area formerly dominated by Coulter pines. Coulters, which have the heaviest cones—weighing up to 5 pounds—of any pine tree in the world, were originally planted here in the 1930s. They are native to California (the nearest natural stand is on Mt. Diablo), but not to Mt. Tamalpais, so MMWD began cutting them in 1987 after they showed signs of disease.

Lakeview bends right and begins climbing steeply. At the bend, Pilot Knob Trail, which climbs the knob's northern flank and accesses the summit, departs left at a signed junction. It offers a loop option.

The fire road enters madrone woodland. Lakeview continues gaining elevation until its end at Eldridge Grade. Left on Eldridge is a descent to Phoenix Lake, right, a climb toward East Peak.

Lakeview FR first appears as a fire trail on the 1925 Northwestern Pacific Railroad map. Trees now block the "lake view" (as on the completely separate Lakeview Trail higher on Tamalpais).

Lower Berry Trail

Bon Tempe Trail to Rock Spring-Lagunitas FR: .47 mile

TERRAIN: Oak-madrone woodland; horses permitted (MMWD)

ELEVATION: From 730 to 980 feet; steep

INTERSECTING TRAIL(S): None

The historical Berry Trail was split by the construction of Rock Spring-Lagunitas FR in the mid-1930s. The lower part became Lower Berry Trail, and the top part, Upper Berry Trail. The middle section, which ran just above Rock Spring-Lagunitas FR, fell into disuse after water pipelines were laid over it to the US Air Force station atop West Peak; this section is now gone. After MMWD closed Upper Berry Trail in 2010, Lower Berry has been known simply as Berry Trail.

Lower Berry rises from Bon Tempe (Shadyside) Trail at the southern tip of Bon Tempe Lake. When circling Bon Tempe clockwise from the Lake Lagunitas parking area, look for the signed trailhead at the near end of the first bridge, past two now-closed former entry points. Lower Berry entry was rerouted in 2001 to ease erosion problems. The entire route is now more gradual than before, some 100 yards longer, and entirely within woodland.

Immediately, the trail enters a quiet, most appealing forest of madrones, maples, laurels, oaks, and tanbarks. Native bunchgrasses still flourish here. Some 200 yards up, the trail briefly passes through a clearing. Look back to see Bon Tempe Lake, White Hill, and Big Rock Ridge. Lower Berry ends when it hits Rock Spring-Lagunitas FR at a signed junction.

Berry Trail, said to have been originally a Miwok path, was "rediscovered" by mountain veteran S. Lucien Berry around the turn of the century. Berry and his friend, Emil Barth, then worked on it. Berry's ashes were scattered along the trail by his widow, son, and father, accompanied by Alice Eastwood and John Forbes. Old Freese maps carried the words "no berries," to forewarn those seeking edibles.

Madrone Trail

Pumpkin Ridge Trail to Concrete Pipeline FR: .92 mile

TERRAIN: Madrone woodland; horses permitted, subject to winter closures (MMWD)

ELEVATION: From 850 to 500 feet; gradual

INTERSECTING TRAIL(S): None

Madrone Trail is perfectly named. For most of its length, it passes through a light-dappled woodland of madrones. Madrone (actually, the Pacific madrone) is a characteristic tree on much of Tamalpais—John Thomas Howell features one on the frontispiece of his *Marin Flora*—but here, north of Bon Tempe and Lagunitas Lakes, they really hold forth. Willis Jepson, who wrote the 1909 classic *A Flora of California*, famously said of madrone, "A tree than which none other in the western woods is more marked by sylvan beauty." Madrone's most distinctive feature is its peeling bark, thought to be a defense against insects. Underlying the bark is a smooth, cool, terra-cotta-colored wood. Leaves are thick and leathery, green above, grayer below. Orange-red fruits appear in fall.

To reach Madrone Trail, climb Pumpkin Ridge Trail .4 mile from the end closer to the Lake Lagunitas parking area. The Madrone Trail intersection is well signed on the ridge.

In the upper reaches of Madrone Trail, redwoods and Douglas-firs prevail. The madrones come into their own .2 mile down, and are the stars the rest of the descent. Their exposed wood feels cool to the touch even on hot summer days. Visitors are invariably enchanted by this woodland. Openings offer views of Bald Hill left, then of Mt. Tam's summit.

Two-thirds of a mile down, Madrone enters an area reworked in 2007 for erosion control. Now, seventeen switchbacks wind Madrone back and forth over a ¼-mile course. Some may find the going a bit tedious, but here, as is so often the case, it is the journey, rather than the destination, that is most rewarding.

Madrone Trail ends at Concrete Pipeline FR near an old sign. Across, left and right, are a pair of water district buildings and the Phoenix gate house and pump station. Shaver Grade is 1 mile to the left, Fish Gulch Trail less than .2 mile to the right.

▨ Meadow Club Road

Bullfrog Road to the Meadow Club: .67 mile

TERRAIN: Grassland (MMWD, bordering private property)

ELEVATION: Around 700 feet; level, with slight rolls

INTERSECTING TRAIL(S): None

There are no trail signs at either end of Meadow Club Road, and the route was not named on older hiking maps, if it appeared at all. It is, however, being increasingly used, particularly by bikers connecting with the Pine Mountain area via Fairfax-Bolinas Road.

Meadow Club Road begins at the big bend left on Bullfrog Road, .2 mile in from the Sky Oaks Meadow parking lot. Bullfrog veers left, Meadow Club Road goes straight, between a pair of oaks. Just in, an MMWD sign listing cycling rules faces riders coming the other way.

The route is flat, then gently rolls. Oaks dot the way. At 300 yards is the first of several white posts marking out-of-bounds for golfers. A golf cart path is just left. The course is among the loveliest anywhere, including tee shots (such as for the fourth hole, which is passed) with dead-on views of Mt. Tamalpais.

In .5 mile, a path goes right, up to the ridge and the Scott Water Tank. Private homes are just over the ridge. At .6 mile, a chain-link fence borders the rest of the way. At its start is a Monterey pine, a type of tree planted on much of the golf course. (The course was originally treeless.)

Continue past the new clubhouse to a gate, which will be considered the end of Meadow Club Road here. It actually goes another 90 yards to the club's paved driveway, where there is a water fountain. Beyond is the parking lot of the private Meadow Club.

On February 24, 1926, MMWD signed an agreement with the newly formed Meadow Club of Tamalpais—Realtor Frank Howard Allen was the club's signer—paving the way for a golf course. The club purchased 7 acres from the district, upon which they built their original clubhouse and some cottages. Alister MacKenzie, the renowned British golf course architect, laid out eighteeen holes on land leased from the district. It was MacKenzie's first United States assignment. (Cypress Point on the Monterey peninsula and, with Bobby Jones, the Augusta National course used in the Masters Golf Tournament followed.) Over the years, there was criticism of the club's lease, which included low annual payments and favorable water rates. In 1976–1977, MMWD deeded the 162-acre golf course to Meadow Club in exchange for some 2,200 acres of watershed above Kent Lake that had been a private hunting preserve.

◼ Pilot Knob Trail

Lake Lagunitas to Lakeview FR: .81 mile

TERRAIN: Madrone woodland (MMWD)

ELEVATION: From 850 to 1,000 to 900 feet; gradual

INTERSECTING TRAIL(S): None

Pilot Knob is a prominent 1,187-foot hill (1,217 feet on some maps) on Lake Lagunitas's northeast shore. The knob's distinctive summit, where its grassy south slope meets the tree-covered north face in a sharp line, is visible from much of Tam and the Ross Valley. Pilot Knob Trail goes near the hill's summit, and a side path leads to the very top. The trail also passes Marin's largest madrone tree.

Two fire roads rise from the old, closed outhouse just above the Lake Lagunitas parking lot. The one skirting the picnic area goes to Lagunitas Dam. Take the other, signed as Lakeview, uphill .2 mile to its crest. Straight ahead, signed, is the start of Pilot Knob Trail.

The early part of the trail passes through both open and lightly wooded stretches. In the clearings are great views of Tam's summit.

In around ¹/₃ mile, in a cleared area to the left, lies a massive old madrone. When it stood, it took the outstretched arms of six people to circle its trunk. Like many other Tam madrones that had their sunlight blocked by redwoods and Douglas-firs, this tree showed signs of stress, and MMWD personnel gave it special care, trying to save it. But it finally fell during a storm in the winter of 2004–2005. Almost miraculously, there is still life in the downed giant, which can be seen in a branch with fresh leaves rising upward. (Window Trail, shown on old Freese maps leading to the tree from Sky Oaks Road, is long gone.)

Pilot Knob Trail continues climbing through mixed woodland. At the route's highest point, ½ mile from the start and before a steady drop down, a steep path goes right. It leads to the top of Pilot Knob itself. Be sure to make this extra 150-yard climb. The open summit is special, a great place to pass a few minutes or a few hours. Lake Lagunitas glistens below, Tam towers above. Pilot Knob's south slope is largely treeless; it receives direct sun and is too dry to support the trees so abundant on the north side. In 2014, MMWD posted a sign that the area right is closed. A plaque honors Teresa Wootton, an old hiking friend who succumbed to cancer.

Return to Pilot Knob Trail and go right. The trail descends through the forest. You'll see a prominent, massive, double-trunked redwood, known as "Supertree." Madrones, however, remain transcendent.

Pilot Knob Trail ends at a signed junction with Lakeview FR. To the right is Lake Lagunitas and to the left, uphill, is Eldridge Grade.

The trail was built in 1955 by the Tamalpais Trail Riders. They originally named it Doris Schmiedell Trail, for one of the equestrian group's co-founders, and MMWD formally recognized the name in 1975. The trail has since been closed to horses, and MMWD maps now show the name "Pilot Knob." Schmiedell was descended on her mother's side from a Donner Party survivor and, on her father's side, from a founder of the San Francisco Stock Exchange. She died in 1993 at age ninety-three. Pilot Knob itself is said to have been named for a similar hill on the New York-Vermont border.

Pumpkin Ridge Trail

Between Sky Oaks Road: .72 mile

TERRAIN: Madrone woodland; horses permitted (MMWD)

ELEVATION: From 730 to 900 to 800 feet; steep

INTERSECTING TRAIL(S): Madrone (.4 mile)

This trail runs atop the madrone-lined crest of Pumpkin Ridge. With its lovely views of Bon Tempe Lake and the mountain, some choice rest sites, and ease of access, Pumpkin Ridge Trail makes for pleasant hiking.

Pumpkin Ridge Trail starts and ends on Sky Oaks Road; I'll describe it from the easier-to-locate trailhead atop Fish Grade. When approaching Lake Lagunitas, Sky Oaks Road makes a final bend right to the parking area. Pumpkin Ridge Trail starts at this bend, across the road from a small parking area.

The trail climbs the grassy hill. Steps made from railroad ties were added to this opening section in 1989. At their top, affixed to a rock left in the second grassland pitch, is a plaque. It reads: *Bruce Stanton Waybur 1916–1960, Who Loved the Hills, the Creatures and Humankind.* Waybur, a University of California graduate (1937) and Rhodes Scholar, died of cancer.

The trail reaches a crest under a stately old madrone tree. Towering redwoods are now blocking its sunlight. At .4 mile, at a signed intersection, Madrone Trail begins its descent to the right.

Pumpkin Ridge Trail continues, fairly level, along the spine of Pumpkin Ridge. A few redwoods break the near-monopoly of madrones. Irises are so abundant here in spring that long-time mountain hike leader and historian Nancy Skinner calls the route "Iris Trail."

You are likely to see or hear deer. The mountain's natives, black-tailed deer, are a subspecies of mule deer. They browse on shrubs, twigs, grass, and flowers, generally in morning and evening. Mating season is in the fall. Males then shed their antlers, soon to begin growing a new set. In early spring, the pregnant does find a secluded site to bear usually two fawns. Seeing the spotted, frisky fawns is always a treat.

In .5 mile, the trail passes an open grassy slope, a choice picnic spot. Here, it forks. The option right, now designated as the actual trail, is the slightly longer of the two, staying in woodland a bit further before dropping to Alex Forman Trail about 50 yards north of the other path.

Pumpkin Ridge Trail descends under an eerie canopy of dead tanbark oaks. It then meets Alex Forman (formerly Sky Oaks-Lagunitas) Trail a few feet from Sky Oaks Road, and ends. A small parking turnout and MMWD "Dogs on leash" and "No bikes" signs mark the junction.

Late MMWD employee and trail-builder Jim Vitek named the trail and ridge for his wife Dorris, a veteran mountain equestrienne whom he fondly called "Punkin'." A misspelling on a map led to "pumpkin." An earlier name was Nebraska Ridge. The trail covers an old district road across the ridgeline.

■ Rock Spring-Lagunitas Fire Road

Lake Lagunitas Parking Area to Ridgecrest Boulevard: 3.39 miles

TERRAIN: Half wooded, half chaparral (MMWD)

ELEVATION: From 730 to 2,080 feet; gradual, lower 1.5 miles very steep

INTERSECTING TRAIL(s): Lake Lagunitas Loop FR (.2 to .3 mile), Lower Berry (.7 mile), Rocky Ridge FR (1.2 miles), Lower Northside (1.8 miles), Cross Country Boys (1.8 miles), Lagoon FR (1.9 miles), Azalea Meadow (2.3 miles), Arturo (2.3 miles), Northside (2.3 miles), Potrero (2.3 miles), Laurel Dell FR (2.6 miles), Benstein (2.9 to 3.0 miles), Mountain Top (3.4 miles)

Rock Spring-Lagunitas FR (or Lagunitas-Rock Spring FR) plays a role in most trips high onto the mountain from the lakes. The fire road has fifteen intersections with thirteen northside trails and fire roads. It is also one of the few routes that crosses Tamalpais's summit ridge, thereby connecting the north and south faces of the mountain. Many hardy hikers use it to walk to Mountain Theater from Lake Lagunitas on play dates. Though both ends of the fireroad are accessible by car, it is described uphill because the Lake Lagunitas trailhead is the more popular starting point.

The fire road begins from the far right side (as you drive in) of the Lake Lagunitas parking area, across the bridge over Lagunitas Creek. At the start, to the right, is Bon Tempe (Shadyside) Trail. Rock Spring-Lagunitas FR rises left, beside Lagunitas Creek. Here is a reminder of how lovely the creek, now dammed to form Lagunitas, Bon Tempe, Alpine, and Kent Lakes, once was.

At the crest of this first hill is Lake Lagunitas, with the dam to the left. Look carefully at the row of logs in the water and you might see western pond turtles warming themselves in the sunshine. Rock Spring-Lagunitas FR runs together with the loop around the lake for 150 yards before veering right and uphill. The next 1.5 miles are very steep. The climb is initially through forest.

In .4 mile above Lagunitas, Lower Berry Trail comes in on the right from Bon Tempe Lake. Berry Trail once went on to Potrero Meadow before the fire road, which severed the route, was built.

The tree cover thins, opening views. At 1.2 miles, the upper end of Rocky Ridge FR joins on the right. It drops to Bon Tempe Dam and offers a loop possibility back. An old bay here accounts for the name, Bay Tree Junction, although Douglas-firs are now dominant. As you continue up, you'll reach a point from which all three of Tam's summits can be seen. The climbing begins to ease.

At 1.75 miles, Lower Northside Trail comes in on the left at a series of steps. This extension of Lower Northside was completed in 1997. Opposite, signed, is Cross Country Boys Trail, which goes to High Marsh.

In another ⅙ mile, once again back in the Douglas-fir forest, is the upper end of Lagoon FR, which descends to Serpentine Knoll. There is a fire hydrant and sign noting the 10,000-gallon capacity of the tank up to the left.

One hundred yards past, on the left, note the stonework, including the steps, at a small pipe from which spring-fed water flows. A TCC plaque that was once attached here encouraged visitors to thank the area's owners for their kindness by appropriately disposing of all litter; the plaque was removed in 1993. MMWD discourages drinking unfiltered water on the mountain. Ferns now thrive here.

In another 100 feet, at the foot of historic Rifle Camp, Azalea Meadow Trail departs right to Cross Country Boys Trail and steps lead up left to Northside and Arturo Trails.

Rifle Camp was once the hub of several camps in the area. The origin of its name is obscure. One often-told story says that a dog named Schneider, owned by Dick Maurer, president of the Down and Outers Club, dug up a rifle here. It is officially called Rifle Picnic Area now, and there are five picnic tables. One of tables is dedicated to Robert P. Howell, a trails advocate and botanist with whom I hiked often on Native Plant Society outings. Another, dedicated to John C. Weitz (1949–2012), well expresses the depth of feeling for Mt. Tamalpais that so many share: *In life he called this mountain his church: In death it must surely be his heaven.*

The unusual tree by the farthest table is what may be the mountain's largest serviceberry (*Amelanchier utahensis*). It was a favorite of the late Fred Sandrock, who for several years published a newsletter, *Fact and Fancies*, filled with accounts of the mountain's history and flora.

A few yards of uphill lead to upper Potrero Meadow, one of the mountain's treasures. The Spanish word *potrero* means "pasture," and the meadow was indeed leased for grazing a century ago. Be sure to stay off the delicate meadow proper; signed Potrero Trail is the only authorized route across it. USAF station buildings, prominent for decades high above on the ridge south, are now gone.

Rock Spring-Lagunitas FR continues left around the meadow. In spring, madrones in bloom stand out across the way, lending a yellow-orange tint to the evergreens. Before leaving the meadow, the fire road meets one end of Laurel Dell FR.

After a bit more uphill, Rock Spring-Lagunitas FR encounters, on the right, Benstein Trail. From this intersection, Benstein descends to Laurel Dell FR above Potrero Camp. The fire road and Benstein run together for 100 yards, then the latter splits off, also to the right, up toward Rock Spring.

A crest is reached, opening southern vistas. Paths depart to the right. Then a second crest is hit and, dramatically, even broader southern views open. This is the divide of the north and south sides of Mt. Tamalpais.

The fire road ends as it drops to Ridgecrest Boulevard at a gate across from a Mountain Theater parking lot. An old sign says the fire road is a route to Ross. Rock Spring is nearby to the right (west), accounting for the fire road's name. Mountain Top Trail goes left, up to the former USAF base site on West Peak.

Rock Spring-Lagunitas FR was built in the 1930s by the Civilian Conservation Corps.

■ Rocky Ridge Fire Road

Alpine Pump FR to Rock Spring-Lagunitas FR: 1.78 miles

TERRAIN: Chaparral; exposed, rocky (MMWD)

ELEVATION: From 720 to 1,410 feet; steep, parts very steep

INTERSECTING TRAIL(S): Stocking (1.4 miles)

Rocky Ridge is a prominent, largely treeless rib on Tam's north side. This fire road tops it, offering access from Bon Tempe Lake to several remote northside trails. The exposed terrain can be blustery in winter winds and hot in summer. Outstanding views compensate.

To reach Rocky Ridge, cross Bon Tempe Dam from the parking area, then veer right on Alpine Pump FR. In 200 feet, Rocky Ridge FR sets off uphill to the left. A signpost points the way to Potrero Meadow. Note that the fire road is sometimes posted as closed to bicyclists during wet conditions.

The most common Mt. Tamalpais trees—bay, Douglas-fir, madrone, tanbark, live oak, redwood, and buckeye—are all found within Rocky Ridge's first ¼ mile. Higher, trees, save for a few isolated Douglas-firs, are rare. The first ½ mile is much the steepest.

The views are immediately sweeping. Gulls regularly fly overhead on their way to and from Bon Tempe, where they dip in the fresh water. The fire road's prominent green, greasy-appearing rocks are serpentine, a metamorphic rock thrust up from the deepest oceanic levels of the Earth's crust. Common on Mt. Tamalpais, its soils are heavy in magnesium and deficient in such essential minerals as calcium, potassium, and aluminum. As a result, serpentine supports only a specialized, low-growing plant community. Abundant loose rocks and prominent rock outcroppings undoubtedly account for the ridge's name.

There are actually three brief downhill stretches. Stocking Trail departs right to Hidden Lake and Kent Trail. This area is ablaze and redolent with ceanothus in early spring.

In another .1 mile there is a clearing on the left. A sign notes a horse trough, water tank, and fire hydrant just uphill left. There is more uphill, then the fire road re-enters shade.

Rocky Ridge FR ends at Rock Spring-Lagunitas FR. The signpost points the way left to Lake Lagunitas, right to Potrero Meadow. The intersection is called Bay Tree Junction for an isolated bay (laurel) that overlooked it; Douglas-firs now prevail. The actual Rocky Ridge continues higher, to West Peak, but the route up, a project of the 1930s Civilian Conservation Corps, is now closed.

William Brewer, working for the original California Geologic Survey, described an ascent of Tamalpais via Rocky Ridge in his book *Up and Down California in 1860–1864*. This lower section was upgraded during construction of Bon Tempe Dam in 1949.

▓ Stocking Trail

From Rocky Ridge FR to Kent Trail: .6 mile

TERRAIN: Deeply wooded beyond rocky opening yards (MMWD)

ELEVATION: Around 1,200 feet; gradual

INTERSECTING TRAIL(S): None

In 2001, MMWD formally closed the historic, ½-mile lower section of Stocking Trail, originally known as Camp Handy Trail, from Bon Tempe Lake to Rocky Ridge FR. The surviving section of Stocking, west of Rocky Ridge, is lovely and easy to follow, an important entry to many deep northside trails.

The signpost for Stocking Trail is 1.4 miles up Rocky Ridge FR. For years, MMWD repeatedly set posts to mark the entry and someone repeatedly sawed them down. The vandal has presumably retired, as the latest sign has stood for some time. Sizable logs and boulders also mark the entrance, just in case.

The sharply spiked shrub chaparral pea, up to 6 feet tall, lines the rocky early yards. Its lovely rose-purple flowers are in bloom in late spring. Bay laurels herald Stocking's re-entrance into forest.

At .2 mile from Rocky Ridge, Stocking descends to a bridge (constructed in 1995) across Van Wyck Creek. Paths cross, up and down, just before the bridge.

Stocking winds through the forest. Particularly enchanting is a grove of towering redwoods. A fallen giant (Stocking once went right through it) is the storied Hogan Tree. The plaque that dedicated this redwood grove to veteran mountain hiker John Hogan, who had Camp Hogan here, is said to be on the tree's underside.

A few yards ahead, the trail skirts a bog marked by a clump of giant chain ferns, the largest on Tam. To the right is Don Richardson Spring; a wooden cover, dated 1933, marks its source. Next to it is a huge, burnt redwood "circle."

Stocking then suddenly comes upon the treasure of Hidden Lake. Proceed quietly—you never know what unusual animal or animal behavior you'll encounter. Mt. Tamalpais is rich in many things, but natural lakes are not among them. This duckweed-covered pond, shrinking in size and drying up in the natural succession of the mountain's terrain, is unique habitat. It was once known as Wildcat Lake. You'll surely want to linger here.

Stocking continues another 100 yards to its junction with Kent Trail. This deep forest is one of the loveliest, most peaceful areas of Mt. Tamalpais. Redwoods, Douglas-firs, tanbark oaks, and madrones grow tall to compete for sunlight. (It was also once one of the mountain's trickier intersections, as here, too, MMWD signs were removed.) Kent rises left, between a redwood and a huge tanbark oak, to Serpentine Knoll and Potrero Camp. Just ahead is the lower end of now-closed Willow Meadow Trail. Kent bends right to continue down to Alpine Lake.

The route was called Swede George Fire Trail on MMWD's 1934 map, and Hidden Lake Trail on the Works Progress Administration 1937 map. After World War II, it was improved to accommodate horses, then renamed to honor Clayton Stocking, a long-time district employee and foreman. He retired in 1962 and died in 1969. He is also honored by a plaque below the lake keeper's residence, where he lived for forty-two years, near Phoenix Dam.

KIRKE WRENCH

FIshing is a popular activity at Bon Tempe Lake.

Taylor Trail

Sky Oaks Ranger Station to Concrete Pipeline FR: .52 mile

TERRAIN: Tanbark oak-madrone woodland; horses permitted (MMWD)

ELEVATION: 700 to 525 feet; steep

INTERSECTING TRAIL(S): None

Taylor Trail offers a pleasant connection between Sky Oaks Ranger Station and Concrete Pipeline FR, avoiding paved, open-to-cars Sky Oaks Road.

The trail descends behind an opening in the wood fence on the east side of the Sky Oaks Ranger Station. There is a water fountain by the building and another by the trailhead, and a trough for horses. Across the employee parking area is the signed start of Alex Forman Trail.

The attractive, tree-lined trail drops steadily almost its entire length. Particularly appealing is the quiet, gently sloping middle section, dominated by madrones. Redwoods are abundant as well. Concrete Pipeline FR, the trail's end, becomes visible well below.

Steps bring Taylor up its sole rise. The trail then has its one steep section as it drops to meet Concrete Pipeline. To the left, in .6 mile, is Fairfax-Bolinas Road. To the right is the upper end of Canyon Trail (75 yards) and Five Corners (¾ mile).

Lawrence B. Taylor, an avid equestrian, was superintendent of the Civilian Conservation Corps camp at Sky Oaks in the 1930s, when the trail was built.

The Coastal Trail follows Bolinas Ridge for several miles as it parallels West Ridgecrest Blvd.

TRAILHEAD THIRTEEN: WEST RIDGECREST BOULEVARD

Directions

Highway 101—Highway 1—Panoramic Highway-Southside (Pantoll) Road *OR* Fairfax-Bolinas Road, from either Fairfax (where it is called Bolinas Road) or from Highway 1 north of Bolinas Lagoon

---

When Ridgecrest Boulevard first opened as a toll road in 1926—$1 per car with two passengers, 25 cents per additional rider—a sign at the northern gate proclaimed it as California's "Most Scenic Drive." Many still think so, as today it is perhaps the number-one locale in the United States for filming automobile commercials. The toll was collected at the Fairfax-Bolinas Road junction, known as Ridgecrest.

An inn, originally Summit House, then Larsen's Lodge, stood at the junction from 1890 until it burned down in 1945. West Ridgecrest was not paved until 1939. The military closed the entire road during World War II and stationed soldiers high on the mountain. Ridgecrest Boulevard reopened to the public after the war, free of charge.

Ridgecrest Boulevard was the vision of San Anselmo financier Miner H. Ballou. Ballou Point, .8 mile northwest along the road from Rock Spring, commands a spectacular vista. A now-gone plaque there read: *M. H. Ballou,*

321

1858–1926. These Surroundings Typify the Character of This Man.

The West Ridgecrest trailhead covers the 3.7 miles of road between Fairfax-Bolinas Road and Rock Spring, where the Pantoll/Southside Road intersects. Rock Spring itself and the 2.9 miles from Rock Spring to the East Peak parking lot (East Ridgecrest) are treated as separate trailheads.

Ridgecrest Boulevard is closed each night by gates at Fairfax-Bolinas Road and at Pantoll. The road is also closed during high fire danger days and, rarely, by snowfall; phone the MTSP information number for a recorded message on its status.

At Fairfax-Bolinas Road, Bolinas Ridge Trail (south) and Bolinas Ridge FR (north) begin their long journeys. Two trails off Bolinas Ridge FR—McCurdy and Randall—are included in this section (although both are also accessible directly from Highway 1). At 1.5 miles toward Rock Spring is the parking area for the new, wheelchair-accessible McKennan Trail. In another .8 mile, Laurel Dell FR departs east and Willow Camp FR to the west. Several trails on Tam's north side, such as Mickey O'Brien, Old Stove, and High Marsh, are reached most easily from this Laurel Dell FR trailhead, which has parking for several cars. East Ridgecrest also has three designated hang glider launching sites.

Suggested Loops from West Ridgecrest Boulevard (elevation 1,800 feet)

1. Laurel Dell FR, 1.6 miles, to broad connector to Barth's Retreat—right, .2 mile, to Mickey O'Brien Trail—right, .7 mile, to Laurel Dell FR—left, .6 mile, to start. **3.1 miles total**

2. Laurel Dell FR, .8 mile, to Bare Knoll Trail—left, .3 mile, to High Marsh Trail—right, 1.8 miles to Cross Country Boys Trail—right, .4 mile, to Kent Trail—right, .4 mile, to Potrero Camp—connector, .1 mile, to Laurel Dell FR—right, 1.7 miles, to start. **5.5 miles total**

3. Willow Camp FR, 1.8 miles, to Avenida Farallone gate—straight, .1 mile, to Belvedere Ave.—left, .4 mile, to Matt Davis Spur—Matt Davis Trail uphill, 2.4 miles, to Coastal Trail—left, 1.4 miles, to Willow Camp FR—right, .1 mile, to start. **6.2 miles total**

4. McCurdy Trail, 2.0 miles, to Bolinas Ridge FR—left, 1.5 miles, to Randall Trail—left, 1.6 miles, to Highway 1—cross road and Randall Spur, .4 mile to Olema Valley Trail—left, 2.3 miles, to start. **7.8 miles total**

Bare Knoll Trail

Laurel Dell FR to High Marsh Trail: .32 mile

TERRAIN: Mostly grassland (MMWD)

ELEVATION: From 1,690 to 1,750 to 1,700 feet; steep

INTERSECTING TRAIL(S): None

Note: The 2004 MMWD Trails Plan calls for closing Bare Knoll.

This trail accesses the "Bare Knoll," actually a pair of isolated, grassy hilltops with extraordinary views. Most of the route is fire-road-width, but is open to cyclists only in its southern half.

From Laurel Dell, follow Laurel Dell FR north and uphill for 275 yards. Broad "Bare Knolls" Trail departs to the left. The MMWD signpost here notes "No Through Access" for cyclists.

The early yards are through light Douglas-fir woodland. At a rather sharp demarcation, the broad trail enters grassland. Immediately, views open.

The route's first crest is in 200 yards. The vistas are outstanding, including a rare look at Kent Lake. Straight ahead is Pine Mountain. Just to its left is Barnabe Peak. Due west, atop the ridge, is Ridgecrest Boulevard. Almost all the trees in the near landscape are Douglas-firs.

The trail drops to a saddle, then mounts the second knoll. Though slightly lower, this knoll affords views, no less glorious, of an entirely pristine landscape.

The trail now plunges steeply down to its end at High Marsh Trail, where the sign reads "Bare Knoll" (singular). There is also a "No Bikes" warning at this junction.

High Marsh Trail goes right to Kent Trail and High Marsh itself and left to Cataract Trail.

The route appears on old maps as a fire road from Laurel Dell FR to the summit. It is not clear why it was first cleared. When High Marsh Trail was built in the 1960s, the connection to it was worn in.

Bolinas Ridge Fire Road

Fairfax-Bolinas Road to Shafter Grade: 6.04 miles*

TERRAIN: Southern part redwood and Douglas-fir forest mixed with chaparral; middle section deep redwood forest; northern section lightly wooded and grassland (GGNRA, MMWD)

ELEVATION: From 1,520 to 1,320 feet; rolling

INTERSECTING TRAIL(S): McCurdy (3.4 miles), Randall (5.0 miles)

*Bolinas Ridge FR continues an additional 6 miles north of Shafter Grade to Sir Francis Drake Boulevard near Mile Marker 21.20.

The Bolinas Ridge FR (called Bolinas Ridge Trail on some signs, although it is broad throughout and open to bicyclists) is one of the most spectacular routes in the entire San Francisco Bay Area. Its daunting length of 12 miles and its remote location and difficulty of access (except at either end) ensure tranquility. Indeed, it is possible to travel its full length on weekdays or in poor weather conditions and not see a single other traveler, or hear a car save near the two trailheads. With a shuttle, long-distance runners, hikers, and bikers can enjoy a net downhill journey on a smooth, duff-covered surface in cool shade. Indeed, there are likely more redwood trees along the ridge than in all of Muir Woods National Monument.

The south end of Bolinas Ridge FR is at the junction of Fairfax-Bolinas Road and Ridgecrest Boulevard. There is parking for a few cars across the road. From the parking area, Coastal (or Bolinas Ridge) Trail departs south to Matt Davis Trail and Pantoll.

Bolinas Ridge FR opens with a gentle rise through a forest of Douglas-firs. When foggy, as is common, the area has a particularly haunting quality. Just in, the fire road meets a miles-long low fence built in 1987 to keep Tamalpais's feral pigs from crossing to the Point Reyes peninsula. The fence worked, and the pig population was then eradicated by hunting and trapping.

The repeating pattern of the fire road's first miles is set early: ups and downs (too many to mention), manzanita-dominated chaparral, views alternating with deep woodland. The first views, about ⅓ mile in, are over Bolinas to the Pacific. Be sure to look back as well, as the summit ridge of Tamalpais can be seen from high points such as the crest at 1 mile. You can decide if you are "on" Mt. Tamalpais or not. At .6 mile is an MMWD boundary sign, notable only because there are so few manmade landmarks on the route.

At 1.4 miles, a stop sign marks a PG&E maintenance route through the dense shrubbery. This cut can be seen when looking at the otherwise trailless, wooded east wall of Bolinas Ridge from San Geronimo Ridge. Also here is an old yellow-topped post with an MMWD boundary sign. These posts, placed to mark a planned cross-California riding and hiking trail, were once common on Tamalpais. Soon after is an MMWD "BF1" sign marking the crossing of a seep. At 1.6 miles, Bolinas Ridge FR goes directly under PG&E's 60 kilovolt Ignacio-Bolinas Power Line No. 1. In another .1 mile, perhaps the biggest tree on the entire route, a massive double-trunked redwood, is to the left.

The fire road then enters an almost unbroken redwood forest. Bolinas Ridge, foggy and usually in receipt of abundant rain, is ideal habitat for redwoods. During Gold Rush days, the ridge was heavily logged; ox-drawn carts carried logs down to sawmills. From a wharf on Bolinas Lagoon, shallow draft lighters departed for San Francisco and beyond. In the late 1960s, timber rights for a section of Bolinas Ridge on the McCurdy Ranch were leased to an Oregon logging firm. There was a strong local backlash; in 1969, cutting was halted and a tough Marin County logging law followed. A few years later, the new Golden Gate National Recreation Area absorbed all the Bolinas Ridge ranches.

Still in deep woodland, the fire road passes an old water tank with ferns growing from its base. Opposite is one of several old, long-gone roads down the west slope of Bolinas Ridge.

At 3.3 miles is another candidate for "biggest redwood," a giant that encircles a hollowed "mother" tree. Bolinas Ridge FR has its first true intersection, with McCurdy Trail, .1 mile later. The junction is well signed, and there are two posts to hitch horses. McCurdy descends 2 miles to Highway 1.

The next section north on Bolinas Ridge FR, between McCurdy and Randall Trails, runs 1.5 miles, entirely in deep redwood forest. It's about as quiet and remote as you get on any route in this book. Although you are on the ridge top, the trees are sufficiently dense and tall to block views. Indeed, there is just a single true vista point on this stretch, ¼ mile from McCurdy, where a slight clearing on the right opens views to San Geronimo Ridge and beyond. Redwoods overwhelmingly dominate, with a few Douglas-firs and dying tanbark oaks mixed in. Sword ferns line the fire road's edge. The route trends downward.

The second junction, at 5.0 miles, is with Randall Trail, actually a broad road open to bicycles. Randall, the last option left (west), drops to Highway 1 by Mile Marker 20.6. There is a sign and old stile at the intersection. Here, a parallel ranch path runs just below the fire road, behind a fence. One hundred yards past Randall, to the right, is a contender for grandest Douglas-fir on the route, a battered, multi-trunked giant. Ahead, taller bikers might need to duck under the branches of a tanbark oak that leans over the fire road.

The route becomes increasingly open. By ½ mile past Randall, the terrain at left is all grassland with views across to Inverness Ridge. Cattle grazing continues on the west slope under a lease arrangement with the National Park Service.

Bolinas Ridge FR meets Shafter Grade, its first right-bound option. This is the northern boundary of the Tamalpais Lands Collaborative and this book's coverage. Shafter Grade descends to Kent Lake and Sir Francis Drake Boulevard (Mile Marker 15.25). A GGNRA sign on the left says it is 4.8 miles straight to Jewell Trail, the next intersection, and 6.1 miles to the end of Bolinas Ridge FR (but not of Bolinas Ridge itself) at Sir Francis Drake Boulevard, Mile Marker 21.20.

The origin of the place name "Bolinas" is unclear. Louise Teather, in her book *Place Names of Marin*, seems to favor the theory that it is of Coast Miwok origin. Or it might refer to early 1600s Spanish mariner Francisco de Bolanos. Or it may come from *ballenas*, the Spanish word for whales.

■ Bolinas Ridge Trail

Junction of Fairfax-Bolinas and Ridgecrest Roads to Matt Davis Trail: 4.60 miles

TERRAIN: Mostly grassland with forested sections (MTSP, GGNRA; part of Bay Area Ridge Trail)

ELEVATION: From 1,520 to 1,800 to 1,510 feet; mostly gradual and gently rolling

INTERSECTING TRAIL(s): McKennan (2.1 miles), Willow Camp FR (3.2 miles)

The designations for Coast and Coastal trails in Marin can be confusing. For decades, the 9.4-mile section of trail between the summit of Fairfax-Bolinas Road south to Highway 1 (at Mile Marker 7.35) was called Coastal Trail. Now, its 4.6 miles to Matt Davis Trail is designated as Bolinas Ridge Trail and the remaining descent to Highway 1 as Matt Davis Trail, Deer Park FR, and the new Coast View Trail.

As of early 2016, most signs along these first 4.6 miles still say Coastal Trail. Also, there is a Bolinas Ridge FR to the north. (The Coastal Trail described in this book's Muir Beach chapter connects Muir Beach to Rodeo Beach, and Point Reyes' Coast Trail runs between Palomarin and Limantour Road.) Here, I'll use the hybrid Coastal/Bolinas Ridge nomenclature. No matter the distance or name, this remains one of Marin's top destination trails.

We'll start by heading south on the trail from the intersection of Fairfax-Bolinas and Ridgecrest Roads; there is parking here for only a few cars. This intersection was the site of a lodge, variously called Summit House (it stood at the highest point on the old San Rafael-Bolinas stage route), Larsen's, Consy's, or Wright's (after its successive owners). The lodge was originally a resting place for stage travelers. The abandoned lodge burned in the big 1945 fire.

The trailhead sign is inviting, indicating, for example, that it is 15 miles to Tennessee Valley. Also inviting is the nearly 12-mile Bolinas Ridge FR across the pavement, a combined-use (pedestrian, biker, equestrian) section of the Bay Area Ridge Trail. Coastal/Bolinas Ridge Trail is a hiker and, for part of the way, equestrian section, of that trail.

The route starts in a redwood/Douglas-fir forest, close beside Ridgecrest Boulevard. Coastal Trail/Bolinas Ridge Trail goes right between several close pairs of towering redwoods. It then drops from the road and crosses through a fence; the gate is now removed. The fence was constructed in 1987 to keep Tam's then-growing feral pig population from expanding to Point Reyes National Seashore. The hardy pigs were a menace to vegetation, particularly bulbous plants such as the mountain's orchids. One captured boar was 6 feet, 7 inches from snout to tail, and weighed 330 pounds!

A downhill leads to a haunting forest of laurels. (The initial 1-mile-long section was once known as Laurel Trail.) At the base, in a gully on the right, Old

Bolinas-San Rafael Trail is now posted as closed. The historic trail, dating from the 1830s or even earlier and perhaps the oldest on the mountain, connected the mission at San Rafael to the coastal settlement at Bolinas.

Coastal/Bolinas Ridge Trail begins climbing over switchbacks. The trail then moves from the deep forest into an isolated area of mixed chaparral, grassland, and bay trees. There are ocean views, and pitcher sage is redolent.

The trail trends back toward Ridgecrest Boulevard, recrosses the pig fence, then comes within a few yards of the boulevard at the head of Morse's Gulch. Just below is an old orchard, still yielding a few apples. The trees were planted by John Wright, who named the grove Fountainhead Orchard for the spring a few yards southwest. Look at the trail's edge here for some brickwork, remnants of Wright's residence.

Coastal/Bolinas Ridge Trail now enters grassland, where it remains most of the rest of the way. But the grassland here, as in other parts of Mt. Tam, is changing. No longer grazed by livestock, the slopes are home to ever-growing numbers of Douglas-firs. There are still many years to enjoy the non-stop stunning ocean views, however. The sunny southern exposure and ocean's warming influence are boons to wildflowers. The first come in January, and at least a few poppies remain in bloom into December. A path, marked with a sign, joins on the left. It directs horse riders on the Bay Area Ridge Trail up left, off the continuing Coastal/Bolinas Ridge Trail.

The route returns to the vicinity of the pig fence. One hundred fifty yards beyond, a gate in the fence marks the top of a now-overgrown old route. Just ahead, another path rises to Ridgecrest Boulevard.

When the trail comes closest to the fence, look carefully for remnants of the McKennan Gulch Copper Prospect. For years, a barren pile of tailings, a change in the color of the dirt (from brownish to gray-black), and a depression five yards to the left could be seen here. Now seemingly nothing is left. The filled tunnel entrance is below the fence. All date from a 1930s test cut, but there was never a working mine here.

The trail again approaches Ridgecrest Boulevard, this time meeting it at a small parking area. From the parking area, McKennan (or McKennan Gulch) Trail, entirely wheelchair accessible, goes .12 mile (so not separately described) to a wonderful stone bench with a knockout view. Hugh McKennan, a '49er from Ireland, bought land around Bolinas Lagoon in 1867 and was soon supplying San Francisco with eggs from his 2,500 ducks.

Coastal/Bolinas Ridge Trail is on Ridgecrest Boulevard for 100 yards before departing from the asphalt to the right (west). It continues through grassland, then enters a woodland atop Stinson Gulch. Many of the downed trees here fell during a storm in 1990; they took out the bridge as well. The bridge was rebuilt and its plaque—*In Memory of Mike Amoroso, Mill Valley Lions Club 1978*—was restored to the far side. Amoroso was a Mill Valley liquor-store owner who was involved in civic projects. In 2014, another storm toppled a giant bay tree onto the bridge—the planks over the gully held—and this section, between McKennan and Willow Camp FR, was posted as closed.

The trail rises out of the woods back into the grassland. In .1 mile from the bridge, look right for the stone Cook Memorial Bench, one of the mountain's revered spots. A plaque reads:

Robert B. Cook 1959–1979
This Scenic 4.3 Mile Section of Pacific Coast Trail, Between the Matt Davis and Laurel Trails, Is Dedicated to the Memory of Bob Cook. It Was Conceived as His Eagle Scout Project and, through His Persistence and Determination, Was Built with Volunteer Labor Over a Two-Year Period.

Cook started building the trail soon after the area became open to the public, and support remains to name it after him. He died in an airplane crash on his way to do more trail work in Idaho. The plaque was unveiled in a ceremony on June 1, 1980. Rest at this special place and enjoy the wonderful view down to Stinson Beach, Bolinas, and the Pacific. Also savor the serenity and the sounds of the laurel-lined rivulet just ahead and of the ocean surf.

The trail rises. Another old cattle drinking tub and some calla lilies (*Zantedeschia aethiopica*, in the Arum family) are further reminders that the area was privately owned and grazed into the early 1970s. The wall of grass upslope, dotted with boulders, is most impressive.

One-quarter mile from the Cook Bench, Coastal/Bolinas Ridge Trail crosses Willow Camp FR. It's a stiff .1 mile uphill to Ridgecrest Boulevard, or a long, steep, but gorgeous drop right toward Stinson Beach, where a tough loop can be made with Matt Davis Trail.

The trail continues to meander around the gulches of Tam's west face. Several isolated and haunting groves of laurel trees are passed. A rusted 1941 Pontiac lies beneath a laurel, as it has for decades; how it got there a mystery.

Coastal/Bolinas Ridge Trail rises to its high point of 1,800 feet. On a fog-free day, the views from this long open section are magnificent. Indeed, there are few more glorious stretches of trail anywhere in the region. In thick fog, the area has an entirely different feel, and you need to be careful to not lose your way.

There is a descent. A sign marks the stretch just passed as the Bob Cook Memorial Section. A few yards beyond, just before another laurel grove, Matt Davis Trail drops right to Stinson Beach. This junction is now considered to be the southern end of Coastal/Bolinas Ridge Trail. Straight is Matt Davis Trail to Pantoll.

▦ Helen Markt Trail

Cataract Trail to Kent Trail: 1.75 miles

TERRAIN: Coniferous forest (MMWD)

ELEVATION: From 1,080 to 670 feet; rolling, parts steep

INTERSECTING TRAIL(S): None

Helen Markt (the "t" is silent) Trail was essentially built by just by one man, Jim Vitek, in the early 1950s. It is one of the mountain's lovelier, more remote trails, winding above the isolated southwest shore of Alpine Lake. Since even its shortest loop possibility (with Kent, High Marsh, and Cataract Trails) is some 8 miles and strenuous, Helen Markt is little visited. (In 1988, I led a hike over that loop for now-defunct Marin Discoveries. Pamela Neill was among the participants. We married the next year.) The nearest trailheads are distant: 2.3 miles from either Sky Oaks or Rock Spring, 1.6 miles from West Ridgecrest Road, or a very steep .6 mile uphill on Cataract Trail from Fairfax-Bolinas Road (Mile Marker 8.09). I'll describe the latter approach, as it is shortest.

Climb .6 mile up Cataract Trail to the bridge over Cataract Creek. About 25 yards above the bridge, an MMWD signpost points the way left to the start of Helen Markt Trail. Cataract Trail continues uphill right toward Laurel Dell.

Helen Markt begins with a short downhill, passing a remnant of an older, steeper connection to the Cataract Creek bridge. The trail rolls through deep woodland. Indeed, for a quiet forest walk, Helen Markt has few equals on Tamalpais. The area above (south) is one of the largest on Tam without a maintained trail. Many of the huge Douglas-firs at the trail's edge, left undisturbed by Vitek, are blackened, a reminder of the fire that roared through here in 1945.

The trail crests at a grassy area. In 1/3 mile, after a descent into a grove of redwoods, look carefully at the trail's left margin, and listen, for Broko Spring. It emerges from the ground through the clay as a (presumably) safe source of cool water almost all year. "Broko" was Joe Vitek's nickname; Jim Vitek's brother, he was also a volunteer trail worker. This is a favorite resting spot. Note the massive redwood stump, nearly encircled by younger root-sprouted "offspring." The stream just ahead cuts through Blake Canyon, named for Arthur H. Blake, a Bay Area hiker and environmentalist who died in 1957.

Beyond, the trail slices through masses of huckleberry shrubs that are covered with tasty berries in late summer and fall. Tanbark oak is also abundant throughout. The longest downhill of the route leads, at 1.2 miles, to the bridge over Swede George Creek, one of the strongest streams on the mountain. The

329

bridge was designed and built by Jim Vitek, who floated logs on Alpine Lake to the remote site. A new plaque was installed in 1999, and the bridge was completely rebuilt in 2003. Swede George Creek, which flows year-round, is usually a torrent in winter. Its name comes from a nineteenth-century woodsman who worked here.

The trail climbs steeply and hits a short clearing at the edge of chaparral. Look left over the manzanita to see Alpine Dam at the far end of the lake. It then descends back into the woods and touches the shore of Alpine Lake, another place to pause. Starflower (*Trientalis latifolia*), with its single pink flower supported on the slenderest of stems, is abundant here in spring. (This is my favorite wildflower.)

Helen Markt ends when it meets Kent Trail at a signpost. Kent goes straight ahead to Bon Tempe Dam and uphill to Serpentine Knoll, High Marsh, and Potrero Camp.

From hiking it for sixty-five years and his career with MMWD, Jim Vitek knew the north side of Tamalpais better than anyone. He built this trail to provide a new long-loop possibility from Bon Tempe Lake. Vitek died in 2007.

Frank and Helen Markt were toll takers on Ridgecrest Boulevard in the 1930s, when a fee was still charged. They lived in a house (destroyed in the 1945 fire) at the junction of Ridgecrest and Fairfax-Bolinas Road. The couple later resided beside Lake Lagunitas, where Frank served as lake keeper from 1940 until his retirement in 1965. Helen died while Vitek was working on this trail, so it was named in her honor.

■ High Marsh Trail

Cataract Trail to Kent Trail: 2.21 miles

TERRAIN: Heavily wooded, some chaparral and grassland (MMWD)

ELEVATION: From 1,700 to 1,520 feet; gradual and rolling, short parts steep

INTERSECTING TRAIL(S): Bare Knoll (.2 mile), connector to Laurel Dell FR (.6 mile), Old Stove (.8 mile), Cross Country Boys (2.0 mile)

It takes an effort to hike the full length of High Marsh Trail—at least 6 miles roundtrip, more for a loop—from any place reachable by car. This assures that the trail, already in one of the remotest parts of the mountain, will be peaceful and quiet even on summer weekends. The rolling trail covers a variety of terrain, has several great views, and, of course, passes High Marsh.

High Marsh Trail leaves Cataract Trail .3 mile below Laurel Dell. An old bench and newer signpost mark the junction. The trail then emerges from the forest to a grassy hillside. This is one of the lovelier places on Mt. Tamalpais, with gently contoured hills, pastoral views (including a glimpse of Kent Lake), and a riot of wildflowers in spring. You'll find orange poppies and fiddlenecks, yellow creamcups and buttercups; white woodland-stars and wild cucumbers; blue eyed grass, baby blue eyes, and blue lupines; and pink and reds from geraniums and scarlet pimpernels.

As High Marsh Trail crests near the end of the grassland, look right for the base of Bare Knoll Trail. It rises to a pair of view knolls and on to Laurel Dell FR. Twenty-five yards later, High Marsh Trail reenters woodland.

At the top of the next uphill, a signpost marks a 75-yard connector right and uphill to Laurel Dell FR. High Marsh levels, and passes through a haunting stretch of manzanita shrubs.

The top of the next major uphill, the highest point on the trail, marks the divide between the drainages of Cataract and Swede George Creeks. A sign marks entry to Old Stove Trail up to the right. It goes to Laurel Dell FR.

Fifty yards later, High Marsh Trail descends steps. There are sweeping views above the chaparral shrubs to Tomales Bay, Mt. St. Helena, and beyond. The trail returns to a forest canopy, then rises to another clearing in the chaparral.

The trail meets the west fork of Swede George Creek and a trail sign. The route right, along the creek, looks good but is badly deteriorated and has been closed. High Marsh continues across the creek, which sometimes requires a leap in winter.

Few parts of the mountain are farther from a road than this next section of High Marsh. The deep forest, in which no signs of civilization are heard or seen, takes the sense of wilderness still further. One of the treasures is a moss-covered "rock garden," just beyond a pair of towering boulders.

The trail passes through a massive downed Douglas-fir, then crosses (or fords) a stream. At a signpost, the option down left, the one-time Willow Meadow Trail, is clear but is not an MMWD-designated route. Follow the arrow for High Marsh Trail veering right and up.

Finally (or all-too-quickly) the trail meets High Marsh itself, somewhat obscured, to the left. The marsh, like Hidden Lake ½ mile north, is a drainage-collecting slump resulting from the huge Potrero landslide—almost 2 miles long and 3,500 feet wide—of some 1,000 years ago. High Marsh has been noticeably shrinking and drying in recent decades, evolving naturally into a meadow; it already appears as a meadow in the summer. It is still, however, a most appealing stopping place.

At High Marsh itself, Cross Country Boys Trail rises steeply uphill to the right. High Marsh Trail veers left. It is then a level 200 yards to High Marsh Trail's end at a signed intersection. Kent Trail goes left to Alpine Lake and right to Potrero Camp. The still-evident route directly across is the former lower section of Azalea Meadow Trail; only its upper end is now officially designated by MMWD.

High Marsh Trail was built almost single-handedly by Bob Murray in the 1960s. It was originally called Gracie Trail.

■ Laurel Dell Fire Road

Ridgecrest Boulevard to Potrero Meadow: 2.20 miles

TERRAIN: Grassland, forest, and chaparral; part riparian (MMWD)

ELEVATION: From 1,920 to 1,640 to 2,020 feet; gradual, rolling

INTERSECTING TRAIL(s): Ray Murphy (.3 mile), Cataract (.6 mile), Bare Knoll (.8 mile), connector to High Marsh Trail (.8 mile), Old Stove (.9 mile, 1.3 miles), connector to Mickey O'Brien (1.4 miles), broad connector to Barth's Retreat (1.6 miles), Music Stand (1.6 miles), broad connector to Potrero Camp (1.8 miles), Benstein (1.8 miles), connector to Potrero Camp (2.0 miles)

Laurel Dell FR provides access to some of the famous sites on the north side of the mountain, including Laurel Dell itself, Barth's Retreat, Music Camp, the two Potrero Meadows, and Rifle Camp. There are also exceptional vista points.

The fire road sets off from West Ridgecrest Boulevard at a gate beside a parking turnout, 1.4 miles from Rock Spring. Here across Ridgecrest is also an entry to Willow Camp Fire Road.

Laurel Dell FR descends in a sweeping arc and enters woodland. In ⅓ mile, the signed Ray Murphy Trail, all of 200 feet long, forks to the right. It crosses Cataract Creek over Ray Murphy Bridge to meet Cataract Trail. Just before the fire road drops to the creek, look left, at the edge of the woodland, for an old fenced enclosure. It was built to protect Laurel Dell's one-time water source from the cattle that used to graze here.

The fire road fords Cataract Creek at the edge of Laurel Dell Meadow, where Barth's Creek joins. The crossing can be quite wet, even impassable, after winter rains. If necessary, retreat to Cataract via the Ray Murphy Bridge and descend. A bridge over Barth's Creek provides dry passage. Nearby to the right, Mickey O'Brien Trail sets off up to Barth's Retreat.

The tree-ringed meadow at Laurel Dell is immensely appealing. Long-time Tam hikers recall the famous dogwood tree that once stood there. Cataract Trail comes in through the grassland.

The Laurel Dell picnic area is just ahead on the left. There are two entrances, one on the other side of an incongruous plum tree, the other, with the famous "Laurel Dell" sign, opposite the outhouses. Laurel Dell has been, with good reason, a favorite destination for generations. Five picnic tables sit beside Cataract Creek amidst the laurels, but the old water fountain is gone. Cataract Trail to High Marsh Trail and Alpine Dam continues downhill from the picnic area.

Laurel Dell FR now heads uphill, into a forest of Douglas-firs. Some 250 yards from Laurel Dell, broad but unsigned Bare Knoll Trail climbs left to a pair of grassy crests. In another couple of hundred feet is a signed, 75-yard-long connector to High Marsh Trail. Forty yards on the left is signed Old Stove Trail. It begins up wooden steps. Old Stove forks, one option left to High Marsh Trail, the other back to Laurel Dell FR.

As the route climbs, tree cover opens. You can look back to the gate at Ridgecrest Boulevard where the fire road begins. On a level section in the chaparral, Old Stove Trail rejoins Laurel Dell FR. (The distance between the Old Stove-Laurel Dell junctions is signed as just .02 mile different via the trail or fire road.) To the right here is a small clearing, once an old campsite.

The fire road rises into forest again, then drops back into chaparral. At the bottom of the dip, a classic sign atop a connector fire road points the way right, down to Barth's Retreat, where Simmons and Mickey O'Brien Trails meet. The latter offers a loop option. To the left, directly opposite, is the unsigned top of Music Stand Trail.

Laurel Dell FR crests just ahead. The views to the north are outstanding. On the clearest of winter days, snow-capped Snow Mountain, 100 miles away in Mendocino County, may be visible. Closer sights include Point Reyes peninsula and Alpine Lake.

The fire road returns to woodland, then passes a broad connector on the left that drops to Potrero Camp. Fifty yards past, Benstein Trail begins its journey to Rock Spring.

Part of lower Potrero Meadow is visible to the left. Then, the larger upper Potrero Meadow is met. A signpost marks a path left to Potrero Camp. Just past is an old sign pointing the way to Mill Valley, Ross, and Fairfax. Laurel Dell FR ends when it meets Rock Spring-Lagunitas FR.

Laurel Dell was earlier known as Old Stove Camp, for the stove that was once there. It was renamed Laurel Dell by J. H. Cutter, first president of the Tamalpais Conservation Club. The California bay laurel may be the most common tree on Tamalpais. The CCC built Laurel Dell FR in the 1930s over parts of Old Stove Trail.

■ McCurdy Trail

From Bolinas Ridge FR to Highway 1/Mile Marker 18.17: 1.99 miles

TERRAIN: Chaparral, light woodland, grassy meadows (GGNRA)

ELEVATION: From 1,380 to 210 feet; very steep

INTERSECTING TRAIL(S): None

Note: Open to bicycles

McCurdy Trail has many characters. The upper part is very eroded and narrow. A middle section cuts through redwood groves. Below that is a broad, grass-surfaced stretch unlike any other route in this book. The lowermost part of McCurdy is less than 1 foot wide.

Although the base of McCurdy Trail is directly off Highway 1 and its upper end is remote, the route will be described downhill because Randall Trail, essentially McCurdy's only loop partner, with similar logistics, is described uphill. McCurdy is also a bit easier to follow downhill. (Some may prefer the reverse route, climbing McCurdy and descending Randall.)

McCurdy is the first trail encountered when going north on Bolinas Ridge FR from Fairfax-Bolinas Road, albeit 3.4 miles away. When traveling south, McCurdy is 1.5 miles from the top of Randall Trail. The McCurdy trailhead, though in deep forest, is easy to spot: the sign is large and there are two hitching posts for horses. The sign says it is 1.8 miles to Woodville, also known as Dogtown. Rerouting of lower McCurdy has lengthened the distance.

Set off downhill on the narrow route. Just past the McCurdy hitching post, look for salal (*Gaultheria shallon*), a shrub with large, glossy, smooth-edged leaves. (Nearby tanbark leaves have serrated edges.) Salal is in the same family, Ericaceae, as manzanita and huckleberry, which are also abundant here, but is more associated with Point Reyes than Mt. Tamalpais.

The descent is immediately steep. The towering Douglas-firs of Bolinas Ridge give way to far shorter and fewer specimens. This opens ocean views, but you may be looking down to avoid ankle-twisting gullies. Runners lured by the long downhill will not enjoy this section. A further problem is encroaching vegetation, including the sharp-pointed shrub chaparral pea.

About ⅓ mile down, bishop pines begin appearing, and there are hundreds more ahead. Bishop pines are native to, and abundant on, the Point Reyes peninsula but are found naturally in only a few areas of Mt. Tamalpais. They have paired needles and their cones are tightly wrapped asymmetrically around their branches.

At .9 mile, McCurdy cuts through groves of redwoods. Near the end of this stretch is a massive, ancient Douglas-fir. Huge limbs droop, touching the ground. Look up to spot the remains of a tree house. You can see Inverness Ridge across

Olema Valley and the San Andreas Fault, literally on a different tectonic plate (the Pacific). McCurdy then enters a wonderful, isolated, most inviting meadow. You'll want to stop and have your snack here.

Almost all the rest of the descent is through the grassland of a former dairy ranch. At 1.4 miles, McCurdy meets another broad, grassy path coming in from the right. (When ascending, veer right past the small boulder.) McCurdy here more resembles a British steeplechase course than a Tamalpais trail.

At just over 1.5 miles, the first sign encountered directs hikers left, off the broad route heading down to Highway 1, and onto a narrow clearing through the grassland. You can see historic structures of the former Teixeira-Strain Ranch across the road, including the main residence built in the 1880s. A couple of fences and a warning sign to keep off a shortcut direct you on the now-meandering, gradual descent.

There is a last clump of trees at the edge of Cronin Gulch, named for early settler Timothy Cronin, who was hanged in 1868 for the murder of his wife. McCurdy Trail exits onto Highway 1 just north of Mile Marker 18.17, where there is a large sign and a small parking pullout. Directly across Highway 1 is a sign, "Olema Valley Trailhead." When making the McCurdy-Randall trail loop, Olema Valley Trail, though often muddy, is far preferable to walking along Highway 1. Just to the right on Highway 1 is a sign welcoming you to Point Reyes National Seashore. Two miles farther right is the Randall trailhead.

During the 1860s, Samuel McCurdy and partner David McMullin purchased 1,835 acres on the west slope of Bolinas Ridge and began logging and farming. McCurdy became sole owner in 1890, and he and his wife raised seven children on the ranch. The family leased the property in 1905 and moved to Mill Valley. (One son, Alex McCurdy, became Mill Valley's police chief, and his son, William, was the first Marin athlete to win a state track and field title while at Tamalpais High School. William McCurdy later coached track and cross-country at Harvard for thirty years, and the college's track is named for him.)

Dr. Ethel Righetti bought the property in 1935. In the 1960s, Righetti granted timber rights on the ridge to an Oregon logging company. The subsequent public outcry halted the cutting in 1969 and triggered new, highly restrictive logging rules across all of Marin County, as well as a demand to secure Bolinas Ridge as parkland. The National Park Service bought the property (then 1,590 acres) for $2.5 million from Righetti's children in 1974 and incorporated it into GGNRA.

▪ Mickey O'Brien Trail

Laurel Dell to Barth's Retreat: .66 mile

TERRAIN: Deep woodland; riparian (MMWD)

ELEVATION: From 1,690 to 1,940 feet; gradual

INTERSECTING TRAIL(S): Connector to Laurel Dell FR (.6 mile)

This is an enchanting trail, through deep forest beside a stream in one of the quietest parts of the mountain. Since Mickey O'Brien connects two of Tam's landmarks, Laurel Dell and Barth's Retreat, it is part of many northside loop walks.

Follow either Laurel Dell FR or Cataract Trail to Laurel Dell itself; Mickey O'Brien begins to the east at the meadow's southern (near) edge.

The trail immediately plunges into woodland. Huckleberry is the common shrub, and Douglas-firs and tanbarks are the main trees. Barth's Creek, which joins Cataract Creek at Laurel Dell, is to the left. It remains a companion the whole way.

In .2 mile, the trail enters its only sizable clearing at the foot of a grassy, serpentine hillside. Until around 2002, what were officially recognized as the world's two largest Sargent cypress trees stood here. One, dubbed the Master Sargent, was 85 feet tall, with a circumference of 10 feet, 2 inches. The second giant was 96 feet tall but had a smaller circumference. Several tree guidebooks list the Sargent cypress's height limit as 40 or 50 feet; John Thomas Howell, in his *Marin Flora*, wrote "up to 50 feet tall." The preeminence of these two giants was only recognized in 1980 by the late Thomas Harris. Now, the two trees, dead, lie neatly stacked beside the trail, but the bases of their trunks still stand. Another sizable Sargent cypress a few yards downstream also appears ready to topple.

At this same serpentine clearing, the creek can be followed uphill ¼ mile to the remaining wreckage of a US Navy Corsair fighter plane. (A sign at the wreckage warns that it is a federal crime to disturb the historic site.) It dates from a two-plane collision over Tam on October 4, 1945. Both pilots parachuted to safety. The engine from the other plane is in Cataract Creek, a few yards upstream from Ray Murphy Bridge.

There is more uphill on the remainder of Mickey O'Brien. The trail passes a massive five-trunked oak, and azaleas border the trail's left margin.

Mickey O'Brien crosses a pair of rivulets. In 2003, Eagle Scouts of San Rafael's Troop 101 added a footbridge; the trail then squeezes between two boulders. The unexpected signpost here used to point to a .2-mile connector (now overgrown) heading left across Barth's Creek to Laurel Dell FR. Continue uphill without crossing the creek. A marked path leads up right to an abandoned outhouse.

The trail terminates at a bridge over Barth's Creek. The bridge is dedicated to the memory of veteran mountain worker and hiker Harold Atkinson, who helped build Mickey O'Brien Trail in 1930 and lived to toil on its rerouting in 1971.

From the bridge's near side, Simmons Trail begins its journey to Rock Spring. Across the bridge is Barth's Retreat (see Simmons Trail description) and a connector fire road up to Laurel Dell FR.

Michael Francis "Mickey" O'Brien was a native San Franciscan who devoted himself to Mt. Tamalpais. A charter member of the Tamalpais Conservation Club, he served as its president in 1925–1926; edited its newsletter, *California Out of Doors*, for eight years; and was on the executive committee for thirty years. In 1947, at age sixty-nine, he suffered a heart attack after a work session on Hoo-Koo-E-Koo Trail. Returning to the mountain just three weeks later to continue his trail work, he collapsed again, and died at Alpine Lodge, beside Panoramic Highway. This trail, once called Barth's Creek Trail, then K.C. Trail, was dedicated to him in 1948.

Old Stove Trail

From High Marsh Trail to Laurel Dell FR, plus spur: .33 mile

TERRAIN: Mostly chaparral; overgrown (MMWD)

ELEVATION: From 1,780 to 1,960 feet; gradual to steep

INTERSECTING TRAIL(s): None

Today's Old Stove Trail is a remnant of a once-longer and well-used route now largely covered by Laurel Dell FR. In recent years, Old Stove has been somewhat improved and, oddly, signed at three ends.

One signed trailhead is at the highest point of High Marsh Trail, .8 mile from Cataract Trail. Old Stove climbs through dying manzanitas, which narrow the way. In .1 mile, easy to miss, a spur enters on the right. This spur is also signed as Old Stove Trail and rises from Laurel Dell FR $1/8$ mile from Laurel Dell itself. There are ten wood steps at the start. (On a November morning as fog was lifting after a night of rain, I saw 500 or more spiderwebs densely packed over Old Stove's opening yards here.)

The .12-mile spur quickly rises out of the forest into chaparral; the transition is abrupt. Just before meeting the High Marsh entry is an unexpected grove of young knobcone pines. As John Thomas Howell wrote in the 1969 supplement to his *Marin Flora*, "The knobcone pines planted on the north side of Mount Tamalpais in the chaparral between Laurel Dell and Potrero Meadow were killed in the fire of 1945 but a new cone-bearing generation now thrives there."

The combined forks of Old Stove rise through manzanita and chamise, one dominant, then the other, with little mixing. Yerba santa also grows at trail's edge. At a crest, Laurel Dell FR comes into sight. Old Stove Trail descends through tall manzanita to meet it, then ends. The MMWD signpost here says it is .64 mile right to Laurel Dell via the fire road and .62 mile via Old Stove (using the spur). Barth's Retreat is to the left.

Old Stove Trail dates to around 1910 as a connection from Laurel Dell to Potrero Meadow. Laurel Dell was originally called Old Stove Camp, for an old stove there. (Using a metal detector, and with permission from the water district, Phil Frank uncovered what appears to be that stove.) There was also an Old Stove Extension, which ran from Laurel Dell across Cataract Creek up to Bolinas Ridge. Already faint, it was all but obliterated after a storm in December 1987.

▇ Randall Trail

From Highway 1 (Mile Marker 20.6) to Bolinas Ridge FR: 1.65 miles

TERRAIN: Lower half Douglas-fir forest, upper half redwood forest (GGNRA)

ELEVATION: From 1,270 to 330 feet; gradual to steep

INTERSECTING TRAIL(S): None

Note: Open to bicycles

Over the nearly 12 miles of Bolinas Ridge FR, from Fairfax-Bolinas Road to Sir Francis Drake Boulevard, only two officially designated routes, McCurdy and Randall Trails, drop west. (Only two descend east, Shafter Grade and Jewell Trail). As the tops of McCurdy and Randall are only 1.5 miles apart, they are natural loop partners, but they are quite different. While much of McCurdy is very steep, rocky, and narrow, Randall is entirely broad and well graded. Indeed, if you don't mind nearly 1,000 feet of elevation change, Randall is one of the most enjoyable routes on Tamalpais to travel, up or down, by foot, bicycle, or horse.

The Randall trailhead, though signed, is very easy to miss when driving on Highway 1 at 55 miles per hour. It's at Mile Marker 20.6, at a gate and stile behind a big "Slower Traffic Use Turnouts" sign. Easier to spot is the parking area and sign for the Olema Valley Trail directly across, on the west side of the road. What is called Randall Spur departs from this parking area. Olema Valley lies atop the infamous San Andreas Fault, which marks the boundary between the Pacific and North American Plates.

Enter Randall Trail through the stile. The route is broad and continues so the entire way. It is immediately crossed by an old ranch path; a path then sets off right, from just below the utility pole. Most visitors to Randall exit here, literally 20 yards into the trail. They follow this .2-mile path up through the canyon to manmade Hagmaier Pond, favored by nude sunbathers.

Those venturing deeper on Randall Trail quickly enter a Douglas-fir forest. Randall remains in ever-deepening woodland all the way to the summit.

In ¼ mile, a broad path enters from the right. Fifty yards away is an abandoned cabin, built in the 1960s by the last private owner of Randall Ranch, Alan Sieroty, who served in the California State Assembly and state senate. (There is an Alan Sieroty Beach on Tomales Bay.) There are then few landmarks in the woods. The ascent is gradual, but goes up every step or pedal of the way. The 1-mile mark is at an eight-trunked bay laurel tree on the right.

The transition from more-open Douglas-fir forest into more-shaded redwood forest is relatively clear and begins about 200 yards above the eight-trunked laurel. It can be noticed at a sharp bend right, where one Douglas-fir (lower) and two redwoods (higher) are tucked into the hairpin turn.

The subsequent upper stretch of Randall is utterly enchanting. There are some Douglas-firs and a few madrones in areas where sunlight penetrates, but mostly redwoods rule. Indeed, passage through this forest can be so pleasant that reaching the crest may actually be a disappointment. Bolinas Ridge FR is at the top. There is a stile, an old Randall Trail sign, and a newer MMWD sign, from which you can scan a map and watershed rules. But the forest experience need not end; both directions on Bolinas Ridge FR are also deeply wooded, particularly south. It is 1.5 miles right to McCurdy Trail for a loop (use Olema Valley Trail rather than Highway 1 to complete the loop) and 1 mile left to Shafter Grade.

William Randall and wife Sarah (Seaver) came to California from Vermont in 1850 during the Gold Rush. In 1857, Randall and partner John Nelson paid Mexican land grantee Rafael Garcia $2,000 for 1,400 acres on the west slope of Bolinas Ridge. Randall bought out Nelson in 1860. In June of that year, William Randall was shot and killed by a neighbor, who felt Randall's fence intruded on his property. His widow was left with left five children to raise.

Around 1880, Sarah built the Randall House that still stands, long shuttered, beside Highway 1, ¼ mile north of the Randall trailhead. Sarah died in 1907 and her children sold the ranch four years later. Dairying continued into the early 1970s, when a new owner planned a housing subdivision. In 1974, the National Park Service purchased the property for $1.1 million and incorporated it into GGNRA.

Willow Camp Fire Road

West Ridgecrest Boulevard to Highway 1: 2.82 miles

TERRAIN: Coastal scrub and grassland (MTSP)

ELEVATION: From 1,900 to 15 feet; very steep

INTERSECTING TRAIL(S): Coastal/Bolinas Ridge (.1 mile)

Willow Camp FR offers an unrelentingly steep connection between Bolinas Ridge and Bolinas Lagoon. There are sweeping ocean views most all the way. Because McKennan Trail to the north has been closed, the only remaining loop option is with less-steep Matt Davis Trail to the south. A one-way, downhill shuttle is also possible, as both ends of Willow Camp (as well as an intermediate point) are accessible by car.

There are three entrances to Willow Camp from Ridgecrest Boulevard, all just south of, and across the pavement from, the top of Laurel Dell FR, 1.4 miles from Rock Spring. There is some shoulder parking on both sides of the road. Directly across Laurel Dell FR is the newest signed entrance. One hundred yards to the south, behind a white gate, is the start of the fire road and a parallel trail.

At the top (1,900 feet), the views are broadest, but they remain no less appealing all the way down (except, of course, when summer's coastal fog rolls in). After 150 yards, the entrance from opposite Laurel Dell FR joins on the right. Just below, the parallel trail joins the fire road at an intersection. To the left here, Coastal/Bolinas Ridge Trail departs toward Matt Davis Trail and Pantoll. Twenty yards down, Coastal/Bolinas Ridge separates right to Fairfax-Bolinas Road. Continue downhill toward Stinson Beach.

At .4 mile, the fire road enters a grove of bays; oaks; and massive, lichen-covered Douglas-firs. Douglas irises (*Iris douglasiana*) found in the woodland here are a different species from ground irises (*I. macrosiphon*) that abound on the grassland just a few yards ahead, offering an opportunity to distinguish them. Douglas iris are taller, with stems of 8 inches or more. Their arching leaves are shiny above, dull below. Ground iris grow close to the ground, have similar upper and lower leaf surfaces, and a pleasing fragrance. Just before leaving the forest, on the right, is a magnificent Douglas-fir, killed and reduced in size, perhaps by lightning. Its enormous low branches hint that it may have been the first in the grove. Another giant, with four trunks, is just ahead on the left.

Beyond the grove, back in grassland, there are few obvious landmarks: a string of underground telephone cable markers, a seep, some Douglas-firs. Since there's no getting lost here, just enjoy the views. They can extend from the western half of San Francisco to Point Reyes and out to the Farallon Islands. Check out the trail pattern visible below to avoid confusion later.

The roar of the surf at Stinson becomes audible. Baccharis is much the most common shrub now lining the fire road, at times narrowing it to trail-width. As you go lower, wild cucumber, or manroot, becomes common as well.

Just beneath the level of the prominent water tanks is a junction with an overgrown path (sometimes called Stinson Gulch Trail and not described) following the water pipeline to a dead end in the canyon. A sign with a Bay Area Ridge Trail logo directs travelers going uphill. Veer left. In 25 yards is another fork. A broad road, used by maintenance vehicles, goes left up to the tanks and takes Willow Camp FR down right.

It's then some 300 yards to a gate and large Willow Camp FR sign. Willow Camp now enters GGNRA lands. Behind the gate is a small parking area at the end of Avenida Farralone in Stinson Beach. Exit if you are heading to the beach or to Matt Davis Trail, veer right to continue on Willow Camp.

Willow Camp drops its final mile over a broad, grass-surfaced GGNRA service road. It runs level, then descends through a cool, wooded stretch. There is much non-native vegetation in this disturbed area, but many splendid oaks as well. A trailer houses the Stinson Beach County Water District. Continue past to an old barn and clump of cactus plants. The now-closed lower part of McKennan Trail once set off right here on its own extremely steep climb to Ridgecrest Boulevard.

A huge stand of woodwardia ferns, left, thrives in the gulch's boggy soil. A water district maintenance road right (not described) leads to a water tank. Follow the Willow Camp arrows.

Willow Camp FR ends at a gate by Highway 1, at Mile Marker 13.69. There is a newer GGNRA sign. On the other side of the gate is a small parking area. Bolinas Lagoon, one of the finest bird-watching locales in the Bay Area, is across the road. Bolinas-Stinson School borders on the right and central Stinson Beach is 1.2 miles to the left.

Willow Camp was an early name for the town of Stinson Beach. Indeed, programs and trophies for the Dipsea Race, which ends there, long said "Willow Camp." The town was renamed in 1920 for the Stinson family; Nathan Stinson and partner James Upton paid $30,000 for 1,720 acres here in 1870. Willows still line Easkoot Creek beside the main entry to the popular beach. There was a Willow Camp Trail on the 1898 Mt. Tam Sanborn map; it appears as a fire road on post–World War II maps.

RECREATION

It is the responsibility of visitors to observe the most current rules and regulations. Rules change; published rules and signs at trailheads prevail. Check the various agencies' websites in advance for information.

Hiking

Recreational hiking on Tamalpais began in the late 1870s, when the newly opened North Pacific Coast Railroad, with a ferry connection from San Francisco, made the mountain reasonably accessible. Although all of Tamalpais was privately owned and criss-crossed with fences, some landowners did permit access. Summit registers began appearing atop Tam in the 1880s and filled ever more quickly as time went on. (Some of these registers survive.)

The number of hikers increased dramatically in 1890 after a rail line was laid into Mill Valley, a town born from a land auction. Numbers rose even more when the Mill Valley & Mt. Tamalpais Scenic Railway to near East Peak opened in 1896. Indeed, long lines formed on summer weekends on the Dipsea steps. Refreshment stands sprang up atop the steps and elsewhere to quench hikers' thirst.

Hiking clubs with colorful names such as the Down & Outers and Cross Country Boys had camps on the mountain, where members spent weekends. (Rifle Camp was associated with the Down & Outers.) The Sierra Club, founded in 1892, held some of its first hikes on Tamalpais. Hikers organized the Tamalpais Conservation Club in 1912 with the motto "Guardian of the Mountain"; the organization continues today.

That same year, German-speaking hikers founded a local branch of the Tourist Club, and their lodge still stands beside Redwood Trail. The California Alpine Club was founded in 1913 and their lodge also still stands on Tamalpais. The pioneering Dipsea Women's Hikes of 1918–1922 drew hundreds each year, more than the Dipsea Race itself. In 2014, Friends of Mt. Tam listed 145 free public hikes on the mountain. State park rangers lead short walks (followed by cookies and hot chocolate!) on the first Saturday of each month.

Many other organizations offer nature study walks on Mt. Tamalpais, among them, the Marin chapters of the California Native Plant Society and Audubon Society, Marin County Parks, and the College of Marin.

Mountain Biking

Mt. Tamalpais is generally recognized as the birthplace of mountain biking. A group dubbed the Larkspur Canyon Gang rode heavy, single-speed, balloon-tired Schwinns in Madrone Canyon in the late 1960s. Mt. Tam riders such as Alan Bonds, Joe Breeze, Gary Fisher, Charles Kelly, Tom Ritchey, Marc Vendetti,

Charlie Wirtz, and others began modifying these "clunkers" to create the first true mountain bikes, a term said to have been coined by Kelly. Fisher and Kelly opened the world's very first mountain bike retail store in San Anselmo in 1979.

A Thanksgiving Day ride around Pine Mountain started in 1975, and continues to be popular today. On October 26, 1976, Bonds, the only rider who didn't fall, won the inaugural Repack Race, the hair-raising, 2-mile descent of Cascade Canyon Fire Road that is considered the birth of the sport. (The Repack Race, last held in 1984, has been banned by the Marin Municipal Water District.) Kelly edited the sport's first newsletter, *The Fat Tire Flyer*, which debuted in 1980. The earliest meetings of the National Off-Road Bicycling Association (NORBA) were held in Marin in 1983. The Marin Museum of Bicycling, incorporating the Mountain Bike Hall of Fame, opened in Fairfax in 2015.

The increasing presence of mountain bikes triggered reactions from many hikers and equestrians, and discussions on how Tamalpais land managers should mesh the needs of various user groups ensued. The result was a near-uniform policy, effective across the mountain's public lands. Bicycles are allowed on all fire roads, with speed limits of 15 miles per hour, reduced to 5 miles per hour on blind curves or when passing. They are are barred from most trails. (In this book, trails open to bikes—including several such as Coast View, which was reworked specifically to serve as multi-use—are so noted in the heading.)

Horseback Riding

Horses were the primary mode of transportation on Tamalpais throughout the nineteenth century, and recreational horseback riding on the mountain continued to be popular for decades after. In 1944–1945, the California Riding and Hiking Act was passed to establish a 3,000-mile-long riding and hiking trail that would span the state from north to south. Completed sections of the route were marked with yellow-topped signposts, a handful of which may still be found on Tam. But with limited funding, the project stalled, and the original act was repealed in 1974.

Today, horses are permitted on almost all fire roads across Tamalpais. Horses are also permitted on many trails within the jursidictions of the Golden Gate National Recreation Area (except Muir Woods National Monument) and Marin County Parks. Horses are not allowed on any Mt. Tamalpais State Park trails other than Heather Cutoff and Riding & Hiking. The Marin Municipal Water District permits equestrians on some trails, although there may be seasonal closures.

In 1990, the state park opened the Frank Valley Group Horse Camp not far from the base of Heather Cutoff Trail. Marin Stables operates on leased MMWD land at the start of Canyon Trail, near Fairfax.

Running

Mt. Tamalpais is home to the oldest major cross-country race in the United States, the Dipsea, first held in 1905. Since the race is point-to-point, from Mill Valley to Stinson Beach (then called Willow Camp), staging it in an era before radio service and automobiles was considered remarkable. The Dipsea is now one of the most celebrated races in the nation, and entries far exceed available places. The Dipsea also spawned, in the 1970s, the Double Dipsea and Quadruple Dipsea Races. The Mt. Tam Hillclimb, held at least as early as 1916, was reestablished in the 1980s. The Miwok 100K (62 miles), Marin's longest race, is entirely over trails within this book.

Tamalpa Runners is Marin's largest running club. Tamalpa built the fountain at the Mountain Home parking lot, the starting point for a Saturday morning running group since the 1970s.

Dog Walking

Marin County Parks preserves allow dogs on-leash on trails and off-leash (under voice control) on fire roads, and several of these fire roads, such as Escalon and Southern Marin Line, have become immensely popular. The 2014 Marin County Parks trails plan bars off-trail travel by those with dogs. Dogs are not permitted, on- or off-leash, on trails or fire roads in Mt. Tamalpais State Park or in Muir Woods National Monument. Dogs are permitted, on-leash only, on Marin Municipal Water District lands. Dog rules vary within Golden Gate National Recreation Area—from completely off-limits to areas permitting dogs off-leash under voice control—so signs must be checked.

Fishing

There has been fishing in all of Marin's reservoir lakes since the day they were filled. A California fishing license is required. Remains of a short-lived 1930s fish hatchery can still be seen behind the Lake Lagunitas picnic area. Alpine Lake was open to fishing from boats until World War II. The California Department of Fish and Wildlife regularly stocks Lagunitas and Bon Tempe Lakes with rainbow trout. Bass and bluegill are also caught.

Camping

There are five campgrounds on Mt. Tamalpais—Pantoll (sixteen sites), Bootjack (fifteen sites), Frank Valley Group Horse Camp (up to twelve horses and riders), Steep Ravine Environmental Campground (six campsites, plus ten primitive cabins) and Alice Eastwood Group Camp (up to seventy-five people in two sections), all within the state park. Reservations can be made up to seven months in advance online or over the phone, or by visiting the ranger station at Pantoll.

Walk-ins are also welcome on a first-come basis at Pantoll and Bootjack.

The National Park Service has several walk-in campgrounds in Marin, but none on Tamalpais. Marin County Parks does not operate any campsites in its preserves. The Marin Municipal Water District is closed to visitors at night and does not permit camping. However, the West Point Inn, which is on MMWD land, offers rustic (no electricity) rooms and cabins. These may be reserved up to three months in advance.

Bay Area Ridge Trail/Bay Trail

The goal of the planned 500-mile-long Bay Area Ridge Trail is to provide pedestrians, bikers, and equestrians with a public access route atop the hills surrounding San Francisco and San Pablo Bays. In all, 350 miles are now open, but the full project, originally scheduled for completion in 1998, remains unfinished, with huge gaps in the northern regions.

The first Tamalpais section was dedicated on September 23, 1989, and the hiker's route across the mountain is now complete. Arrows and circular blue signs mark the way. Trails and fire roads within this book that are part of the Bay Area Ridge Trail—Miwok, Redwood Creek, Deer Park/Dipsea FR, Coast View, Matt Davis, Coastal/Bolinas Ridge FR and San Geronimo Ridge FR—are noted in the text. Visit the Bay Area Ridge Trail website to learn more and to download maps.

There is a separate Bay Trail, which is intended to circle San Francisco Bay along the shoreline. The Sausalito-Mill Valley multi-purpose path over the old railroad bed is part of the Bay Trail.

Note that neither Bay Area Ridge Trail nor Bay Trail are separate jurisdictions; rules of the respective land managers prevail.

West Marin Stagecoach

Mt. Tamalpais visitors who wish to reduce their impact, avoid parking fees and full lots, and enjoy one-way jaunts should consider using the West Marin Stagecoach, run by publicly funded Marin Transit. All buses have front-mounted bicycle racks.

The No. 61 bus runs several times a day between Marin City, where there are connections with Golden Gate Transit buses, and Bolinas. (The No. 61 line is extended south to Fort Baker during summer weekends.) It passes within yards of no fewer than two dozen Tamalpais trails (in order heading west): Miwok, Dias Ridge, Dias Spur, Dipsea, Sun, Panoramic, Redwood, Canopy View, Camp Eastwood Road, Trestle, Gravity Car Grade, Hogback, Troop 80, Sierra, Bootjack, Easy Grade, Matt Davis, Alpine, Old Stage Road, Old Mine, Stapelveldt, Deer Park (Dipsea) FR, Steep Ravine, Hill 640, and Willow Camp

FR. The No. 68 bus runs along Sir Francis Drake Boulevard between San Rafael and Inverness, passing the easiest entries to Kent Lake. Visit the West Marin Stagecoach website for more information.

Some Cautions

Ticks

Ticks are eight-legged, blood-sucking arachnids that have long been a nuisance on the mountain. Attracted to mammals' warmth, ticks are brushed off foliage. They then quickly and firmly attach themselves, penetrating the skin with their head; they present a danger of infection.

The tick problem has gotten far more serious in recent years because of the spread of Lyme disease, though it is still rare locally. The disease is caused by a bacterial spirochete (*Borrelia burgdorferi*) discovered in 1983 that is carried by some ticks. If left untreated, Lyme disease—named for Old Lyme, Connecticut, where the disease was first described in 1975—can be debilitating, causing arthritis and heart and nerve problems. Our Lyme-disease-carrying tick is the western black-legged (*Ixodes pacificus*), and it is active just about all year. Tiny (only $\frac{1}{8}$-inch long), it requires close examination to be seen.

Check yourself over, or have a friend check you, for ticks after trips, particularly if you went cross-country in grassland. According to the Mayo Clinic, tick removal is best accomplished by "[using] tweezers to grasp the tick near its head or mouth and [pulling straight back] gently to remove the whole tick without crushing it." Once it's been removed, put the tick in a container and freeze it in case it needs to be examined. If the head remains embedded; if the tick has been lodged for a while; if the area shows any sign of infection; or if a circular, reddish rash forms around the bite (often a diagnostic symptom of Lyme disease), see a physician. Early treatment of Lyme disease with antibiotics is usually successful.

Poison Oak

Contact with the oily sap of poison oak causes dermatitis in most people, though the resulting degree of inflammation and itching varies widely. Poison oak may be the most abundant shrub on Mt. Tamalpais and is common in many habitats. It also takes on a variety of appearances. It may be short or tall, single-stalked or branching, a vine, or even a short tree. The three-lobed leaves, which turn reddish in summer, are diagnostic (the old axiom is "leaves of three, let it be") and all mountain visitors quickly learn to recognize the plant. Even without leaves in winter, poison oak can still be toxic. If you know, or even think, you've touched the plant, wash or shower as soon as you can using a strong soap such as Fels Naptha. The cream Tecnu is a popular aid.

Giardiasis, E. coli

As far as can be determined, there have been no verified cases of giardiasis, an intestinal ailment caused by the protozoan *Giardia lamblia*, resulting from drinking untreated Mt. Tamalpais water. Still, to be safe, Marin Municipal Water District has, on their lands, posted many once-commonly used but untreated water sources as "non-potable." In November 2014, E. coli bacteria was found in the Mountain Theater well, and warning signs were attached to fountains at Bootjack and Mountain Theater. *Take an adequate supply of water on any trip on the mountain.*

Insects

While signs warn of mountain lions, rattlesnakes, and coyotes, insects wreak far more havoc. Yellow jackets are particularly problematic in late summer, when the workers become more defensive in the vicinity of the nest. Many a Mt. Tam lunch break has been shortened by this wasp, whose sting can cause severe reactions, even medical emergencies, in some.

European honeybees are in the same order as wasps and ants (Hymenoptera), and disturbing one of their colonies can have unpleasant consequences. Again, sensitive individuals may require swift medical attention.

Through their spreading of disease, mosquitoes have been, and remain, the world's number-one killer of humans (aside from other humans). Of increasing concern locally is their transmission of the West Nile virus. The disease was first reported in the United States in 1999 and reached the Pacific coast in 2002; several cases are reported annually in Marin.

Spiders, anathema to some, are not really a danger to Tamalpais travelers. Indeed, a not-uncommon joy along mountain trails is to see hundreds of their webs glistening in morning dew.

Rattlesnakes

Rattlesnakes live and breed on Mt. Tamalpais, but bites are extremely rare, and fatal encounters are, so far, nil. The mountain's northern Pacific rattlesnake (*Crotalus oreganus*) is usually 2 to 4 feet long. It has the characteristic broad, triangular head, and rattles, a segment of which is added each time the snake sheds its skin. The warning at Pantoll reads: "Rattlesnakes may be found in the area. They are important members of the natural community. They will not attack, but if disturbed or cornered, they will defend themselves. Give them distance and respect." Bites need to be treated promptly in a medical facility.

Gopher snakes resemble rattlers, including a vibrating tail when aroused. But they, and all other mountain snake species—including rubber boa, king snake, western racer, garter snake, and ringneck snake—are harmless.

Mushrooms

Mushrooms are fungi that produce a fleshy, fruiting body. Hundreds of mushroom species grow on Mt. Tamalpais, particularly in forested areas during the rainy season. Take a walk on any woodland trail after a heavy rain and be dazzled by their numbers and variety. Mushroom collecting on Tam, once unregulated, is now controlled. Check with the managing land authority for current rules.

Some local mushroom species, are, of course, highly toxic, and it is not uncommon to hear of a fatality or two each season somewhere in the Bay Area. The genus *Amanita* is particularly dangerous; deadly poisonous members bear such names as "death cap" (*A. phalloides*) and "destroying angel" (*A. ocreata*). Needless to say, only experienced mycologists should consider sampling wild mushrooms.

Mountain Lions

In 1994, a 150-pound mountain lion killed a runner in the Sierra foothills. Within months, there were several confirmed mountain lion sightings on Tam, after decades of almost none, and fears mounted. There are now mountain lion warnings at several Tam trailheads.

Chances of a meeting a mountain lion are so remote—the total number in all Marin is estimated as fewer than ten, and they are very wary of humans—that no one need alter their behavior on the mountain. The standard GGNRA warning sign reads: "Remain calm—do not run. Pick up small children immediately. Stand upright—maintain eye contact. Back away slowly. Be assertive—if approached, wave your arms, speak firmly or shout, and throw sticks or rocks. If attacked, fight back aggressively."

Coyotes

Coyotes were not even mentioned among the "cautions" in early editions of *Tamalpais Trails*, but their numbers have increased markedly in recent years. Unlike mountain lions, coyotes are less likely to hide from humans; you may well see them sauntering or hunting less than 50 yards away. But, again, there have been no attacks on people in Marin. Dogs, however, have been killed.

Here is the GGNRA's coyote warning sign at the base of Matt Davis Trail: "Keep children close to you. Make loud noises, throw rocks. Stand upright, avoid eye contact, back away slowly, do not run. If attacked, fight back aggressively."

Homo sapiens

The mountain has always been safe, and remains so. Crimes of any sort on Tam are rare. There are occasional car break-ins—don't leave valuables in cars parked at trailheads—but if you lose an item on a trail, it will more likely than not be returned to you. Report suspicious activities.

Fire

Fires have always been a part of Mt. Tamalpais. In 1859, a fire reportedly burned for three months. In 1881, another scorched 65,000 acres. In 1904, 14,000 acres burned. In 1929, a fire destroyed 117 homes in Mill Valley, lit up the night sky of San Francisco, and was visible in Santa Cruz. The last major Tam conflagration was in 1945, clearing 17,000 acres on the north side.

Since lightning is rare in Marin, modern-era fires are usually human-caused. Today, far more homes crowd Tam's lower slopes, and Marin has responded with increased fire-fighting resources, such as the Throckmorton Ridge Fire Station above Mountain Home, controlled burns to diminish potential fuel sources, broom removal, and the clearing of fire breaks.

At all times, but particularly during the hot, rainless months of summer and fall, mountain visitors must exercise exceptional caution regarding potential fire-causing activities. Smoking is now prohibited entirely on MMWD lands and on MCOSD trails. Several times a year, when high temperatures, wind, and low humidity combine, land managers close access roads and, on rare occasions, all trails. There are heavy fines for violators. During fire season, the Marin County Fire Department maintains an information line for daily updates on fire conditions, including Mt. Tamalpais trail and road closures.

Maps

Many wonderful, privately produced maps of Mt. Tamalpais's trails exist, and some are referenced in the text. Here is a partial list.

- The Sanborn Map Company published the first hiker's map of Tamalpais in 1898.
- The Northwestern Pacific Railroad issued a map within a hiker's guide brochure during the 1920s for tourists coming to Marin by rail.
- The original Tamalpais Conservation Club map was largely the work of Dr. C. A. Phillips, who died the year of its publication, 1934. The club revised and reissued the map in 1951, 1974, 1980, and 1984.
- Harry Freese produced a classic map filled with little-known treasures in 1953, and it was the standard for decades. Erickson Maps reissued it in the 1970s and '80s, adding topographic lines.
- B. Q. Charette of Mill Valley released a trail map in the late 1970s.

- Jerry Olmsted, a meticulous researcher, added color and shaded relief in his *Rambler's Guide to the Trails of Mt. Tamalpais and the Marin Headlands*; Kristen Bergstrom was the cartographer. The map debuted in 1983, published by Olmsted Bros. Map Co., then went through ten printings. After Olmsted's death, Ben Pease acquired the rights. In 2014, Pease offered a revised map in Olmsted's style.

- Dewey Livingston, a master cartographer, hand-drew the maps that appeared in each of the five editions (1989 through 2004) of my book *Tamalpais Trails*.

- Tom Harrison of San Rafael continues to produce a series of maps on durable stock.

- Each Mt. Tamalpais jurisdiction offers free maps of the lands they manage; go online to review and download.

CONTACT INFORMATION

The following URLs and phone numbers were correct at press time. However, things change quickly in today's hyperconnected world and you may find that the URL or number you seek is no longer in service.

Unless otherwise noted, all phone numbers are in the 415 area code.

We encourage you to check in with the appropriate sources to get the most up-to-date information on closures, routes, schedules, fees, and more before your visit.

Audubon Canyon Ranch: *www.egret.org*; 868.9244

Bay Area Ridge Trail: *www.ridgetrail.org*; 561-2595

California Alpine Club: *www.californiaalpineclub.org*; 388-9940

Golden Gate National Recreation Area: *www.nps.gov/goga*; 561-4700

Green Gulch Farm Zen Center: *www.sfzc.org/ggf*; 475-936

Marin County Fire Department Information: 945-1195

Marin Municipal Water District: *www.marinwater.org*; 499-7191
> Parking Passes: *www.marinwater.org/191/Parking-Passes*

Marin County Parks/Marin County Open Space District: *www.marincountyparks.org*; 473-6387

Marin Transit: *www.marintransit.org*; 226-0855, TDD 711

Mountain Home Inn: *www.mtnhomeinn.com*; 381-9000

Mt. Tamalpais Conservation Club: *www.tamalpais.org*; 451-1912

Mt. Tamalpais State Park: *www.parks.ca.gov* (search for Mount Tamalpais)
> Ranger Station: 388-2070
> California State Parks campsite reservations:
> *www.reserveamerica.com*; (800) 444-PARK (7275)

Muir Woods National Monument: *www.nps.gov/muwo*;
> Visitor Information 388-2595, TTY 556-2766

Ralston White Retreat: *www.ralstonwhiteretreat.org*;
> Retreat Office 388-0858, Reservations (888) 388-0858

Rock Spring: 499-7191 (recorded message)

Steep Ravine: California State Parks reservation service:
> (800) 444-PARK (7275)

Tourist Club: *www.touristclubsf.org*; 388-9987

West Marin Stagecoach: *www.marintransit.org*; 526-3239

West Point Inn: *www.westpointinn.com*; 388-9955

ACKNOWLEDGMENTS

Since I began working on Tamalpais Trails, many of the mountain's giants who helped me immeasurably—Lincoln Fairley, Randy Hogue, Salem Rice, Fred Sandrock, Ben Schmidt, and Jim Vitek—have passed on, but my gratitude to them endures.

I also wish to acknowledge the help of Larry Brauer, Wilma Follette, Mike Hoy, Matt Leffert, Dewey Livingston, Mia Monroe, Brad Rippe, Nancy Skinner, and Ty Stefan. And special thanks to Pam, Sally, and Lily for all their support and forbearance.

Errors that remain are entirely my own.

❉

BIBLIOGRAPHY

Fairley, Lincoln. 1987. *Mount Tamalpais, A History* (Scottwall Associates). The best modern history of the mountain, with hundreds of historic photographs.

Griffin, L. Martin. 1998. *Saving the Marin-Sonoma Coast* (Sweetwater Springs Press). An account of some of Mt. Tamalpais's environmental battles, by a key participant.

Howell, John Thomas, Frank Almeda, Wilma Follette, Catherine Best. 2007. *Marin Flora* (California Academy of Sciences and Marin Chapter of the California Native Plant Society). The definitive work on Marin's plants, updating Howell's original 1949 work of the same name.

Kelly, Charles. 2014. *Fat Tire Flyer* (Velo Press). A splendidly illustrated, first-hand account of the earliest days of mountain biking on Tamalpais.

Livingston, Dewey. 1995. *A Good Life: Dairy Farming in the Olema Valley* (Historic Resource Study/National Park Service). The definitive work on the historic dairy ranches of Mt. Tamalpais's Bolinas Ridge.

TRAIL & FIRE ROAD INDEX

Trail/Fire Road	Miles	Trailhead	Page
Filter Plant Road	1.00	Sky Oaks	302
Fish Grade	.76	Phoenix Lake	255
Fish Gulch	.57	Phoenix Lake	256
Glen FR	.87	Mill Valley	127
Grassy Slope FR	.82	Kent Lake/Pine Mtn	95
Gravity Car Grade	.93	Mountain Home	150
Green Gulch	1.39	Muir Beach/Hwy 1	175
H-Line FR	.89	Mill Valley	128
Harry Allen	1.15	Phoenix Lake	257
Heather Cutoff	1.46	Muir Woods	199
Helen Markt	1.75	West Ridgecrest	329
Hidden Meadow	.82	Phoenix Lake	258
High Marsh	2.21	West Ridgecrest	330
Hill 640 FR	.30	Pantoll	240
Hillside	.70	Muir Woods	200
Hogback FR	.61	Mountain Home	151
Hoo-Koo-E-Koo	4.04	Old State Hwy	221
Horseshoe FR	.28	Mill Valley	129
Huckleberry	.61	Old State Hwy	225
Indian FR	1.33	Old State Hwy	226
International	.52	East Ridgecrest	74
Junction	.25	Deer Park	65
Kaasi Road	.51	Muir Beach/Hwy 1	176
Kent	3.85	Sky Oaks	303
Kent Pump FR	4.53	Kent Lake/Pine Mtn	96
King Mountain Loop	1.95	Old State Hwy	227
Ladybug	.46	Old State Hwy	229
Lagoon FR	.78	Sky Oaks	305
Lagunitas-Rock Spring FR	3.39	Sky Oaks	314
Lake Lagunitas FR	1.58	Sky Oaks	306
Lakeview FR	.78	Sky Oaks	308
Lakeview Trail	.25	East Ridgecrest	74
Laurel Dell FR	2.20	West Ridgecrest	332
Lost	.52	Muir Woods	201
Lower Berry	.41	Sky Oaks	309
Lower Fern Creek	1.03	Muir Woods	202
Lower Northside	.91	East Ridgecrest	75
Madrone	.92	Sky Oaks	309
Matt Davis	6.70	Mountain Home	152
Maytag	.33	Mill Valley	129
McCurdy	1.99	West Ridgecrest	334
Meadow Club Road	.67	Sky Oaks	310
Mickey O'Brien	.66	West Ridgecrest	336
Middle Green Gulch	2.11	Muir Beach/Hwy 1	177
Middle Peak FR	.62	East Ridgecrest	76
Miller	.68	East Ridgecrest	77
Miwok	3.73	Muir Beach/Hwy 1	179
Monte Vista FR	.32	Mill Valley	130

Trail/Fire Road	Miles	Trailhead	Page
Moore	.43	Deer Park	65
Mountain Theater	.25	Rock Spring	278
Mountain Top	.54	East Ridgecrest	78
Muir Beach	.39	Muir Beach/Hwy 1	181
Music Stand	.28	Rock Spring	279
Nora	.51	Mountain Home	156
Northside	2.66	East Ridgecrest	79
Oat Hill FR	2.70	Kent Lake/Pine Mtn	98
Old Mine	1.49	Rock Spring	280
Old Railroad Grade	6.72	Mill Valley	131
Old Sled	1.03	Kent Lake/Pine Mtn	100
Old Stage Road	1.83	Pantoll	241
Old Stove	.33	West Ridgecrest	337
Old Vee FR	1.09	Kent Lake/Pine Mtn	101
O'Rourke's Bench	.41	Rock Spring	281
Owl	1.09	Muir Beach/Hwy 1	182
Panoramic	.92	Mountain Home	157
Peters Dam FR	1.83	Kent Lake/Pine Mtn	101
Phoenix Lake FR & Ord Trail	2.33	Phoenix Lake	259
Piedmont	.35	Old State Hwy	230
Pilot Knob	.81	Sky Oaks	311
Pine Mountain FR	8.77	Kent Lake/Pine Mtn	103
Pipeline	.27	Mountain Home	158
Plankwalk	.32	East Ridgecrest	81
Potrero	.33	Rock Spring	282
Pumpkin Ridge	.72	Sky Oaks	313
Randall	1.65	West Ridgecrest	338
Redwood	.74	Mountain Home	159
Redwood Creek (Main)	.88	Muir Woods	204
Redwood Creek (Lower)	2.04	Muir Woods	206
Riding & Hiking	.40	Pantoll	242
Rock Spring-Lagunitas FR	3.39	Sky Oaks	314
Rock Spring	1.70	Rock Spring	283
Rocky Point Road	.94	Muir Beach/Hwy 1	183
Rocky Point Trail	.36	Muir Beach/Hwy 1	184
Rocky Ridge FR	1.78	Sky Oaks	316
Ross	.66	Phoenix Lake	261
San Geronimo Ridge FR	6.13	Kent Lake/Pine Mtn	106
Shafter Grade	1.70	Kent Lake/Pine Mtn	109
Shaver Grade	1.69	Phoenix Lake	262
Sierra	1.05	Mountain Home	160
Simmons	.95	Rock Spring	286
Six Points	.57	Deer Park	66
Southern Marin Line FR	2.78	Old State Hwy	231
Stapelveldt	1.02	Pantoll	243
Steep Ravine	2.12	Pantoll	244
Stocking	.60	Sky Oaks	317
Sun	.69	Mountain Home	161
Tavern Pump	.33	East Ridgecrest	82

Trail/Fire Road	Miles	Trailhead	Page
Taylor	.52	Sky Oaks	319
TCC	1.80	Pantoll	247
Temelpa	1.76	Mill Valley	136
Tenderfoot	1.09	Mill Valley	139
Troop 80	1.48	Mountain Home	162
Tucker	1.65	Phoenix Lake	263
Tucker Cutoff	.26	Old State Hwy	232
Upper Fern Creek	.77	East Ridgecrest	83
Verna Dunshee	.68	East Ridgecrest	84
Vic Haun	.47	Mill Valley	164
Warner Canyon	.48	Mill Valley	140
Wheeler	.53	Mill Valley	141
Willow Camp FR	2.82	West Ridgecrest	340
Windy Ridge Trail	.45	Old State Hwy	323
Worn Spring FR	2.51	Phoenix Lake	264
Yolanda	2.23	Phoenix Lake	268
Zig-Zag	.50	Mill Valley	142

Map Legend

▦ Main Road		🅿	Trailhead Parking
▬ Local Road		🅿	Trailhead Parking (Fee)
▢ Parks and Open Space		🚌	Public Transit
▢ Private Land		🚌	Seasonal Transit/Shuttle
▢ Cities and Towns		▲	Peak
▢ Adjacent Parks		■	Point of Interest
▬ ▬ ▬ Multi-use Fire Road (Hiking/Bicycling/Equestrian)		◘	Trailhead (Limited Parking)
▬·▬·▬ Multi-use Trail (Hiking/Bicycling/Equestrian)		⛩	Picnic Area
▬ ▬ ▬ Hiking/Equestrian Trail		⛺	Campground
·········· Hiking Trail		⛺	Group Camp
·········· Minor Hiking Trail		🐎	Stable
		ℹ	Information
		⛑	Ranger Station
		🎭	Theater